D1639477

MONOGRAPHS ON NUMERICAL ANALYSIS

General Editors

E. T. GOODWIN, L. FOX

COMPUTING METHODS FOR SCIENTISTS AND ENGINEERS

BY

L. FOX

AND

D. F. MAYERS

Oxford University Computing Laboratory

CLARENDON PRESS · OXFORD

1968

Oxford University Press, Ely House, London W.1

GLASGOW NEW YORK TORONTO MELBOURNE WELLINGTON
CAPE TOWN SALISBURY IBADAN NAIROBI LUSAKA ADDIS ABABA
BOMBAY CALCUTTA MADRAS KARACHI LAHORE DACCA
KUALA LUMPUR HONG KONG TOKYO

PRINTED IN NORTHERN IRELAND AT THE UNIVERSITIES PRESS, BELFAST

Preface

THIS book is the last publication, at least for some time, stemming from the Summer schools organized by the Delegacy for Extra-mural Studies and the Computing Laboratory at Oxford University. Our general aim has been to exhibit, to those who have scientific problems to solve, the why and how of good computing methods. At the risk of tedious repetition we must explain our reasons for producing these books.

Most computation is performed by scientists, whose mathematical training generally stops, or slows down, before they reach the mathematical 'professional' state. They have, however, studied some mathematics, and have learnt various techniques, for example for solving linear equations, which are justified in mathematical terms but fail when the 'practical' arithmetic of modern computing machines has to be used. The reasons for this failure, and the necessities for and requirements of good computing methods in general, are rarely properly explained in books on elementary numerical analysis. They are explained in a few very good books on particular areas of numerical mathematics, but these tend to be written by professional mathematicians, using mathematics and a mathematical style of writing that tend to frighten and repel those who have most need of their discoveries. We have therefore taken the view that some books were needed at a medium level, which use simple mathematics, which do not make a fetish of mathematical rigour, and which try to communicate to the reader some of the 'numerical sense' that good computing men exhibit.

This aim, though not perhaps the attempt to achieve it, would surely be applauded by those who direct computing services, especially in universities. We are all aware of the growing demand for computing facilities, and are vociferous about the deficiencies of the hardware and software of computing machinery. Very rarely do we talk of the deficiencies of users of such machinery, though we all know perfectly well that considerable time is wasted by solving the wrong problem, using the wrong method, and getting inaccurate and even meaningless answers, of which we are not always immediately aware.

In this book we have therefore included those elementary matters that seem to us basic for the successful computation of problems in many contexts. One outstanding fact emerges, that in spite of the discoveries and achievements of the last two decades, very little exists, in the form of computer programmes, for what we call *physical problems*. Here the data are inexact, with known maximum 'tolerances', and we would like to know worth-while upper bounds for the corresponding uncertainties in the answers. We know few significant results in this field, and their lack may stem from the fact, mentioned earlier, that many of the advances have been made by professional mathematicians who themselves do not solve real scientific problems. The recent work of Moore and his associates on 'interval analysis' is the first major development with some hope of success in this difficult problem. At present our book, and all others we have seen, is incomplete in this respect.

The elementary matters that we do discuss include the necessity for consideration of the 'best' formulation of a given problem, the meaning and nature of inherent instability (or ill-conditioning), which is a function of the problem, and of induced instability, which is a function of the method. Particularly in the first five chapters, on algebraic problems, we have also illustrated the power of 'backward error analysis' in exhibiting the nature and extent of induced instability. For the rest we have tried to include the best methods for a variety of problems involving algebra and the differential calculus, stressing the error analysis of the techniques rather than their mathematical derivation or justification. We have 'covered' the treatment of recurrence relations, evaluation of zeros of polynomials, the solution of linear equations and the determination of eigensolutions of matrices, some topics in the approximation of functions including Chebyshev approximation, interpolation and numerical integration, and the numerical solution of ordinary differential equations; and we have tried to show how the same causes of induced instability can occur in apparently quite different contexts.

With a sound knowledge of this material we believe that the scientist has the numerical sense that will enable him to tackle more difficult problems, such as the solution of integral equations and partial differential equations, though he will have to do more mathematical reading at this stage. To disseminate this knowledge we have written quite deliberately in terms of elementary mathematics that all scientists, with the relevant problems to solve, should certainly have or take steps to acquire. Even if the computing laboratories were equipped with library programmes to cover every possible eventuality, it is emphasized that the computer user must have this mathematical and numerical knowledge unless he is prepared to hand every one of his problems to an 'expert'. This is at present impossible, and computing, especially inefficient computing, is *very* expensive.

Some scientists claim that their time is valuable, and should not be spent on things that the machine can do perfectly well. It is therefore legitimate, they assert, to use inefficient codes and inefficient numerical methods. There is some truth in this, but it avoids two important facts. The first is the machine saturation that we have already mentioned. The second is the meaning of 'inefficient'. A method that produces good results in a long time is better, for scientific purposes, than one that produces poor results in any period of time, and too often the scientist's claim leads him to the use of inefficiencies in this sense. With engineers who claim that '10 per cent accuracy is all they require, so that almost any method will do', we have no sympathy whatever. The analysis that guarantees 10 per cent is always as difficult as that which guarantees 0·0001 per cent. It is also equally important. The 'scientific method' proceeds by building up theories from observations and testing the theories on additional observations. In this respect errors of measurement have to be separated from errors of computation, and if the latter are too big, or cannot reasonably be estimated, the 'scientific method' becomes a meaningless shambles.

We therefore dedicate our book to those research scientists who want to improve their computing methods, to undergraduate students, who will subsequently need to use computing methods, and to those who have the job of running computing services and getting the best from them in the true meaning of the word.

We are very grateful for the assistance of Mrs. Linda Hayes, who checked and corrected the whole of the first draft, and who verified that our examples and exercises were both accurate and meaningful.

L. Fox

D. F. Mayers

Contents

1

Problem Formulation and Choice of Method

Introduction

1. THE solution of a problem involving any kind of numerical computation sufficiently laborious or repetitive to warrant the use of a modern digital computer is performed in four major steps.

(i) We must formulate the problem in mathematical terms, as a set of formulae, equations, inequalities, and so on.

(ii) We must decide what particular method or combination of methods, perhaps both mathematical and numerical, is most suitable for our formulated problem. The word 'suitable' will be clarified in the sequel.

(iii) We must carry out the programming and coding of our choice. The word 'programming' has an infinity of meanings. Here we refer to the construction of a logical diagram (block-diagram or flow-diagram) of the computing process, and to the writing in any sort of language of the set of instructions, the *programme*. The word 'coding' implies the transcription of the instructions, together with all necessary 'red-tape' additions, in the precise form (language) acceptable by our particular machine, for example 'Autocode', 'Fortran', or 'Algol', together with 'terminal' instructions.

(iv) We must test our programme, and produce our results from the correct version, by operating the machine in the relevant manner.

Summarizing, the steps are

(i) formulation,
(ii) choice of method,
(iii) programming and coding,
(iv) operation.

2. It is, of course, important that items (iii) and (iv) should be performed adequately. A poor programme can spoil a good method, leading to excessive time of computation and significant inaccuracy of results. Moreover, checks should be used, more than would seem to be current practice, to ensure that the correct data enter the machine, that the correct answers are emitted, and that any possible copying of results is done correctly. (Readers, punches, paper and magnetic tapes, and human beings are at present generally less reliable than the electronic equipment.)

Most scientists who compute regularly do, in our experience, learn the programming and coding quite easily and well, and are assisted in this respect by satisfactory books on programming and machine manuals. Not a few scientists, indeed, become fascinated with this new discipline and spend hours in devising coding techniques to save machine time and space, an enthusiasm that is well rewarded in the case of basic programmes in frequent use.

Far fewer computors, however, have the energy and determination to learn about numerical analysis and allied mathematics. Few books, moreover, are available to assist this endeavour, and some of them are written in terms of abstract mathematics that not all scientists can appreciate.

In our opinion computing success depends far more on adequate attention to steps (i) and (ii), the formulation and choice of method, than on brilliant performance with steps (iii) and (iv). In this book, therefore, we concentrate on steps (i) and (ii), with particular attention to (ii). We do not discuss methods for every conceivable problem: indeed we do not mention at all the solution of partial differential equations. Instead we restrict ourselves to a few basic ideas, relevant in almost all contexts, and illustrate them by examples in the fields of linear algebra, approximation, and the solution of ordinary differential equations.

Formulation

3. Considering first the question of 'formulation', we stress at the outset that little can be accomplished without an adequate knowledge of some parts of mathematics. Scientists who solve algebraic or differential equations, for example, should know *something* of the relevant theories. *Some* knowledge of numerical methods, moreover, will help us to formulate the problem most conveniently for numerical purposes. *Some* knowledge of both theory and practice, in fact, should be our ideal.

There are no general basic rules about how to formulate a problem, and we give here some fairly simple examples to indicate the sort of thing that can be done and the importance of taking a little thought before rushing to the computer.

Example 1

4. Consider the simultaneous first-order differential equations

$$
\left.
\begin{aligned}
\frac{dy_1}{dx} &= a_{11}y_1 + a_{12}y_2 + \ldots + a_{1n}y_n \\
\frac{dy_2}{dx} &= a_{21}y_1 + a_{22}y_2 + \ldots + a_{2n}y_n \\
&\quad\cdot \\
&\quad\cdot \\
&\quad\cdot \\
\frac{dy_n}{dx} &= a_{n1}y_1 + a_{n2}y_2 + \ldots + a_{nn}y_n
\end{aligned}
\right\}, \qquad (1)
$$

with given initial values of $y_1(0)$, $y_2(0)$,..., $y_n(0)$. We want to know the *nature* of the solution for large values of x, that is whether the functions oscillate, with or without bound, or whether they tend monotonically to infinity or to zero.

Faced with such a problem, many scientists instinctively snatch from the programme library the Runge–Kutta routine which (Chapter 10) proceeds to compute approximations to $y_1(x)$, $y_2(x)$,..., $y_n(x)$ at selected intervals in x. Now the Runge–Kutta method is not particularly fast, and suffers from certain kinds of instability, and without due attention to the latter we can by this method reach quite the wrong conclusions.

Our mathematical knowledge, however, tells us that the *general* solution of (1) is given by

$$
y_r(x) = b_{r1}e^{\lambda_1 x} + b_{r2}e^{\lambda_2 x} + \ldots + b_{rn}e^{\lambda_n x}, \qquad r = 1, 2, \ldots, n, \qquad (2)
$$

(provided the λ_r are distinct) where the λ_r are the eigenvalues of the matrix

$$
\mathbf{A} =
\begin{bmatrix}
a_{11} & a_{12} & \ldots & a_{1n} \\
a_{21} & a_{22} & \ldots & a_{2n} \\
\multicolumn{4}{c}{\cdots\cdots\cdots\cdots\cdots} \\
a_{n1} & a_{n2} & \ldots & a_{nn}
\end{bmatrix}. \qquad (3)
$$

The b_{rs} are constants to be determined from the given initial conditions. Now the λ_r are precisely what we need to answer the given question, and the programme library will almost certainly include a routine which solves the algebraic eigenvalue problem very rapidly and very accurately.

The particular solution, incorporating the initial conditions, is not much harder to obtain, and we return to this point in § 9.

Example 2

5. Consider next the evaluation, for successive integer values $r = 1, 2,...,$ of the definite integral

$$I_r = \int_0^1 e^{\frac{4}{3}(x-1)}x^{r+3} \, dx. \tag{4}$$

Again there are various possibilities. First, we might perform numerical integration, say by Simpson's rule, separately for each value of r (but noting that one factor of the integrand is independent of this parameter). Second, with a view to avoiding inaccuracies due to the truncation error of Simpson's rule (see Chapter 9), we might observe that the integral can be expressed as a finite series by successive integration by parts.

The series is

$$I_r = \tfrac{3}{4}\{1 - \tfrac{3}{4}(r+3) + (\tfrac{3}{4})^2(r+3)(r+2) - ... + (-1)^r(\tfrac{3}{4})^{r+2}(r+3)! \,+$$
$$+ (-1)^{r+1}(\tfrac{3}{4})^{r+3}(r+3)! \, (1 - e^{-\frac{4}{3}})\}, \tag{5}$$

and we observe various difficulties in computing its numerical value for any particular r. First we notice the alternation in sign, with the result that we are going to lose significant figures by cancellation. Even for r as small as 5 the largest individual term exceeds 4000, while I_r is of course very much smaller. Second we note the corresponding necessity for great accuracy in the individual terms, including that of $e^{-\frac{4}{3}}$. In fact double-precision arithmetic is certainly necessary for even moderate values of r.

6. A better approach is to observe that, with a single integration by parts, we can find the two-term recurrence relation

$$I_r = 0 \cdot 75 - 0 \cdot 75(r+3)I_{r-1}, \tag{6}$$

which, with one given value I_s which we compute separately, can be used to produce the required results with a relatively trivial amount of work. Some care is in fact needed with the use of (6), as we shall prove and demonstrate in Chapter 3. In fact it is best to use the condition $I_r \to 0$ as $r \to \infty$, which is easily obtained from the observation that I_r is monotonic decreasing as r increases. The selected condition $I_N = 0$, for some sufficiently large N, then enables us to find accurate values from (6) expressed in the form

$$I_{r-1} = (0 \cdot 75 - I_r)/\{0 \cdot 75(r+3)\}, \qquad r = N, N-1, N-2,\ldots, 1,$$
$$\tag{7}$$

that is by *backward recurrence*. This is a fast and accurate method, needing no special attention in the arithmetic.

Example 3

7. In the previous example we turned the integral formulation into the solution of a *difference equation*. Quite commonly we might use a *differential equation* in a similar way. For example, the function

$$f(x, y) = \int_0^\infty e^{-k}\{J_0(kx)\cosh ky - 1\}\operatorname{cosech} k\, dk \tag{8}$$

satisfies the elliptic partial differential equation

$$\frac{\partial^2 f}{\partial x^2} + \frac{1}{x}\frac{\partial f}{\partial x} + \frac{\partial^2 f}{\partial y^2} = 0. \tag{9}$$

Some years ago one of us was asked to tabulate (8) at points in the rectangle $x = 0$, $x = a$, $y = 0$, $y = b$ for certain values of a and b. It turned out to be easier to solve (9) numerically, with the help of boundary conditions obtained from (8), than to apply quadrature formulae for (8) at every pair of values (x, y). Moreover (9) was the original formulation of the problem, and the client, quite properly applying his mathematical knowledge to deduce (8), lacked the computing experience to appreciate the numerical advantages of (9)!

Choice of method

8. These examples indicate that in one sense 'formulation' and 'choice of method' are not strictly separable, and that consultation at an early stage between scientist and numerical analyst is very important. The heading of this section, however, is more concerned with the details of the solution of the well-formulated problem. For example, having decided that the determination of the eigenvalues of (3), or the use of the recurrence (6) or differential equation (9) are better formulations of the given respective problems, how do we select the most suitable of the various possible numerical methods for their solution?

In an ideal world we might envisage that the programme library would contain routines, written by experts, to cover every conceivable situation. Unfortunately this is not the case, and probably never will be. There exist certain routines in connection with certain problems. For example, we are likely to have programmes for solving linear equations, finding eigenvalues and vectors of matrices, performing certain kinds of numerical quadrature, solving certain classes of differential equations, solving certain statistical and curve-fitting problems, and perhaps finding zeros of polynomials. Outside this short list there is very little, and the scientist usually has to carry out at least our steps (i)–(iii) for himself. (We are not considering here large-scale computation in say chemical crystallography or nuclear physics, in which programmes usually exist that are written by experts and used time and again. We are concerned with everyday computations that arise in many scientific contexts.) We must then consider separately the use of the programme library and the construction of new *ad hoc* programmes.

The programme library

9. At first sight the use of the programme library is a straight-forward operation. A little thought, however, reveals the necessity for close familiarity with the details of the relevant programmes and of the problem we are trying to solve.

Consider, for example, the solution of linear simultaneous algebraic equations (Chapter 5). The associated matrix may be 'general', or it may have special properties such as symmetry, with or without positive-definiteness. It may be diagonal, or triple diagonal, or have a similar favourable 'sparse' nature. It may be general but too large for the machine store, or it may be very large and sparse. There may be several different right-hand sides, and new right-hand sides might be generated during the computation as in the process of 'inverse iteration' (Chapter 5). The equations might be 'ill-conditioned' so that the answers have few accurate figures, and we may wish to correct a first approximation and even to find out whether such a correction is worth while. The choice of the library programme clearly depends on many things.

For eigenvalue problems we have similar sets of parameters, in that the matrix may have any of the properties already mentioned. Here there are still more possibilities relevant to our requirements. For example, we may need only one particular eigensolution, we may need some eigenvalues but not the eigenvectors and vice versa, we may need all the solutions, we may or may not want to make corrections, and so on. It is uneconomic to obtain either more or less than we need.

As an illustration consider an extension of the problem of Example 1, in which we now seek not only the λ_r but also the b_{rs} in equation (2). If we use $\mathbf{y}(x)$ to denote the vector of solutions with components $y_r(x)$, then equation (2) can be written

$$\mathbf{y}(x) = \sum_{s=1}^{n} \alpha_s e^{\lambda_s x} \mathbf{b}^{(s)}, \tag{10}$$

where $\mathbf{b}^{(s)}$ is the normalized eigenvector for the eigenvalue λ_s, and the α_s are constants depending on the initial conditions. At $x = 0$ we have

$$\mathbf{y}(0) = \sum_{s=1}^{n} \alpha_s \mathbf{b}^{(s)}, \tag{11}$$

and the α_s can therefore be obtained by solving a set of linear algebraic equations.

On the other hand we know that if we have the eigenvectors $\mathbf{c}^{(s)}$ of the transposed matrix $\mathbf{A}'$ of $\mathbf{A}$, then the biorthogonality properties give immediately the required solution

$$\alpha_s = \mathbf{c}^{(s)'} \mathbf{y}(0) / \mathbf{c}^{(s)'} \mathbf{b}^{(s)}. \tag{12}$$

The most convenient library eigenvalue programme would then compute the eigenvalues of $\mathbf{A}$, assumed unsymmetric, and the eigenvectors of both $\mathbf{A}$ and $\mathbf{A}'$, and this could be our choice if we had an efficient routine of this kind.

10. Similar considerations apply to the solution of ordinary differential equations (Chapter 10). While the Runge–Kutta method, or one of its variants, is a useful general-purpose routine for non-linear first-order equations, there are many circumstances in which other methods are preferable. This is true, for example, for linear equations of the form

$$y'' + f(x)y' + g(x)y = k(x), \tag{13}$$

particularly when the conditions are of boundary-value type, for equations

$$y'' + g(x)y = k(x), \tag{14}$$

which lack the first derivative, and for the eigenvalue problem with differential equation

$$y'' + (f(x) - \lambda)y = 0. \tag{15}$$

For (13)–(15) we might prefer some form of finite-difference method, and when the functions $f(x)$, $g(x)$, and $k(x)$ are polynomials in x we might do better to find an expansion in terms of Chebyshev polynomials. Questions of stability, which may depend on the nature of the solution, must also be taken into account in selecting the library programme, and all these things are discussed in Chapter 10.

New programmes

11. When no suitable library programme exists we must write our own, and for this purpose we must know something about numerical analysis. The library programmes written by experts have been carefully thought out, and we must know the reasons why particular techniques are used and why others are discarded, so that we can apply the basic principles to our new situation. (In passing we should remark that not all library programmes have been compiled by experts, and the compiler's name is a very important piece of information!)

The basic aim, of course, is to produce meaningful results as economically as possible. We have discussed in the preface various philosophical questions about the need for 'absolute perfection' in computed results, and about the relative values of 'human' and 'machine' time. Here, of course, we ignore such questions, and discuss what our maximum objectives should be.

The first important consideration concerns the phrase 'meaningful results', and here we have to make an important distinction between *mathematical* and *physical* problems. In the former all data are exact, and answers can in theory be obtained with unlimited precision. In a mathematical problem a meaningful result is therefore one that is accurate to the number of figures we need for any specific purpose. For example, a mathematical table, say of the exponential function e^x, is precisely of this kind. There are many such published tables, with varying numbers of figures for use in different contexts, but in each case the aim of the compiler of the table is to produce results accurate to the number of figures quoted.

A physical problem is quite different. Here at least some of the data are uncertain, by which we usually mean that a particular datum x is known only to lie within some interval $(x-\varepsilon_1, x+\varepsilon_2)$. The solutions will lie in corresponding intervals. For example we may be able to show that a solution y is contained in the interval $(y-\eta_1, y+\eta_2)$. This is all we can meaningfully ask, and if $y = 2\cdot0$, $\eta_1 = \eta_2 = 0\cdot1$, it is meaningless to ask for a 'solution' correct to three significant figures. For example, if $1\cdot5 \leqslant x \leqslant 2\cdot5$, then $y = x^{10}$ is in the approximate interval $57\cdot6 \leqslant y \leqslant 9536\cdot7$, and the 'solution' is not known for certain even to one significant figure. On the other hand $y = x^{0.1}$ is in the interval $1.04 < y < 1.10$, and the three-figure 'solution' 1.07 is certainly 'correct' to within 3 per cent. The engineers' rule of thumb, that the number of 'correct' figures in the results is equal to the number of 'correct' figures in the data, is in fact quite worthless. There may, of course, be some probability distribution of x in its 'datum interval', and a corresponding distribution of y in its 'solution interval', and this information (if it can be found) *is* meaningful.

Some measure of the effect on the solution of uncertainties in the data is called the *degree of condition* of the problem. If it is large the problem is *ill-conditioned*, and if it is small the problem is *well-conditioned*. The condition is a function only of the given problem, and is quite independent of the method of solution. We give many examples of ill-conditioned situations in the following chapters.

12. The second consideration refers to the degree of certainty with which we can guarantee that our *method* will give meaningful results in the two senses quoted. Some methods suffer from *induced instability*, which means that they introduce sources of error that may produce very unsatisfactory results. *Stable methods* do not have these defects, or at least have them in much smaller degree, and the numerical analyst is constantly striving to invent such methods. These topics, also, we discuss in subsequent chapters.

Here we note briefly some circumstances that can produce instability. In the problems of a discrete variable, the algebraic problems, errors arise solely through our inability to perform exact arithmetic. The necessary use of 'digital numbers', for example those of 'floating-point' arithmetic, inevitably gives rise to inexact arithmetic. Without going into quantitative details at this stage, in unstable methods the growth of the unavoidable individual rounding errors causes a significant and unwarranted error in the computed solution. We shall discuss, in the sequel, two methods of error analysis that give comparative evaluation of various techniques from a determination of the magnitude of the induced rounding errors.

In problems of a continuous variable, such as those involved in approximation, the evaluation of definite integrals, and the solution of differential equations of all kinds, we generally solve an approximating discrete problem. For this we want to use a stable technique, in the sense of the preceding paragraph, but we must also be concerned with the extent to which the accurate solution of the discrete problem differs from that of the continuous problem.

The general nature of this difference is associated with the term 'truncation error'. This will depend on various things, but in particular on the number of discrete points which, in any given context, is adequate to represent the continuous variation of the dependent variable. We shall find it necessary, in the later chapters of this book, to pay some close mathematical attention to the various types of truncation error and their consequences.

13. The term 'truncation error' can also be stretched to include certain topics in the algebraic problem. For example, in the summation of a series, such as

$$S = 1 - \tfrac{1}{2} + \tfrac{1}{3} - \tfrac{1}{4} + ..., \tag{16}$$

we can clearly take only a finite number of terms and must *truncate* the series at some point. It is important that we make adequate mathematical investigation of the *remainder*. The 'machine' test, of stopping at the first term that is smaller than the tolerable error, is quite unsatisfactory. Certainly, in (16), the difference between S and the sum of the first n terms is indeed smaller than the next term, and the machine criterion is valid. The same criterion, however, would give a 'sum' to the divergent series

$$T = 1 + \tfrac{1}{2} + \tfrac{1}{3} + \tfrac{1}{4} + ..., \tag{17}$$

which is manifest nonsense.

Somewhat analogous, but less obvious, is the danger of too early termination of an iterative process, which for various reasons we may want to use even in *linear* algebraic problems. Here we are also effectively summing an infinite series, and the convergence may be so slow that the 'remainder' is very much larger than the first neglected term. The problem is less obvious than that of (16) because the terms of the series are not known in advance, and each may require extensive computation. In the days of machine saturation it is tempting to take 25 iterates even though 250 are really necessary.

14. Finally, we must include a note about the dangers of extrapolating, without explicit justification, from a particular problem that has possibly been solved satisfactorily, to another of apparently very similar form. For example, we can solve the integral equation

$$f(x) = g(x) + \int_0^1 k(x, y) f(y) \, dy, \tag{18}$$

in terms of an approximating algebraic problem, by replacing the integral by a linear combination of values $f(y_r)$, the y_r being particular points in the interval $(0, 1)$. The problem

$$0 = g(x) + \int_0^1 k(x, y) f(y) \, dy \tag{19}$$

can apparently be treated in precisely the same way. The mathematical properties of these 'similar' equations, however, are completely different, and this method applied to (19) can give completely spurious results.

As a second example consider the problem of interpolation, in a table giving the values of the Bessel function $J_0(x)$ at integer values of x. A rather powerful method of interpolating at the 'half-way points' is obtained from the fact that $y(x) = J_0(x)$ satisfies the differential equation

$$y'' + \frac{1}{x} y' + y = 0. \tag{20}$$

Using the simplest expressions for derivatives in terms of differences (see Chapter 8), we can replace (20) by the approximating algebraic equation

$$\frac{4r+1}{4r+2} y_r - \frac{7}{4} y_{r+\frac{1}{2}} + \frac{4r+3}{4r+2} y_{r+1} = 0, \qquad y_r = y(r), \qquad r = 1, 2, ... \tag{21}$$

Interpolating for $y(2 \cdot 5)$, from given values at $x = 2$ and $x = 3$, the formula gives

$$y(2 \cdot 5) = \tfrac{22}{35} y(3) + \tfrac{18}{35} y(2), \tag{22}$$

and with $J_0(3) = -0 \cdot 26005$, $J_0(2) = 0 \cdot 22389$, correct to five decimal places, this produces the approximation $y(2 \cdot 5) = -0 \cdot 04832$. The error is only $0 \cdot 00006$ compared with $J_0(2 \cdot 5)$.

For a function as 'consistently smooth' as $J_0(x)$ one might suppose that one would obtain comparable absolute accuracy (here the important criterion), at any other 'half-way' point. For $x = 1 \cdot 5$, however, equation (21) gives

$$y(1 \cdot 5) = \tfrac{10}{21} y(1) + \tfrac{14}{21} y(2) = 0 \cdot 51364, \tag{23}$$

which differs from $J_0(1 \cdot 5)$ by the much larger value $0 \cdot 00181$.

The point here is that various contributions to the error terms in the algebraic equation are quite large at this interval of unity. In the region $(2, 3)$ they tend fortuitously to cancel, whereas in $(1, 2)$ they reinforce each other. Again, therefore, one must use a method that is known to be accurate, and this almost always requires actual computation of the error terms or their upper bounds.

In all cases, we repeat, 'intuition', 'reasonable expectation', and 'rules of thumb' are no substitute for proper mathematical investigation.

Exercise 1

1. Suggest economic formulations of the following computing problems.
(i) The evaluation of

$$I_r = e^{-1} \int_0^1 x^r e^x \, dx$$

for positive integral values of r.
(ii) The evaluation of

$$I_{p,q} = \int_0^1 x^p (1+x)^q \, dx$$

for positive integral values of p and q.
(iii) The tabulation, for $x = 1(0 \cdot 01)2$ (which means $x = 1$ to 2 in intervals of $0 \cdot 01$) of the function

$$f(x) = \int_0^\infty \frac{e^{-u^2}}{u+x} \, du \qquad \text{(Goodwin and Staton, 1948)}.$$

(Hint: Express $f(x)$ as the solution of a first-order differential equation.)
(iv) The evaluation of the slowly-convergent series

$$S = 1 - \tfrac{1}{2} + \tfrac{1}{3} - \tfrac{1}{4} + \dots = \sum_{r=0}^\infty \frac{(-1)^r}{r+1} = \sum_{r=0}^\infty (-1)^r u_r.$$

(Hint: Use the Euler transformation $\displaystyle\sum_{r=n}^\infty (-1)^r u_r = \sum_{s=0}^\infty \frac{(-1)^{n+s}}{2^{s+1}} \Delta^s u_n$, where $\Delta^s u_n$ is the sth forward difference of u_n (see Chapter 8), starting with a convenient value of n.)
(v) The evaluation of the slowly-convergent series

$$S = \frac{1}{1^2} + \frac{1}{2^2} + \dots = \sum_{r=1}^\infty \left(\frac{1}{r^2}\right) = \sum_{r=1}^\infty u_r.$$

(Hint: Use the Euler–Maclaurin asymptotic formula

$$\tfrac{1}{2} u_n + \sum_{r=n+1}^\infty u_r = \int_n^\infty u(x) \, dx - \{\tfrac{1}{12} u'(n) - \tfrac{1}{720} u'''(n) + \dots \},$$

(valid when $u(x)$ and all its derivatives vanish as $x \to \infty$) starting with a convenient value of n.)

(vi) The test for 'stability', that all the roots of the polynomial

$$p_n(x) = a_0 x^n + a_1 x^{n-1} + \ldots + a_{n-1} x + a_n$$

should have negative real parts.
(Hint: use Routh's criterion, that *all* the determinants

$$T_2 = \begin{vmatrix} a_1 & a_0 \\ a_3 & a_2 \end{vmatrix}, \quad T_3 = \begin{vmatrix} a_1 & a_0 & 0 \\ a_3 & a_2 & a_1 \\ a_5 & a_4 & a_3 \end{vmatrix}, \quad T_4 = \begin{vmatrix} a_1 & a_0 & 0 & 0 \\ a_3 & a_2 & a_1 & a_0 \\ a_5 & a_4 & a_3 & a_2 \\ a_7 & a_6 & a_5 & a_4 \end{vmatrix}, \ldots,$$

with $T_0 = a_0$, $T_1 = a_1$, should be positive. See Chapter 5 for an economic method of evaluating successive determinants of this kind when, for $r > 1$, T_{r+1} is obtained from T_r by 'bordering' with an extra row and column.)
(vii) The evaluation at $x = 0$ of successive derivatives of the function

$$y = (1 + x + x^2)^{\frac{1}{2}}.$$

(Hint: use 'logarithmic' differentiation and the theorem of Leibnitz to produce a recurrence relation for the required quantities.)

2. The zeros of $x^2 - 2x + 0 \cdot 19$ are $x_1 = 1 \cdot 9$, $x_2 = 0 \cdot 1$. If the 'physical' quadratic is $x^2 - (2 + \varepsilon)x + (0 \cdot 19 + \eta)$, with $|\varepsilon| \leqslant 0 \cdot 05$, $|\eta| \leqslant 0 \cdot 005$, show that we can at best guarantee that

$$1 \cdot 844 \leqslant x_1 \leqslant 1 \cdot 956, \qquad 0 \cdot 094 \leqslant x_2 \leqslant 0 \cdot 106.$$

Are the greatest 'errors' in x_1 and x_2 achieved simultaneously?

3. Find the formula corresponding to (21) for interpolating at $x = 0$ from given values of $y(0 \cdot 5)$ and $y(-0 \cdot 5)$. (Hint: since $x = 0$, and $J_0(x)$ is perfectly 'well-behaved', then also $y'(0) = 0$. The value of $y'(x)/x$ at $x = 0$ is then just $y''(0)$, by the rule of de l'Hospital. The equation becomes $y''(0) + \frac{1}{2} y(0) = 0$, giving the approximating algebraic equation $y(\frac{1}{2}) + y(-\frac{1}{2}) - \frac{15}{8} y(0) = 0$. Also $y(\frac{1}{2}) = y(-\frac{1}{2})$ since $J_0(x)$ is an even function. Hence $y(0) = \frac{16}{15} y(\frac{1}{2})$. With $J_0(\frac{1}{2}) = 0 \cdot 93847$, this gives the approximation $J_0(0) = 1 \cdot 00103$, compared with the true value of unity.)

4. Consider the integral equation

$$f(x) = \tfrac{1}{3} \{ x^3 - (1 + x^2)^{\frac{3}{2}} \} + \int_0^1 (x^2 + y^2)^{\frac{1}{2}} f(y) \, dy.$$

For any particular $x = x_r$, this can be written as

$$f(x_r) = \tfrac{1}{3} \{ x_r^3 - (1 + x_r^2)^{\frac{3}{2}} \} + \int_0^1 (x_r^2 + y^2)^{\frac{1}{2}} f(y) \, dy,$$

and the integral can be expressed approximately in the form

$$\int_0^1 (x_r^2 + y^2)^{\frac{1}{2}} f(y) \, dy = \sum_{s=1}^n \alpha_s (x_r^2 + y_s^2)^{\frac{1}{2}} f(y_s).$$

By taking x_r in turn equal to $y_1, y_2, \ldots, y_n$, we obtain a set of simultaneous algebraic equations for the unknowns $f(x_1), f(x_2), \ldots, f(x_n)$.

Use Simpson's rule, with successive intervals $h = \frac{1}{2}, \frac{1}{4}, \frac{1}{8}, \ldots$, and observe the convergence of the solutions to definite values.

Repeat with the equation

$$0 = \tfrac{1}{3}\{x^3 - (1+x^2)^{\frac{3}{2}}\} + \int_0^1 (x^2+y^2)^{\frac{1}{2}} f(y) \, dy,$$

whose true solution is $f(x) = x$, and observe the lack of convergence, and the violent oscillations in the results for $h < \frac{1}{4}$. (By this process Fox and Goodwin (1953) obtained the values

$f(0)$	$f(\frac{1}{8})$	$f(\frac{1}{4})$	$f(\frac{3}{8})$	$f(\frac{1}{2})$	$f(\frac{5}{8})$	$f(\frac{3}{4})$	$f(\frac{7}{8})$	$f(1)$
0·0448		0·2124		0·5992		0·7185		1·0329
0·0216	0·1098	0·2360	0·5117	−0·3507	1·3618	−0·7614	1·2992	0·6004

See Baker *et al.* (1964) for an explanation of this phenomenon.)

2

Error Analysis and Floating-point Arithmetic

Introduction
1. WE CAN regard most problems in numerical analysis as variations on the theme represented by the equation

$$f(x) = y. \tag{1}$$

The operator f may be a matrix, and x and y vectors; it may be a combination of derivatives or integrals of a function of a continuous variable x; it may represent a polynomial or more complicated function of one or more variables represented by x, or it may represent a host of analogous things.

With such an equation we have two main problems. The first, the *direct problem*, is the evaluation of y for a given operator f and argument x. The evaluation of a polynomial, or the premultiplication of a vector by a matrix, are two obvious examples. The second is the *inverse problem*, in which we seek to evaluate x for given f and y. This involves the inversion of the operator f. Obvious examples are the solution of linear algebraic equations (in which we may not *necessarily* complete the practical process of inversion), the solution of a differential equation, and the determination of the zeros of a polynomial.

The aim of any error analysis, of course, is to find the error or to estimate an upper bound or statistical expectation for it, in the quantity we seek to compute, y in the direct problem and x in the inverse problem. The error is the accumulated effect of inherent uncertainties in the data (f and x in the direct problem, f and y in the inverse problem), and the results of inexact computation (including truncation error in its various forms).

For algebraic problems we have two main forms of error analysis, the *forward* and *backward* methods, which we discuss in the next few sections. The results are expressed in terms of certain numbers representing rounding errors in the data and in machine arithmetic; and in the second part of the chapter we investigate the nature and magnitudes of these errors.

Forward error analysis

2. For algebraic problems every computation can be represented by a precisely-defined sequence of the fundamental arithmetic operations of addition, subtraction, multiplication, and division. It is therefore possible in theory, starting from any given data, to follow closely every operation and to bound the error of the result of any single operation and hence of the final result. We exclude from this discussion, of course, questions of truncation error, which require some extra *mathematical* attention.

The computation, both for the direct and inverse problems, can again be represented by the single equation

$$z_r = g_r(z_{r-1}), \tag{2}$$

where, from successively computed quantities $z_1, z_2, ..., z_{r-1}$, we produce z_r with the operation g_r. Our process is inevitably finite, so that equation (2) holds for $r = 1, 2, ..., N$. Note that z_r is not necessarily just a single number; it may be called the *state* of the rth step in the computation. For example z_0 represents the initial data.

Now we may not start with the correct z_0. In a physical problem, for example, z_0 has uncertainties denoted by $\delta_P z_0$ of known upper bound, the suffix P representing 'physical'. In a mathematical problem the use of finite storage registers forces the use of a z_0 with errors $\delta_M z_0$ (M for 'mathematical'), in theory known exactly. In each case we start with the initial state $\bar{z}_0 = z_0 + \zeta_0$, say, which is what the machine actually stores. We call the elements of $\bar{z}_0$ *digital numbers*.

In the computation of z_1 we use $\bar{z}_0$ instead of z_0, giving one source of error, and in the computation of $g_1(\bar{z}_0)$ we make further rounding errors, to produce the number $\bar{z}_1$. We can write

$$\bar{z}_0 = z_0 + \zeta_0, \qquad \bar{z}_1 = \overline{g_1(\bar{z}_0)} = g_1(\bar{z}_0) + \eta_1 = g_1(z_0) + \zeta_1, \tag{3}$$

and the general step is represented by the similar formula

$$\bar{z}_r = \overline{g_r(\bar{z}_{r-1})} = g_r(\bar{z}_{r-1}) + \eta_r = g_r(z_{r-1}) + \zeta_r. \tag{4}$$

The notation in (3) and (4) has the following meaning. A bar over any symbol or combination of symbols, denoting some numerical operation, means that this is what the machine actually produces and stores. It is the *digital equivalent* of the exact number we are trying to obtain, the best, as it were, that the machine can do for us. The quantity η_r is the difference between the machine result and the exact value of the *current* operation involved. The quantity ζ_r is the difference between the state after r steps of the computation and what we would have obtained with the use of exact initial data and exact computation throughout. It is, so to speak, the accumulated effect of the initial ζ_0 and the various η_r. We can say that $\bar{z}_N$ is the digital state at the Nth stage resulting from uncertainties in the initial state and further errors in the computation, z_N is the ideal exact state, and $\zeta_N = z_N - \bar{z}_N$. We seek an upper bound for $|\zeta_N|$.

In simple problems we can perform this by *forward analysis*, but in many cases the inter-relations between the various rounding (and truncation) errors are so complicated that this process becomes prohibitive. Attempts in some directions have been made with the use of 'range arithmetic' (Dwyer, 1951), and with the rather similar new 'interval arithmetic' of Moore (1966). The reader should watch for further papers on this topic.

Backward error analysis

3. In many cases it turns out to be easier (if not always so informative) to use *backward error analysis*. Here we accept the 'solution' $\bar{z}_N$, and try to find a 'neighbouring' problem, a 'perturbation' of the given problem, which would produce $\bar{z}_N$ with the use of exact arithmetic at all stages. For this purpose we no longer concentrate on the ζ_r in (4), but consider the local error η_r and attempt to find a perturbation operator $g_r + \delta g_r$ so that the equation

$$\bar{z}_r = \overline{g_r(\bar{z}_{r-1})} = g_r(\bar{z}_{r-1}) + \eta_r = (g_r + \delta g_r)(\bar{z}_{r-1}) \tag{5}$$

is satisfied exactly.

The interesting thing is that the relations between the various δg_r in (5) are often far simpler than those between the ζ_r in (4). In fact, returning to our original problem (1), we can often say that we have obtained an *exact* solution of the perturbed problem

$$(f + \delta f)(x + \delta x) = y + \delta y, \tag{6}$$

where the perturbations δf and δx in the direct problem, and δf and δy in the inverse problem, are simple functions of the 'local' perturbations δg_r.

4. We can now interpret (6) as follows. In the direct problem we are given f and x, but may have to start with digital $\bar{f}$ and $\bar{x}$, either through physical uncertainties or through our inability to store exactly

mathematical f and x. We are likely to use $\bar{x}$ throughout, and further perturbations are induced only in f. Equation (6) can then be written in the form

$$(\bar{f}+\delta_T f)(\bar{x}) = (f+\delta_{PM}f+\delta_T f)(x+\delta_{PM}x) = y+\delta y = \bar{y}, \qquad (7)$$

where PM means the initial combination of mathematical and physical errors, and $\delta_T f$ is the perturbation induced by our particular technique of computation, some combination of the δg_r in (5). Here we seek δy, and obtain immediately

$$\bar{y}-y = \delta y = (f+\delta_{PM}f+\delta_T f)(x+\delta_{PM}x)-f(x)$$
$$= (\delta_{PM}f+\delta_T f)(x)+(f+\delta_{PM}f+\delta_T f)(\delta_{PM}x), \qquad (8)$$

at least if f is a linear operator. If we have upper bounds for all the δ quantities we have an upper bound for the error in the required quantity. Note that if either $\delta_{PM}f(x)$ or $f(\delta_{PM}x)$ is large we may have an *ill-conditioned direct problem*, and if $\delta_T f(x)$ is large we have *induced instability*.

In the inverse problem we are given f and y in (1), and seek x. Here we start with digital $\bar{f}$ and $\bar{y}$, and again solve exactly a problem defined by

$$(\bar{f}+\delta_T f)(\bar{x}) = (f+\delta_{PM}f+\delta_T f)(x+\delta x) = y+\delta_{PM}y+\delta_T y = \bar{y}+\delta_T y, \quad (9)$$

in which we may have to perturb the initial $\bar{y}$ by a further $\delta_T y$.

The error in x, the quantity we seek, is now given by

$$\delta x = (f+\delta_{PM}f+\delta_T f)^{-1}(y+\delta_{PM}y+\delta_T y)-f^{-1}(y), \qquad (10)$$

and the situation is here more complicated. Even if we have determined upper bounds for the δ quantities we cannot immediately determine an upper bound to δx. For this depends on the inverse f^{-1} of f and of the effects of perturbations in f on its inverse, for which results are not always available from theoretical considerations. In particular if these effects are large the problem is likely to be ill-conditioned. On the other hand we see that the backward error analysis gives a relative evaluation of techniques, for those for which $\delta_T f$ and $\delta_T y$ are small are certainly better than those for which these perturbations are large.

5. Not only is the backward method usually easier to perform, but it has some interesting by-products not shared by the direct method. With the latter, for example, and particularly with the inverse problem, we may find, even with stable techniques and with well-conditioned problems, that in the early stages computed quantities diverge far and fast from those we should obtain with exact arithmetic.

At least partial recovery is certain, but the analysis is so prohibitively involved that we wrongly class such techniques as unstable. The backward analysis will often reveal this fact and evaluate properly the technique. In subsequent chapters we give some simple examples of forward and backward analysis and of the phenomenon just mentioned.

Floating-point arithmetic

6. To be able to perform the error analysis, in any particular context, we must attach some numerical values to the quantities η_r in an equation like (5), and hence to the local perturbation δg_r. In theory these can usually be determined precisely, but the computation may be lengthy and we shall normally be content with computed upper bounds for these quantities. As a result we shall be able to give upper bounds to the *actual error* ζ_N in the direct problem, and upper bounds to the *perturbations* in the inverse problem.

We consider here algebraic problems, and concentrate on the errors induced by floating-point arithmetic, the style almost always used in modern digital computers. The first significant fact is that we must store every number in floating-point form

$$x = 2^b \cdot a \quad \text{(or } 10^b \cdot a \text{ in the decimal scale),} \tag{11}$$

where b is a positive or negative integer (or zero) and a is a fraction in the range

$$0.5 \leqslant |a| < 1.0 \quad (0.1 \leqslant |a| < 1.0 \text{ in the decimal scale).} \tag{12}$$

(We shall ignore here inessential features, such as the precise method of storing negative numbers, whether equality can be allowed in any part of (12), the differences in different rounding methods, and so on. Our examples, moreover, will usually use the scale of 10, since mental arithmetic is more familiar in this scale.)

The fractional part is compressed into a finite register of t digits, and this implies immediately that only few numbers can be stored exactly. For example, numbers like $2^{\frac{1}{2}}$, π, or 0.6 in the decimal scale, can be stored in our machine only in rounded form. Whereas, in a four-digit decimal machine, the number 4976 is stored exactly as $10^4(0.4976)$, and -0.0004976 is stored exactly as $10^{-3}(-0.4976)$, any number whose significant part lies in the range 49755000... to 4976499... is also stored with a fractional part of 0.4976, the digital equivalent of any number in this interval. We write, for example,

$$\bar{x} = fl(x) = 10^4(0\cdot4976), \tag{13}$$

where the bar has been used earlier in this chapter for the same purpose, and where the symbol fl (for 'floating-point'), means the floating-point digital representation of the number in brackets. Then

$$\pi = 3\cdot14159..., \qquad \bar{\pi} = fl(\pi) = 10^1(0\cdot3142), \tag{14}$$

where of course the number is properly rounded before expression in digital form. There follows the result

$$\bar{\pi} - \pi = fl(\pi) - \pi = 10^1(0\cdot000040...), \tag{15}$$

the number on the right being the rounding error in the floating-point representation of π, analogous to the η rounding error in equation (4).

The worst absolute rounding error in the decimal scale is five units in the first neglected figure, but in the floating-point representation it is clearly more convenient to consider the worst possible *relative error*. Since the fractional part of the number can be as small as $0\cdot1$ the relative error can be as much as five units in the last figure, and we can certainly write, in the decimal scale,

$$\bar{x} = fl(x) = x(1+\varepsilon), \qquad |\varepsilon| \leqslant 5.10^{-t} = \tfrac{1}{2}.10^{1-t}. \tag{16}$$

The error ε is of course zero when the number x has exact digital representation in t figures, and we call such an x a *digital number*.

It is worth noting that rounding is a more ruthless operation in the decimal than in the binary scale, and we easily see that in the latter the ε of equation (16) is bounded by

$$|\varepsilon| \leqslant 2^{-t}, \tag{17}$$

the lower limit for $|a|$ in (12) being $0\cdot5$, the same as the maximum rounding error in the tth binary place.

Following this first formula of digital arithmetic we can now examine various arithmetic processes, and in particular determine upper bounds for the errors involved in more elaborate operations in digital arithmetic.

Addition and subtraction

7. First we consider the addition $x = x_1 + x_2$ of two digital numbers

$$x_1 = 2^{b_1}.a_1, \qquad x_2 = 2^{b_2}.a_2, \tag{18}$$

in which we assume $b_1 \geqslant b_2$. The machine performs the addition in the form

$$x = 2^{b_1}(a_1 + 2^{b_2-b_1}a_2), \tag{19}$$

so that the first operation 'shifts' a_2 to the right by $b_1 - b_2$ places. The addition is then performed in a double-length accumulator, if necessary the result is shifted up or down (*standardized*) to put it in the standard range (12) with adjustment of the exponent, and the fractional part is finally rounded to t figures (that is to single-length precision). Some examples will clarify this process, using a four-figure decimal machine.

If $b_1 - b_2 > t$ the second number obviously makes no contribution to the digital sum, which is satisfactory since the double-length sum may not be formed exactly in the machine. In the limiting case we have something like

$$fl[10^4(0\cdot4976) + 10^{-1}(-0\cdot9999)] = fl\{10^4(0\cdot4976 - 0\cdot000009999)\}$$
$$= fl\{10^4(0\cdot497590001)\} = 10^4(0\cdot4976).$$
$$(20)$$

If $b_1 - b_2 = t$ the double-length sum can be formed exactly, as in

$$fl\{10^4(0\cdot4976) + 10^0(-0\cdot9999)\} = fl\{10^4(0\cdot4976 - 0\cdot00009999)\}$$
$$= fl\{10^4(0\cdot49750001)\} = 10^4(0\cdot4975).$$
$$(21)$$

The addition

$$fl\{10^4(0\cdot1000) + 10^0(-0\cdot8726)\} = fl\{10^4(0\cdot1000 - 0\cdot00008726)\}$$
$$= fl\{10^4(0\cdot09991274)\} = fl\{10^3(0\cdot99912740)\} = 10^3(0\cdot9991),$$
$$(22)$$

requires a *left* shift as well as a rounding. We may need as many as t left shifts, as in

$$fl\{10^4(0\cdot1001) + 10^4(-0\cdot1000)\} = fl\{10^4(0\cdot0001)\} = 10^0(1\cdot0000). \quad (23)$$

Note also that cancellation can help to give an exact sum even with different exponents in the two numbers, as in

$$fl\{10^4(0\cdot1001) + 10^3(-0\cdot9999)\} = fl\{10^4(0\cdot1001 - 0\cdot09999)\}$$
$$= fl\{10^4(0\cdot00011)\} = 10^1(0\cdot1100),$$
$$(24)$$

with no error. On the other hand we can clearly never obtain more than one right shift, as in

$$fl\{10^0(0\cdot4976) + 10^0(0\cdot5368)\} = fl\{10^0(1\cdot0344)\} = 10^1(0\cdot1034), \quad (25)$$

and absence of rounding error is much less likely.

Finally, we observe the curious fact that the result of forming $x-y$, where x and y are positive *non-digital* numbers, can give a result greater than x. For example, if

$$x = 48 \cdot 29501, \qquad y = 0 \cdot 00497629, \tag{26}$$

the machine produces

$$fl\{fl(x)-fl(y)\} = fl\{10^2(0 \cdot 4830)-10^{-2}(0 \cdot 4976)\}$$
$$= fl\{10^2(0 \cdot 4830-0 \cdot 00004976)\} = fl\{10^2(0 \cdot 48295024)\} = 48 \cdot 30. \tag{27}$$

8. We can now find a general formula for the sum or difference of two digital numbers x_1 and x_2, defined in (18). If the exact result is given by

$$x_1 \pm x_2 = 2^{b_3} \cdot a_3, \tag{28}$$

then the rounding error in the digital representation is at most $2^{b_3}(0 \cdot 5 \times 2^{-t})$, and the argument which produced (17) gives the similar result

$$fl(x_1 \pm x_2) = (x_1 \pm x_2)(1+\varepsilon), \qquad |\varepsilon| \leqslant 2^{-t}. \tag{29}$$

In the decimal scale we easily find that $|\varepsilon|$ cannot exceed 5.10^{-t}.

Multiplication and division

9. For the multiplication of the digital numbers x_1 and x_2 in (18), the machine adds b_1 and b_2, forms the double-length product a_1a_2, shifts to the left if necessary, obviously by at most one place, adjusts the exponent, and rounds the fractional part to single length. For example, if

$$x_1 = 10^4(0 \cdot 4976), \qquad x_2 = 10^{-3}(0 \cdot 4976), \tag{30}$$

we have

$$fl(x_1x_2) = fl(10^{4-3} \times 0 \cdot 24760576) = 10^1(0 \cdot 2476), \tag{31}$$

while if

$$x_1 = 10^4(0 \cdot 4976), \qquad x_2 = 10^{-3}(0 \cdot 1294), \tag{32}$$

we have

$$fl(x_1x_2) = fl(10^1 \times 0 \cdot 06438944) = 10^0(0 \cdot 6439). \tag{33}$$

Again we can easily see, just as for addition and subtraction, that

$$fl(x_1x_2) = x_1x_2(1+\varepsilon), \qquad |\varepsilon| \leqslant 2^{-t}, \tag{34}$$

with (16) still applying in the decimal scale.

The division x_1/x_2, not allowed if $x_2 = 0$, is only slightly more complicated. If $|a_1| > |a_2|$ we shift a_1 one place to the right in a double-length accumulator, divide $2^{-1}a_1$ by a_2 and round correctly to single length, and take the exponent b_1-b_2+1. If $|a_1| < |a_2|$

we divide without shifting, and the exponent is $b_1 - b_2$. In both cases our results are standardized.

For example, if

$$x_1 = 10^4(0\cdot4976), \qquad x_2 = 10^3(0\cdot3824), \tag{35}$$

we find

$$fl(x_1/x_2) = fl\{10^2(0\cdot04976000/0\cdot3824)\}$$
$$= fl\{10^2(0\cdot13012...)\} = 10^2(0\cdot1301), \tag{36}$$

and

$$fl(x_2/x_1) = fl\{10^{-1}(0\cdot38240000/0\cdot4976)\}$$
$$= fl\{10^{-1}(0\cdot768488...)\} = 10^{-1}(0\cdot7685). \tag{37}$$

Again, it is clear, we can write

$$fl(x_1/x_2) = (x_1/x_2)(1+\varepsilon), \qquad |\varepsilon| \leqslant 2^{-t}, \tag{38}$$

with $|\varepsilon|$ bounded by (16) in the decimal scale.

Extended additions and multiplications

10. Consider next the evaluation of $x_1+x_2+...+x_n$, where the x_r are digital numbers. In standard floating-point operation we must perform a process of 'nested addition', more easily represented in the bar notation in the form

$$fl(x_1+x_2+...+x_n) = \overline{\overline{(x_1+x_2}+x_3}+x_4+...). \tag{39}$$

Using previous theorems we have

$$\left. \begin{aligned} \overline{x_1+x_2} &= (x_1+x_2)(1+\varepsilon_2) \\ \overline{\overline{(x_1+x_2}+x_3)} &= \{(x_1+x_2)(1+\varepsilon_2)+x_3\}(1+\varepsilon_3),... \end{aligned} \right\}, \tag{40}$$

and ultimately deduce

$$fl(x_1+x_2+...+x_n) = (x_1+x_2)(1+E_2)+x_3(1+E_3)+...+x_n(1+E_n), \tag{41}$$

where

$$\left. \begin{aligned} 1+E_2 &= (1+\varepsilon_2)(1+\varepsilon_3)...(1+\varepsilon_n) \\ 1+E_3 &= (1+\varepsilon_3)...(1+\varepsilon_n),..., \qquad 1+E_n = 1+\varepsilon_n \end{aligned} \right\}, \tag{42}$$

where each $|\varepsilon_r| \leqslant 2^{-t}$. If $|\varepsilon|$ is the upper bound to the $|\varepsilon_r|$, we have

$$(1-|\varepsilon|)^{n-r+1} < 1+E_r < (1+|\varepsilon|)^{n-r+1}, \qquad r = 2, 3,..., n, \tag{43}$$

and for reasonable values of n, small in comparison with ε^{-1}, we can write

$$|E_r| < (n-r+1)\,|\varepsilon|, \qquad r = 2, 3, \ldots, n, \tag{44}$$

where $|\varepsilon|$ is given in (16) and (17). (This inequality is not strictly true, and should include a factor slightly larger than unity on the right-hand side. The effect is so small that we ignore it in all cases.)

11. For extended multiplications and divisions we have similarly

$$fl(x_1 x_2 \ldots x_n) = (\overline{\overline{\overline{x_1 x_2 x_3 x_4 \ldots}}}), \tag{45}$$

and the successive application of (34) gives easily the result

$$\left.\begin{aligned} fl(x_1 x_2 \ldots x_n) &= (x_1 x_2 \ldots x_n)(1+E) \\ 1+E &= (1+\varepsilon_2)(1+\varepsilon_3)\ldots(1+\varepsilon_n) \end{aligned}\right\}. \tag{46}$$

Again, to a very close approximation, we produce for the upper bound to $|E|$ the expression

$$|E| < (n-1)\,|\varepsilon|, \qquad |\varepsilon| < 2^{-t}. \tag{47}$$

In virtue of (38) we shall obtain for mixed multiplications and divisions the same result

$$fl(x_1^{\pm 1} x_2^{\pm 1} \ldots x_n^{\pm 1}) = (x_1^{\pm 1} x_2^{\pm 1} \ldots x_n^{\pm 1})(1+E), \tag{48}$$

with $|E|$ bounded by (47).

In the extended operations the actual rounding error, though not the upper bounds quoted in (44), (47), and (48), obviously depend on the ordering of the terms, since the individual ε_r depend on the numbers involved in every operation. For division and multiplication the order is relatively unimportant, but for extended addition it is clear from (41) and (44) that we would like to associate the smaller E_r with the larger x_r, so that treatment of the terms in *increasing* order of magnitude gives the smallest error.

For example, we have

$$10^4(0{\cdot}3827)+10^2(0{\cdot}1254)+10^1(0{\cdot}1567) = 10^4(0{\cdot}3841107), \tag{49}$$

with $10^4(0{\cdot}3841)$ as its correct four-figure digital equivalent. Floating arithmetic in the order given in (49), however, produces

$$\left.\begin{aligned} fl\{10^4(0{\cdot}3827)+10^2(0{\cdot}1254)\} &= fl\{10^4(0{\cdot}383954)\} = 10^4(0{\cdot}3840) \\ fl\{10^4(0{\cdot}3840)+10^1(0{\cdot}1567)\} &= fl\{10^4(0{\cdot}3841567)\} = 10^4(0{\cdot}3842) \end{aligned}\right\}, \tag{50}$$

with an error of nearly one unit in the last figure. In the reverse order we have smaller rounding errors, for

$$\begin{aligned} fl\{10^1(0\cdot1567)+10^2(0\cdot1254)\} &= fl\{10^2(0\cdot14107)\} = 10^2(0\cdot1411) \\ fl\{10^2(0\cdot1411)+10^4(0\cdot3827)\} &= fl\{10^4(0\cdot384111)\} = 10^4(0\cdot3841) \end{aligned} \Bigg\}, \quad (51)$$

a much better result.

12. Finally, we consider the error arising from the floating-point evaluation of $\sum_{r=1}^{n} x_r y_r$, where the x_r and y_r are digital numbers, an operation occurring in many computing contexts. Again we consider the 'nested' form

$$fl(x_1y_1+x_2y_2+\ldots+x_ny_n) - fl(\overline{x_1y_1}+\overline{x_2y_2}+\ldots+\overline{x_ny_n})$$

$$= (\overline{x_1y_1}+\overline{x_2y_2}+\overline{x_3y_3}+\ldots). \quad (52)$$

Previous results give

$$\overline{x_1y_1} = x_1y_1(1+\varepsilon_1), \quad \overline{x_2y_2} = x_2y_2(1+\varepsilon_2) \\ fl(\overline{x_1y_1}+\overline{x_2y_2}) = \{x_1y_1(1+\varepsilon_1)+x_2y_2(1+\varepsilon_2)\}(1+\eta_2) \Bigg\}, \quad (53)$$

etc., and we easily deduce

$$fl(x_1y_1+\ldots+x_ny_n) = x_1y_1(1+E_1)+x_2y_2(1+E_2)+\ldots+x_ny_n(1+E_n), \quad (54)$$

where

$$1+E_1 = (1+\varepsilon_1)(1+\eta_2)\ldots(1+\eta_n), \quad 1+E_2 = (1+\varepsilon_2)(1+\eta_2)\ldots(1+\eta_n) \\ 1+E_r = (1+\varepsilon_r)(1+\eta_r)\ldots(1+\eta_n), \quad r = 3,4,\ldots,n \Bigg\}. \quad (55)$$

Here all the $|\varepsilon_r|$ and $|\eta_r|$ are bounded by the same $|\varepsilon|$, and we can write

$$|E_1| \leqslant n\,|\varepsilon|, \quad |E_2| \leqslant n\,|\varepsilon| \\ |E_r| \leqslant (n-r+2)\,|\varepsilon|, \quad r = 3,\ldots,n \Bigg\}, \quad (56)$$

where ε is given by (16) or (17).

More accurate floating-point arithmetic

13. So far we have assumed that in the computation of $x_1+x_2+x_3$, say, the machine adds x_1 and x_2, temporarily to double length, and rounds to a single-length digital number before adding x_3. This is the standard practice, which is usually performed in the arithmetic instructions of languages like ALGOL and FORTRAN. In certain contexts, however, we may prefer to form all the additions in a double-length accumulator, perhaps with a final single rounding to standard single length. Similar considerations apply to the computations

$$c = \sum_{r=1}^{n} x_r y_r, \qquad e = \left(\sum_{r=1}^{n} x_r y_r \right) \Big/ d, \qquad (57)$$

where in the first we would like to accumulate to double length the double-length products, with or without a final rounding to single length. In the second of (57) we would often prefer to keep the numerator to double length before dividing by the single-length d, and finally round to single length.

Such operations may be available in basic machine language (though not in compiled languages), and though they take longer to perform they have significant advantages, particularly in linear algebra. Since the exponents of the various terms may differ considerably we can rarely form exact double-length accumulations, but the errors are now restricted to the last few digits in the second register, that is they are small multiples of 10^{-2t} or 2^{-2t}. Wilkinson (1963) refers to these operations by the symbol $fl_2(\ )$.

The analysis is virtually the same as that for $fl(\ )$ arithmetic, except for one almost inessential detail. Consider the evaluation by this process of $fl(x_1 y_1 + x_2 y_2)$, where in exact double-length form

$$\left. \begin{aligned} x_1 y_1 &= 10^2(0 \cdot 98734824), \qquad x_2 y_2 = 10^1(0 \cdot 14672806) \\ x_1 y_1 + x_2 y_2 &= 10^3(0 \cdot 1002021046) \end{aligned} \right\}. \qquad (58)$$

To form the fl_2 addition we must round the second number to $10^2(0 \cdot 01467281)$, and the addition gives $10^2(1 \cdot 00202105)$, which may perhaps be rounded to the standard double length number $10^3(0 \cdot 10020211)$. The first rounding error has affected the second, and it is easy to see that the maximum relative error of the result is here

$$|\varepsilon| \leqslant 0 \cdot 55 \times 10^{1-2t} (\text{decimal}), \qquad |\varepsilon| \leqslant 1 \cdot 5 \times 2^{-2t} (\text{binary}), \qquad (59)$$

the new upper bounds corresponding to (29).

Without further detailed proof we can then easily see, for fl_2 arithmetic, that the results of §§ 10 and 12 apply with the new bounds (59) for $|\varepsilon|$, the results being in double-length form. If we want these in rounded single length we merely multiply by a final $(1+\varepsilon')$, with $|\varepsilon'|$ bounded by (16) or (17). The final single-length results are then little inferior, in terms of rounding error, to those of (16) and (17) for a simple rounding operation. In analogy with the remark at the end of § 10 we shall write

$$fl_2\left(\sum_{r=1}^{n} x_r\right) = \left(\sum_{r=1}^{n} x_r\right)(1+\varepsilon) \\ fl_2\left(\sum_{r=1}^{n} x_r y_r\right) = \left\{\sum_{r=1}^{n} (x_r y_r)\right\}(1+\varepsilon), \qquad |\varepsilon| \leqslant 2^{-t} \tag{60}$$

with a similar result for the second of (57).

Exercises 2

1. Consider the arguments of § 2 in respect of the computation of $\sum\limits_{r=0}^{N} x_r$, where the x_r are given non-digital numbers. Show that we can take

$$z_0 = x_0, x_1, \ldots, x_N \quad \text{(a set of numbers, the initial state)}$$

and then $\bar{z}_0 = z_0 + \zeta_0$ gives

$$\zeta_0 = \zeta_0^{(0)}, \zeta_0^{(1)}, \ldots, \zeta_0^{(N)}, \quad \text{where} \quad |\zeta_0^{(r)}| \leqslant 2^{-t} |x_r|.$$

Show that we can perform the computation from

$$z_1 = x_0 + x_1, \qquad z_2 = z_1 + x_2, \ldots,$$

so that equation (2) is here given by $z_r = z_{r-1} + x_r$, and each z_r, $r \geqslant 1$, is a single number. Then

$$\bar{z}_1 = fl(\bar{x}_0 + \bar{x}_1) = (\bar{x}_0 + \bar{x}_1)(1+\varepsilon_1), \quad \text{where} \quad |\varepsilon_1| \leqslant 2^{-t}.$$

Show that, in equation (3),

$$|\eta_1| \leqslant 2^{-t}(|\bar{x}_0| + |\bar{x}_1|), \qquad |\zeta_1| \leqslant 2^{1-t}(|x_0| + |x_1|),$$

and find corresponding bounds for η_r and ζ_r in equation (4).

From (42) and (44) deduce that if the x_r are digital (so that $\bar{x}_r = x_r$), then *forward* analysis gives for the error in the result the bound

$$|\zeta_N| = \sum_{r=0}^{N} |x_r| E_r, \qquad E_0 = E_1 \leqslant N \cdot 2^{-t}, \qquad E_r \leqslant (N-r) \cdot 2^{-t},$$

and *backward* analysis shows that our result is the exact value of the sum $\sum\limits_{r=0}^{N} x'_r$, where $x'_r = (1+E_r)x_r$, with the same definitions of E_r. What are the corresponding results for non-digital x_r?

2. Discuss, in the spirit of exercise 1, the results of §§ 11 and 12. Notice, in the computation of the product $x_1 x_2 \ldots x_n$, that the backward analysis shows that we have the exact result of the product $x_1' x_2' \ldots x_n'$, where

$$x_1' x_2' \ldots x_n' = (x_1 x_2 \ldots x_n)(1+E), \qquad |E| \leqslant (n-1) \cdot 2^{-t},$$

and that we can share the perturbation just as we please among the individual x_r, the choice depending on the particular context!

3. In § 7 we observed that cancellation can still provide the exact sum of two digital numbers with different exponents, provided that a double-length accumulator is available for the addition, as in our fl arithmetic. Show, with illustration from (24), that this is not true if only a single-length accumulator is available, so that one number has to be rounded before the addition.

Show also that the relative error of $fl(x_1 + x_2 + x_3)$, where each x is a digital number, can be large even in the standard fl arithmetic. Consider, for example, the sum
$$10^4(0 \cdot 1000) + 10^2(0 \cdot 1234) - 10^4(0 \cdot 1013),$$
with the addition performed in the given order on a four-digit decimal machine.

Show finally that the relative error of $fl(x_1 + x_2)$ can be large if x_1 and x_2 are not digital. Consider, for example, the sum $10^4(0 \cdot 10014) + 10^3(-0 \cdot 99996)$ in a four-digit decimal machine.

4. Compute in four-decimal fl arithmetic the sum

$$10^1(0 \cdot 1000) + 10^1(0 \cdot 1000) + 10^0(0 \cdot 5000) + 10^0(0 \cdot 1667) + 10^{-1}(0 \cdot 4167),$$

the digital numbers representing the first five terms of the series for e. Verify that addition in the reverse order gives a smaller rounding error.

5. We can sometimes obtain sharper bounds when we know in advance something about the magnitude of the numbers involved. For example, if x_1, x_2, and x_3 are digital numbers we have from the analysis of § 12 the result

$$fl(x_1 x_2 + x_3) = \{x_1 x_2(1+\varepsilon_2) + x_3\}(1+\varepsilon_3),$$

where $|\varepsilon_2|$, $|\varepsilon_3| \leqslant 5 \cdot 10^{-t}$ in a decimal machine. Then, to a close approximation

$$|fl(x_1 x_2 + x_3) - (x_1 x_2 + x_3)| \leqslant |\varepsilon_2 x_1 x_2| + |(x_1 x_2 + x_3)\varepsilon_3| \leqslant 5 \cdot 10^{-t}\{|x_1 x_2| + |x_1 x_2 + x_3|\}.$$

If we know that both $x_1 x_2$ and $x_1 x_2 + x_3$ are less than unity in modulus this gives an upper bound to the error of 10 units in the last place.

Show, however, that if $|x_1 x_2| \leqslant 1$, $|x_1 x_2 + x_3| \leqslant 1 - 0 \cdot 5 \cdot 10^{-t}$, then the error cannot in fact exceed one unit in the last place. Construct an example to show that this upper bound is possible.

(Hint: start with $\overline{x_1 x_2} = x_1 x_2 + \eta_2$, and since $|x_1 x_2| \leqslant 1$ then $|\eta_2| \leqslant 0 \cdot 5 \times 10^{-t}$. We are here better advised to examine the *absolute* rather than the *relative* error.)

3

Computations with Recurrence Relations

Introduction

1. In this and the following two chapters we shall discuss some techniques, and the error analysis thereof, for certain classes of algebraic problems. Our aim is to illustrate the circumstances that lead to ill-conditioning, and also to demonstrate the use of error analysis not only for finding the errors in the computed results but also to make comparative evaluation of techniques from the point of view of induced instability.

We start with the treatment of recurrence relations, which are rather important because they occur in many different contexts. For example, they may be involved in an algebraic approximation to a differential equation; and their properties are indeed very similar to those of ordinary differential equations. The general linear *recurrence relation* (or *difference equation*) of order n is given by

$$a_{r,0}y_r + a_{r,1}y_{r+1} + \ldots + a_{r,n}y_{r+n} = b_r, \qquad r = 0, 1, \ldots, \qquad (1)$$

where the coefficients $a_{r,s}$ and b_r are functions of r. If $b_r \equiv 0$ the equation is *homogeneous*. The general solution of (1) is given by

$$y_r = \sum_{s=1}^{n} A_s y_r^{(s)} + y_r^{(0)}, \qquad (2)$$

where $y_r^{(1)}$, $y_r^{(2)}, \ldots, y_r^{(n)}$ are independent 'complementary' solutions of the homogeneous form of (1), and $y_r^{(0)}$ is any particular solution of (1). The arbitrary constants A_s in (2) are determined from n given conditions on y_r. The most common conditions specify y_r at n different points, though we may also be given specified linear combinations of two or more values. In any case the solution exists, and is unique, if we can solve uniquely the corresponding linear equations for the A_s, and this we shall take to be possible in all cases. If $b_r \equiv 0$ the particular solution $y_r^{(0)}$ in (2) is also identically zero.

In the special case in which the coefficients on the left of (1) are constants, independent of r, the complementary functions are obtained in terms of the roots of the polynomial equation

$$a_0 + a_1 p + a_2 p^2 + \ldots + a_n p^n = 0. \qquad (3)$$

In particular, if the roots $p_1, p_2, \ldots, p_n$ are distinct, then

$$y_r^{(s)} = p_s^r, \qquad y_r = \sum_{s=1}^{n} A_s p_s^r + y_r^{(0)}. \tag{4}$$

2. We shall not discuss the general case in detail, but concentrate on the first-order or two-term recurrence relation

$$y_{r+1} = a_r y_r + b_r, \tag{5}$$

and the second-order or three-term recurrence written in the form

$$y_{r+1} + a_r y_r + b_r y_{r-1} = c_r. \tag{6}$$

With (5) we need one associated condition to produce a unique solution, and the specification of y_s for some particular s is the most usual condition.

For (6) we need two conditions, and here there are two main possibilities. In the first, giving the so-called *initial-value* problem, we are provided with two adjacent values y_s and y_{s+1} for some s, or possibly y_s and some linear combination of y_{s-1}, y_s, and y_{s+1}. In either case we can clearly compute in succession the sequence $y_{s+1}, y_{s+2}, \ldots$ by *forward recurrence*, or the sequence $y_{s-1}, y_{s-2}, \ldots$ by *backward recurrence*.

The second possibility, giving the so-called *boundary-value* problem, is the specification say of y_0 and y_n, the values at the two ends of some range, and we seek to find $y_1, y_2, \ldots, y_{n-1}$.

First-order equations. Conditioning

3. For the first-order equation (5) we immediately proceed to illustrate that the combination of (5) and a specified value of y_0 can give rise to a very ill-conditioned situation. The recurrence system (equation plus condition) given by

$$y_{r+1} = 0{\cdot}75 - 0{\cdot}75(r+4)y_r, \qquad y_0 = \alpha, \tag{7}$$

produces for different values of α the results shown in Table 3.1. We have used four-figure floating-decimal arithmetic according to the definition of Chapter 2.

TABLE 3.1

$y_0 = \alpha$	0·1700	0·1800	0·1900	0·2000	0·2100	0·2200	0·1957
y_1	0·2400	0·2100	0·1800	0·1500	0·1200	0·0900	0·1629
y_2	−0·1500	−0·0375	0·0750	0·1875	0·3000	0·4125	0·1391
y_3	1·425	0·9188	0·4125	−0·09380	−0·6000	−1·106	0·1240
y_4	−6·731	−4·074	−1·416	1·243	3·900	6·556	0·09900
y_5	41·14	25·19	9·246	−6·708	−22·65	−38·59	0·1560
y_6	−276·9	−169·2	−61·66	46·03	153·7	261·3	−0·3030

The results show that y_r is extremely sensitive, for large r, to small changes in the initial condition, and this recurrence *system* is very ill-conditioned. In fact the interval that contains y_r, corresponding to an interval $(y_0 - \varepsilon,\ y_0 + \varepsilon)$ containing the initial value, increases rapidly and unboundedly with r for any ε, however small.

4. On the other hand the similar recurrence system

$$y_r = \frac{1}{0 \cdot 75(r+4)}(0 \cdot 75 - y_{r+1}), \qquad y_N = \beta, \qquad (8)$$

in which we start with a specified value at $r = N$ and recur *backwards*, gives a very well-conditioned problem. This is illustrated in the results of Table 3.2.

TABLE 3.2

$y_6 = \beta$	0·1700	0·2200	0
y_5	0·08593	0·07852	0·1111
y_4	0·1107	0·1119	0·1065
y_3	0·1218	0·1215	0·1226
y_2	0·1396	0·1397	0·1394
y_1	0·1628	0·1628	0·1628
y_0	0·1957	0·1957	0·1957

As r decreases, the results become increasingly insensitive to small changes in the given condition, and the interval containing y_r, generated by the initial interval $(y_N - \varepsilon,\ y_N + \varepsilon)$, decreases very rapidly as r decreases.

Effect on problem formulation

5. Now it is clear that if our knowledge of the solution of our particular problem is contained only in the recurrence system (7), in which α is specified and we wish to compute $y_1,\ y_2,...,$ then the *physical* problem, in which α has small uncertainties, is extremely ill-conditioned. But it is important to observe that this phenomenon will make it very difficult to find a satisfactory solution to the corresponding *mathematical* problem, in which α is presumed known exactly. For in the first place we may not be able to store this number exactly, and in the second place the inevitable appearance of rounding errors in floating-point arithmetic will affect significantly our computed 'digital' results. They will diverge more and more from the correct values which we would obtain with exact α and exact arithmetic.

On the other hand we note that the first six solutions in Table 3.1 all have the same general nature. At some stage they begin to oscillate with increasing amplitude, and small changes in the initial value, or subsequent rounding errors, mainly affect the size of these amplitudes without giving misleading information about the nature of the solution. In a *relative* sense, in fact, as we shall see more clearly in § 11, the problem is not disturbingly ill-conditioned for most starting values y_0.

6. But inspection of the signs in Table 3.1 reveals the possibility, for some particular value of $\alpha = y_0$, of a solution that does not have this unbounded oscillatory behaviour. There is in fact one value of α in (7) for which the solution is monotonic decreasing, and the components of this solution are the values of the definite integral

$$y_r = \int_0^1 e^{\frac{4}{3}(x-1)} x^{r+3}\, dx, \qquad r = 0, 1, 2, \ldots, \tag{9}$$

which we discussed in §§ 5 and 6 of Chapter 1. The corresponding value of α is

$$y_0 = \int_0^1 e^{\frac{4}{3}(x-1)} x^3\, dx = \tfrac{1}{128}(243 e^{-\frac{4}{3}} - 39) = 0 \cdot 1957352 \ldots \tag{10}$$

The resulting *mathematical* problem, formulated as in (7) with this given value of y_0, is clearly extremely difficult to solve accurately. This is revealed in the last solution of Table 3.1, in which the small starting error in y_0 produces results which, as early as y_5, have not even the first significant figure correct and which then begin to oscillate without bound. The corresponding physical problems become more and more ill-conditioned, in a relative as well as an absolute sense, as $\alpha = y_0$ approaches this critical value.

We conclude that this formulation of the problem defined by (9) is unsatisfactory, in that we have produced an ill-conditioned version of the problem. It is, of course, possible to start with a very accurate y_0 and use double or higher precision arithmetic, but this is lengthy, inelegant, and merely postpones the dilemma. A better method is to reformulate the problem, and Table 3.2 provides a significant clue. We can here recur backwards with perfect safety, and apparently almost any starting condition will do! Mathematically we easily find from (9) that $y_r \to 0$ as $r \to \infty$, and the new formulation

$$y_r = \frac{1}{0 \cdot 75(r+4)}\, (0 \cdot 75 - y_{r+1}), \qquad y_N = 0 \quad \text{for some sufficiently large } N, \tag{11}$$

produces a very well-conditioned version of our problem. We shall see in § 10 how to select N, and no special care is needed with regard to the arithmetic.

We note, finally, that it is meaningless to talk of an ill-conditioned recurrence relation. The phrase can be applied only to the way in which it is used, that is to the recurrence *system*.

Forward error analysis

7. In computing with the two-term recurrence relation (5), whose associated condition gives essentially a problem of initial-value type, it is quite practicable to perform some *forward* error analysis. The data are the given coefficients a_r, b_r, $r = 0, 1, \ldots$, and the initial value y_0. We assume that they might all have both mathematical (rounding) and physical (inherent) error, so that we must use throughout the digital

$$\bar{a}_r = a_r + \delta a_r, \qquad \bar{b}_r = b_r + \delta b_r, \tag{12}$$

and start with the digital

$$\bar{y}_0 = y_0 + \delta y_0, \tag{13}$$

with known upper bounds for $|\delta a_r|$, $|\delta b_r|$ and $|\delta y_0|$. We seek an upper bound for the error in the computed $\bar{y}_N$.

In the first step we try to compute $y_1 = \bar{a}_0 \bar{y}_0 + \bar{b}_0$. The machine produces

$$\bar{y}_1 = fl(\bar{a}_0 \bar{y}_0 + \bar{b}_0) = \bar{a}_0 \bar{y}_0 + \bar{b}_0 + \eta_1, \tag{14}$$

where η_1 is the 'local rounding error' needed to make (14) an identity. With fl_2 arithmetic, discussed in § 13 of Chapter 2, $|\eta_1|$ will hardly exceed half a unit in the last figure of $\bar{y}_1$. For example, in a four-decimal machine we might have

$$\bar{a}_0 = 0\!\cdot\!8234, \qquad \bar{y}_0 = 0\!\cdot\!2345, \qquad \bar{b}_0 = 10^{-1}(0\!\cdot\!8456), \tag{15}$$

and we find

$$fl_2(\bar{a}_0 \bar{y}_0 + \bar{b}_0) = fl_2(0\!\cdot\!19308730 + 0\!\cdot\!08456)$$
$$= fl_2(0\!\cdot\!27764730) = 0\!\cdot\!2776, \tag{16}$$

and $\eta_1 = -0\!\cdot\!00004730$. With standard fl arithmetic we should have extra roundings, finding $fl(0\!\cdot\!1931 + 0\!\cdot\!08456) = 0\!\cdot\!2777$, $\eta_1 = 0\!\cdot\!00005270$. We discuss this further in § 28, but assume for the moment that η_1 is bounded by half a unit in the last figure of $\bar{y}_1$.

8. The error after the first step is then

$$\bar{y}_1 - y_1 = \bar{a}_0 \bar{y}_0 + \bar{b}_0 + \eta_1 - (a_0 y_0 + b_0) = a_0 \delta y_0 + \varepsilon_1, \tag{17}$$

where

$$\varepsilon_1 = \bar{y}_0 \delta a_0 + \delta b_0 + \eta_1, \tag{18}$$

and again we can find at least an upper bound for ε_1. The error (17) has two parts, one the propagated effect of the initial error $\varepsilon_0 = \delta y_0$

in y_0, and the other an extra error ε_1 arising from digital errors in the new coefficients and another rounding η_1. (If δa_0 and δb_0 are both zero, ε_1 is just this rounding error.) At the next step the error arises from the propagation of both ε_0 and ε_1 and a new error $\varepsilon_2 = \bar{y}_1 \delta a_1 + \delta b_1 + \eta_2$.

This pattern persists, and we can assert that the final error is given by

$$\bar{y}_N - y_N = \varepsilon_0 E_N(0) + \varepsilon_1 E_N(1) + \ldots + \varepsilon_N E_N(N), \tag{19}$$

where $E_N(s)$ is the error at point N, caused by unit error at point s, in the recurrence (5). Clearly $E_N(N) = 1$, and

$$\varepsilon_s = \bar{y}_{s-1} \delta a_{s-1} + \delta b_{s-1} + \eta_s. \tag{20}$$

It is easy to see that the quantities $E_r(s)$, $r \geq s$, propagate according to the *homogeneous* form of the equation. For if z_r is a solution of the recurrence, and there is an error of amount $E_r(s)$ at point $r > s$, caused by unit error $E_s(s)$ at point s, then

$$z_{r+1} + E_{r+1}(s) = a_r\{z_r + E_r(s)\} + b_r = z_{r+1} + a_r E_r(s), \tag{21}$$

giving the general relation

$$E_{r+1}(s) = a_r E_r(s). \tag{22}$$

In particular we find

$$E_N(s) = a_{N-1} a_{N-2} \ldots a_s. \tag{23}$$

In (20) the errors δa_{s-1}, δb_{s-1} and η_s can all be independent and so can the corresponding ε_s, so that the upper bound for the error is given finally by

$$|\bar{y}_N - y_N| \leqslant |\varepsilon_N| + |\varepsilon_{N-1} a_{N-1}| + \ldots + |\varepsilon_0 a_{N-1} a_{N-2} \ldots a_0|, \tag{24}$$

where ε_s is defined in (20).

9. We can now find some estimate for the error of $\bar{y}_5$, say, obtained in the last column of Table 3.1. Here the a_r and b_r are exact and can be stored exactly, so that in (19) and (24) each ε_r ($r \geq 1$) is just the local rounding error η_r. To sufficient accuracy we easily find

$$\left. \begin{array}{lll} E_5(5) = 1, & E_5(4) = -6, & E_5(3) = 31\cdot5 \\ E_5(2) = -142, & E_5(1) = 532, & E_5(0) = -1595 \end{array} \right\}. \tag{25}$$

It follows from (19) that the initial error in $\bar{y}_0$ alone contributes an error of about $0\cdot056$ in $\bar{y}_5$. The error in $\bar{y}_5$ is in fact about $0\cdot061$, so that the other terms contribute very little. This is perhaps a little surprising, since the arithmetic was performed in the fl mode, so that the local rounding errors could exceed $0\cdot5$ units in the last figure of $\bar{y}_r$, and even with this restriction the contribution could be as much as $5.10^{-5}(1+6+31\cdot5+142+532) \sim 0\cdot036$. Apart from the fact that we shall not normally have the worst combination of signs and extreme rounding errors, we here have some 'savings' in virtue of the simple and exact nature of the coefficients in the recurrence relations. Here many of the η_r are in fact zero, including the most important η_1.

10. The error analysis of the backward recurrence process (8) can be performed in precisely the same way. For the general form (5), recurring backwards from $r = N$, with $y_N = 0$, we produce the estimate

$$|\bar{y}_{N-s}-y_{N-s}| \leqslant |(a_{N-1}a_{N-2}...a_{N-s})^{-1}\varepsilon_N|+|(a_{N-2}...a_{N-s})^{-1}\varepsilon_{N-1}|+$$
$$+|(a_{N-s})^{-1}\varepsilon_{N-s+1}|+|\varepsilon_{N-s}|, \quad (26)$$

where ε_N is the error in y_N, and the other ε_r have definitions analogous to those of (20). If the a_r and b_r are digitally exact, then the ε_r, for $r < N$, are just the local rounding errors η_r.

We can now estimate the smallest value of N for which the assumption $y_N = 0$ will produce a $\bar{y}_5$, say, whose discrepancy from the true y_5 given by the *mathematical* problem (9), solved by the formulation (11), is within some prescribed tolerance. It is clear that $\bar{y}_4, \bar{y}_3,..., \bar{y}_0$ are then also satisfactory approximations to the true values.

Since y_r is known to be monotonic decreasing, and we assume that we can compute $y_0 = 0\cdot1957...$, it is clear that $\varepsilon_N < 0\cdot2$ for any N. A little calculation then shows that the contribution from the first term in (26) is in absolute value at most

$$0\cdot2[(\tfrac{3}{4})^{N-5}\{9.10.11...(N+3)\}]^{-1} = \frac{(0\cdot2)8!}{(N+3)!}(\tfrac{4}{3})^{N-5}, \quad (27)$$

and the smallest N for which this quantity is less than $0\cdot5\times10^{-4}$ is $N = 10$. (In fact $N = 9$ will do, because at this point $\varepsilon_N < 0\cdot1$.) We can further deduce quite easily, with this value of N and assuming that $|\varepsilon_r| \leqslant 0\cdot5\times10^{-4}$, that the contribution from the other terms in (26) cannot exceed about $0\cdot6\times10^{-4}$, so that the maximum error of our result hardly exceeds one unit in the fourth decimal place.

In practice one might well select two or more trial values of N, and observe the behaviour of the computed results. Consistency is here a satisfactory criterion of accuracy.

11. Finally, we note that the general solution (2) of our recurrence relation (5) is clearly given by

$$y_r = y_r^{(0)} + A(-\tfrac{3}{4})^r \prod_{s=0}^{r} (4+s), \quad (28)$$

where $y_r^{(0)}$ is the particular solution given by the definite integral (9), which decreases slowly but monotonically to zero. The complementary solution is rapidly increasing (and oscillating). Rounding errors are propagated as multiples of this solution, and their *absolute* effect increases without bound. But provided the constant A is of reasonable size, that is compared with an individual initial error or subsequent local rounding error, the propagated error cannot grow *relatively* large, and in this sense, as we indicated in § 5, the problem is not particularly ill-conditioned. Conditioning gets worse, in both absolute and relative senses, when A is only of the same order of magnitude as the initial or local errors. It is *catastrophic* when we want to have $A = 0$, giving the particular solution $y_r^{(0)}$, since then the introduction of any error ultimately, and indeed very rapidly, produces a 'solution' quite different from the one we 'want'.

Second-order equations. Initial-value problem

12. Turning now to the second-order equation (6), we consider first the initial-value problem in which it is sufficient to take initial conditions specifying

$$y_0 = \alpha, \qquad y_1 = \beta. \tag{29}$$

The general solution of (6) is

$$y_r = y_r^{(0)} + A_1 y_r^{(1)} + A_2 y_r^{(2)}, \tag{30}$$

where $y_r^{(0)}$ is a particular solution of (6), and $y_r^{(1)}$ and $y_r^{(2)}$ are independent solutions of the homogeneous form of (6) (with $c_r = 0$), the complementary solutions. The constants A_1 and A_2 are determined from the given initial conditions.

The homogeneous case. Ill-conditioning and problem formulation

13. Possibilities of ill-conditioning are immediately obvious from our discussion of the first-order system. Consider, for example, a homogeneous equation with constant coefficients, given by

$$y_{r+1} - 10 \cdot 1 y_r + y_{r-1} = 0, \tag{31}$$

whose general solution is

$$y_r = A_1 10^r + A_2 10^{-r}. \tag{32}$$

If we are given initial values y_0 and y_1, then any initial uncertainties in these values, and any rounding errors, will propagate in multiples of 10^r and 10^{-r}. If the true solution contains a reasonable component of 10^r, the resulting errors will be absolutely large but relatively fairly constant. If y_0 and y_1 are such, however that the constant A_1 is really zero, and we 'want' the solution 10^{-r}, then rounding errors will 'swamp' the computation, and the problem is ill-conditioned in both absolute and relative senses.

If we are given y_n and y_{n-1}, for use with backward recurrence, the situation is completely reversed. We here obtain accurately the solution $A_2 10^{-r}$, since the contaminant $A_1 10^r$ is *decreasing* in this direction. If the conditions try to suppress A_2, backward recurrence will introduce a multiple of this solution and 'swamp' the required $A_1 10^r$.

14. Again, therefore, we obtain accurately the solution that dominates in the direction of recurrence, and if we want to suppress this solution we must, if the necessary conditions are available, recur in the reverse direction. This device has been used extensively in practical computation, for example for the Bessel function $J_r(x)$ for fixed x and integer values of r. This function satisfies the homogeneous second-order recurrence

$$y_{r+1} - \frac{2r}{x} y_r + y_{r-1} = 0. \tag{33}$$

Now if we consider the constant-coefficient equation

$$y_{r+1} - 2a y_r + y_{r-1} = 0, \tag{34}$$

we know that the general solution is

$$y_r = A_1 p_1^r + A_2 p_2^r, \qquad p_1, p_2 = a \pm \sqrt{(a^2 - 1)}. \tag{35}$$

If $|a| < 1$ we substitute $a = \cos\theta$, and if $|a| > 1$ we write $a = \cosh\theta$, and find the respective solutions

$$y_r = A_1 e^{ir\theta} + A_2 e^{-ir\theta} \quad (|a| < 1), \qquad y_r = A_1 e^{r\theta} + A_2 e^{-r\theta} \quad (|a| > 1). \tag{36}$$

In the first case the solutions oscillate like $\cos r\theta$ and $\sin r\theta$, with bounded amplitude, and in the second case have combinations of increasing and decreasing exponential forms. In the first case neither solution 'grows' and 'swamps' the other, but in the second we have an ill-conditioned situation when we want a solution for which $A_1 = 0$.

For the equation (33), with non-constant coefficients, we therefore reasonably expect that in the region for which $r < x$ the solutions are of oscillatory form, and when $r > x$ one solution will increase and the other will decrease exponentially. This is indeed true, the general solution of (33) being

$$y_r = A_1 J_r(x) + A_2 Y_r(x). \tag{37}$$

It is known that both $J_r(x)$ and $Y_r(x)$ have bounded oscillation for $r < x$, and for $r > x$ the function $J_r(x)$ decreases monotonically to zero and $Y_r(x)$ increases monotonically to infinity.

15. By forward recurrence, with 'correct' values of $y_0 = J_0(x)$, $y_1 = J_1(x)$, we shall therefore fail to produce satisfactory values for $J_r(x)$ much beyond $r = x$. Knowing that $J_r(x) \to 0$ as $r \to \infty$, however, we can *reformulate the problem*, starting with $y_N = 0$ and the arbitrary $y_{N-1} = 1$, for some sufficiently large N, and solve by backward recurrence. With a 'check' value at some r, say $r = 0$, we can scale our 'trial' solution to satisfy this condition.

Certainly our starting conditions imply that the computed solution is a linear combination $A_1 J_r(x) + A_2 Y_r(x)$, but if N is large then A_2 must be very small, since otherwise we could not have y_{N-1} as small as unity. In the backward recurrence, moreover, $J_r(x)$ 'dominates' as far as $r = x$, and the errors introduced are virtually negligible. As r decreases each computed y_r is more nearly $A_1 J_r(x)$, and provided that A_1 is not small we obtain a good solution. Corresponding to the analysis of § 10 we can find a best N for which $y_r, y_{r-1}, \dots y_0$, suitably scaled, agree with $J_r(x)$. The rigorous analysis is complicated, however, and it is usually easier to vary N and inspect the results.

16. For $x = 2$, with $J_0(2) = 0 \cdot 22389\dots$, $J_1(2) = 0 \cdot 57672\dots$, we use four-decimal floating-point arithmetic, starting with $\bar{y}_0 = 0 \cdot 2239$, $\bar{y}_1 = 0 \cdot 5767$, and proceed with forward recurrence to compute the values shown in Table 3.3. Comparison with $J_r(2)$ shows a rapidly increasing divergence with increasing r. Until the very last step there are no *local* rounding errors, in virtue of the 'exact' nature of $2r/x = r$.

TABLE 3.3

r	0	1	2	3	4	5
$\bar{y}_r$	$0 \cdot 2239$	$0 \cdot 5767$	$0 \cdot 3528$	$0 \cdot 1289$	$0 \cdot 0339$	$0 \cdot 0067$
$J_r(2)$	$0 \cdot 2239$	$0 \cdot 5767$	$0 \cdot 3528$	$0 \cdot 1289$	$0 \cdot 0340$	$0 \cdot 0070$

r	6	7	8	9	10
$\bar{y}_r$	$-0 \cdot 0004$	$-0 \cdot 0091$	$-0 \cdot 0633$	$-0 \cdot 4973$	$-4 \cdot 413$
$J_r(2)$	$0 \cdot 0012$	$0 \cdot 0002$	$0 \cdot 0000$	$0 \cdot 0000$	$0 \cdot 0000$

With backward recurrence, starting say with $\bar{y}_{10} = 0$, $\bar{y}_9 = 1$, we find the results shown in the second row of Table 3.4. The third row is obtained by multiplying $\bar{y}_r$ by a constant k so that $k\bar{y}_0 = J_0(2)$ to four figures. We observe that the results are everywhere virtually correct to four decimal places, that is to four figures after the decimal point.

TABLE 3.4

r	10	9	8	7	6	5
$\bar{y}_r$	0	1	9	71	488	2857
$k\bar{y}_r$	0	0·0000	0·0000	0·0002	0·0012	0·0070

r	4	3	2	1	0
$\bar{y}_r$	13790	52300	143100	233900	90800
$k\bar{y}_r$	0·0340	0·1290	0·3529	0·5768	0·2239

In the values of $\bar{y}_r$ in Table 3.4 there are some local rounding errors, at $r = 4$, 3, and 2, but these have very little effect on the final results. In general, of course, a less convenient value of x will involve digital errors in the coefficient (r/x), and this will cause local small errors in the final answers.

Non-homogeneous case

17. In the non-homogeneous case we may be unable to find a *particular* solution by recurrence in either direction. Consider, for example, the relation

$$y_{r+1} - 10 \cdot 1 y_r + y_{r-1} = -1 \cdot 35 r, \tag{38}$$

whose general solution is

$$y_r = A_1 10^r + A_2 10^{-r} + \tfrac{1}{6} r. \tag{39}$$

If the initial conditions y_0 and y_1, for use with forward recurrence, or y_N and y_{N-1} for backward recurrence, are such that both A_1 and A_2 are theoretically zero, then one or other of the complementary functions will dominate the computation in either direction, and initial or rounding errors will ultimately 'swamp' the required solution.

For example, with $y_0 = 0$, $y_1 = \tfrac{1}{6}$, or in the reverse direction with $y_9 = \tfrac{3}{2}$, $y_8 = \tfrac{4}{3}$, we expect to produce $y_r = \tfrac{1}{6} r$. Table 3.5 gives the results of four-decimal floating-point arithmetic, and we observe the very rapid failure in both cases.

TABLE 3.5

r	0	1	2	3	4	5	6
$\bar{y}_r$	0	0·1667	0·3340	0·5060	0·7270	1·437	7·030

r	9	8	7	6	5	4
$\bar{y}_r$	1·500	1·333	1·160	0·9400	0·2340	−5·327

In fact equation (38), with specified y_0, y_1 is an ill-conditioned system for the determination of the solution (39) with $A_1 = 0$; equation (38), with specified y_N, y_{N-1} is ill-conditioned for the solution (39) with $A_2 = 0$; and equation (38), with either set of initial conditions, is ill-conditioned for the solution (39) with $A_1 = A_2 = 0$. If the latter solution is required, then some other formulation of the problem is necessary. We need more or at least different information, and in this case a satisfactory formulation is given by equation (38) together with *specified boundary values* $y_0 = 0$, $y_N = \frac{1}{6}N$. We return to this point in §§ 21 and 22.

We remark also that the nature of the complementary solutions might vary in different parts of any relevant range of r. Equation (33) is an example of this, in which the solutions are of oscillatory type for $r < x$ and of exponential type for $r > x$. The nature of the solution, at any value of r, is essentially given by the roots of the 'characteristic' equation of type (3) in which the coefficients are 'locally constant'. Such knowledge will again enable us, in certain circumstances in which some extra information is available, to reformulate our problem to give a well-conditioned situation. This we discuss later in §§ 26 and 27.

Forward error analysis

18. As in the forward error analysis of §§ 7–9 for the first-order case, so here we can find upper bounds for the error of $\bar{y}_N$, obtained by forward recurrence from the system

$$y_{r+1} + a_r y_r + b_r y_{r-1} = c_r, \qquad y_0 = \alpha, \qquad y_1 = \beta. \tag{40}$$

We assume, as in § 7, that all the given data have either physical or mathematical errors or both, and the following notation is an obvious extrapolation of that of § 7. We start with

$$\bar{y}_0 = y_0 + \varepsilon_0, \qquad \bar{y}_1 = y_1 + \varepsilon_1, \tag{41}$$

and find

$$\left.\begin{array}{l} \bar{y}_2 = y_2 - a_1\varepsilon_1 - b_1\varepsilon_0 + \varepsilon_2 \\ \varepsilon_2 = -\bar{y}_1\delta a_1 - \bar{y}_0\delta b_1 + \delta c_1 + \eta_2 \\ \bar{y}_3 = y_3 + a_2(a_1\varepsilon_1 + b_1\varepsilon_0 - \varepsilon_2) - b_2\varepsilon_1 + \varepsilon_3 \\ \varepsilon_3 = -\bar{y}_2\delta a_2 - \bar{y}_1\delta b_2 + \delta c_2 + \eta_3 \end{array}\right\}, \tag{42}$$

etc. It is perhaps easiest to represent this in the pictorial form

$$\left.\begin{array}{ccccc}
 & \varepsilon_0 & \varepsilon_1 & \varepsilon_2 & \varepsilon_3\ldots \\
\bar{y}_0 - y_0 & 1 & 0 & 0 & 0\ldots \\
\bar{y}_1 - y_1 & 0 & 1 & 0 & 0\ldots \\
\bar{y}_2 - y_2 & -b_1 & -a_1 & 1 & 0\ldots \\
\bar{y}_3 - y_3 & a_2 b_1 & a_2 a_1 - b_2 & -a_2 & 1\ldots
\end{array}\right\}. \tag{43}$$

We deduce that the general contribution to $\bar{y}_N - y_N$ is $\varepsilon_s E_N(s)$, where now $E_N(s)$ is the error at point N caused by zero error at point $s-1$ and unit error at point s. The quantity $E_r(s)$ is generated, for $r > s$, according to the homogeneous form of the recurrence relation. This general contribution holds for $s = 1, 2, 3, ..., N$, but for $s = 0$ we have a special case which can be included with ε_2. We write finally

$$\bar{y}_N - y_N = \varepsilon_1 E_N(1) + \varepsilon_2' E_N(2) + \varepsilon_3 E_N(3) + ... + \varepsilon_N E_N(N), \qquad (44)$$

where $E_N(s)$ is defined by

$$\left. \begin{aligned} E_{r+1}(s) + a_r E_r(s) + b_r E_{r-1}(s) = 0, \quad r > s \\ E_{s-1}(s) = 0, \qquad E_s(s) = 1 \end{aligned} \right\} , \qquad (45)$$

where

$$\varepsilon_s = -\bar{y}_{s-1}\, \delta a_{s-1} - \bar{y}_{s-2}\, \delta b_{s-1} + \delta c_{s-1} + \eta_s, \qquad s = 1, 2, 3, ... \qquad (46)$$

and

$$\varepsilon_2' = \varepsilon_2 - b_1 \varepsilon_0. \qquad (47)$$

Again, if the coefficients a_r, b_r, and c_r are known and can be stored exactly, then ε_3, ε_4,... are single rounding errors, ε_0 and ε_1 are the respective physical and/or mathematical uncertainties in the initial values of y_0 and y_1, and ε_2' is a rounding error minus $b_1 \varepsilon_0$.

19. The determination of the $E_N(s)$, by means of (45), would require the computation of $N-s$ steps of a recurrence relation for each value of s. With N fixed, however, we can determine all the required quantities with one recurrence of $N-1$ steps. Equation (45) gives a relation between $E_{r+1}(s)$, $E_r(s)$ and $E_{r-1}(s)$ for fixed s. We seek a similar relation between $E_N(s-1)$, $E_N(s)$ and $E_N(s+1)$ for fixed N.

Suppose there is a relation of the form

$$E_N(s+1) + \alpha_s E_N(s) + \beta_s E_N(s-1) = 0. \qquad (48)$$

Now if $p_r^{(1)}$ and $p_r^{(2)}$ are two independent solutions of

$$p_{r+1} + a_r p_r + b_r p_{r-1} = 0, \qquad (49)$$

which is satisfied by $p_r = E_r(s)$ with the initial conditions of (45), then the general solution of the system (45) is

$$E_r(s) = A_1 p_r^{(1)} + A_2 p_r^{(2)}. \qquad (50)$$

The initial conditions (45) then give

$$A_1 = -p_{s-1}^{(2)}/W_s, \qquad A_2 = p_{s-1}^{(1)}/W_s, \qquad W_s = p_{s-1}^{(1)} p_s^{(2)} - p_{s-1}^{(2)} p_s^{(1)}, \qquad (51)$$

where W_s is the 'Wronskian'. From the equations

$$p_{s+1}^{(1)} + a_s p_s^{(1)} + b_s p_{s-1}^{(1)} = 0, \qquad p_{s+1}^{(2)} + a_s p_s^{(2)} + b_s p_{s-1}^{(2)} = 0, \qquad (52)$$

we can eliminate a_s and find

$$W_{s+1} = b_s W_s. \tag{53}$$

Substituting into (48) from (50) and (51), and using (53), we find

$$\alpha_s = a_{s-1}/b_s, \qquad \beta_s = 1/b_s, \tag{54}$$

and deduce that the required quantities can be computed by *backward* recurrence with the system

$$\left.\begin{aligned} E_N(s-1) + a_{s-1} E_N(s) + b_s E_N(s+1) &= 0 \\ E_N(N+1) = 0, \qquad E_N(N) &= 1 \end{aligned}\right\}, \tag{55}$$

the initial conditions being self-explanatory.

We note that an exactly similar analysis could be used for the first-order case (5), and we would find the recurrence

$$E_N(s-1) = a_{s-1} E_N(s), \qquad E_N(N) = 1, \tag{56}$$

whose solution is obviously (23).

20. We can now understand the catastrophic failure of the results of the first part of Table 3.5 to produce the particular integral $y_r = \tfrac{1}{6} r$ of the system (38). Equation (55) is here given by

$$E_N(s-1) = 10 \cdot 1 E_N(s) - E_N(s+1), \qquad E_N(N+1) = 0, \qquad E_N(N) = 1, \tag{57}$$

and this we can solve exactly to find

$$E_N(s) = (0 \cdot 99)^{-1}(10^{N-s} - 10^{-N-2+s}). \tag{58}$$

For $N = 6$ the required values are, approximately,

$$\left.\begin{aligned} E_N(1) = 10^5, \qquad E_N(2) = 10^4, \qquad E_N(3) &= 10^3 \\ E_N(4) = 10^2, \qquad E_N(5) = 10, \qquad E_N(6) &= 1 \end{aligned}\right\}. \tag{59}$$

The initial uncertainty $\delta y_1 = \varepsilon_1 = 0 \cdot 000033$ alone contributes something like $3 \cdot 3$ units in $\bar{y}_6$, and the local rounding error ε_2, with a computed value of $0 \cdot 00033$, contributes another $3 \cdot 3$ units, giving about $6 \cdot 6$ from these main terms. The 'error' in $\bar{y}_6$ is in fact about $6 \cdot 0$.

Second-order equations, boundary-value problem. A stable method

21. Turning now to the boundary-value problem, given by (6) with $y_0 = \alpha$, $y_n = \beta$, we see immediately that this can be solved in terms of the linear simultaneous algebraic equations

$$\left.\begin{aligned}
a_1 y_1 + y_2 \qquad\qquad &= c_1 - b_1 \alpha \\
b_2 y_1 + a_2 y_2 + y_3 \qquad &= c_2 \\
b_3 y_2 + a_3 y_3 + y_4 &= c_3 \\
\cdots\cdots\cdots\cdots\cdots & \\
b_{n-2} y_{n-3} + a_{n-2} y_{n-2} + y_{n-1} &= c_{n-2} \\
b_{n-1} y_{n-2} + a_{n-1} y_{n-1} &= c_{n-1} - \beta
\end{aligned}\right\}. \tag{60}$$

With a more general condition at the first point, such as

$$p_0 y_0 + p_1 y_1 = r, \tag{61}$$

or

$$q_{-1} y_{-1} + q_0 y_0 = s, \tag{62}$$

we can produce simultaneous algebraic equations by obvious adjustments in the early rows of (60). For (61) the first two rows of the new equations of type (60) can be writen as

$$\left.\begin{aligned}
p_0 y_0 + p_1 y_1 \qquad &= r \\
b_1 y_0 + a_1 y_1 + y_2 &= c_1
\end{aligned}\right\}, \tag{63}$$

from which we can, if we wish, eliminate y_0 and produce (60) with a new first equation. A similar device can be applied to (62), with the equations

$$\left.\begin{aligned}
q_{-1} y_{-1} + q_0 y_0 \qquad &= s \\
b_0 y_{-1} + a_0 y_0 + y_1 &= c_0
\end{aligned}\right\}, \tag{64}$$

and here it is probably convenient to eliminate y_{-1} immediately.

22. The solution of linear algebraic equations, by methods which we illustrate and analyse in Chapter 5, is one of the most satisfactory of all numerical methods. With some attention to detail, we can guarantee that the computed solution $\bar{x}$ of the linear equations

$$\mathbf{Ax} = \mathbf{b} \tag{65}$$

is the exact solution of a 'perturbed problem'

$$(\mathbf{A} + \delta\mathbf{A})\bar{\mathbf{x}} = \mathbf{b} + \delta\mathbf{b}. \tag{66}$$

We can, moreover, guarantee that the perturbing matrix $\delta\mathbf{A}$ and perturbing vector $\delta\mathbf{b}$ have very small elements relative to those of $\mathbf{A}$ and $\mathbf{b}$, so that we certainly get a good solution whenever the problem is well-conditioned. In other words this method does not suffer from *induced instability*.

As a simple illustration of this consider the problem of equation (38), with the boundary conditions

$$y_0 = 0, \qquad y_5 = \tfrac{5}{6}. \tag{67}$$

Using four-digit floating-point arithmetic, we solve the linear equations

$$\left.\begin{aligned}
-10\!\cdot\!1y_1 + y_2 \qquad\quad &= -1\!\cdot\!35 \\
y_1 - 10\!\cdot\!1y_2 + y_3 \quad &= -2\!\cdot\!70 \\
y_2 - 10\!\cdot\!1y_3 + y_4 &= -4\!\cdot\!05 \\
y_3 - 10\!\cdot\!1y_4 \quad &= -6\!\cdot\!233
\end{aligned}\right\} , \tag{68}$$

(in which the last right-hand side already has a digital error), and by the standard elimination process (see Chapter 5) obtain the results

$$y_1 = 0\!\cdot\!1666, \quad y_2 = 0\!\cdot\!3334, \quad y_3 = 0\!\cdot\!4999, \quad y_4 = 0\!\cdot\!6666, \tag{69}$$

which are very close indeed to the required solution $y_r = \tfrac{1}{6}r$.

An unstable method and its analysis

23. We come now to the first illustration of a method with possible *induced instability*. In theory it is possible and even attractive to solve the boundary-value problem by a combination of initial-value techniques. If we compute by forward recurrence the two trial solutions $y_r^{(1)}$ and $y_r^{(2)}$, defined by the systems

$$\left.\begin{aligned}
y_{r+1}^{(1)} + a_r y_r^{(1)} + b_r y_{r-1}^{(1)} = c_r, &\qquad y_0^{(1)} = \alpha, \qquad y_1^{(1)} = 0 \\
y_{r+1}^{(2)} + a_r y_r^{(2)} + b_r y_{r-1}^{(2)} = 0, &\qquad y_0^{(2)} = 0, \qquad y_1^{(2)} = 1
\end{aligned}\right\} , \tag{70}$$

then it is clear that the combination

$$y_r = y_r^{(1)} + \lambda y_r^{(2)} \tag{71}$$

satisfies the given recurrence and the first condition. The constant λ is obtained from the other boundary condition, and is given by

$$\beta = y_n^{(1)} + \lambda y_n^{(2)}, \qquad \lambda = (\beta - y_n^{(1)})/y_n^{(2)}. \tag{72}$$

Before analysing the method we illustrate its failure, using four-digit floating-point arithmetic, for the system

$$y_{r-1} - 10\!\cdot\!1y_r + y_{r+1} = -1\!\cdot\!35r, \qquad y_0 = 0, \qquad y_5 = 0\!\cdot\!8333, \tag{73}$$

solved satisfactorily by the simultaneous equations approach in § 22. The computed 'trial solutions' are shown in Table 3.6.

TABLE 3.6

r	0	1	2	3	4	5
$\bar{y}_r^{(1)}$	0	0	$-1{\cdot}35$	$-16{\cdot}34$	$-167{\cdot}6$	-1682
$\bar{y}_r^{(2)}$	0	1	$10{\cdot}1$	$101{\cdot}0$	1010	10100

The value of λ is then given by

$$-1682+10100\lambda = 0{\cdot}8333, \tag{74}$$

and with floating-point arithmetic the *computed* value is

$$\bar{\lambda} = fl\{(1682+0{\cdot}8333)10100\} = fl\{1683/10100\} = 0{\cdot}1666. \tag{75}$$

The computed $\bar{y}_r$ is then

$$
\left.
\begin{array}{ccccccc}
r & 0 & 1 & 2 & 3 & 4 & 5 \\
\bar{y}_r & 0 & 0{\cdot}1666 & 0{\cdot}3330 & 0{\cdot}4900 & 0{\cdot}7000 & 1{\cdot}0000
\end{array}
\right\}. \tag{76}
$$

The error increases rapidly with r, and even the given boundary-value y_5 is not obtained accurately! If we use the $\bar{\lambda}$ given by (75), but use *exact* arithmetic at this stage to compute $\bar{y}_r^{(1)}+\bar{\lambda}\bar{y}_r^{(2)}$, we obtain the four-decimal values

$$
\left.
\begin{array}{ccccccc}
r & 0 & 1 & 2 & 3 & 4 & 5 \\
\bar{\bar{y}}_r & 0 & 0{\cdot}1666 & 0{\cdot}3327 & 0{\cdot}4866 & 0{\cdot}6660 & 0{\cdot}6600
\end{array}
\right\}, \tag{77}
$$

which show no particular improvement.

The reasons for this failure, of course, are connected with the rapid growth in absolute *value* of the trial solutions, followed by the subtraction of nearly equal large numbers and the corresponding loss of significant digits. Notice that the 'constant' term $1{\cdot}35r$ in (73) is not 'allowed' to enter with its full weight after a few steps, and that we should obtain precisely the same result for any given value of y_5 in the range $0{\cdot}5001$ to $1{\cdot}4999$.

This phenomenon is therefore most manifest whenever the trial solutions, and hence at least one of the complementary solutions of the recurrence relation, increases very rapidly. It is *not*, however, connected with the corresponding *growth* of absolute *error* in the trial solutions, but is connected solely with the *size* of the *local* errors. This becomes clear as a result of the following analysis, our *first application of backward error analysis*.

24. Consider first the computation of $y_r^{(1)}$. At each step we commit a *local* rounding error η_r, so that we always satisfy exactly an equation of the form

$$\bar{y}_{r+1}^{(1)}+a_r\bar{y}_r^{(1)}+b_r\bar{y}_{r-1}^{(1)} = c_r+\eta_r^{(1)}, \tag{78}$$

assuming that the a_r, b_r, and c_r are digital numbers, and where we can find an upper bound for $\eta_r^{(1)}$. In the aggregate the computed $\bar{y}_r^{(1)}$ therefore satisfy exactly the algebraic equations

$$\left.\begin{aligned}
a_1\bar{y}_1^{(1)}+\bar{y}_2^{(1)} &= c_1-b_1\alpha+\eta_1^{(1)} \\
b_2\bar{y}_1^{(1)}+a_2\bar{y}_2^{(1)}+\bar{y}_3^{(1)} &= c_2+\eta_2^{(1)} \\
\text{---} \\
b_{n-2}\bar{y}_{n-3}^{(1)}+a_{n-2}\bar{y}_{n-2}^{(1)}+\bar{y}_{n-1}^{(1)} &= c_{n-2}+\eta_{n-2}^{(1)} \\
b_{n-1}\bar{y}_{n-2}^{(1)}+a_{n-1}\bar{y}_{n-1}^{(1)}+\bar{y}_n^{(1)} &= c_{n-1}+\eta_{n-1}^{(1)}
\end{aligned}\right\}, \tag{79}$$

though of course $\bar{y}_1^{(1)}$ is zero and we obtain $\bar{y}_2^{(1)}$, $\bar{y}_3^{(1)}$,... in succession.

The computed $\bar{y}_r^{(2)}$ satisfy very similar equations, with α and c_r replaced by zero, $\bar{y}_1^{(2)}=1$, and $\eta_r^{(2)}$ replaces $\eta_r^{(1)}$. Then from (72) we shall find $\bar{\lambda}$ using the computed $\bar{y}_n^{(1)}$ and $\bar{y}_n^{(2)}$, and make a rounding error so that we solve exactly the equation

$$\bar{y}_n^{(1)}+\bar{\lambda}\bar{y}_n^{(2)} = \beta-\eta_n, \tag{80}$$

where η_n is a rounding error with computable upper bound. We can finally assert that the solution

$$\bar{y}_r = \bar{y}_r^{(1)}+\bar{\lambda}\bar{y}_r^{(2)}, \tag{81}$$

assuming that this is computed exactly (as in (77)) satisfies exactly the equations

$$\left.\begin{aligned}
a_1\bar{y}_1+\bar{y}_2 &= c_1-b_1\alpha+\eta_1^{(1)}+\bar{\lambda}\eta_1^{(2)} \\
b_2\bar{y}_1+a_2\bar{y}_2+\bar{y}_3 &= c_2+\eta_2^{(1)}+\bar{\lambda}\eta_2^{(2)} \\
\text{---} \\
b_{n-2}\bar{y}_{n-3}+a_{n-2}\bar{y}_{n-2}+\bar{y}_{n-1} &= c_{n-2}+\eta_{n-2}^{(1)}+\bar{\lambda}\eta_{n-2}^{(2)} \\
b_{n-1}\bar{y}_{n-2}+a_{n-1}\bar{y}_{n-1} &= c_{n-1}-\beta+\eta_{n-1}^{(1)}+\bar{\lambda}\eta_{n-1}^{(2)}+\eta_n
\end{aligned}\right\}. \tag{82}$$

If the original set of linear equations has the matrix form

$$\mathbf{Ay} = \mathbf{c}, \tag{83}$$

(which we could solve, of course, by the method of § 22), we can write (82) as the perturbation

$$\mathbf{A\bar{y}} = \mathbf{c}+\delta\mathbf{c} \tag{84}$$

of this original set.

The stability of the technique therefore depends on the magnitude of the induced perturbation $\delta\mathbf{c}$, which is effectively $\boldsymbol{\eta}^{(1)}+\bar{\lambda}\boldsymbol{\eta}^{(2)}$ in obvious vector notation, with an extra η_n in the last component of $\delta\mathbf{c}$.

The *technique* is good, that is the induced instability is small, if $\eta^{(1)}$, $\eta^{(2)}$, and η_n are small and $\bar{\lambda}$ is of the order of unity. *The first criteria depend on the local errors, and we are not concerned with their propagated effect.* The size of $\bar{\lambda}$ depends on the degree of ill-conditioning of the problem, to which we shall refer in due course. In our case $\bar{\lambda}$ is satisfactorily small, and of course it is always determined as part of the computation.

Now in the computation of Table 3.6 the η_r become quite large. For example, in the production of y_4 we are trying to compute

$$(-16.34)(10{\cdot}1)+1{\cdot}35-3(1{\cdot}35) = -167{\cdot}734, \tag{85}$$

and the errors of floating-point arithmetic produce an $|\eta_4|$ of large amount $0{\cdot}134$. Similarly the η_n, involved in the computation of $\bar{\lambda}$, is found to be $0{\cdot}1733$. In this example we have therefore perturbed the linear equations by large amounts on the right-hand sides, and we cannot therefore expect to get good results. There is, of course, a further rounding error in the floating-point computation of (81), and this is in fact quite significant though obviously easily avoidable.

25. To demonstrate that the *local* rounding errors, rather than their propagated effect, are here the important quantities, we repeat the computation of Table 3.6 (using recurrence in the reverse direction because the 'exact' nature of the coefficients and starting values hides the effect for forward recurrence), and postulate a computing machine that has to round to four-decimal places but can store any number of figures to the left of the decimal point. We find the results of Table 3.7.

TABLE 3.7

r	5	4	3	2	1	0
$\bar{y}_r^{(1)}$	0·8333	0	−6·2333	−67·0063	−673·2303	−6733·9697
$\bar{y}_r^{(2)}$	0	1	10·1000	101·0100	1010·1010	10101·0101

We now compute λ very accurately from the equation

$$-6733{\cdot}9697+10101{\cdot}0101\lambda = 0, \tag{86}$$

obtaining $\bar{\lambda} = 0{\cdot}66666300$, and make no further errors in the computation of y_r, finding the very good results

$$\left.\begin{array}{ccccccc} r & 5 & 4 & 3 & 2 & 1 & 0 \\ y_r & 0{\cdot}8333 & 0{\cdot}6667 & 0{\cdot}5000 & 0{\cdot}3333 & 0{\cdot}1667 & 0{\cdot}0000 \end{array}\right\}. \tag{87}$$

(This *accurate* computation is, of course, essential.)

Here the local rounding errors are at most five units in the fifth decimal place. We cannot, however, conclude that the results of Table 3.7 are those that would be obtained by exact arithmetic. By accident there are no rounding errors in $y_r^{(2)}$, but the *correct* four-decimal values of $y_r^{(1)}$, starting with $y_5^{(1)} = \frac{5}{6}$, are in fact

$$
\begin{array}{ccccccc}
r & 5 & 4 & 3 & 2 & 1 & 0 \\
y_r^{(1)} & 0{\cdot}8333 & 0 & -6{\cdot}2333 & -67{\cdot}0067 & -673{\cdot}2340 & -6734{\cdot}0067
\end{array}\Bigg\},
$$

(88)

and we see that the $y_0^{(1)}$ of Table 3.7 is already in error by about $0{\cdot}04$. This discrepancy is subsequently multiplied by about 10 at each step, and in a longer range would soon be very large indeed.

Effectively this does not matter because the computed $\bar{\lambda}$ has a corresponding error compared with its exact value, and the combination $\bar{y}_r^{(1)} + \bar{\lambda}\bar{y}_r^{(2)}$ is here correct at every point. Here we have our first example of the phenomenon mentioned in § 5 of Chapter 2. The *forward* error analysis might class the method as unstable because consecutive numbers, computed by our 'new' machine, in the early part of the computation diverge more and more from the true values obtained by exact arithmetic. The fact that this does not matter is difficult to explain by forward analysis, but becomes obvious when we use *backward* error analysis. Only the local errors matter, and with our strange computer (for example, a desk-machine!) we have been able to restrict them to five units in the fifth decimal place.

We do not, of course, propose to use this bogus computer and the method outlined, because the solution of simultaneous equations, at least over a finite range, is the best general all-purpose method, and when properly used needs no special arithmetical attention.

Ill-conditioned boundary-value problems

26. We have shown that solution by a combination of step-by-step computations is likely to fail when these trial solutions have a rapidly increasing part. This will happen, for example, as we mentioned in the latter part of § 17, for the equation

$$
y_{r-1} - 2a_r y_r + y_{r+1} = c_r,
$$

(89)

when $a_r > 1$. Paradoxically, it is in just these circumstances that the boundary-value problem is well-conditioned (see Chapter 5).

Not all boundary-value problems, of course, are well-conditioned. The linear equations of type (60) may have a matrix that is singular or nearly singular, so that small changes in the data, the coefficients and right-hand sides, may cause large changes in the solution. If the matrix is singular, for the case of given boundary *values*, the trial solution $y_r^{(2)}$, starting with $y_0^{(2)} = 0$, $y_1^{(2)} = 1$, will also have a zero value $y_n^{(2)}$. In fact $y_n^{(2)}$ is proportional to the determinant $|\mathbf{A}|$ of the matrix, and $|\mathbf{A}|^{-1}$ is a factor of the inverse $\mathbf{A}^{-1}$ of $\mathbf{A}$. In the combination of step-by-step solutions ill-conditioning is therefore revealed by a small value of $y_n^{(2)}$, that is by a large and poorly-determined value of λ in an equation like (72). In the solution by linear equations we find, correspondingly, evidence of large elements in $\mathbf{A}^{-1}$.

Now if the conditions specify *boundary values* we cannot have a singular matrix corresponding to (89) for fixed $a_r > 1$. For in this case the complementary solutions are $e^{r\theta}$ and $e^{-r\theta}$, and $y_r^{(2)}$ is therefore given by

$$y_r^{(2)} = k(e^{r\theta} - e^{-r\theta}), \tag{90}$$

for some constant k, and this cannot vanish at any non-zero value of r. By analogy we deduce, for an equation like (89) with given boundary values, that the problem is well-conditioned in any region in which the non-constant $a_r > 1$.

The case $a_r < 1$ is quite different. In the constant-coefficient case the complementary solutions are $\cos r\theta$ and $\sin r\theta$, and $y_r^{(2)}$ is therefore given by

$$y_r^{(2)} = k \sin r\theta, \tag{91}$$

which vanishes at many points, $\theta = n\pi/r$. In this case, of course, the solution by combination of trial solutions is not likely to exhibit *induced* instability, because the numbers do not increase rapidly in size, and this method may then be just as stable as the linear-equation method. Indeed we may here have to exhibit some special care with the latter, because a leading submatrix of the matrix $\mathbf{A}$ may be singular or nearly singular, and some linear-equation-solving methods have induced instability in this case (see Chapter 5).

Problem reformulation: infinite range

27. These general considerations suggest that it is advisable, whenever possible, to use linear-equation-solving methods in regions of exponential behaviour, and step-by-step methods in regions of oscillatory behaviour of the complementary solutions. The latter, we note, are usually faster and easier to programme, and these remarks indicate the desirability, whenever the appropriate conditions exist, of reformulating the problem accordingly.

Consider, for example, the solution of

$$y_{r-1} - 2a_r y_r + y_{r+1} = c_r, \qquad y_0 = \alpha, \qquad y_n = \beta, \tag{92}$$

in which $a_r > 1$ for $r < r_c$, $0 < a_r < 1$ for $r_c < r < r_d$, and $a_r > 1$ for $r > r_d$. Here we have an oscillatory region sandwiched between two exponential regions. We can solve a full set of linear algebraic equations, but it is attractive, and possibly faster, to use the following variation.

Suppose that we take the arbitrary value $y_{r_d} = 1$ at the second point at which the solution changes its character. We can then confidently solve by linear equations in the range $r_d < r < n$. This then provides two starting values for use with backward recurrence from r_d to r_c, which is satisfactory in this oscillatory region. The computed value at r_c, and the given $y_0 = \alpha$, then provide boundary values for solution by linear equations in this first sub-range. The only equation left unsatisfied is (92) at $r = r_c$. By repeating the whole process with $y_{r_d} = 0$, say, we can find a linear combination of these two trial solutions for which everything is satisfied. If the problem is well-conditioned the constants of this combination are well-determined, and since we have not induced any instability in any part of the range we have achieved a satisfactory result.

This process is a special case of the technique of 'matching in the middle', which is discussed further in Chapter 10 in relation to the corresponding solution of certain types of ordinary differential equations.

Floating-point analysis

28. Finally, we return to the error analysis of §§ 7 and 18, in which we took the local rounding error to be about half a unit in the last figure of any computed $\bar{y}_r$, and consider this estimate in relation to the floating-point error analysis of Chapter 2.

In the computation of (14), for example, in which $\bar{a}_0$, $\bar{y}_0$, and $\bar{b}_0$ are digital numbers, our floating-point analysis would give

$$\bar{y}_1 = fl(\bar{a}_0 \bar{y}_0 + \bar{b}_0) = \{\bar{a}_0 \bar{y}_0 (1 + \varepsilon_1') + \bar{b}_0\}(1 + \varepsilon_2'), \tag{93}$$

where each $|\varepsilon'| \leqslant 2^{-t}$ in the binary scale and $\frac{1}{2}.10^{1-t}$ in the decimal scale. Ignoring second-order quantities, this gives

$$\bar{y}_1 - (\bar{a}_0 \bar{y}_0 + \bar{b}_0) = \bar{a}_0 \bar{y}_0 \varepsilon_1' + (\bar{a}_0 \bar{y}_0 + \bar{b}_0)\varepsilon_2', \tag{94}$$

and ε_1' and ε_2' are independent rounding errors.

Now we shall normally take the worst combination of values for the ε' terms, which will imply that both the signs and the sizes of their factors are 'worst possible'. In this simple case, however, we observe that $\bar{a}_0\bar{y}_0\varepsilon'_1$ is the *absolute* rounding error in $fl(\bar{a}_0\bar{y}_0)$, and $(\bar{a}_0\bar{y}_0+\bar{b}_0)\varepsilon'_2$ is the absolute rounding error in $fl(\bar{a}_0\bar{y}_0+\bar{b}_0)$, and we can find these values, or a very good approximation to them, by inspecting the fifth digit in our four-figure computation. In the fl computation (16), for example, we have, rounded in the fifth figure,

$$\bar{a}_0\bar{y}_0\varepsilon'_1 = 0\cdot00001, \quad (\bar{a}_0\bar{y}_0+\bar{b}_0)\varepsilon'_2 = 0\cdot00004, \quad \eta = 0\cdot00005, \quad (95)$$

which is accurate enough for our purpose.

In the particular case when $a_0y_0 < 1$, $a_0y_0+b_0 < 1$, we can show that the total rounding error can never exceed one unit in the last figure, though this can be attained and is twice our postulated bound assumed in § 7. For example (Wilkinson, 1963),

$$fl\{10^0(0\cdot6247)\times10^0(0\cdot5000)+10^{-2}(0\cdot3150)\}$$
$$= fl\{10^0(0\cdot3124)+10^{-2}(0\cdot3150)\} = 10^0(0\cdot3156), \quad (96)$$

if each rounding is done to the nearest even number, and this has an error of 10^{-4} compared with the correct value $10^0(0\cdot3155)$. A proof of this result is indicated in Exercise 5 of Chapter 2.

For the second-order recurrence relation the corresponding basic computation is given by

$$-\bar{y}_{r+1} = fl(\bar{a}_r\bar{y}_r+\bar{b}_r\bar{y}_{r-1}-\bar{c}_r) =$$
$$= [\{\bar{a}_r\bar{y}_r(1+\varepsilon'_1)+\bar{b}_r\bar{y}_{r-1}(1+\varepsilon'_2)\}(1+\varepsilon'_3)-\bar{c}_r](1+\varepsilon'_4), \quad (97)$$

and with neglect of second-order quantities we have

$$-\bar{y}_{r+1}-(\bar{a}_r\bar{y}_r+\bar{b}_r\bar{y}_{r-1}-\bar{c}_r) = (\bar{a}_r\bar{y}_r)\varepsilon'_1+(\bar{b}_r\bar{y}_{r-1})\varepsilon'_2+$$
$$+(\bar{a}_r\bar{y}_r+\bar{b}_r\bar{y}_{r-1})\varepsilon'_3+(\bar{a}_r\bar{y}_r+\bar{b}_r\bar{y}_{r-1}-\bar{c}_r)\varepsilon'_4. \quad (98)$$

The absolute error is the sum of the individual absolute rounding errors in the floating-point evaluation of the four partial sums given in brackets in (98).

If all these partial sums are less than unity in absolute value, a little calculation reveals that the total error can hardly exceed $1\frac{1}{2}$ units in the last figure.

Exercises 3

1. Find a particular solution and the two complementary solutions of the recurrence

$$y_{r+1} - (2 + h^2)y_r + y_{r-1} = h^2.$$

(Hint: write $h = 2 \sinh \theta/2$.)
Repeat the analysis with h^2 replaced by $-h^2$.

2. Find the complementary solutions of the recurrence

$$y_{r+3} - 4y_{r+2} + 5y_{r+1} - 2y_r = 0.$$

3. Show that $I_r = \int_0^1 e^{\frac{4}{3}(x-1)} x^{r+3} \, dx$ tends to zero monotonically as $r \to \infty$.

4. In the exercises for Chapter 1 we asked for economic formulations of the problem of determining, for positive integer values of r, the values of

$$I_r = e^{-1} \int_0^1 x^r e^x \, dx.$$

We expected the suggested use of the recurrence relation

$$I_{r+1} = 1 - (r+1)I_r.$$

Starting with $I_0 = 0{\cdot}4$, $0{\cdot}5$, $0{\cdot}6$, $0{\cdot}7$, and $0{\cdot}8$, compute successive values by forward recurrence, as in Table 3.1.
    Then use a backward recurrence system, corresponding to equation (8), and compute a corresponding Table 3.2. Discuss the results of both tables.

5. Perform the analysis of §§ 9, 10 and 11 on the results of Exercise 4.

6. For the computation of $I_{p,q} = \int_0^1 x^p (1+x)^q \, dx$, for positive integer values of p and q, show that

$$\left. \begin{aligned} (p+1)I_{p,q} &= 2^q - qI_{p+1,q-1} \\ (q+1)I_{p,q} &= 2^{q+1} - pI_{p-1,q+1} \end{aligned} \right\}.$$

It would appear that we could use either of these formulae, by recurrence along lines $p + q = $ constant, with prior computed values along either $p = 0$ or $q = 0$. Discuss the stability of both suggested methods.

7. The successive derivatives at $x = 0$ of the function $y = (\pi + x + x^2)^{\frac{1}{2}}$ satisfy the recurrence relation

$$\pi y_{r+1} + (r - \tfrac{1}{2})y_r + r(r-2)y_{r-1} = 0.$$

(See Exercise 1, (vii) of Chapter 1, the π being inserted here to produce some rounding error.)

Use the analysis of § 19 to find the values of $E_N(s)$ for $N = 6$, and estimate from § 18 the maximum possible error in y_6 computed from the recurrence relation, with $y_0 = \pi^{\frac{1}{2}}$, $y_1 = \frac{1}{2}\pi^{-\frac{1}{2}}$.

What can one say about the nature of the complementary solutions of this recurrence?

8. The function $y_r = r$ satisfies the recurrence relation

$$y_{r+1} - 2 \cdot 5y_r + y_{r-1} + 0 \cdot 5r = 0.$$

Compare the results, using four-digit floating-decimal arithmetic, obtained by
    (i) forward recurrence with $y_0 = 0$, $y_1 = 1$ (up to $r = 10$),
    (ii) backward recurrence with $y_{10} = 10$, $y_9 = 9$,
    (iii) using the boundary conditions $y_0 = 0$, $y_{10} = 10$, with
        (a) combination of step-by-step solutions starting at $r = 0$,
        (b) combination of step-by-step solutions starting at $r = 10$,
        (c) solution of linear algebraic equations.

9. Compare the amount of work, measured by the number of multiplications, in the solution of a boundary-value problem by combination of step-by-step solutions and by solving linear equations.

10. Prove the statement of § 26, that the value $y_n^{(2)}$ of the step-by-step solution is proportional to the value of the determinant of the matrix of the linear equations.

11. Prove that the boundary-value problem defined by

$$y_{r+1} - 1 \cdot 5y_r + y_{r-1} = c_r, \qquad y_0 = \alpha, \qquad y_n = \beta,$$

is particularly ill-conditioned for some values of n. What are these values?

12. Show that the boundary-value problem defined by

$$y_{r+1} - (2 - \lambda)y_r + y_{r-1} = c_r, \qquad y_0 = \alpha, \qquad y_5 = \beta,$$

is particularly ill-conditioned for some values of λ. What are these values?

13. Show that the boundary-value problem defined by

$$y_{r+1} - 2 \cdot 5y_r + y_{r-1} = c_r, \qquad y_0 = 0, \qquad \alpha y_5 + y_4 = 0, \qquad r < 5,$$

is particularly ill-conditioned for some value of α. What is this value? (Note that ill-conditioning, with this equation, is not possible with given values of y_0 and y_5, as stated in § 26.)

14. Prove the last remark of § 28.

15. The induced instability of the method of § 23 can be lessened by the process of 'matching in the middle'. In place of equations (70) and (71) we could use the equations

$$\left. \begin{aligned} y_{r+1}^{(f)} + a_r y_r^{(f)} + b_r y_{r-1}^{(f)} &= c_r, & y_0^{(f)} &= \alpha, & y_1^{(f)} &= 0 \\ z_{r+1}^{(f)} + a_r z_r^{(f)} + b_r z_{r-1}^{(f)} &= 0, & z_0^{(f)} &= 0, & z_1^{(f)} &= 1 \end{aligned} \right\},$$

for the *forward* recurrence, and

$$\left. \begin{aligned} y_{r+1}^{(b)} + a_r y_r^{(b)} + b_r y_{r-1}^{(b)} &= c_r, & y_n^{(b)} &= \beta, & y_{n-1}^{(b)} &= 0 \\ z_{r+1}^{(b)} + a_r z_r^{(b)} + b_r z_{r-1}^{(b)} &= 0, & z_n^{(b)} &= 0, & z_{n-1}^{(b)} &= 1 \end{aligned} \right\},$$

for the *backward* recurrence. We then take the solutions

$$y_r = y_r^{(f)} + \lambda^{(f)} z_r^{(f)}, \qquad x > x_0 \Big\rbrace$$
$$y_r = y_r^{(b)} + \lambda^{(b)} z_r^{(b)}, \qquad x < x_n \Big\rbrace,$$

and match them at two adjacent intermediate points x_k, x_{k+1}, so that the coefficients are obtained from

$$y_k^{(f)} + \lambda^{(f)} z_k^{(f)} = y_k^{(b)} + \lambda^{(b)} z_k^{(b)} \Big\rbrace$$
$$y_{k+1}^{(f)} + \lambda^{(f)} z_{k+1}^{(f)} = y_{k+1}^{(b)} + \lambda^{(b)} z_{k+1}^{(b)} \Big\rbrace.$$

Try this for the problem of equation (73), and attempt its analysis by the methods of §§ 24–25.

(This technique is virtually the same as that of § 50, in Chapter 10, for solving certain types of differential equations. The best matching points depend (how and why?) on the nature of the complementary solutions of the recurrence relations.)

4

Computations with Polynomials

Introduction

1. POLYNOMIALS occur in two contexts. First, there is the *direct* problem of evaluating a given polynomial for particular values of its argument. The polynomial may come from many sources, but one important case is the polynomial approximation of more complicated functions, for use in computer library subroutines. Important considerations here are the speed of evaluation and the determination of bounds for the errors arising in the various forms discussed in Chapter 2.

The second, more interesting, problem is the *inverse* problem of determining zeros of polynomials. Here we are concerned with inherent instability (ill-conditioning), the stability or induced instability of our numerical methods, and the precision with which we can hope to compute our results. Almost all useful methods are iterative, and in general we shall give statements, without proofs, about the existence and rates of convergence of various processes. Proofs can be found in other texts, to which we give reference where this is relevant. In particular, much of our treatment is adapted from that of Wilkinson (1963), who gives more detailed information.

Evaluation of polynomials. Error analysis

2. We consider first the evaluation of the polynomial

$$p_n(z) = a_0 z^n + a_1 z^{n-1} + \ldots + a_n, \tag{1}$$

for a given argument $z = z_0$. We could evaluate (1) term by term, which would involve $2n-1$ multiplications and n additions. Preferably we use the technique of 'nested multiplication' defined by the recurrence scheme

$$p_0 = a_0, \qquad p_r = z_0 p_{r-1} + a_r, \qquad r = 1, 2, \ldots, n, \qquad p_n = p_n(z_0), \tag{2}$$

which requires only n multiplications and n additions.

A by-product of this method is that the p_r satisfy the equation

$$\frac{p_n(z)}{z - z_0} = p_0 z^{n-1} + p_1 z^{n-2} + \ldots + p_{n-1} + \frac{p_n}{z - z_0}, \tag{3}$$

which is easily proved by multiplying through by $z-z_0$ and equating corresponding coefficients of z^r on each side, for $r = 0, 1,..., n$. This fact is useful in various contexts.

3. We have already given, in §§ 7 and 8 of Chapter 3, some *forward* error analysis for the determination of the difference between p_n and $\bar{p}_n$, where $\bar{p}_n$ is obtained from floating-point arithmetic and with possible mathematical roundings and physical uncertainties in the data, a_r and z, (which in the sequel is used without ambiguity in place of z_0). Referring to that analysis, with $\bar{a}_r = a_r + \delta a_r$, $\bar{z} = z + \delta z$, we easily produce the result

$$\bar{p}_n - p_n = \varepsilon_0 E_n(0) + \varepsilon_1 E_n(1) + ... + \varepsilon_n E_n(n) \\ \varepsilon_0 = \delta a_0, \qquad \varepsilon_r = \delta z \bar{p}_{r-1} + \delta a_r + \eta_r, \qquad E_n(r) = z^{n-r} \Big\}, \tag{4}$$

and η_r is a local rounding error which makes the statement

$$\bar{p}_r = fl(\bar{z}\bar{p}_{r-1} + \bar{a}_r) = \bar{z}\bar{p}_{r-1} + \bar{a}_r + \eta_r \tag{5}$$

into an identity, with the full meaning of equality.

We can then write

$$\bar{p}_n - p_n = \sum_{r=0}^{n} (\delta z \bar{p}_{r-1} + \delta a_r + \eta_r) z^{n-r}. \tag{6}$$

4. We could have obtained the same result by the method of back-ward error analysis. At some stage we have computed $\bar{p}_{r-1}$, and then

$$\bar{p}_r = fl(\bar{z}\bar{p}_{r-1} + \bar{a}_r) = fl\{(z + \delta z)\bar{p}_{r-1} + a_r + \delta a_r\} \\ = z\bar{p}_{r-1} + \delta z \bar{p}_{r-1} + a_r + \delta a_r + \eta_r. \tag{7}$$

This is precisely the value we would have obtained by *exact* arithmetic from a *perturbed polynomial* whose coefficient of z^{n-r} is

$$a'_r = a_r + \delta z \bar{p}_{r-1} + \delta a_r + \eta_r. \tag{8}$$

There is no interaction between these various perturbations, and we deduce that

$$\bar{p}_n = a'_0 z^n + a'_1 z^{n-1} + ... + a'_n, \qquad a'_r = a_r + \delta z \bar{p}_{r-1} + \delta a_r + \eta_r. \tag{9}$$

The error is then

$$\bar{p}_n - p_n = \sum_{r=0}^{n} (a'_r - a_r) z^{n-r}, \tag{10}$$

which reduces exactly to (6).

5. In the case of exact digital a_r and z, the error is just

$$\bar{p}_n - p_n = \sum_{r=0}^{n} \eta_r z^{n-r}, \tag{11}$$

where η_r is the local rounding error. Consider, as an example, the polynomial

$$p_4(z) = 1 \cdot 259 z^4 + 0 \cdot 6373 z^3 - 2 \cdot 469 z^2 + 0 \cdot 01236 z + 1 \cdot 367, \tag{12}$$

evaluated at $z = 0 \cdot 92$ by four-figure floating-decimal arithmetic. We find

$$\bar{p}_0 = p_0 = 1 \cdot 259, \qquad \eta_0 = 0, \qquad a_0' = a_0 = 1 \cdot 259. \tag{13}$$

Then

$$
\left.
\begin{aligned}
&\bar{p}_1 = fl\{(1 \cdot 259)(0 \cdot 92) + 0 \cdot 6373\} = 1 \cdot 795 \\
&\eta_1 = -0 \cdot 00058, \qquad a_1' = 0 \cdot 63672 \\
&\bar{p}_2 = fl\{(1 \cdot 795)(0 \cdot 92) - 2 \cdot 469\} = -0 \cdot 8180 \\
&\eta_2 = -0 \cdot 0004, \qquad a_2' = -2 \cdot 4694 \\
&\bar{p}_3 = fl\{(-0 \cdot 8180)(0 \cdot 92) + 0 \cdot 01236\} = -0 \cdot 7402 \\
&\eta_3 = 0, \qquad a_3' = 0 \cdot 01236 \\
&\bar{p}_4 = fl\{(-0 \cdot 7402)(0 \cdot 92) + 1 \cdot 367\} = 0 \cdot 6860 \\
&\eta_4 = -0 \cdot 000016, \qquad a_4' = 1 \cdot 366984
\end{aligned}
\right\}, \tag{14}
$$

and we easily confirm that $\bar{p}_4$ is the exact value of

$$
\left.
\begin{aligned}
&\bar{p}_4(z) = 1 \cdot 259 z^4 + 0 \cdot 63672 z^3 - 2 \cdot 4694 z^2 + 0 \cdot 01236 z + 1 \cdot 366984 \\
&z = z_0 = 0 \cdot 92
\end{aligned}
\right\}. \tag{15}
$$

For this favourable case we can find an upper bound for η_r, which is given by

$$
\begin{aligned}
\eta_r &= fl(z\bar{p}_{r-1} + a_r) - (z\bar{p}_{r-1} + a_r) \\
&= \{z\bar{p}_{r-1}(1 + \varepsilon_1) + a_r\}(1 + \varepsilon_2) - (z\bar{p}_{r-1} + a_r), \tag{16}
\end{aligned}
$$

where $|\varepsilon_1|$, $|\varepsilon_2|$ are bounded by 2^{-t} or $5 . 10^{-t}$. This gives, effectively,

$$\eta_r = z\bar{p}_{r-1}\varepsilon_1 + (z\bar{p}_{r-1} + a_r)\varepsilon_2 = z\bar{p}_{r-1}\varepsilon_1 + p_r\varepsilon_2, \tag{17}$$

and

$$|\eta_r| \leqslant |\varepsilon| \{|z\bar{p}_{r-1}| + |p_r|\}, \qquad |\varepsilon| \leqslant 2^{-t} \quad \text{or} \quad 5 . 10^{-t}. \tag{18}$$

The bound (18) will rarely be attained, and (17), which gives η_r as the sum of the digital rounding errors in $z\bar{p}_{r-1}$ and p_r, is a better estimate. With fl_2 arithmetic, of course, the upper bound for η_r is little more than half a unit in the last figure of $\bar{p}_r$.

6. Consider finally the case in which a_r and z have only mathematical (rounding) errors, and let us seek an upper bound for the error in terms of the original data, rather than in terms of the intermediate quantities $\bar{p}_r$. We seek here the difference between

$$p_n(z) = a_0 z^n + a_1 z^{n-1} + \ldots + a_n, \qquad (19)$$

and its digital equivalent

$$q_n(\bar{z}) = \bar{a}_0 \bar{z}^n + \bar{a}_1 \bar{z}^{n-1} + \ldots + \bar{a}_n, \qquad (20)$$

obtained by fl arithmetic with

$$\bar{a}_r = a_r(1+\varepsilon_r), \qquad \bar{z} = z(1+\zeta), \qquad |\varepsilon_r|, |\zeta| \leqslant 2^{-t} \quad \text{or} \quad 5 . 10^{-t}. \qquad (21)$$

In the evaluation of $q_n(\bar{z})$ we compute the sequence

$$\bar{q}_0 = \bar{a}_0 = a_0(1+\varepsilon_0), \qquad \bar{q}_r = fl(\bar{z}\bar{q}_{r-1} + \bar{a}_r), \qquad (22)$$

and therefore seek a bound for the difference between $\bar{q}_n$ and p_n. We have

$$\bar{q}_1 = \{z(1+\zeta)a_0(1+\varepsilon_0)(1+\eta_0) + a_1(1+\varepsilon_1)\}(1+\xi_1)$$
$$= a_0 z(1+\zeta)(1+\varepsilon_0)(1+\eta_0)(1+\xi_1) + a_1(1+\varepsilon_1)(1+\xi_1), \qquad (23)$$

and then, with a little bit of manipulation,

$$\bar{q}_2 = a_0 z^2(1+\zeta)^2(1+\varepsilon_0)(1+\eta_0)(1+\eta_1)(1+\xi_1)(1+\xi_2) +$$
$$+ a_1 z(1+\zeta)(1+\varepsilon_1)(1+\eta_1)(1+\xi_1)(1+\xi_2) + a_2(1+\varepsilon_2)(1+\xi_2), \qquad (24)$$

where all the ε, ζ, η, and ξ have the upper bounds of (21). We easily deduce the result

$$\bar{q}_n = a_0(1+E_0)z^n + a_1(1+E_1)z^{n-1} + \ldots + a_{n-1}(1+E_{n-1})z + a_n(1+E_n), \qquad (25)$$

where, to a good approximation,

$$|E_0| \leqslant (2n+1)|\varepsilon| + n|\zeta|, \qquad |E_r| \leqslant 2(n-r+1)|\varepsilon| + (n-r)|\zeta|, \qquad r = 1, 2, \ldots, n, \qquad (26)$$

and we have indicated separately the contributions from ζ and the other rounding errors. Then

$$|\bar{q}_n - p_n(z)| \leqslant |a_0| \{(2n+1)|\varepsilon| + n|\zeta|\} |z|^n +$$
$$+ \sum_{r=1}^{n} |a_r| \{2(n-r+1)|\varepsilon| + (n-r)|\zeta|\} |z^{n-r}|. \qquad (27)$$

In the particular case when $\zeta = 0$, so that z is digital, (27) reduces to

$$|\bar{q}_n - p_n(z)| < |\varepsilon| \left\{ (2n+1) |a_0 z^n| + \sum_{r=1}^{n} (2n-2r+2) |a_r z^{n-r}| \right\}$$

$$\leqslant |\varepsilon| \sum_{r=0}^{n} (2n-2r+2) |a_r z^{n-r}|. \tag{28}$$

7. The corresponding argument for 'physical' a_r, in which ε_r in (21) can be quite large, is rather involved and probably less satisfactory than that of the backward analysis of § 4. For physical a_r and exact digital z, however, we easily produce from (28) the upper bound

$$|\bar{q}_n - p_n(z)| < |\varepsilon| \sum_{r=0}^{n} (2n-2r+2) |a_r z^{n-r}| + |\sum_{r=0}^{n} \delta a_r z^{n-r}|,$$

$$|\varepsilon| \leqslant 2^{-t} \quad \text{or} \quad 5.10^{-t}. \tag{29}$$

Here we have separated the 'arithmetical' from the 'physical' errors, and of course the last term in (29), representing the *inherent* error, will usually be much greater than the *induced* error represented by the first of (29).

Zeros of polynomials. Ill-conditioning and problem formulation

8. We turn to a consideration of the zeros of polynomials, and we discuss first the degree of inherent instability, that is the effect on the zeros of small changes in the coefficients. Theoretically, if

$$p_n(z) = \prod_{r=0}^{n} (z - z_r) = \sum_{s=0}^{n} a_s z^{n-s}, \tag{30}$$

the degree of conditioning can be expressed in terms of the *condition numbers*

$$k_{rs} = \delta a_s \frac{\partial z_r}{\partial a_s}, \tag{31}$$

the changes in the zeros z_r resulting from small changes δa_s in the coefficients a_s. In practice, of course, it is rarely possible to compute the k_{rs}, and in fact we have no general theory about the circumstances which give rise to severe ill-conditioning.

Certainly we know from mathematical theory that if z_r is an isolated zero of $p_n(z)$, and $z_r(\varepsilon)$ is a zero of the perturbed polynomial

$$p_n(z) + q_n(z) = \sum_{s=0}^{n} a_s z^{n-s} + \varepsilon \sum_{s=0}^{n} b_s z^{n-s}, \tag{32}$$

then

$$z_r(\varepsilon) - z_r = \frac{-\varepsilon\, q_n(z_r)}{p_n'(z_r)} + 0(\varepsilon^2). \qquad (33)$$

Moreover, if z_r is a zero of multiplicity m, that is $p_n(z)$ has a factor $(z-z_r)^m$, then (33) is replaced by

$$z_r(\varepsilon) - z_r = \left\{ \frac{-\epsilon\, m!\, q_n(z_r)}{p_n^{(m)}(z_r)} \right\}^{\frac{1}{m}} + 0\left(\varepsilon^{\frac{2}{m}}\right), \qquad (34)$$

the m perturbed zeros being obtained from the m interpretations of the term with exponent $(1/m)$. Here the individual effects on the m zeros z_r can be quite large, even for small ϵ, though we can show that

$$\sum_{r=1}^{m} z_r(\varepsilon) - mz_r = 0(\varepsilon), \qquad (35)$$

so that the perturbations are not independent and their combined effect is of the same order as the single effect on an isolated zero.

9. We should therefore expect that equal zeros are very ill-conditioned, and that nearly equal zeros, by analogy, might change rather a lot in respect of small changes in the coefficients. But it turns out that reasonably well-separated zeros can also be very ill-determined. We give some examples from Wilkinson (1963).

(i) For the polynomial

$$p_{20}(z) = (z-1)(z-2)...(z-20) = z^{20} - 210z^{19} + ... + 20!, \qquad (36)$$

with a linear distribution of zeros, the larger zeros are very sensitive, the smaller zeros fairly stable, with respect to small changes in the coefficients. In particular, if the coefficient of z^{19} in (36) is changed to $210 + 2^{-23} \sim 210{\cdot}0000001$, the original zeros 16 and 17 become the complex pair

$$z_{16}, z_{17} \sim 16{\cdot}73... \pm i2{\cdot}81.... \qquad (37)$$

(ii) For the polynomial

$$p_{20}(z) = (z-2^{-1})(z-2^{-2})...(z-2^{-20}), \qquad (38)$$

with a geometric distribution of zeros, small *relative* changes in the coefficients have no great effect on the *relative* accuracy of any zero, though again the smaller zeros are least affected. Small *absolute* changes in the coefficients will, of course, have a much more serious effect. This is easily seen by observing that the constant term in (38) is 2^{-210}, and this is the product of the zeros. If this number were merely doubled, which represents a very small *absolute* change, the product of the zeros is doubled and at least one of them has suffered a large *relative* change.

(iii) The zeros of the Chebyshev polynomial

$$p_n(z) = \cos(n \cos^{-1}z), \qquad -1 \leq z \leq 1, \qquad (39)$$

are reasonably well-conditioned, the changes in any zero being smaller than the change in any coefficient.

The zeros of

$$z^n - 1 = 0, \quad \text{integer } n, \qquad (40)$$

are also well-conditioned, and these two examples are very similar. The zeros of (39) are the projections on the real axis of the points on the unit circle at which $\cos n\theta = 0$, and those of (40) are the points on the unit circle at which $e^{in\theta} = 1$.

Generally, polynomials with complex zeros seem to be more stable, from this point of view, than those with real zeros.

Examples (i) and (ii) suggest that for real zeros the ratios $|z_s/z_r|$ are more important than the differences $|z_s - z_r|$. With respect to (i), for example, the polynomial

$$q_{20}(z) = (z-9)(z-8)...(z+10) \qquad (41)$$

is more 'stable' than the $p_{20}(z)$ of (36), and we have observed generally that small zeros are better conditioned. This suggests, for a *mathematical problem* in which all the data are exact but not necessarily digital, that we might with advantage make a change of origin, for example writing $Z = z-10$ in (36). The computation of $p_{20}(Z)$, however, must be performed with great accuracy, and this is not a trivial task.

10. Another important point is with respect to the formulation of problems. Due to the possibility of ill-conditioning we ought if possible to avoid formulation in terms of the computation of zeros of polynomials. An important case is the evaluation of the eigenvalues of a matrix **A**, which can be formulated as the determination of the zeros of the determinant of $(\mathbf{A} - \lambda \mathbf{I})$, expanded in the *characteristic polynomial equation*

$$\det(\mathbf{A} - \lambda \mathbf{I}) = \lambda^n + p_1 \lambda^{n-1} + ... + p_n = 0. \qquad (42)$$

It might happen that the eigenvalues are relatively insensitive to small changes in the *matrix* elements, whereas the computed *polynomial*, with rounded coefficients, is badly conditioned with respect to small random changes in the coefficients. In fact, whereas the uncertainties in the matrix elements a_{rs} may be random, those in the coefficients p_r are highly correlated, and unless we compute the p_r very accurately, bringing out this correlation, at least some of the zeros of our computed polynomial may have very little relation with the eigenvalues of the matrix **A**.

Computation of zeros

11. The importance of the error analysis for the computation of a polynomial, and of the question of ill-conditioning, lies in the fact that all methods for the computation of zeros, except for trivial problems and special cases, are of an iterative nature and involve at least the evaluation of $p_n(z)$ for several values of the argument. The favoured methods, for real zeros, include the following.

(i) Between any two arguments x_r and x_s, for which $p_n(x_r)$ and $p_n(x_s)$ have opposite signs, there is at least one real zero. We can obtain this by the method of bisection, incorporated in an algorithm, which starts from arguments a and b, $b > a$, with $p_n(a) < 0$ and $p_n(b) > 0$, and proceeds as follows.

$$x_0 = a, \quad y_0 = b; \qquad p_n(x_r) \leq 0, \quad p_n(y_r) > 0$$

$$\left. \begin{array}{l} \text{If} \quad p_n\{\tfrac{1}{2}(x_r+y_r)\} \leq 0, \qquad x_{r+1} = \tfrac{1}{2}(x_r+y_r), \qquad y_{r+1} = y_r \\[2mm] \text{If} \quad p_n\{\tfrac{1}{2}(x_r+y_r)\} > 0, \qquad x_{r+1} = x_r, \qquad y_{r+1} = \tfrac{1}{2}(x_r+y_r) \end{array} \right\} . \quad (43)$$

There is at least one real zero in every interval (x_r, y_r), and for a mathematical problem, and with exact arithmetic, we locate the zero in an interval of width $2^{-r}(b-a)$ in r steps.

(ii) We compute $p_n(x)$ for values $x_r = x_0 \pm rh$, where r is an integer and h the constant 'interval'. If $p_n(x)$ changes sign in this range, we can compute an x for which $p_n(x) = 0$ by the process of 'inverse interpolation' (see Chapter 8).

(iii) In the neighbourhood of an isolated zero x, the Newton iterative method, defined by

$$x_{r+1} = x_r - p_n(x_r)/p_n'(x_r), \qquad (44)$$

converges to the zero at a quadratic rate. This means that

$$(x_{r+1}-x) = k_r(x_r-x)^2, \qquad k_r \to p_n''(x)/2p_n'(x) \quad \text{as} \quad x_r \to x. \quad (45)$$

Ultimately the error at any stage is proportional to the square of the error at the previous stage. It is often argued that the number of correct figures therefore doubles at each iteration, but this statement clearly depends on the size of k_r and certainly cannot be guaranteed. In fact the early rate of convergence can be very slow, as indicated by a geometric picture of the process (Fig. 4.1).

Starting from a point P_0, we draw the tangent that meets the real axis at Q_1. From P_1, the corresponding point of the curve, the tangent produces the point Q_2, etc. If the first tangent is nearly horizontal, and the others almost vertical, we may perform many steps before Q_r is as accurate as Q_0.

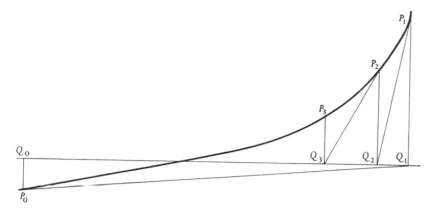

Fig. 4.1.

Moreover, the same reasoning shows that if there is a zero between a and b, and other real zeros elsewhere, we do not necessarily converge to the required zero even if the starting point lies between a and b.

(iv) Laguerre's method is defined by the iterative sequence

$$\left.\begin{aligned} x_{r+1} &= x_r - \frac{np_n(x_r)}{p'_n(x_r) \pm \{H(x_r)\}^{\frac{1}{2}}} \\ H(x_r) &= (n-1)^2\{p'_n(x_r)\}^2 - n(n-1)p_n(x_r)p''_n(x_r) \end{aligned}\right\}, \qquad (46)$$

and this gives two sequences of zeros, starting from a common point $x = a$, which converge to the nearest zeros $> a$ and $< a$ respectively. This avoids the last-mentioned difficulty of Newton's process (though not necessarily the first) and has *cubic* convergence in the limit. The amount of computation, of course, is quite a bit greater at each step.

12. For complex roots methods (i) and (ii) of § 11 are not possible, and Newton's method (iii) can converge only if we start with a complex approximation, giving rise to much time-consuming complex arithmetic. In such circumstances we usually replace Newton's method by Bairstow's method, which computes a quadratic factor $z^2 - pz - l$ of $p_n(z)$, and p and l are real for real zeros or for a pair of conjugate complex zeros.

Corrections to a first approximation $z^2 - pz - l$ are obtained in the following steps. First, $p_n(z)$ is divided by $z^2 - pz - l$ to produce

$$p_n(z) = (z^2 - pz - l)q_{n-2}(z) + s_1 z + s_0. \qquad (47)$$

Here $q_{n-2}(z)$ is a polynomial $\sum\limits_{r=0}^{n-2} q_r z^{n-r-2}$, and its coefficients are determined from the recurrence

$$q_0 = a_0, \quad q_1 = a_1 + pq_0, \quad q_r = a_r + pq_{r-1} + lq_{r-2}, \quad r = 2, 3, \dots, n-2 \atop s_1 = a_{n-1} + pq_{n-2} + lq_{n-3}, \quad s_0 = a_n + lq_{n-2}},$$

$$(48)$$

which is demonstrated exactly like that of (3).

Next, $q_{n-2}(z)$ is divided by $z^2 - pz - l$, by exactly the same process, to produce

$$q_{n-2}(z) = (z^2 - pz - l) \sum_{r=0}^{n-4} t_r z^{n-r-4} + u_1 z + u_0. \qquad (49)$$

Then a better quadratic factor, $z^2 - (p + \delta p)z - (l + \delta l)$, is obtained by solving the two simultaneous equations

$$D\delta p = u_1 s_0 - u_0 s_1, \qquad D\delta l = lu_1 s_1 - s_0(u_0 + pu_1), \qquad (50)$$

where

$$M = lu_1 + p(u_0 + pu_1), \qquad D = u_0^2 + pu_0 u_1 - lu_1^2. \qquad (51)$$

(For a proof see *Modern Computing Methods*, 1961.)

Accuracy of computed zeros

13. It is now clear that the accuracy with which we can compute zeros depends essentially on the accuracy with which we can evaluate the polynomial for given values of the argument. Consider first a mathematical polynomial, for which the analysis is that of § 6. If z is digital, the attempt to compute $p_n(z)$ produces the exact value of the perturbed polynomial

$$\bar{q}_n(z) = \sum_{r=0}^{n} a_r(1 + E_r)z^{n-r}, \quad |E_0| < (2n+1)2^{-t}, \quad |E_r| < 2(n-r+1)2^{-t}.$$

$$(52)$$

The actual perturbation, represented by the numbers E_r, depends on the particular z, and (52) gives upper bounds for E_r. At each stage of an iterative process we are attempting to compute a zero of $\bar{q}_n(z)$, and that of $p_n(z)$ lies somewhere in a 'domain of dependence' corresponding to the extreme perturbations.

This domain might be an interval of the real axis, corresponding to an isolated real zero z_k of $p_n(z)$, or it might consist of two circular regions surrounding a complex root and its complex conjugate. If two zeros of $p_n(z)$ are very close together, it might happen that the domain of dependence includes both roots, which can then not be separated.

14. We give some easy examples of these phenomena. Consider first the 'digital' polynomial

$$p_2(z) = z^2 - 2 \cdot 029z + 1 \cdot 028, \tag{53}$$

of which the larger root is very nearly $z_1 = 1 \cdot 0493$. With nested multiplication, and four-figure floating-decimal arithmetic, a little experiment shows that the computed value of the polynomial is zero for every value of z in the range

$$1 \cdot 042 \leq z \leq 1 \cdot 055. \tag{54}$$

For example, if $z = 1 \cdot 042$, nested multiplication gives

$$\left. \begin{array}{l} p_0 = 1, \; \bar{p}_1 = 1 \cdot 042 - 2 \cdot 029 = -0 \cdot 9870 \\ \bar{p}_2 = fl\{(-0 \cdot 9870)(1 \cdot 042) + 1 \cdot 028\} \\ \quad = fl\{-1 \cdot 028 + 1 \cdot 028\} = 0 \end{array} \right\}, \tag{55}$$

and if $z = 1 \cdot 055$, then

$$p_0 = 1, \qquad \bar{p}_1 = 1 \cdot 055 - 2 \cdot 029 = -0 \cdot 9740, \qquad \bar{p}_2 = 0. \tag{56}$$

In this example, of course, the region of dependence is governed by the zeros of the polynomials

$$\bar{q}_n(z) = z^2 - 2 \cdot 029z + (1 \cdot 028 \pm 0 \cdot 0005), \tag{57}$$

which include the maximum floating-point perturbations with these coefficients and for z in the region of $1 \cdot 04$. Computation easily gives the approximate bounds

$$1 \cdot 0412 < z < 1 \cdot 0559 \tag{58}$$

for the computed zero of this 'physical' polynomial.

For the slightly different quadratic

$$p_2(z) = z^2 - 2 \cdot 029z + 1 \cdot 029, \tag{59}$$

with exact zeros 1 and $1 \cdot 029$, the same kind of computation gives intervals for the zeros bounded by those of the quadratics

$$z^2 - 2 \cdot 029z + 1 \cdot 0285 = 0, \qquad z^2 - 2 \cdot 029z + 1 \cdot 0295 = 0. \tag{60}$$

The first of (60) gives

$$0 \cdot 9878 < z < 1 \cdot 0412, \tag{61}$$

and the second gives

$$z = 1 \cdot 0145 \pm 0 \cdot 0170i. \tag{62}$$

We therefore cannot separate the two real zeros, since $p_2(z) = 0$, in fl arithmetic, for any z in the interval $(0 \cdot 988, 1 \cdot 041)$, and moreover the region of dependence includes part of the complex plane.

15. It is clear that the limits of the interval $(z - h_1, z + h_2)$, in which we can locate the real zeros, or the boundaries of a region containing complex zeros, are governed by the difference between the *true* value of $p_n(z-h_1)$, for example, and the computed value of this quantity. If we have the correct signs at h_1 and h_2 then the zero lies in this interval. The sign will be incorrect when the error becomes just larger than the true value, and of opposite sign. Within the interval of dependence the function may not be zero everywhere, as in our simple examples, but will be quite random, and we shall have the situation typified in Fig. 4.2, in which AB is the interval of dependence.

$$- - - - - \overset{A}{|} + - - + + + - + \overset{B}{|} + + + +$$

FIG. 4.2.

An upper bound for the error in the computation of the polynomial, and hence maximum widths for the interval of dependence, can be obtained from (52). The true value of the polynomial and the upper bound for the error are respectively

$$p_n(z) = \sum_{r=0}^{n} a_r z^{n-r}, \qquad |e_n(z)| \leq \sum_{r=0}^{n} 2.2^{-t}(n-r+1)\, |a_r z^{n-r}|, \qquad (63)$$

and interest attaches to the points at which $|e_n(z)|$ is of nearly the same size as the computed value of $p_n(z)$.

We should stress, however, that the method of nested multiplication exhibits little in the way of induced instability. Even if n is of the order of 100 the largest coefficient in $e_n(z)$ affects only the last 8 binary figures of a_r, and in most machines the word-length easily absorbs this (that is effectively keeps 'guarding' figures) for most practical problems. With fl_2 arithmetic, of course, the perturbation will hardly affect more than the last binary place. The most important consideration, therefore, as we saw in the examples of § 14, is the sensitivity of zeros with respect to small changes in the given data. In fact, for the polynomial (53),

$$p_2(z) = z^2 - 2 \cdot 029z + 1 \cdot 028 = z^2 - 2 \cdot 029z + b, \qquad (64)$$

the condition of a zero, measured by a small change δb in b, is given by

$$|\delta z| = \frac{|\delta b|}{|2z - 2 \cdot 029|}, \qquad (65)$$

and for z near $1 \cdot 049$, an approximate zero of $p_2(z)$, we have

$$|\delta z| \sim 14 \delta b. \qquad (66)$$

In such circumstances, with a mathematical problem, we may have to use double- or triple-precision arithmetic, not only to keep *induced* rounding errors to a minimum, but so that we can make small the digital errors in the storage of the mathematical data. For a physical problem, of course, it may happen that the sensitivity of some zeros is so great that no significant figures are worth quoting. In the physical case some idea of the region of dependence is obtained by considering the 'error' $\sum_{r=0}^{n} \delta a_r z^{n-r}$, the physical part of (29), and comparing this with the computed value of the polynomial.

Computational comments

16. It is interesting to consider the numerical behaviour of the methods (i) and (iii) of § 11 for real zeros. Four-figure floating-point

TABLE 4.1

r	x	y	$p_2(x)$	$p_2(y)$	$\frac{1}{2}(x+y)$	$p_2\{\frac{1}{2}(x+y)\}$
0	1·0	1·5	—	+	1·25	+
1	1·0	1·25	—	+	1·125	+
2	1·0	1·125	—	+	1·062	+
3	1·0	1·062	—	+	1·031	—
4	1·031	1·062	—	+	0·046	0
5	1·046	1·062	0	+	1·054	0
6	1·054	1·062	0	+	1·058	+
7	1·054	1·058	0	+	1·056	+
8	1·054	1·056	0	+	1·055	0
9	1·055	1·056	0	+		

arithmetic, for the larger zero of $p_2(z)$ in (53), is shown in Table 4.1.

We have converged on one of the end points of the interval of dependence, though this cannot be guaranteed. Certainly our computed $p_2(z)$ always has the correct *sign* for z outside this interval, but inside the interval it is usually fairly random (in this simple case $p_2(z)$ is always zero). Whatever sign we take for the value in this interval, a little experiment shows (and indeed the result can be proved rigorously) that our final result will lie within the interval.

The computation, however, by itself gives no indication of the size of this interval, and the Newton method is a little more informative. Corresponding to Table 4.1 we have results of Table 4.2 for Newton's method with different starting approximations.

TABLE 4.2

r	0	1	2	3	4	5	6
x_r	1·5	1·259	1·138	1·081	1·058	1·047	1·047...
x_r	1·041	1·060	1·049	1·049...			
x_r	1·042	1·042...					

6

In this simple example, of course, the process ends as soon as we enter the interval of dependence, since $fl(p_2(z))$ is then exactly zero. More commonly, the iterates move steadily towards a zero until we reach the interval of dependence, after which the results oscillate within this interval, more or less at random, with a possible occasional 'jump' to an external point. Rounding errors in the computation of $p_n(z)$, of course, will affect seriously the quadratic nature of the convergence in the region of the interval of dependence.

Deflation. Induced instability

17. We have decided that the computation of the polynomial, by nested multiplication, produces little in the way of induced instability. This is not true of the method of 'deflation', which after the computation of some particular zero z_0 proceeds to 'divide out' this zero to produce a polynomial of degree $n-1$ whose zeros are theoretically the remaining zeros of $p_n(z)$. The relevant formula is that of (3), and of course everything is exact if z_0 is an exact zero and no further errors are made in the arithmetic. In the practical process of deflation we *accept* the *computed* $p_0, \ldots, p_{n-1}$ of equation (3) as 'satisfactory' coefficients of our deflated polynomial, and *assume* that $p_n = 0$.

We first give a simple example to show what can happen. Consider the polynomial

$$p_3(z) = z^3 - 11 \cdot 1 z^2 + 11 \cdot 1 z - 1. \tag{67}$$

The zeros are $0 \cdot 1$, 1, and 10, and are reasonably stable with respect to small relative changes in the coefficients. Suppose that we have computed the approximation $0 \cdot 1001$ to the smallest root. The deflated quadratic is obtained from the array

$$\left. \begin{array}{cccc} 1 & -11 \cdot 10 & 11 \cdot 10 & -1 \cdot 000 \\ & 0 \cdot 1001 & -1 \cdot 1011 & 1 \cdot 0008999 \\ \hline 1 & -11 \cdot 00 & 9 \cdot 999 & 0 \cdot 001 \end{array} \right\}, \tag{68}$$

in which the first row contains the coefficients a_r, the second the exact quantities $z_0 \bar{p}_{r-1}$, and the last the floating-point quantities $\bar{p}_r$, as defined in equations (1), (2), and (3). The accepted quadratic is

$$p_2(z) = z^2 - 11 \cdot 00z + 9 \cdot 999 = (z - 10 \cdot 0001\ldots)(z - 0 \cdot 9999\ldots), \tag{69}$$

and the deflation has been very successful.

Take next, as a start, the approximation 1·001 to the middle zero. The previous array becomes

$$\left.\begin{array}{cccc} 1 & -11{\cdot}10 & 11{\cdot}10 & -1{\cdot}000 \\ & 1{\cdot}001 & -10{\cdot}1101 & 0{\cdot}99099 \\ \hline 1 & -10{\cdot}10 & 0{\cdot}9900 & -0{\cdot}009000 \end{array}\right\}. \qquad (70)$$

The accepted quadratic is

$$p_2(z) = z^2 - 10{\cdot}10z + 0{\cdot}9900 = (z - 10{\cdot}001...)(z - 0{\cdot}0990...), \quad (71)$$

and the deflation is not quite so successful.

Taking finally the approximation 10·01 to the largest root, we obtain

$$\left.\begin{array}{cccc} 1 & -11{\cdot}10 & 11{\cdot}10 & -1{\cdot}000 \\ & 10{\cdot}01 & -10{\cdot}9109 & 1{\cdot}9019 \\ \hline 1 & -1{\cdot}090 & 0{\cdot}1900 & 0{\cdot}902 \end{array}\right\}. \qquad (72)$$

The accepted quadratic is now

$$p_2(z) = z^2 - 1{\cdot}090z + 0{\cdot}1900 = (z - 0{\cdot}872...)(z - 0{\cdot}218...), \quad (73)$$

and we have induced very significant errors in the determination of the other zeros of (67).

18. The method of backward error analysis throws light on these different results. From the array (68) we deduce that the $p_2(z)$ of (69) would be produced exactly from the perturbed original polynomial

$$p_3(z) = z^3 - 11{\cdot}1001z^2 + 11{\cdot}1001z - 1{\cdot}0008999, \qquad (74)$$

and the corresponding computations for (70) and (72) give respectively

$$p_3(z) = z^3 - 11{\cdot}101z^2 + 11{\cdot}1001z - 0{\cdot}99099, \qquad (75)$$

and

$$p_3(z) = z^3 - 11{\cdot}10z^2 + 11{\cdot}1009z - 1{\cdot}9019. \qquad (76)$$

These are the polynomials whose zeros we are effectively producing, and we observe the perturbations compared with the given polynomial. The important point, of course, is the effect of the perturbations compared with those given in (52) entailed by floating-point computation of the given polynomial, since we can hardly expect our deflation method to give smaller errors in the zeros. In this respect (74) is quite satisfactory, (75) is less good particularly in the constant term, and (76) has a very large perturbation in this term.

Now it is clear from (3) that, apart from 'arithmetic' deflation errors, the error in the constant in equations corresponding to (74)–(76) is just

$$p_n(z_0) = \sum_{r=0}^{n} a_r z_0^{n-r}. \qquad (77)$$

Moreover, if our accepted z_0 is within the region of dependence of the corresponding zero of $p_n(z)$, it is clear from our previous discussion that $p_n(z_0)$ is of much the same size as the error in the corresponding quantity obtained by nested multiplication with the original polynomial, that is

$$p_n(z_0) \sim \sum_{r=0}^{n} a_r E_r z_0^{n-r}, \qquad |E_0| \le (2n+1)2^{-t}, \qquad |E_r| \le 2(n-r+1)2^{-t}, \qquad (78)$$

obtained from (52).

The errors involved in the deflation are typified by

$$|fl(z_0 p_{r-1}+a_r)-(z_0 p_{r-1}+a_r)| = |\varepsilon| \{|2z_0 p_{r-1}| + |a_r| \}, \qquad |\varepsilon| \le 2^{-t}, \qquad (79)$$

which are not particularly significant unless $|z_0 p_{r-1}|$ is large compared with a_r.

It follows, on both counts, that if $|z_0| < |z_i|$, where z_i is any other zero of the original polynomial, then the deflation has introduced no larger perturbations than those involved in the direct evaluation of $p_n(z_i)$, whereas if $|z_0| > |z_i|$ these perturbations can be very much larger. In consequence, deflation will *induce* significant instability, even in well-conditioned zeros, unless it is performed in the proper order, in *increasing absolute value* of successive zeros.

19. In general, of course, we cannot guarantee that our iterative methods will produce zeros in this 'correct order', and we may prefer to avoid deflation altogether. One of the virtues of deflation is that we eliminate one zero and therefore cannot converge wastefully to this in subsequent iterations. This can also be achieved by Newton's method by working with the formulae

$$p_n(z) = g(z) \prod_{i=1}^{r} (z-z_i), \quad \frac{p_n'(z)}{p_n(z)} = \frac{g'(z)}{g(z)} + \sum_{i=1}^{r} \left(\frac{1}{z-z_i} \right). \qquad (80)$$

Here $p_n'(z)/p_n(z)$ can be found from $p_n(z)$ and earlier computed zeros z_i, and even if the latter are not very accurate the zeros of $g(z)$ are certainly also zeros of $p_n(z)$. This procedure avoids all problems connected with the induced instability of deflation. It is, of course, also applicable for finding the zeros of a non-polynomial function $f(z)$.

Exercises 4

1. Compute, by nested multiplication with four-figure floating-decimal arithmetic, the polynomial

$$p_3(x) = 0 \cdot 1296 x^3 + 0 \cdot 3424 x^2 - 0 \cdot 2134 x + 0 \cdot 7892, \qquad x = 0 \cdot 1,$$

and show that the computed result is the exact value of the polynomial

$$\bar{p}_3(x) = 0 \cdot 1296 x^3 + 0 \cdot 34244 x^2 - 0 \cdot 21344 x + 0 \cdot 78919.$$

2. Show that, in the fl computation of the polynomial $p_n(z)$ defined in (1), with digital (real) z and mathematical coefficients, the error cannot exceed

$$2.2^{-t} \{ q_n(|z|) + |z| \, q_n'(|z|) \},$$

where

$$q_n(z) = |a_0| \, z^n + |a_1| \, z^{n-1} + \dots + |a_{n-1}| \, z + |a_n|.$$

3. Note the presence of the modulus signs in Exercise 2. In particular, for the computation of e^x from its truncated Taylor's series, the *relative* error for positive x cannot exceed $2.2^{-t}(1+x)$. Note, however, that for e^{-x} the absolute error is proportional to e^x, and the relative error has a much larger factor proportional to e^{2x}. How would you compute e^{-x}, with a relative error no greater than that of the computation of e^x from the truncated Taylor's series, *without* using multi-length arithmetic?

4. In the spirit of Exercise 3, how would you determine the roots of the quadratic equation $ax^2 + 2bx + c = 0$, assumed real, so that both have the same relative error?

5. Equation (11) gives the error in the nested evaluation of a polynomial with digital data, and (18) gives an upper bound for the η_r in (11). This bound depends, of course, on the worst combination of signs and values, and will rarely be attained. For the polynomial (12), for example, show that the bounds give

$$\eta_1, \eta_2, \eta_3, \eta_4 = 10^{-4}(15, 12, 7, 7),$$

compared with the actual $10^{-4}(6, 4, 0, 0)$ of equation (14).

Since η_r is just the sum of the digital rounding errors in $z p_{r-1}$ and p_r, with due regard to sign, we could get more realistic values by remembering just a single discarded figure in these quantities. For example, in (14) we have

$$fl(z p_0) = fl\{(0 \cdot 92)(1 \cdot 259)\} = 1 \cdot 158(+0 \cdot 00028)$$

$$fl(p_1) = fl(z p_0 + a_1) = fl(1 \cdot 158 + 0 \cdot 6373) = 1 \cdot 795(+0 \cdot 0003),$$

and the single discarded figures give the estimate $\eta = -0 \cdot 0003 - 0 \cdot 0003 = -0 \cdot 0006$. Find, in a similar way, good approximations to η_2, η_3, and η_4.

6. In the analysis of § 6 the ε_r and ζ represent the original uncertainties in the data, and these may be to some extent 'random'. The errors of type η and ξ are induced by the computation, are theoretically completely determinable, and should perhaps be treated separately. They come respectively from

$$fl(\bar{z}\bar{q}_{r-1}) = \bar{z}\bar{q}_{r-1}(1+\eta_{r-1}), \quad \text{and} \quad fl(\bar{z}\bar{q}_{r-1}+\bar{a}_r) = \{fl(\bar{z}\bar{q}_{r-1})+\bar{a}_r\}(1+\xi_r),$$

and in the spirit of Exercise 5 can be estimated satisfactorily by looking at a single discarded figure. If these are so small that we can write

$$\prod_{r=1}^{p}\prod_{s=1}^{q}(1+\eta_r)(1+\xi_s) = 1+\sum_{r=1}^{p}\eta_r+\sum_{s=1}^{q}\xi_s,$$

show that we have actually computed, corresponding to (25) and (26), the quantity

$$\bar{q}_n = \bar{a}_0\bar{z}^n\left(1+\sum_{s=0}^{n-1}\eta_s+\sum_{s=1}^{n}\xi_s\right)+\sum_{r=1}^{n}\bar{a}_r\bar{z}^{n-r}\left(1+\sum_{s=r}^{n-1}\eta_s+\sum_{s=r}^{n}\xi_s\right).$$

7. Verify equations (34) and (35) for the quadratics

$$p_2(x) = (x-1)^2, \qquad q_2(x) = -(x+1)^2.$$

8. The quartic

$$p_4(z) = z^4+1{\cdot}011z^3-1{\cdot}434z^2-0{\cdot}3256z+0{\cdot}09299$$

has a real zero between $z = 0{\cdot}88$ and $0{\cdot}89$. Using four-figure floating-decimal arithmetic, and evaluation of any relevant polynomial by nested multiplication, try to determine the zero to four significant figures by the bisection method of § 11(i).

(Rounding to the nearest even number where necessary, we obtain the sequence

0·88	0·89	0·885	0·8875	0·8862	0·8868	0·8865	0·8866).
−	+	−	+	−	+	zero	+

Show that, in the vicinity of $z = 0{\cdot}8865$, even if the worst possible combination of rounding errors occurs the values of the η_r defined in §§ 3 and 5 cannot possibly exceed

$$|\eta_0| = 0, \quad |\eta_1| = 0{\cdot}0005, \quad |\eta_2| = 0{\cdot}0005, \quad |\eta_3| = 0{\cdot}0005, \quad |\eta_4| = 0{\cdot}000005.$$

By examining the derivative, and applying (33), show that the uncertainty in the computed zero cannot therefore exceed five units in the fourth figure. Show that, at $z = 0{\cdot}8865$,

$$\eta_0 = 0, \quad \eta_1 = +0{\cdot}0005, \quad \eta_2 = +0{\cdot}000423,$$
$$\eta_3 = -0{\cdot}0000385, \quad \eta_4 = -0{\cdot}00000385,$$

so that the error in this estimated zero is in fact just under three units in the fourth decimal.

(The zero is $0{\cdot}8868$ correct to four figures, so that our error is here not far short of the maximum possible. Observe the signs in the table

0·8862	0·8863	0·8864	0·8865	0·8866	0·8867	0·8868	0·8869	0·8870
−	−	−	0	+	+	+	+	+

obtained by floating arithmetic. In the region 0·8865–0·8867 all the true values are negative, and in each case the error in the computation is greater than the true value.)

9. The quartic in Exercise 8 has another real zero near $z = 0\cdot17$. Compute this, by four-figure floating-decimal arithmetic, using Newton's method, starting at $z = 0\cdot2$. (We find the sequence $0\cdot2$, $0\cdot1735$, $0\cdot1728$, with no further change, and observe the quadratic convergence.) Show that in the vicinity of this zero the maximum values of the η_r are again those of Exercise 8, and that the maximum error in the computed zero is here less than half a unit in the fourth significant figure.

10. Compute, by Bairstow's method, a quadratic factor, in the neighbourhood of $z^2 + 2z + 0\cdot6$, of the quartic of Exercise 8. Discuss the accuracy of the computed result.

11. The other zeros of the quartic of Exercise 8 are approximately $-1\cdot717$ and $-0\cdot353$. Find the values obtained by Newton's method, using four-digit arithmetic, and estimate their error.

12. For the quartic of Exercise 8, perform the deflation process for roots in the vicinity of $-1\cdot717$, $0\cdot887$, $-0\cdot353$ and $0\cdot173$, and then in the reverse order, verifying the conclusions of §§ 17 and 18.

(Starting with the approximation $z = -1\cdot717$, Newton's method gives no change to this precision and the deflated cubic is $z^3 - 0\cdot7060z^2 - 0\cdot2220z + 0\cdot05560$. Newton's method, starting with the approximation $0\cdot887$, gives the value $0\cdot8857$ for a root of this cubic, and the deflated quadratic is $z^2 + 0\cdot1797z - 0\cdot06280$, with zeros $-0\cdot3561$ and $0\cdot1764$.

Working in the reverse order, the results (which depend, of course, slightly on the first approximation in the Newton process) we find to be

$$\begin{array}{ll} 0\cdot1728, & z^3 + 1\cdot184z^2 - 1\cdot229z - 0\cdot5380; \\ -0\cdot3534, & z^2 + 0\cdot8306z - 1\cdot523; \\ 0\cdot8870, & z + 1\cdot718; \\ -1\cdot718, & \end{array}$$

which are considerably more accurate.

13. If the quartic of Exercise 8 is 'physical', with uncertainties of $\pm0\cdot005$ in the coefficients, including that of z^4, show that the possible uncertainties in the zeros, in decreasing order of magnitude, are approximately $\pm0\cdot015$, $\pm0\cdot008$, $\pm0\cdot009$, and $\pm0\cdot008$ respectively. (Note that this is a fairly well-conditioned case, and in particular the first derivative suffers little 'physical' change.)

14. Some zeros may be 'badly conditioned', and some 'well-conditioned'. For example, the cubic $p_3(z) = (z-1)^2(z-2) = z^3 - 4z^2 + 5z - 2$ has ill-conditioned zeros at $z = 1$ and a well-conditioned zero at $z = 2$. With fl arithmetic, the computed value of $p_3(z)$ can be very small for a wide range of z in the region of $z = 1$, and this zero is therefore badly determined. After first deflation, it might be thought that the next computed zero should be corrected ('purified') by iterating in the original polynomial, thereby bypassing errors of deflation. *This is almost always a retrograde step.*

With the given cubic, for example, $p_3(1\cdot027) = 0$ in four-digit fl arithmetic, so we accept $z_1 = 1\cdot027$ as a zero. The deflated quadratic is $z^2 - 2\cdot973z + 1\cdot947$, whose zeros are $z_2 = 0\cdot974$ and $z_3 = 1\cdot999$. Note the correlated errors in z_1 and z_2, that $z_1 + z_2$ is effectively correct (illustrating (35)), and that z_3 is accurate in spite of the error in z_1 and the deflation.

15. The method (ii) of §11 for computing real zeros can be changed into a process of successive linear interpolation. If we have obtained x_r and x_{r+1} such that $p_n(x_r) < 0$ and $p_n(x_{r+1}) > 0$, then there is a zero between x_r and x_{r+1}. If the

function is assumed linear in this region, the zero would be at

$$x_{r+2} = \frac{x_r p_n(x_{r+1}) - x_{r+1} p_n(x_r)}{p_n(x_{r+1}) - p_n(x_r)}.$$

By computing $p_n(x_{r+2})$, and observing its sign, we can repeat the process with x_{r+2} replacing x_r or x_{r+1}, and so on until a required accuracy is reached. Try this for the zero of $p_4(z)$, in Exercise 8, which lies between $z = 0 \cdot 88$ and $z = 0 \cdot 89$.

16. Muller (1956) effectively uses successive quadratic interpolation. If x_{r-2}, x_{r-1}, and x_r are three estimates of a zero, then we take the next estimate x_{r+1} to be the relevant zero of the quadratic $a + bx + cx^2 = 0$, where

$$p_n(x_s) = a + bx_s + cx_s^2, \qquad s = r - 2, \, r - 1, \, r.$$

The process is repeated with x_{r+1} replacing x_{r-2}. Try this for the computation of Exercise 15. (The method can be used, of course, also to find complex roots.)

5

Computation with Matrices

Introduction
1. THE main problems involving matrices, and the only ones we discuss here, are the solution of linear algebraic equations, the evaluation of determinants, and the computation of eigenvalues (latent roots) and eigenvectors (latent vectors). As in previous chapters we look at the questions of inherent instability and of induced instability, and illustrate the power of backward error analysis for the evaluation of methods with regard to their degree of induced instability. Since this is a very large subject we cannot prove or even discuss everything, and occasionally we give only summaries of methods and procedures, with due reference to more extensive published literature.

Though the linear equation problem and the eigenvalue problem are quite considerably connected, we examine them separately and make appropriate cross references. We also examine briefly the problem of 'least-squares' solutions, illustrating both good (stable) methods and poor (unstable) methods for this computation.

I. Linear equations

Ill-conditioning. Physical problem
2. It is convenient to start with a few examples of ill-conditioning for the linear-equations problem. Consider the equations

$$\left.\begin{array}{l} \frac{1}{2}x_1+\frac{1}{3}x_2+\frac{1}{4}x_3+\frac{1}{5}x_4 = b_1+\varepsilon_1 \\ \frac{1}{3}x_1+\frac{1}{4}x_2+\frac{1}{5}x_3+\frac{1}{6}x_4 = b_2+\varepsilon_2 \\ \frac{1}{4}x_1+\frac{1}{5}x_2+\frac{1}{6}x_3+\frac{1}{7}x_4 = b_3+\varepsilon_3 \\ \frac{1}{5}x_1+\frac{1}{6}x_2+\frac{1}{7}x_3+\frac{1}{8}x_4 = b_4+\varepsilon_4 \end{array}\right\}, \tag{1}$$

in which the coefficients on the left are exact but the right-hand sides b_r have possible uncertainties of known maximum amounts. (For example, if the b_r are measurements of distance, with an instrument that is accurate to half a unit of distance, then $|\varepsilon_r|$ would be at most 0·5 in this unit, and ε_r in (1) could be either positive or negative.)

Now the inverse of the matrix $\mathbf{A}$ in (1) is exactly

$$\mathbf{A}^{-1} = \begin{bmatrix} 200 & -1200 & 2100 & -1120 \\ -1200 & 8100 & -15120 & 8400 \\ 2100 & -15120 & 29400 & -16800 \\ -1120 & 8400 & -16800 & 9800 \end{bmatrix}, \qquad (2)$$

and from this we can investigate the effect on the solution of the 'tolerances' ε_r. In particular if each $|\varepsilon_r|$ has the same upper bound η, and if the worst combination of magnitudes and signs can happen, we find that the quantities δx_r, defined in obvious notation by

$$\mathbf{A}\mathbf{x} = \mathbf{b}, \qquad \mathbf{A}(\mathbf{x}+\delta\mathbf{x}) = \mathbf{b}+\boldsymbol{\epsilon}, \qquad (3)$$

can be as large as

$$\begin{aligned} |\delta x_1| &= 4620\eta, & |\delta x_2| &= 32820\eta \\ |\delta x_3| &= 63420\eta, & |\delta x_4| &= 36120\eta \end{aligned} \Big). \qquad (4)$$

If we take $\eta = 10^{-4}$ we see that the absolute uncertainties in the answers, *even though the arithmetic has been performed exactly*, may be approximately as large as

$$|\delta x_1| = 0{\cdot}46, \qquad |\delta x_2| = 3{\cdot}28, \qquad |\delta x_3| = 6{\cdot}34, \qquad |\delta x_4| = 3{\cdot}61. \quad (5)$$

It is traditional to regard the linear-equation problem as ill-conditioned when the absolute errors *can* be large, that is if the elements of the inverse matrix $\mathbf{A}^{-1}$ are large for reasonably-sized $\mathbf{A}$. But in practice the degree of ill-conditioning clearly depends on the solution of the problem. For example, if the quantities b_r are such that the solutions are of order of magnitude

$$x_1 = +4000, \quad x_2 = -32000, \quad x_3 = +63000, \quad x_4 = -36000, \quad (6)$$

then the *relative* errors due to the perturbing ε_r terms are at most only about 1 part in 10^4, and we would hardly regard this, at least for many purposes, as a poor result. Right-hand sides

$$b_1 = 1, \qquad b_2 = -1, \qquad b_3 = 1, \qquad b_4 = -1 \qquad (7)$$

would in fact produce solutions of this magnitude.

If $\mathbf{A}^{-1}$ has large elements, however, there are always some right-hand sides, of normal size, which give small solutions. For example, the right-hand sides of comparable size given by

$$b_1 = b_2 = b_3 = b_4 = 1 \qquad (8)$$

give the much smaller results

$$x_1 = -20, \quad x_2 = 180, \quad x_3 = -420, \quad x_4 = 280. \quad (9)$$

The possible absolute error is still given by (5), and the relative error is here much larger, varying between 1 part in 40 and 1 part in 70. The right-hand sides

$$b_1 = 1, \quad b_2 = 0\cdot7227, \quad b_3 = 0\cdot5697, \quad b_4 = 0\cdot4714, \quad (10)$$

again of comparable size with (7) and (8), give the results

$$x_1 = 1\cdot162, \quad x_2 = -0\cdot234, \quad x_3 = 2\cdot436, \quad x_4 = -0\cdot560, \quad (11)$$

and in this case the effects of uncertainties of amount 10^{-4} in the right-hand sides, which may change the answers by the absolute amounts (5), are so relatively large that *not a single figure is meaningful* in the answers (11). The ill-conditioning is here extreme!

3. It is also worth remarking that the uncertainties in the individual x_r are highly correlated, and a linear combination

$$y = \sum_{r=1}^{4} \alpha_r x_r, \quad (12)$$

often required in physical problems, may be less uncertain, that is 'better conditioned', than the individual x_r. For example, if $\alpha_r = 1$, $r = 1, 2, 3, 4$, we find

$$y = \sum_{r=1}^{4} x_r, \quad \delta y = \sum_{r=1}^{4} \delta x_r, \quad (13)$$

and $|\delta y|$ is at most 900η, smaller by a factor of 70 than the maximum uncertainty $|\delta x_3|$ in the solutions of the linear equations. Even the results (11) then give some useful figures, for here

$$y = 2\cdot804, \quad |\delta y| < 0\cdot09, \quad (14)$$

and the relative error in y is at most 1 part in about 30.

We see again that the term ill-conditioning must be used with care. To say that a matrix is ill-conditioned is meaningless. The matrix of (1), for example, while in some cases ill-conditioned from the point of view of solving linear equations, may be quite satisfactory for other purposes. We repeat that only the *particular problem* has a 'condition'.

4. It is not difficult, at least for symmetric matrices, to throw some analytical light on the results of the last two sections. The solution of

$\mathbf{Ax} = \mathbf{b}$, for symmetric $\mathbf{A}$, is

$$\mathbf{x} = \sum_{r=1}^{n} \left(\frac{\mathbf{x}^{(r)\prime}\mathbf{b}}{\lambda_r} \right) \mathbf{x}^{(r)}, \tag{15}$$

where $\mathbf{x}^{(r)}$ is an eigenvector of $\mathbf{A}$, with normalization $\mathbf{x}^{(r)\prime}\mathbf{x}^{(r)} = 1$, corresponding to the eigenvalue λ_r. The problem is likely to be ill-conditioned if any λ_r is very small, for the 'tolerance' $\delta\mathbf{b}$ in $\mathbf{b}$ produces an uncertainty in the solution given by

$$\delta\mathbf{x} = \sum_{r=1}^{n} \left(\frac{\mathbf{x}^{(r)\prime}\,\delta\mathbf{b}}{\lambda_r} \right) \mathbf{x}^{(r)}, \tag{16}$$

which might be quite large for a small λ_r. The ill-conditioning may be relatively tolerable if $\mathbf{x}$ is also large, that is when $\mathbf{x}^{(r)\prime}\mathbf{b}$ is not small.

But it may happen that $\mathbf{x}^{(r)\prime}\mathbf{b}$ *is* very small, for small λ_r and reasonably-sized $\mathbf{b}$, and this is true if $\mathbf{b}$ is nearly orthogonal to the eigenvector $\mathbf{x}^{(r)}$ corresponding to small λ_r. In this event $|\mathbf{x}^{(r)\prime}\,\delta\mathbf{b}|$ may be much larger than $|\mathbf{x}^{(r)\prime}\mathbf{b}|$, and the problem is ill-conditioned in both absolute and relative senses. (See § 38 for a very analogous situation in the problem of determining eigenvectors of matrices.)

Similarly, if we seek the linear combination

$$y = \sum_{r=1}^{n} c_r x_r = \mathbf{c}'\mathbf{x}, \tag{17}$$

in obvious matrix notation, then

$$y = \sum_{r=1}^{n} \left(\frac{\mathbf{x}^{(r)\prime}\mathbf{b}}{\lambda_r} \right) \mathbf{c}'\mathbf{x}^{(r)} = \mathbf{b}' \sum_{r=1}^{n} \left(\frac{\mathbf{c}'\mathbf{x}^{(r)}}{\lambda_r} \right) \mathbf{x}^{(r)}. \tag{18}$$

The 'tolerance' in y is then

$$\delta y = (\delta\mathbf{b})' \sum_{r=1}^{n} \left(\frac{\mathbf{c}'\mathbf{x}^{(r)}}{\lambda_r} \right) \mathbf{x}^{(r)}, \tag{19}$$

and δy may or may not be small relative to y. The important thing here, of course, is the size of the term $\mathbf{c}'\mathbf{x}^{(r)}$ relative to small λ_r.

Ill-conditioning. Mathematical problem

5. We have remarked previously that there is no real meaning to the term 'ill-conditioned mathematical problem', except that when the physical problem is ill-conditioned it is difficult to get an accurate solution to the mathematical problem for which such a solution exists and is meaningful.

Consider, for example, the solution of the linear equations

$$\begin{aligned}
\tfrac{1}{2}x_1 + \tfrac{1}{3}x_2 + \tfrac{1}{4}x_3 + \tfrac{1}{5}x_4 + \tfrac{1}{6}x_5 &= 1 \\
\tfrac{1}{3}x_1 + \tfrac{1}{4}x_2 + \tfrac{1}{5}x_3 + \tfrac{1}{6}x_4 + \tfrac{1}{7}x_5 &= 1 \\
\tfrac{1}{4}x_1 + \tfrac{1}{5}x_2 + \tfrac{1}{6}x_3 + \tfrac{1}{7}x_4 + \tfrac{1}{8}x_5 &= 1 \\
\tfrac{1}{5}x_1 + \tfrac{1}{6}x_2 + \tfrac{1}{7}x_3 + \tfrac{1}{8}x_4 + \tfrac{1}{9}x_5 &= 1 \\
\tfrac{1}{6}x_1 + \tfrac{1}{7}x_2 + \tfrac{1}{8}x_3 + \tfrac{1}{9}x_4 + \tfrac{1}{10}x_5 &= 1
\end{aligned}\right\}, \qquad (20)$$

in which the matrix is that of (1) with an extra row and column. All the data are exact. In computing practice, however, we rarely use fractions, and have to represent numbers in the form typified by

$$\tfrac{1}{3} = 0.3333\ldots. \qquad (21)$$

With a computing machine of finite word-length we have seen that we cannot store (21) exactly, and have to round it to a given number of digits, with the implicit assumption that the neglected digits are all zero. The question arises as to how many figures we have to keep to ensure a result of specified accuracy to the mathematical problem.

In Table 5.1 we show the exact solution and the results obtained by rounding the coefficients of the matrix to various numbers of digits. Apart from this rounding the computation has been performed so accurately that the method introduces no further errors to the number of digits quoted.

TABLE 5.1

	x_1	x_2	x_3	x_4	x_5
Exact values	30	−420	1680	−2520	1260
Coefficients rounded					
to 4 decimals	−8·8	90·5	−196	58·9	75·6
5	55·3	−746·5	2854·9	−4105·2	1976·9
6	13·1	−229·9	1042·7	−1696·4	898·1
7	25·9	−373·7	1524·4	−2318·6	1171·4
8	29·65	−416·02	1666·62	−2502·69	1252·39

We observe that rounding to four decimals *produces the wrong sign* in most components of the solution, and even with eight decimals we still have relative errors of about 1 part in 100. Instead of solving exactly the equations $\mathbf{Ax} = \mathbf{b}$ we have solved exactly the *perturbed equations*

$$(\mathbf{A} + \delta_r \mathbf{A})\mathbf{y} = \mathbf{b}, \qquad r = 4, 5, 6, 7, 8. \qquad (22)$$

(When $r = 4$, for example, the (1, 2) element of $\delta_4\mathbf{A}$ is $-0.0000333\ldots$.) The solutions are so sensitive to small changes in the data that $\delta\mathbf{A}$ must be very small to ensure that $\mathbf{y}$ is a good approximation to $\mathbf{x}$.

Induced instability

6. We turn now to the question of induced instability, and immediately give an example of a fairly well-conditioned problem 'solved' badly by a method exhibiting induced instability, the method being effectively that described in books on abstract algebra and which would be perfectly satisfactory with exact arithmetic. Consider the equations

$$
\left.
\begin{aligned}
-1{\cdot}732y_1+y_2 \qquad\quad &= 0{\cdot}100\\
y_1-1{\cdot}732y_2+y_3 \qquad &= 0{\cdot}100\\
y_2-1{\cdot}732y_3+y_4 &= 0{\cdot}100\\
\text{-----------------------------------}&\\
y_7-1{\cdot}732y_8+y_9 &= 0{\cdot}100\\
y_8-1{\cdot}732y_9 &= 0{\cdot}100
\end{aligned}
\right\}. \tag{23}
$$

By adding a multiple of the first equation to the second we can produce a new second equation containing only y_2 and y_3, and adding a multiple of this to the third of (23) we produce a new third equation containing only y_3 and y_4. Successive repetitions of this process ultimately produce a new set of equations of upper triangular form, and with four-figure floating-point arithmetic we find the results

$$
\left.
\begin{array}{rll}
 & -1{\cdot}732y_1+y_2 & = 0{\cdot}1000\\
0{\cdot}5774 & -1{\cdot}155y_2+y_3 & = 0{\cdot}1577\\
0{\cdot}8658 & -0{\cdot}8662y_3+y_4 & = 0{\cdot}2365\\
1{\cdot}154 & -0{\cdot}5780y_4+y_5 & = 0{\cdot}3729\\
1{\cdot}730 & -0{\cdot}002000y_5+y_6 & = 0{\cdot}7451\\
500{\cdot}0 & 498{\cdot}3y_6+y_7 & = 372{\cdot}7\\
-0{\cdot}002007 & -1{\cdot}734y_7+y_8 & = -0{\cdot}6480\\
0{\cdot}5767 & -1{\cdot}155y_8+y_9 & = -0{\cdot}2737\\
0{\cdot}8658 & -0{\cdot}8662y_9 & = -0{\cdot}1370
\end{array}
\right\}, \tag{24}
$$

where the numbers on the left are the successive 'multipliers'.

We complete the solution by working backwards in (24) (*back substitution*) and obtain the results

r	9	8	7	6	5	4	3	2	1
y_r	0·1582	0·3739	0·5894	0·7467	0·8000	0·7389	0·5800	0·3656	0·1533

$$\tag{25}$$

They are clearly inaccurate in the last two figures, since examination of (23) reveals a symmetry ($y_1 = y_9$, $y_2 = y_8$, etc.) not exhibited by (25). Note here, incidentally, that the existence of symmetry in the *computed* solutions does not *necessarily* imply their accuracy! The inaccuracy is due to *induced* and not to *inherent* instability, and we improve the method very considerably, producing a result with an error of not more than a few units in the fourth figure, if we carry out a similar process *after* removing the third row in (23) from its original place and attaching it to the end of the list of equations.

Elimination. Backward error analysis

7. The failure of the method of the first part of § 6 is revealed by a backward error analysis, which we indicate here for a matrix of order four. We start with the array

$$\begin{array}{ccccccc}
\text{multipliers} & & \mathbf{A}^{(1)} & & & \mathbf{b}^{(1)} \\
 & a_{11}^{(1)} & a_{12}^{(1)} & a_{13}^{(1)} & a_{14}^{(1)} & b_1^{(1)} \\
m_{21} & a_{21}^{(1)} & a_{22}^{(1)} & a_{23}^{(1)} & a_{24}^{(1)} & b_2^{(1)} \\
m_{31} & a_{31}^{(1)} & a_{32}^{(1)} & a_{33}^{(1)} & a_{34}^{(1)} & b_3^{(1)} \\
m_{41} & a_{41}^{(1)} & a_{42}^{(1)} & a_{43}^{(1)} & a_{44}^{(1)} & b_4^{(1)}
\end{array} \right\} . \qquad (26)$$

If $a_{11}^{(1)}$ is not zero, we use the first row as *pivotal* row, with $a_{11}^{(1)}$ as *pivot*, and add a multiple m_{r1} of this row, $r = 2, 3, 4$, to the rth row to eliminate $a_{r1}^{(1)}$, $r \neq 1$. Clearly

$$m_{r1} = -a_{r1}^{(1)}/a_{11}^{(1)}, \qquad (27)$$

and we obtain the new array

$$\begin{array}{ccccccc}
\text{multipliers} & & \mathbf{A}^{(2)} & & & \mathbf{b}^{(2)} \\
 & a_{11}^{(1)} & a_{12}^{(1)} & a_{13}^{(1)} & a_{14}^{(1)} & b_1^{(1)} \\
 & 0 & a_{22}^{(2)} & a_{23}^{(2)} & a_{24}^{(2)} & b_2^{(2)} \\
m_{32} & 0 & a_{32}^{(2)} & a_{33}^{(2)} & a_{34}^{(2)} & b_3^{(2)} \\
m_{42} & 0 & a_{42}^{(2)} & a_{43}^{(2)} & a_{44}^{(2)} & b_4^{(2)}
\end{array} \right\} . \qquad (28)$$

Here, for example,

$$a_{43}^{(2)} = a_{43}^{(1)} + m_{41} a_{13}^{(1)}, \qquad b_3^{(2)} = b_3^{(1)} + m_{31} b_1^{(1)}. \qquad (29)$$

If $a_{22}^{(2)}$ is not zero we perform a similar process with rows two to four of the array (28), producing the array

$$
\begin{array}{c}
\text{multipliers} \qquad\qquad \mathbf{A}^{(3)} \qquad\qquad \mathbf{b}^{(3)} \\
\left.\begin{array}{ccccc}
a_{11}^{(1)} & a_{12}^{(1)} & a_{13}^{(1)} & a_{14}^{(1)} & b_1^{(1)} \\
& a_{22}^{(2)} & a_{23}^{(2)} & a_{24}^{(2)} & b_2^{(2)} \\
& & \underline{a_{33}^{(3)}} & a_{34}^{(3)} & b_3^{(3)} \\
m_{43} & & a_{43}^{(3)} & a_{44}^{(3)} & b_4^{(3)}
\end{array}\right\}.
\end{array}
\tag{30}
$$

A final step, with the same qualification, produces the upper triangular set

$$
\begin{array}{c}
\mathbf{A}^{(4)} \qquad\qquad \mathbf{b}^{(4)} \\
\left.\begin{array}{ccccc}
a_{11}^{(1)} & a_{12}^{(1)} & a_{13}^{(1)} & a_{14}^{(1)} & b_1^{(1)} \\
& a_{22}^{(2)} & a_{23}^{(2)} & a_{24}^{(2)} & b_2^{(2)} \\
& & a_{33}^{(3)} & a_{34}^{(3)} & b_3^{(3)} \\
& & & a_{44}^{(4)} & b_4^{(4)}
\end{array}\right\},
\end{array}
\tag{31}
$$

which we can solve easily by back-substitution.

8. Now in practice we make rounding errors in the arithmetic, even if we can store exactly the original data, so that instead of (27), for example, and the first of (29), we actually compute the digital quantities given by

$$
\left.\begin{array}{l}
\bar{m}_{r1} = -a_{r1}^{(1)}/a_{11}^{(1)} + \eta_{r1} \\
\bar{a}_{43}^{(2)} = a_{43}^{(1)} + \bar{m}_{41}a_{13}^{(1)} + \varepsilon_{43}^{(2)}
\end{array}\right\}.
\tag{32}
$$

To examine the effect of all these rounding errors we consider more closely the relation between corresponding elements of successive matrices $\mathbf{A}^{(r)}$.

An element $a_{rs}^{(k)}$ on or above the diagonal, that is for which $r \leqslant s$, is changed in successive stages until $k = r$, at which stage no further change occurs. We have

$$
\left.\begin{array}{l}
\bar{a}_{rs}^{(2)} = a_{rs}^{(1)} + \bar{m}_{r1}a_{1s}^{(1)} + \varepsilon_{rs}^{(2)} \\
\bar{a}_{rs}^{(3)} = \bar{a}_{rs}^{(2)} + \bar{m}_{r2}\bar{a}_{2s}^{(2)} + \varepsilon_{rs}^{(3)} \\
\hdashline
\bar{a}_{rs}^{(r)} = \bar{a}_{rs}^{(r-1)} + \bar{m}_{r,r-1}\bar{a}_{r-1,s}^{(r-1)} + \varepsilon_{rs}^{(r)}
\end{array}\right\}.
\tag{33}
$$

Adding equations (33), we find

$$\bar{a}_{rs}^{(r)} = a_{rs}^{(1)} + \bar{m}_{r1}a_{1s}^{(1)} + \bar{m}_{r2}\bar{a}_{2s}^{(2)} + \ldots + \bar{m}_{r,r-1}\bar{a}_{r-1,s}^{(r-1)} + \varepsilon_{rs}^{(2)} + $$
$$+ \varepsilon_{rs}^{(3)} + \ldots + \varepsilon_{rs}^{(r)}. \tag{34}$$

For an element $a_{rs}^{(k)}$ below the diagonal, that is for which $r > s$, changes are made until $k = s$, at which stage $a_{rs}^{(s)}$ is used to produce a multiplier and is taken to be zero in all subsequent stages. Corresponding to (33) we then find

$$\left. \begin{array}{l} \bar{a}_{rs}^{(2)} = a_{rs}^{(1)} + \bar{m}_{r1}a_{1s}^{(1)} + \varepsilon_{rs}^{(2)} \\[4pt] \bar{a}_{rs}^{(3)} = \bar{a}_{rs}^{(2)} + \bar{m}_{r2}\bar{a}_{2s}^{(2)} + \varepsilon_{rs}^{(3)} \\[4pt] \text{------------------------------} \\[4pt] \bar{a}_{rs}^{(s)} = \bar{a}_{rs}^{(s-1)} + \bar{m}_{r,s-1}\bar{a}_{s-1,s}^{(s-1)} + \varepsilon_{rs}^{(s)} \\[4pt] 0 = \bar{a}_{rs}^{(s)} + \bar{m}_{rs}\bar{a}_{ss}^{(s)} + \varepsilon_{rs}^{(s+1)} \end{array} \right\}, \tag{35}$$

where the last equation has been obtained from the 'multiplier equation'

$$\bar{m}_{r,s} = \frac{-\bar{a}_{rs}^{(s)}}{\bar{a}_{ss}^{(s)}} + \eta_{rs}, \qquad \varepsilon_{rs}^{(s+1)} = -\bar{a}_{ss}^{(s)}\eta_{rs}. \tag{36}$$

Adding equations (35), we obtain corresponding to (34) the result

$$0 = a_{rs}^{(1)} + \bar{m}_{r1}a_{1s}^{(1)} + \ldots + \bar{m}_{rs}\bar{a}_{ss}^{(s)} + \varepsilon_{rs}^{(2)} + \varepsilon_{rs}^{(3)} + \ldots + \varepsilon_{rs}^{(s+1)}. \tag{37}$$

Now the elements $\bar{a}_{rs}^{(r)}$, for $r \leqslant s$, are the elements in the upper triangular matrix $\mathbf{A}^{(n)}$, in which $n = 4$ in § 7. The zeros on the left of equations like (37) are the zero elements below the diagonal in this matrix. All these quantities, and the multipliers $\bar{m}_{rs}$, are digital numbers, the quantities actually stored in the machine. Equations (34) and (37), moreover, contain none of the 'subsidiary' terms in the elimination process, such as $a_{32}^{(2)}$ or $a_{34}^{(2)}$. It follows that the elimination would have been performed *exactly*, with *exact multipliers* and *exact final elements* in $\mathbf{A}^{(n)}$, if the *original* data had been changed to values typified by

$$\left. \begin{array}{ll} a_{rs}^{(1)} + \delta a_{rs}^{(1)} = a_{rs}^{(1)} + \varepsilon_{rs}^{(2)} + \ldots + \varepsilon_{rs}^{(r)}, & r \leqslant s \\[4pt] a_{rs}^{(1)} + \delta a_{rs}^{(1)} = a_{rs}^{(1)} + \varepsilon_{rs}^{(2)} + \ldots + \varepsilon_{rs}^{(s+1)}, & r > s \end{array} \right\}, \tag{38}$$

that is by $r-1$ rounding errors of type ε_{rs} for $r \leqslant s$, and by s such errors, one coming from the 'multiplier equation', for $r > s$. The column $\mathbf{b}$ on the right-hand side is effectively similar, for the purpose of this analysis, to the last column of the matrix.

9. As an example of this analysis, consider the reduction to upper triangular form of the matrix $\mathbf{A}^{(1)}$, and the corresponding operations on the right-hand vector $\mathbf{b}^{(1)}$, given by

$$\left.\begin{matrix} & \mathbf{A}^{(1)} & & \mathbf{b}^{(1)} \\ 0\cdot 9 & 0\cdot 8 & -0\cdot 4 & 0\cdot 1 \\ 0\cdot 2 & -0\cdot 5 & 0\cdot 3 & 0\cdot 1 \\ 0\cdot 4 & -0\cdot 1 & 0\cdot 4 & 0\cdot 1 \end{matrix}\right\}, \tag{39}$$

using one-figure floating-decimal arithmetic. The first multipliers are $-0\cdot 2$ and $-0\cdot 4$, and the first reduced array, and the perturbations in the original data which would produce it exactly, are given by

$$\left.\begin{matrix} & \mathbf{\bar{A}}^{(2)} & & \mathbf{\bar{b}}^{(2)} & \delta_1\mathbf{A} & & & \delta_1\mathbf{b} \\ 0\cdot 9 & 0\cdot 8 & -0\cdot 4 & 0\cdot 1 & 0\cdot 0 & 0\cdot 0 & 0\cdot 0 & 0\cdot 0 \\ & -0\cdot 7 & 0\cdot 4 & 0\cdot 08 & -0\cdot 02 & -0\cdot 04 & 0\cdot 02 & 0\cdot 0 \\ & -0\cdot 4 & 0\cdot 6 & 0\cdot 06 & -0\cdot 04 & 0\cdot 02 & 0\cdot 04 & 0\cdot 0 \end{matrix}\right\}. \tag{40}$$

The final multiplier is $-0\cdot 6$, and the final array and the *additional* perturbations involved are given by

$$\left.\begin{matrix} & \mathbf{\bar{A}}^{(3)} & & \mathbf{\bar{b}}^{(3)} & \delta_2\mathbf{A} & & & \delta_2\mathbf{b} \\ 0\cdot 9 & 0\cdot 8 & -0\cdot 4 & 0\cdot 1 & 0\cdot 0 & 0\cdot 0 & 0\cdot 0 & 0\cdot 0 \\ & -0\cdot 7 & 0\cdot 4 & 0\cdot 08 & 0\cdot 0 & 0\cdot 0 & 0\cdot 0 & 0\cdot 0 \\ & & 0\cdot 4 & 0\cdot 01 & 0\cdot 0 & -0\cdot 02 & 0\cdot 04 & -0\cdot 002 \end{matrix}\right\}. \tag{41}$$

The perturbations are additive, and we deduce, and can easily verify, that the *final array*, and *all* the multipliers, would be obtained by exact arithmetic from the original perturbed array given by

$$\left.\begin{matrix} & \mathbf{A}^{(1)}+\delta\mathbf{A} & & \mathbf{b}^{(1)}+\delta\mathbf{b} \\ 0\cdot 9 & 0\cdot 8 & -0\cdot 4 & 0\cdot 1 \\ 0\cdot 18 & -0\cdot 54 & 0\cdot 32 & 0\cdot 1 \\ 0\cdot 36 & -0\cdot 10 & 0\cdot 48 & 0\cdot 098 \end{matrix}\right\}. \tag{42}$$

10. It remains to evaluate the size of the rounding errors induced by floating-point arithmetic. Starting with digital data, the general equation corresponding to the second of (32) gives

$$\bar{a}_{rs}^{(k)} = fl(\bar{a}_{rs}^{(k-1)}+\bar{m}_{r,k-1}\bar{a}_{k-1,s}^{(k-1)}) = \{\bar{a}_{rs}^{(k-1)}+\bar{m}_{r,k-1}\bar{a}_{k-1,s}^{(k-1)}(1+\varepsilon_1)\}(1+\varepsilon_2), \tag{43}$$

with $|\varepsilon_1|$, $|\varepsilon_2| \leqslant 2^{-t}$, so that

$$\varepsilon_{rs}^{(k)} = \bar{a}_{rs}^{(k)} - (\bar{a}_{rs}^{(k-1)} + \bar{m}_{r,k-1}\bar{a}_{k-1,s}^{(k-1)})$$

$$= \bar{a}_{rs}^{(k)} - \frac{\bar{a}_{rs}^{(k)}}{1+\varepsilon_2} + \bar{m}_{r,k-1}\bar{a}_{k-1,s}^{(k-1)}\varepsilon_1. \tag{44}$$

Then, with neglect of 2^{-2t}, we find the bound

$$|\varepsilon_{rs}^{(k)}| \leqslant 2^{-t}[|\bar{a}_{rs}^{(k)}| + |\bar{m}_{r,k-1}\bar{a}_{k-1,s}^{(k-1)}|]. \tag{45}$$

This result applies to all the equations in (33) and all but the last equation in (35). For the latter we have

$$\bar{m}_{rs} - fl(-\bar{a}_{rs}^{(s)}/\bar{a}_{ss}^{(s)}) = -\bar{a}_{rs}^{(s)}(1+\varepsilon)/\bar{a}_{ss}^{(s)}, \tag{46}$$

so that

$$\varepsilon_{r,s}^{(s+1)} = -(\bar{a}_{rs}^{(s)} \mid \bar{m}_{rs}\bar{a}_{ss}^{(s)}) = c\bar{a}_{rs}^{(s)}, \qquad |\varepsilon_{r,s}^{(s+1)}| \leqslant 2^{-t}|\bar{a}_{rs}^{(s)}|. \tag{47}$$

From these results it is clear that the rounding errors may be large if either the multipliers, or the elements in successive 'reduced' matrices, or both, are large. The 'classical mathematical' method takes remedial action only if a pivot is zero, so that the multipliers cannot be formed and the process breaks down. This remedy consists in selecting some other row as pivotal row, and it is now clear that we must perform some corresponding action not only to prevent breakdown but also to minimize the induced instability of the method. The poor results of the example of § 6 are due to the failure to take this appropriate action.

Pivoting and stability

11. The easiest remedial action is to eliminate x_1, x_2,... in this order, but to select as pivotal row the row whose relevant first term is largest in absolute value. This ensures that every $|\bar{m}_{rs}| \leqslant 1$, and it also helps to restrict the growth of successive $|\bar{a}_{rs}^{(k)}|$. In fact the latter cannot exceed $2^{k-1}|a_{rs}^{(1)}|$, and in practice the observed growth is very much smaller. In practice, also, the technique is performed by interchanging the row originally in the pivotal position with the one we wish to use as pivot. For the example of § 6 this is found to involve the interchange of rows three and four, then of the new four and five, etc., with the effect that the original third row is gradually pushed to the bottom of the list. The final result is that we have reduced to upper triangular form a row permutation of the original equations, and in passing we note that the value of the determinant is $(-1)^p$ times the product of the selected pivotal elements, where p is the number of row interchanges.

This process is often called 'partial pivoting', and one might also consider the process called 'total pivoting', in which we select as pivot, at each stage, the element of largest absolute value in all the relevant part of the matrix, that is in those rows and columns that have not previously been 'pivotal'. The multipliers are still not greater than unity in absolute value, and the upper bound to the growth of the $|\bar{a}_{rs}^{(k)}|$, though not known exactly, is considerably smaller than that induced by partial pivoting. This method is used only rarely, however, because the machine work involved is rather larger, the partial pivoting is generally satisfactory, and the latter can be made still better, by the use of fl_2 arithmetic described in the next section, in a manner which cannot easily be performed with total pivoting.

We might mention in passing that there are various other methods, for example using orthogonal matrices, which guarantee that succcessive elements do not grow in size, but these are also too lengthy in computation to compete successfully with 'elimination with partial pivoting', and their use is reserved for the corresponding problem of determining eigenvalues and eigenvectors, discussed in the second part of this chapter.

Compact method, fl_2 arithmetic

12. Examination of equations (34) and (37) shows that if the pivots can be taken in natural order the elimination process effectively produces, for a set of equations of order four, and with exact arithmetic, the result

$$
\begin{bmatrix}
a_{11}^{(1)} & a_{12}^{(1)} & a_{13}^{(1)} & a_{14}^{(1)} & b_1^{(1)} \\
a_{21}^{(1)} & a_{22}^{(1)} & a_{23}^{(1)} & a_{24}^{(1)} & b_2^{(1)} \\
a_{31}^{(1)} & a_{32}^{(1)} & a_{33}^{(1)} & a_{34}^{(1)} & b_3^{(1)} \\
a_{41}^{(1)} & a_{42}^{(1)} & a_{43}^{(1)} & a_{44}^{(1)} & b_4^{(1)}
\end{bmatrix}
=
\begin{bmatrix}
1 & & & \\
-m_{21} & 1 & & \\
-m_{31} & -m_{32} & 1 & \\
-m_{41} & -m_{42} & -m_{43} & 1
\end{bmatrix}
\times
$$

$$
\times
\begin{bmatrix}
a_{11}^{(1)} & a_{12}^{(1)} & a_{13}^{(1)} & a_{14}^{(1)} & b_1^{(1)} \\
 & a_{22}^{(2)} & a_{23}^{(2)} & a_{24}^{(2)} & b_2^{(2)} \\
 & & a_{33}^{(3)} & a_{34}^{(3)} & b_3^{(3)} \\
 & & & a_{44}^{(4)} & b_4^{(4)}
\end{bmatrix},
\tag{48}
$$

which in general can be written in the form

$$
[\mathbf{A}^{(1)}, \mathbf{b}^{(1)}] = \mathbf{L}[\mathbf{A}^{(n)}, \mathbf{b}^{(n)}].
\tag{49}
$$

Here $\mathbf{A}^{(n)}$ is the upper triangular matrix, henceforth called $\mathbf{U}$, obtained by the elimination process, $\mathbf{b}^{(n)}$ is the final vector on the right-hand side, and $\mathbf{L}$ is a unit lower triangular matrix whose other elements are the negatives of the multipliers in the appropriate positions.

Due to the rounding errors we actually perform instead the decomposition

$$[\mathbf{A}^{(1)} + \delta\mathbf{A}^{(1)}, \mathbf{b}^{(1)} + \delta\mathbf{b}^{(1)}] = \overline{\mathbf{L}}[\overline{\mathbf{A}}^{(n)}, \overline{\mathbf{b}}^{(n)}], \tag{50}$$

where, according to (34) and (37), $\delta a_{rs}^{(1)}$ is the sum of $r-1$ rounding errors for $r \leqslant s$, and of s such errors for $r > s$, with bounds (45) and (47) for these errors. With the multipliers restricted to unity in absolute value, we see that $|\varepsilon_{rs}^{(k)}| \leqslant 2.2^{-t} |g|$ in all cases, where $|g|$ is the maximum of all the elements in successive matrices. Then

$$\left. \begin{aligned} |\delta a_{rs}^{(1)}| &\leqslant 2(r-1).2^{-t} |g|, & r \leqslant s \\ |\delta a_{rs}^{(1)}| &\leqslant 2s.2^{-t} |g|, & r > s \end{aligned} \right\}, \tag{51}$$

and by the same argument we have

$$|\delta b_r^{(1)}| \leqslant 2(r-1).2^{-t} |h|, \tag{52}$$

where $|h|$ is the maximum element ever appearing on the right-hand side.

13. Now the factors r and s in (51) and (52) arise through the piecemeal way in which the elements of $\overline{\mathbf{A}}^{(n)} = \overline{\mathbf{U}}$ are produced. In equation (48), for example, the element $a_{44}^{(4)}$ is effectively obtained from the product of the last rows and columns of $\overline{\mathbf{L}}$ and $\overline{\mathbf{U}}$ in the form

$$a_{44}^{(4)} = a_{44}^{(1)} + m_{41} a_{14}^{(1)} + m_{42} a_{24}^{(2)} + m_{43} a_{34}^{(3)}. \tag{53}$$

In the standard elimination process the computation is performed according to the scheme

$$a_{44}^{(4)} = [\{(a_{44}^{(1)} + m_{41} a_{14}^{(1)}) + m_{42} a_{24}^{(2)}\} + m_{43} a_{34}^{(3)}], \tag{54}$$

the elements in each bracket being calculated and rounded to single length by standard fl arithmetic. Successive partial sums are in fact the unwanted elements $a_{44}^{(2)}$, $a_{44}^{(3)}$ in the elimination method.

This we can avoid by forgetting about elimination, seeking directly the decomposition (49), and using fl_2 arithmetic in the process. If all $|m_{rs}| < 1$, the elements of $\mathbf{L}$ and $\mathbf{U}$ can be computed in the natural order, and it is not difficult to see that the $\overline{\mathbf{L}}$ and $\overline{\mathbf{U}}$ (and the column $\mathbf{b}^{(n)}$) so computed satisfy (50) with the omission from (51) and (52) of the factors containing r and s. If some of the $|m_{rs}|$ exceed unity with this natural ordering we can, quite easily, determine in the course of the computation the necessary row interchanges of $\mathbf{A}^{(1)}$ and $\mathbf{b}^{(1)}$ so that the required effect can be achieved. This method, details of which are given, for example, in Fox (1964) and Wilkinson (1965), is the one most often used when fl_2 arithmetic is available.

Completing the solution

14. To obtain the solution of the linear equations we have still to perform the back-substitution, that is to solve the upper triangular equations of type (31). This is obviously effected quite easily by working backwards, and for example we produce x_2 from the equation

$$a_{22}^{(2)}x_2 + a_{23}^{(2)}x_3 + a_{24}^{(2)}x_4 = b_2^{(2)}, \tag{55}$$

in which everything except x_2 is already known.

This again cannot be done by exact arithmetic and we can show (see, for example, Wilkinson, 1965) that the effect of these rounding errors can also be 'thrown back' into the data, so that the computed solution $\mathbf{\bar{x}}$ is the exact solution of an equation

$$(\mathbf{A}^{(1)} + \delta_1\mathbf{A}^{(1)} + \delta_2\mathbf{A}^{(1)})\mathbf{\bar{x}} = \mathbf{b}^{(1)} + \delta_1\mathbf{b}^{(1)} + \delta_2\mathbf{b}^{(1)}. \tag{56}$$

Again the perturbations $\delta_2\mathbf{A}^{(1)}$, $\delta_2\mathbf{b}^{(1)}$ induced by the back-substitution turn out to be small if the equations of type (31) have been produced with the equivalent of partial pivoting from the original set, and again we do better, where possible, to use fl_2 arithmetic in the evaluation, for example, of x_2 from (55).

We conclude that the method of elimination with partial pivoting induces little instability unless there is a substantial growth in the size of successive elements (which in practice is very rare), and that this is still further reduced with the use of the 'compact' method with fl_2 arithmetic.

Special cases

15. There are two special cases, of frequent occurrence, in which pivoting is not necessary. First, our equations may have a matrix that is symmetric and positive definite, obtained for example in the method of 'least squares'. In this case it is easy to show that the basic triangular decomposition can be written in the form

$$\mathbf{A} = \mathbf{LL'}, \tag{57}$$

where the upper triangle $\mathbf{L'}$ is the transpose of the lower triangle $\mathbf{L}$, and only one has to be calculated. The matrix $\mathbf{L}$ corresponds to the matrix of multipliers in (49), but is no longer a unit triangular matrix. However if every $|a_{rs}| \leqslant 1$, which can always be arranged by suitable scaling of the rows and columns, it can also be shown that every element of $\mathbf{L}$ does not exceed unity in absolute value, and this guarantees the essential stability of the method. The technique is virtually identical with that of the general case, equation (49) being replaced by

$$[\mathbf{A}^{(1)}, \mathbf{b}^{(1)}] = \mathbf{L}[\mathbf{L}', \mathbf{b}^{(n)}], \tag{58}$$

the elements of $\mathbf{L}$ and $\mathbf{b}^{(n)}$ are computed successively, and we back-substitute in $\mathbf{L}'\mathbf{x} = \mathbf{b}^{(n)}$ to obtain the required answers.

We note in passing that even in the general case it is desirable that all rows and columns of $\mathbf{A}$, and also of $\mathbf{b}$, should be of reasonable size, say such that each has at least one element lying between $0 \cdot 5$ and $1 \cdot 0$ in absolute value. This can always be arranged, though unfortunately not uniquely in the general unsymmetric case, by appropriate scaling of the rows and columns.

The technique represented by (58) can be performed if $\mathbf{A}$ merely has symmetry, but in this case the method will involve complex arithmetic and may have significant induced instability. It should by now be clear that the main ingredient of induced instability is the vanishing or near-vanishing of a principal minor of the matrix $\mathbf{A}$, and this is impossible if $\mathbf{A}$ is definite. Without this property it is undesirable to take advantage of the symmetry, and we should perform pivoting as in the general case.

16. For our second special case we consider the triple-diagonal form, which we have already met in Chapter 3 in connection with three-term recurrence relations, and which we used in § 6 to illustrate an example of induced instability. The general triple-diagonal matrix has the form

$$\mathbf{A} = \begin{bmatrix} b_1 & c_1 & & & & \\ a_2 & b_2 & c_2 & & & \\ & a_3 & b_3 & c_3 & & \\ & & & \cdots\cdots\cdots & & \\ & & & a_{n-1} & b_{n-1} & c_{n-1} \\ & & & & a_n & b_n \end{bmatrix}, \tag{59}$$

and we are interested especially in the size of the multipliers in an elimination process with pivots taken down the diagonal. We have seen that these multipliers are effectively the elements of the $\mathbf{L}$ matrix in the decomposition

$$
\mathbf{A} =
\begin{bmatrix}
b_1 & c_1 & & & & \\
a_2 & b_2 & c_2 & & & \\
& a_3 & b_3 & & c_3 & \\
& & & \text{-----} & & \\
& & & a_{n-1} & b_{n-1} & c_{n-1} \\
& & & & a_n & b_n
\end{bmatrix}
=
\mathbf{L}
\begin{bmatrix}
1 & & & & \\
l_2 & 1 & & & \\
& l_3 & 1 & & \\
& & & \ddots & \\
& & & l_n & 1
\end{bmatrix}
\times
$$

$$
\times \quad
\mathbf{U}
\begin{bmatrix}
u_1 & v_1 & & & \\
& u_2 & v_2 & & \\
& & u_3 & v_3 & \\
& & & \ddots & \\
& & & & u_n
\end{bmatrix}. \tag{60}
$$

Equating the elements in the rth row we find the equations

$$
a_r = l_r u_{r-1}, \qquad b_r = l_r v_{r-1} + u_r, \qquad c_r = v_r, \tag{61}
$$

which serve to determine in succession l_r, u_r, and v_r. We can eliminate u_r and v_r and find the non-linear recurrence relation

$$
l_{r+1} = \frac{a_{r+1}}{b_r - l_r c_{r-1}}. \tag{62}
$$

If l_{r+1} is always less than unity in absolute value we have guaranteed stability, and an obvious important case is provided by the special *diagonally-dominant* system for which

$$
a_r = c_r = k, \qquad |b_r| > 2k \quad \text{for all } r. \tag{63}
$$

In this case, of course, the roots of the characteristic quadratic relevant to the corresponding recurrence relation are locally real, and the solutions of the recurrence relation are of exponential type. This confirms a remark in § 26 of Chapter 3 about this type of equation. When (63) is not satisfied some l_r can be arbitrarily large or even infinite, and we have the possibility of breakdown or induced instability as exemplified in § 6. This can be avoided by pivoting, and again we refer back to a remark at the end of § 26 of Chapter 3.

For the case (63), moreover, there is no inherent instability, whereas if this inequality is not satisfied the last pivot, even with row interchanges, may be zero or very small, and the matrix correspondingly singular or nearly singular. This, again, we noted in different terms in Chapter 3.

Accuracy and correction of solution

17. We have indicated a method, elimination (compact or otherwise) with interchanges, which exhibits little in the way of induced instability, but this does not tell us immediately how accurate our solution is. At the risk of some repetition it is convenient to summarize the situation. We are proposing to solve the linear equations

$$\mathbf{Ay} = \mathbf{b}. \tag{64}$$

The data may have physical uncertainties, and in any case may be incapable of exact storage, so that we actually start with the problem defined by

$$(\mathbf{A}+\delta_P\mathbf{A}+\delta_M\mathbf{A})\mathbf{x} = \mathbf{b}+\delta_P\mathbf{b}+\delta_M\mathbf{b}. \tag{65}$$

Here the suffix P means 'physical', M represents 'mathematical'. In a physical problem we can effectively ignore $\delta_M\mathbf{A}$ and $\delta_M\mathbf{b}$, since these are likely to be much smaller than $\delta_P\mathbf{A}$ and $\delta_P\mathbf{b}$ and can be incorporated in these quantities. In a mathematical problem the δ_P terms are zero, and the δ_M terms represent roundings at the less significant end of the storage registers. In this problem, moreover, we can make the δ_M terms as small as we please by using 'multiprecision' arithmetic, whereas the δ_P terms are always of a definite size, probably with known upper bounds.

Consider now the technique of solution. We have shown that we solve exactly the perturbed system

$$(\mathbf{A}+\delta_P\mathbf{A}+\delta_M\mathbf{A}+\delta_T\mathbf{A})\bar{\mathbf{x}} = \mathbf{b}+\delta_P\mathbf{b}+\delta_M\mathbf{b}+\delta_T\mathbf{b}. \tag{66}$$

Here T means 'technique', and the δ_T terms have upper bounds depending on the particular technique or method of solution. In methods which do not exhibit induced instability the δ_T terms are small, and in particular with fl_2 arithmetic they are only small multiples of the δ_M terms. Even with fl arithmetic they are likely to be much smaller than the δ_P terms unless the number n of equations is very large. For these various

reasons it is satisfactory to write (65) and (66) in the respective forms
(Physical)

$$(\mathbf{A}+\delta_P\mathbf{A})\mathbf{x} = \mathbf{b}+\delta_P\mathbf{b}, \qquad (\mathbf{A}+\delta_P\mathbf{A}+\delta_T\mathbf{A})\bar{\mathbf{x}} = \mathbf{b}+\delta_P\mathbf{b}+\delta_T\mathbf{b}, \qquad (67)$$

(Mathematical)

$$(\mathbf{A}+\delta_M\mathbf{A})\mathbf{x} = \mathbf{b}+\delta_M\mathbf{b}, \qquad (\mathbf{A}+\delta_M\mathbf{A}+\delta_T\mathbf{A})\bar{\mathbf{x}} = \mathbf{b}+\delta_M\mathbf{b}+\delta_T\mathbf{b}. \qquad (68)$$

18. Consider now the question of accuracy of the computed solution of the *mathematical* problem, that is the difference between $\bar{\mathbf{x}}$ and $\mathbf{y}$ in equations (68) and (64). If the corresponding physical problem is ill-conditioned this difference may be large even when the δ_M and δ_T terms are small.

The most important point to note is that the size of the residuals of $\bar{\mathbf{x}}$, defined by the components of the vector

$$\mathbf{r} = \mathbf{b}-\mathbf{A}\bar{\mathbf{x}}, \qquad (69)$$

does not necessarily give any indication of the difference between $\mathbf{y}$ and $\bar{\mathbf{x}}$. In particular small residuals do not guarantee an accurate solution, and indeed it can be shown (see Wilkinson, 1963) that the method of computation *automatically produces small residuals* whenever the solution is 'small'. We must do some extra work to determine the accuracy of our alleged solution, and if necessary to improve it.

For this purpose, of course, we prefer to avoid a significant amount of multiprecision arithmetic, and we can proceed as follows. We hope and expect that the solution $\bar{\mathbf{x}}$ of (68) is a reasonable approximation to the required $\mathbf{y}$ of (64). With this approximation, we carry out the following iterative process.

(i) Compute residuals $\mathbf{r} = \mathbf{b}-\mathbf{A}\mathbf{x}^{(0)}$, $\mathbf{x}^{(0)} = \bar{\mathbf{x}}$, using for this purpose accurate fl_2 arithmetic *without* rounding finally to single length. The elements of $\mathbf{r}$ will have many zeros in the most significant single-length part, and we can therefore scale to a single-length number with only small rounding error in the least significant part. Call this vector $\mathbf{r}^{(0)}$.

(ii) Solve $\mathbf{A}\,\delta\mathbf{x}^{(0)} = \mathbf{r}^{(0)}$, using the single-precision $\mathbf{L}$ and $\mathbf{U}$ matrices, say, already used in the production of $\mathbf{x}^{(0)}$. By this device the amount of work involved at this stage is small.

(iii) Form $\mathbf{x}^{(1)} = \mathbf{x}^{(0)}+\delta\mathbf{x}^{(0)}$, round to single length, and repeat the iteration, using $\mathbf{x}^{(1)}$ instead of $\mathbf{x}^{(0)}$, in (i).

19. In the case in which $\mathbf{A}$ and $\mathbf{b}$ in (64) are digital, so that the δ_M terms in (68) are zero, it can be shown (Wilkinson 1963, Moler 1967) that this process tends to a correct single-length solution whenever the first approximation is sufficiently accurate, say has one correct significant figure.

As an example, consider the equations with symmetric matrix and right-hand side given by

$$
\begin{array}{cc}
\mathbf{A}^{(1)} & \mathbf{b}^{(1)}
\end{array}
$$

$$
\left.\begin{array}{ccccc}
0{\cdot}5001 & 0{\cdot}7001 & 0{\cdot}6001 & 0{\cdot}5001 & 0{\cdot}2300 \\
0{\cdot}7001 & 1{\cdot}000 & 0{\cdot}8001 & 0{\cdot}7001 & 0{\cdot}3200 \\
0{\cdot}6001 & 0{\cdot}8001 & 1{\cdot}000 & 0{\cdot}9001 & 0{\cdot}3300 \\
0{\cdot}5001 & 0{\cdot}7001 & 0{\cdot}9001 & 1{\cdot}000 & 0{\cdot}3100
\end{array}\right\} . \tag{70}
$$

Using four-decimal fl_2 arithmetic we compute the triangle $\mathbf{L}$ in $\mathbf{A} = \mathbf{LL}'$, and find

$$
\mathbf{L} = \begin{bmatrix}
0{\cdot}7072 & & & \\
0{\cdot}9900 & 0{\cdot}1411 & & \\
0{\cdot}8486 & -0{\cdot}2836 & 0{\cdot}4466 & \\
0{\cdot}7072 & -0{\cdot}0001984 & 0{\cdot}6715 & 0{\cdot}2213
\end{bmatrix} . \tag{71}
$$

The column $\mathbf{b}^{(n)}$ of equation (58) is then obtained from $\mathbf{Lb}^{(n)} = \mathbf{b}^{(1)}$, effectively a process of forward substitution, and we find

$$
\mathbf{b}^{(n)\prime} = 0{\cdot}3252,\ -0{\cdot}01381,\ 0{\cdot}1122,\ 0{\cdot}02112. \tag{72}
$$

The solution of $\mathbf{L}'\mathbf{x}^{(0)} = \mathbf{b}^{(n)}$ then gives the first approximation

$$
\mathbf{x}^{(0)\prime} = 0{\cdot}06900,\ 0{\cdot}1187,\ 0{\cdot}1077,\ 0{\cdot}09544. \tag{73}
$$

The residuals of this approximation are exactly

$$
(\mathbf{b}-\mathbf{Ax}^{(0)})' = 10^{-4}(0{\cdot}30916,\ 0{\cdot}04786,\ 0{\cdot}15686,\ 0{\cdot}1046), \tag{74}
$$

and for the second approximation we take the new right-hand sides

$$
10^{-4}(0{\cdot}3092),\ 10^{-5}(0{\cdot}4786),\ 10^{-4}(0{\cdot}1569),\ 10^{-4}(0{\cdot}1046), \tag{75}
$$

and repeat the computations which gave rise to (72) and (73). With obvious notation we find

$$
\delta\mathbf{b}^{(n)\prime} = 10^{-4}(0{\cdot}4372),\ 10^{-3}(-0{\cdot}2728),\ 10^{-3}(-0{\cdot}2212),\ 10^{-3}(0{\cdot}5785), \tag{76}
$$

and the correction

$$
\delta\mathbf{x}^{(0)\prime} = 10^{-1}(0{\cdot}1792),\ 10^{-1}(-0{\cdot}1083),\ 10^{-2}(-0{\cdot}4426),\ 10^{-2}(0{\cdot}2614). \tag{77}
$$

We should now proceed with the *single-length* addition

$$
\mathbf{x}^{(1)\prime} = \mathbf{x}^{(0)\prime}+\delta\mathbf{x}^{(0)\prime} = 0{\cdot}08692,\ 0{\cdot}1079,\ 0{\cdot}1033,\ 0{\cdot}09805, \tag{78}
$$

repeating all the steps. The new residuals corresponding to (75) are

$$10^{-4}(-0\cdot3462), \ 10^{-4}(-0\cdot4783), \ 10^{-4}(-0\cdot4629), \ 10^{-4}(-0\cdot3981), \quad (79)$$

and the process gives the very small correction

$$\delta\mathbf{x}^{(1)'} = 10^{-4}(-0\cdot3864), \ 10^{-5}(-0\cdot6321), \ 10^{-4}(-0\cdot1890), \ 10^{-6}(0\cdot9535).$$
$$(80)$$

At this stage we reasonably conclude that we have the answer correct to single length. It is interesting and important to observe that the residuals (74) corresponding to the first approximation (73), which has significant errors, are in fact *smaller* than the residuals (79) corresponding to the very accurate solution (78). We cannot in fact expect the residuals to get very small, for in any case we have rounded to single length the sum of $\mathbf{x}^{(0)}$ and $\delta\mathbf{x}^{(0)}$. What actually happens is that the 'shape' of the residual vector changes, so that it effectively becomes nearly orthogonal to the eigenvectors corresponding to the small eigenvalues, the latter being the cause of the 'ill-conditioning'.

20. This correction of the first approximation is always worth while, not only for the mathematical problem but also for the physical problem. In the former case the correction is valuable in its own right, and in the latter case it gives at least some indication of the number of figures worth quoting in the answers to the physical problem. Here, for example, we know that (78) is virtually the exact solution of (70). We know also, from our previous analysis, that the first approximation (73) is the exact solution of some small perturbation of (70), the perturbation having a maximum value of half a unit in the last figures of (70). It follows that if (70) is uncertain to within half a unit in its last figures then the 'solution' is meaningful only to the extent, at most, to which (73) and (78) are in agreement. If the physical uncertainties are larger than this, say half a unit in the third figure of (70), we would expect the uncertainty in the solution to be greater by at least the factor 10, etc.

Finally, if the mathematical error $\delta_M\mathbf{A}$ and $\delta_M\mathbf{b}$ is not zero, so that the original data cannot be stored exactly, we would expect our process to give satisfactory results if we took extra care with the computation of the residuals, for example multiplying the single-length first approximation by a double length $\mathbf{A}+\delta_M\mathbf{A}$, and subtracting from a double-length $\mathbf{b}+\delta_M\mathbf{b}$. We use the same matrix decomposition throughout, and the amount of multiple-length arithmetic is kept to a minimum.

The inverse and the determinant

21. In connection with the solution of linear equations it is neither necessary nor desirable to compute either the inverse or the determinant of the relevant matrix. Even if we have the same matrix with a number of different right-hand sides it is faster to perform the triangular decomposition, once and for all, followed by a forward and back-substitution for each right-hand side. The solution of linear equations as the ratios of two determinants (Cramer's rule) is slower by the factor n than the direct elimination method.

We *may* need the inverse in its own right, for example in connection with correlation in least-squares processes. Its computation is performed, one column at a time, by solving linear equations with the same matrix on the left and successive columns of the unit matrix on the right. The only important point is that we cannot now be deceived, in regard to the accuracy of the alleged inverse, by the smallness of residuals. The residuals are here given by the matrix

$$\mathbf{R} = \mathbf{I} - \mathbf{AX}, \qquad (81)$$

where $\mathbf{X}$ is the alleged inverse and $\mathbf{I}$ is the unit matrix. If $\mathbf{R}$ has small elements, for an $\mathbf{A}$ of 'normal size', then the computed inverse must be quite accurate. We recall that in the linear-equation case 'small' residuals are associated with 'small' solutions, and these depend on particular right-hand sides $\mathbf{b}$ such that $\mathbf{A}^{-1}\mathbf{b}$ is small even when $\mathbf{A}^{-1}$ is large. In the case when $\mathbf{b}$ is successively the columns of the unit matrix, then at least one vector $\mathbf{A}^{-1}\mathbf{b}$ must be large if $\mathbf{A}^{-1}$ is large and $\mathbf{b}$ of 'normal' size. In other words the inversion must reveal the 'ill-conditioning'. For the columns of the unit matrix are independent vectors, and we cannot have n independent vectors orthogonal, or very nearly orthogonal, to a particular eigenvector.

22. With regard to the determinant, we effectively seek its evaluation mainly for the purpose of finding a zero of some function expressed in determinantal form. For example, the eigenvalues of a matrix are the roots of the equation

$$f(\lambda) = \det(\mathbf{A} - \lambda\mathbf{I}) = 0, \qquad (82)$$

and we may compute a zero by evaluating $f(\lambda)$ for different values of λ, followed by a process of inverse interpolation (see Chapter 8). More generally the element λ appears, perhaps non-linearly, in every element of the determinant of a matrix, and evaluation and interpolation might then be the only feasible method. (There are, of course, many other methods for the solution of the *particular* problem (82).)

Iterative methods

23. The methods so far discussed are called *direct*, the point being that if we work throughout with unlimited precision we obtain the correct result (at least to a mathematical problem) in a finite number of numerical operations. Iterative methods, on the other hand, seek to approximate successively to the solution, theoretically in an infinite sequence of operations but practically in a finite sequence which terminates when the approximation is contextually correct.

Iterative methods are used most often for large 'sparse' matrices, and we do not propose to discuss the various techniques nor to analyse their efficiency. We shall merely use the idea of iteration to give a further warning about the danger of too early truncation of an infinite series. Here, of course, the fact that we are effectively summing an infinite series is less obvious than in the explicit case mentioned in § 13 of Chapter 1.

The basic iterative method for solving linear equations $\mathbf{Ax} = \mathbf{b}$ is given by the iteration

$$\mathbf{Mx}^{(r+1)} = \mathbf{Nx}^{(r)} + \mathbf{b}, \qquad \mathbf{A} = \mathbf{M} - \mathbf{N}, \tag{83}$$

and one of the main differences between various methods is contained in the choice of the matrices $\mathbf{M}$ and $\mathbf{N}$ in the splitting of $\mathbf{A}$. The other variation is in the possible dependence of $\mathbf{M}$ and $\mathbf{N}$ on the index r of the iteration, but we shall not consider this case.

If (83) converges, it converges to the solution of $\mathbf{Mx} = \mathbf{Nx} + \mathbf{b}$, that is $\mathbf{Ax} = \mathbf{b}$, and the error $\mathbf{e}^{(r)} = \mathbf{x} - \mathbf{x}^{(r)}$ satisfies the equation

$$\mathbf{e}^{(r)} = \mathbf{M}^{-1}\mathbf{Ne}^{(r-1)} = \dots = (\mathbf{M}^{-1}\mathbf{N})^r\mathbf{e}^{(0)}. \tag{84}$$

We therefore have convergence, from an arbitrary start $\mathbf{x}^{(0)}$, if and only if all the eigenvalues of the matrix $\mathbf{M}^{-1}\mathbf{N}$ are less than unity in absolute value. If the largest modulus is ρ, the rate of convergence depends on the size of ρ, and the choice of $\mathbf{M}$ and $\mathbf{N}$ is decided with the intention of making ρ as small as possible.

24. Now we consider the common case in which the largest eigenvalue of $\mathbf{M}^{-1}\mathbf{N}$ is real, equal to λ_1, and all other eigenvalues have smaller modulus. We can then consider the series

$$\mathbf{x} = \mathbf{x}^{(r)} + (\mathbf{x}^{(r+1)} - \mathbf{x}^{(r)}) + (\mathbf{x}^{(r+2)} - \mathbf{x}^{(r+1)}) + \dots. \tag{85}$$

This is effectively the way in which the computation is performed,

with the addition of successive 'increments' to a starting approximation. We proceed to demonstrate the possibly slow convergence of this
series, and the danger of premature truncation, for example at a stage
at which the next increment is smaller than the 'tolerance' we are
prepared to accept in our result.

Consider the linear equations

$$0 \cdot 7652x_1 - 0 \cdot 5664x_2 = 0 \cdot 1988 \atop -0 \cdot 5664x_1 + 0 \cdot 4348x_2 = -0 \cdot 1316 \Bigg\}. \qquad (86)$$

The iteration defined by

$$\mathbf{x}^{(r+1)} = \begin{bmatrix} 0 \cdot 2348 & 0 \cdot 5664 \\ 0 \cdot 5664 & 0 \cdot 5652 \end{bmatrix} \mathbf{x}^{(r)} + \begin{bmatrix} 0 \cdot 1988 \\ -0 \cdot 1316 \end{bmatrix}, \qquad (87)$$

that is with $\mathbf{M} = \mathbf{I}$ in (83), converges to the true solution $x_1 = 1$,
$x_2 = 1$.

Suppose, however, that we start with $x_1^{(0)} = 0 \cdot 8$, $x_2^{(0)} = 0 \cdot 8$, and ask
that the iteration should stop when the maximum component of the
current increment is smaller in magnitude than $0 \cdot 0025$. We find the
results

$$\begin{matrix} r & 0 & 1 & 2 & 3 & 4 & 5 \\ x_1^{(r)} & 0 \cdot 8 & 0 \cdot 8398 & 0 \cdot 8342 & 0 \cdot 8373 & 0 \cdot 8386 & 0 \cdot 8403 \\ x_2^{(r)} & 0 \cdot 8 & 0 \cdot 7737 & 0 \cdot 7814 & 0 \cdot 7825 & 0 \cdot 7849 & 0 \cdot 7870 \end{matrix} \Bigg\}, \qquad (88)$$

and would accept $\mathbf{x}^{(4)}$ as the answer, unaware that its relative error is
about 20 per cent. This lack of awareness, of course, is more common
with modern computation in which, unlike desk-machine work, we
probably do not print out the successive approximations that certainly
reveal to the discerning eye a very slow rate of convergence.

25. We can analyse the problem by finding a relation between
successive increments. From (83) there easily follows the result

$$\boldsymbol{\Delta}^{(r)} = \mathbf{M}^{-1}\mathbf{N}\boldsymbol{\Delta}^{(r-1)} = (\mathbf{M}^{-1}\mathbf{N})^r\boldsymbol{\Delta}^{(0)}, \qquad \boldsymbol{\Delta}^{(r)} = \mathbf{x}^{(r+1)} - \mathbf{x}^{(r)}. \quad (89)$$

Now suppose that $\boldsymbol{\Delta}^{(0)}$ is expanded in the form

$$\boldsymbol{\Delta}^{(0)} = \sum_{s=1}^{n} \alpha_s \mathbf{y}^{(s)}, \qquad (90)$$

where $\mathbf{y}^{(s)}$ is an eigenvector of $\mathbf{M}^{-1}\mathbf{N}$ with eigenvalue λ_s. Then, for
sufficiently large r and with λ_1 real such that $|\lambda_1| > |\lambda_2| > ... > |\lambda_n|$,
we have

$$\boldsymbol{\Delta}^{(r)} \sim \alpha_1 \lambda_1^r \mathbf{y}^{(1)}, \qquad (91)$$

and successive increments are merely multiplied by λ_1. Equation (85) can then be written as

$$\mathbf{x} = \mathbf{x}^{(r)} + (\mathbf{x}^{(r+1)} - \mathbf{x}^{(r)})(1 + \lambda_1 + \lambda_1^2 + \ldots)$$
$$= \mathbf{x}^{(r)} + (1 - \lambda_1)^{-1}(\mathbf{x}^{(r+1)} - \mathbf{x}^{(r)}), \tag{92}$$

provided $|\lambda_1| < 1$.

It follows that the 'current' increment should be multiplied by $(1 - \lambda_1)^{-1}$ to give the realistic increment at this stage, and if λ_1 is very near to unity, which is quite common in practice, this factor can be very large.

In our simple example λ_1 is approximately 0·99, and the 'true' correction is approximately 100 times the 'current' correction. From (88), for example, we find

$$\mathbf{x}^{(4)} = (0·8386, 0·7849), \qquad 100(\mathbf{x}^{(5)} - \mathbf{x}^{(4)}) = (0·1700, 0·2100), \tag{93}$$

and the sum is within 1 per cent of the true result.

This situation pertains, of course, when the physical problem is ill-conditioned. In our example the 'solution' $\mathbf{x}^{(4)}$ gives residuals of about 0·0017 and 0·0021, and the effects of these residuals are very great. The phenomenon, however, is quite common in the solution by finite-difference methods of elliptic partial differential equations, and our simple example is given as a warning of what can happen.

II. The eigenvalue problem

26. Turning to our second batch of matrix computations, we seek the eigenvalues and eigenvectors of a matrix $\mathbf{A}$, that is the numbers λ_r and vectors $\mathbf{x}^{(r)}$ for which the set of linear homogeneous equations

$$(\mathbf{A} - \lambda_r \mathbf{I})\mathbf{x}^{(r)} = \mathbf{0} \tag{94}$$

has non-trivial solutions $\mathbf{x}^{(r)} \neq \mathbf{0}$. This is a much larger problem than the solution of linear equations, and we cannot do justice to it in the space available. A full account is given in Wilkinson (1965), and here we state, usually without proof, a selection of results which are in some sense similar to those discussed in more detail for linear equations, and which are proved by essentially similar techniques of backward error analysis. We give a little more detail on some particular points that have some connection with the work of Chapters 3 and 4 on polynomials and recurrence relations. In all cases we assume that the eigenvalues are distinct.

With linear equations we usually require just the solution thereof. With the eigenvalue problem there are more possibilities. For example we may seek only eigenvalues, with little or no interest in the eigenvectors, or we may require only a few smallest (or largest) eigenvalues, with or without the eigenvectors. There is also a larger variety of methods, and we should learn enough about them so that we can select the most appropriate for our particular problem.

Ill-conditioning

27. For a physical problem we are concerned with the differences between the eigensolutions of the matrix $\mathbf{A}$ and of the perturbed matrix $\mathbf{A}+\delta\mathbf{A}$, and the following statements have been proved.

(i) If $\mathbf{A}$ is symmetric, of order n, and the maximum element of $\delta\mathbf{A}$ does not exceed ε in absolute value, then the effect of $\delta\mathbf{A}$ changes an eigenvalue λ_r of $\mathbf{A}$ to $\lambda_r+\delta\lambda_r$, where

$$|\delta\lambda_r| \leqslant n\varepsilon. \tag{95}$$

(ii) The 'error' (95) is easy to evaluate, but the unsymmetric case is far more complicated. Here we have to consider the eigenvectors of both $\mathbf{A}$ and its transpose $\mathbf{A}'$, given by

$$\mathbf{A}\mathbf{x}^{(r)} = \lambda_r\mathbf{x}^{(r)}, \qquad \mathbf{A}'\mathbf{y}^{(r)} = \lambda_r\mathbf{y}^{(r)}. \tag{96}$$

If these are normalized so that $\mathbf{x}^{(r)\prime}\mathbf{x}^{(r)} = \mathbf{y}^{(r)\prime}\mathbf{y}^{(r)} = 1$, then with the same notation as before we find

$$|\delta\lambda_r| \leqslant n\varepsilon/(\mathbf{y}^{(r)\prime}\mathbf{x}^{(r)}). \tag{97}$$

This quantity can be large if $\mathbf{y}^{(r)\prime}\mathbf{x}^{(r)}$ is small compared with ε. (In the symmetric case $\mathbf{y}^{(r)} = \mathbf{x}^{(r)}$, and the denominator in (97) is unity.)

(iii) For the perturbed matrix $\mathbf{A}+\varepsilon\mathbf{B}$, where every $|b_{rs}| \leqslant 1$, the first-order perturbation in the eigenvector $\mathbf{x}^{(r)}$ is given by

$$\delta\mathbf{x}^{(r)} = \varepsilon \sum_{s\neq r}\left\{\frac{\mathbf{y}^{(r)\prime}\mathbf{B}\mathbf{x}^{(r)}}{(\lambda_r-\lambda_s)\mathbf{y}^{(s)\prime}\mathbf{x}^{(s)}}\right\}\mathbf{x}^{(s)}. \tag{98}$$

The eigenvector $\mathbf{x}^{(r)}$ is therefore ill-conditioned, in the symmetric case, when λ_r is near to any other λ_s. In the unsymmetric case any small $\mathbf{y}^{(s)\prime}\mathbf{x}^{(s)}$ may also produce ill-conditioning even when no λ_s is close to λ_r. (The qualification 'may' is included because more than one $\mathbf{y}^{(s)\prime}\mathbf{x}^{(s)}$ may be small, and their effect on the eigenvector can then be less severe, reduced by cancellation.)

8

Stable methods, similarity transforms

28. Corresponding to the 'direct methods' for linear equations, we have various techniques for reducing the problem to one of simpler form. In the elimination method of § 7 for linear equations, further examination shows that we reduce the equation $\mathbf{A}^{(1)}\mathbf{x} = \mathbf{b}^{(1)}$ to the form $\mathbf{A}^{(n)}\mathbf{x} = \mathbf{b}^{(n)}$, where $\mathbf{A}^{(n)}$ is upper triangular, by successive pre-multiplications with certain simple matrices. These include the 'multiplier' matrices, for example

$$\mathbf{P}_1 = \begin{bmatrix} 1 & & & \\ m_{21} & 1 & & \\ m_{31} & 0 & 1 & \\ m_{41} & 0 & 0 & 1 \end{bmatrix}, \tag{99}$$

which in § 7 produces the array $\mathbf{A}^{(2)}$ and $\mathbf{b}^{(2)}$, and the 'row-changing' matrices, for example

$$\mathbf{Q}_{1,3} = \begin{bmatrix} 0 & 0 & 1 & 0 \\ 0 & 1 & 0 & 0 \\ 1 & 0 & 0 & 0 \\ 0 & 0 & 0 & 1 \end{bmatrix}, \tag{100}$$

which interchanges the first and third rows with a view, say, to bringing the selected pivot into the diagonal position. Then $\mathbf{A}^{(1)}$ is reduced to $\mathbf{A}^{(n)} = \mathbf{U}$ in $n-1$ steps represented by the sequence

$$\mathbf{A}^{(r+1)} = \mathbf{P}_r\mathbf{Q}_{rs}\mathbf{A}^{(r)} = \mathbf{S}_r\mathbf{A}^{(r)}, \qquad r = 1, 2,..., n-1; \qquad s \geqslant r. \tag{101}$$

If no interchanges are necessary we have effected the triangular decomposition

$$\mathbf{A} = \mathbf{LU}, \tag{102}$$

where $\mathbf{L}^{-1}$ is the product $\mathbf{P}_{n-1}...\mathbf{P}_3\mathbf{P}_2\mathbf{P}_1$ of the lower triangular matrices of type (99), $\mathbf{A} = \mathbf{A}^{(1)}$ and $\mathbf{U} = \mathbf{A}^{(n)}$. If interchanges take place, and $\tilde{\mathbf{A}}$ is the matrix obtained from $\mathbf{A}$ by performing these interchanges at the very start, then (102) holds with $\mathbf{A}$ replaced by $\tilde{\mathbf{A}}$. The nature of $\mathbf{L}$, in relation to the elements of the $\mathbf{P}$ matrices, is shown in equation (48).

29. For the general eigenvalue problem we can perform virtually the same operation, though with postmultiplication included to preserve similarity, with the sequence

$$\mathbf{A}^{(r)} = \mathbf{S}_r\mathbf{A}^{(r-1)}\mathbf{S}_r^{-1}, \qquad \mathbf{S}_r = \mathbf{P}_r\mathbf{Q}_{rs}, \, r = 2, 3,..., n-1, \qquad s \geqslant r. \tag{103}$$

Here, however, as indicated in the notation, there is no point in eliminating the column elements in the row *immediately* below the pivot, because we can transform $A^{(1)}$ only to Hessenberg or 'nearly' upper triangular form. The first P matrix will then have the form typified by

$$P_2 = \begin{bmatrix} 1 & & & \\ 0 & 1 & & \\ 0 & m_{32} & 1 & \\ 0 & m_{42} & 0 & 1 \end{bmatrix}. \tag{104}$$

With the use of the Q-type row interchanging matrices, to keep the $|m_{rs}| \leqslant 1$, we can then produce, in $(n-2)$ steps, the *upper Hessenberg* form typified by

$$A^{(n-1)} = H = \begin{bmatrix} x & x & x & x \\ x & x & x & x \\ & x & x & x \\ & & x & x \end{bmatrix}. \tag{105}$$

This is a similarity transform of a row and corresponding column permutation of $A^{(1)}$, and therefore has the same eigenvalues as $A^{(1)}$. The corresponding eigenvectors of $A^{(1)}$ are related with those of H through the known matrices of types P and Q. This means that if

$$B = YCY^{-1}, \tag{106}$$

then the eigenvalues of C are the same as those of B, and if y is an eigenvector of B then

$$z = Y^{-1}y \tag{107}$$

is an eigenvector of C.

30. If no interchange takes place, we have effectively performed the matrix decomposition defined by

$$H = L^{-1}AL, \qquad LH = AL, \tag{108}$$

where L^{-1} is the product $P_{n-1}...P_3P_2$ of unit lower triangular matrices of type (104) (and therefore has the first column of the unit matrix as its first column), $A = A^{(1)}$, and $H = A^{(n-1)}$. If there are row and column interchanges, and $\tilde{A}$ is obtained from A by making these interchanges at the very start, then (108) holds with A replaced by $\tilde{A}$.

Two important results follow, similar to those for the linear equations problem. First, we can show by backward error analysis that, with fl arithmetic, the computed result does not satisfy exactly (108), but does satisfy exactly the equation

$$AL - LH = F, \tag{109}$$

where F is a 'perturbing' matrix whose elements are of computable upper bound. As in the linear-equations analysis, the elements of F are of the order of n times the largest element of H, and therefore depend partly on the growth of the numbers in the successive matrices $A^{(r)}$ of (103). Interchanges are necessary here to keep small the elements of matrices like P_2 in (104), which also appear in the analysis.

Equation (109) shows that we have satisfied *exactly* the similarity equation

$$H = L^{-1}(AL - F) = L^{-1}(A - FL^{-1})L, \tag{110}$$

so that the eigenvalues of H are those of $A - FL^{-1}$, a perturbation of A. It is not certain that L^{-1} has small elements, even though no element of L exceeds unity, though in practice it appears that FL^{-1} is usually quite small and the method exhibits little induced instability.

Second, we can compute the elements of L and H in (108), without explicit thought about the factors $P_{n-1}...P_3P_2$ of L^{-1}, directly and with fl_2 arithmetic, and even with the automatic incorporation of effective interchanges to keep all the elements of L not greater than unity. As before, this reduces the size of the elements of F to a maximum of $2^{-t}|h|$, where $|h|$ is the absolute value of the largest element of H.

Again, corresponding to the remark at the end of § 11, we could use orthogonal matrices to effect the similarity transformation to Hessenberg form, and again these have the advantage of complete stability, the perturbation corresponding to FL^{-1} in (110) having guaranteed small values. Again the computation is somewhat more lengthy, so that we generally prefer the economy and take the small risk of inducing a larger perturbation than necessary.

31. The orthogonal transformations come into their own, however, in the important case in which A is symmetric. For we can then transform A into a symmetric triple-diagonal form, with guaranteed stability and with small computing time. Basically we use the successive transformations defined by

$$A^{(r)} = P_r A^{(r-1)} P_r^{-1}, \qquad r = 2, 3, ..., \tag{111}$$

where P_r is an orthogonal matrix, and at each stage $A^{(r)}$ is symmetric, with more zeros than its predecessor.

There are two favoured methods. First, with the method of Givens, we use simple orthogonal matrices to produce zeros typified in the successive matrices

$$\mathbf{A}^{(1)} \qquad\qquad \mathbf{A}^{(2)}$$

$$\begin{bmatrix} x & x & x & x \\ x & x & x & x \\ x & x & x & x \\ x & x & x & x \end{bmatrix}, \qquad \begin{bmatrix} x & x & 0 & x \\ x & x & x & x \\ 0 & x & x & x \\ x & x & x & x \end{bmatrix},$$

$$\mathbf{A}^{(3)} \qquad\qquad \mathbf{A}^{(4)} \qquad\qquad (112)$$

$$\begin{bmatrix} x & x & 0 & 0 \\ x & x & x & x \\ 0 & x & x & x \\ 0 & x & x & x \end{bmatrix}, \qquad \begin{bmatrix} x & x & 0 & 0 \\ x & x & x & 0 \\ 0 & x & x & x \\ 0 & 0 & x & x \end{bmatrix},$$

so that the transformation to triple-diagonal form is accomplished in

$$(n-2)+(n-3)+...+1 = \tfrac{1}{2}(n-2)(n-1) \qquad (113)$$

steps. Second, with the method of Householder, we introduce zeros simultaneously into all the relevant positions of the first row, then of the second row, thereby producing the final form in $(n-1)$ steps, though each involves more arithmetic. An important point is that, as might be expected in analogy with 'compact' methods described earlier for linear equations and for the unsymmetric eigenvalue problem, we can here use fl_2 arithmetic and thereby reduce significantly the magnitude of the perturbation induced.

Completing the solution

32. There remains, effectively, the determination of the eigenvalues and vectors of the transformed matrices, typified by

$$\mathbf{C} = \begin{bmatrix} x & x & & \\ x & x & x & \\ & x & x & x \\ & & x & x \end{bmatrix}, \qquad \mathbf{H} = \begin{bmatrix} x & x & x & x \\ x & x & x & x \\ & x & x & x \\ & & x & x \end{bmatrix}, \qquad (114)$$

for the (symmetric) triple-diagonal case and the nearly triangular case respectively. The eigenvalues, of course, are the zeros of the respective determinantal equations

$$\det(\mathbf{C}-\lambda\mathbf{I}) = 0, \qquad \det(\mathbf{H}-\lambda\mathbf{I}) = 0. \qquad (115)$$

It cannot be stressed too strongly that it is *not* advisable to expand (115) into the relevant polynomial equation

$$\lambda^n + p_1\lambda^{n-1} + \ldots + p_n = 0, \tag{116}$$

and to look for its zeros by one of the methods of Chapter 4. For we have seen how ill-conditioned a polynomial can be with respect to its zeros, and even if the eigenvalues of $\mathbf{C}$ and $\mathbf{H}$ are relatively insensitive to small changes in the coefficients, the use of (116), with coefficients rounded to single length, may give very inaccurate results. The point here is that (116) *is* all right if the coefficients are determined sufficiently accurately, because in that case the possible uncertainties in $\mathbf{C}$ or $\mathbf{H}$ have *correlated* effects in the coefficients p_r. These correlations will have their effect if the p_r are computed to sufficient precision, which may involve double- or treble-length arithmetic. Random roundings in the coefficients, which are involved in the single-length values of p_r, destroy the correlations and can cause large errors in the solution even in a well-conditioned problem.

33. On the other hand we can compute $\det(\mathbf{C} - p\mathbf{I})$ or $\det(\mathbf{H} - p\mathbf{I})$, for a given value of p, by the methods of the first part of this chapter, and we know that the result *is* the correct value of a small perturbation $\det(\mathbf{C} + \delta\mathbf{C} - p\mathbf{I})$ or $\det(\mathbf{H} + \delta\mathbf{H} - p\mathbf{I})$. We do not therefore *induce* any particular instability by *this* method, and any significant errors *are* due to the degree of ill-conditioning of the problem.

In fact we can use special methods for these particular types of matrices. With

$$\mathbf{C} - p\mathbf{I} = \begin{bmatrix} a_1 - p & b_2 & & & \\ b_2 & a_2 - p & b_3 & & \\ & & \text{--------} & & \\ & & b_{n-1} & a_{n-1} - p & b_n \\ & & & b_n & a_n - p \end{bmatrix}, \tag{117}$$

we can compute the determinant from the recurrence

$$\left.\begin{aligned} f_0(p) &= 1, \qquad f_1(p) = a_1 - p \\ f_{r+1}(p) &= (a_{r+1} - p)f_r(p) - b_{r+1}^2 f_{r-1}(p) \end{aligned}\right\}, \tag{118}$$

in which $f_r(p)$ is the determinant of the leading submatrix of order r of $\mathbf{C} - p\mathbf{I}$. For $r = n$ we have $f_n(p) = \det(\mathbf{C} - p\mathbf{I})$.

Again the computed $f_n(p)$ is the exact value of the determinant of a slight perturbation of $\mathbf{C} - p\mathbf{I}$, and this process is very stable. In fact we strictly need only the sign of $f_r(p)$, because the number of equalities in sign of successive members of the sequence $f_0(p)$, $f_1(p), \ldots, f_n(p)$ (a

Sturm sequence) is equal to the number of eigenvalues greater than p, and by using successive values of p, in an obvious 'bisection' method analogous to that of § 11(i) in Chapter 4, we can produce any required eigenvalue. Ultimate convergence can usually be improved by Newton's method, in which we need both $f(p)$ (in value as well as in sign) and its derivative. The latter comes easily from the recurrence relation

$$f_0'(p) = 0, \qquad f_1'(p) = -1, \qquad f_{r+1}'(p) = (a_{r+1}-p)f_r'(p) -$$
$$- b_{r+1}^2 f_{r-1}'(p) - f_r(p), \quad (119)$$

obtained by differentiating (118).

By considering the linear equations $(\mathbf{C}-p\mathbf{I})\mathbf{x} = 0$, and taking the first component x_1 as unity, we find that

$$x_{r+1} - (\quad 1)^r f_r/(b_2 b_3...b_{r+1}), \quad (120)$$

which in theory gives the vector components for $p = \lambda$, the computed eigenvalue. The *instability* of this computation we study in § 37 below.

34. Similarly, for the Hessenberg form

$$\mathbf{H}-p\mathbf{I} = \begin{bmatrix} h_{11}-p & h_{12} & h_{13} & ... & h_{1n} \\ h_{21} & h_{22}-p & h_{23} & ... & h_{2n} \\ & h_{32} & h_{33}-p & ... & h_{3n} \\ & & & & \\ & & & h_{n,n-1} & h_{n,n}-p \end{bmatrix}, \quad (121)$$

in which we assume that $h_{21}, h_{32},..., h_{n,n-1}$ are not zero, the solution of the linear equations, with $x_n = 1$, is obtained from the equations

$$\left. \begin{aligned} h_{n,n-1}x_{n-1}+(h_{n,n}-p) &= 0 \\ h_{n-1,n-2}x_{n-2}+(h_{n-1,n-1}-p)x_{n-1}+h_{n-1,n} &= 0 \end{aligned} \right\}, \quad (122)$$

etc., and we can easily see that the value of $\det(\mathbf{H}-p\mathbf{I})$ is given by

$$\det(\mathbf{H}-p\mathbf{I}) = (-1)^{n-1}\{(h_{11}-p)x_1+h_{12}x_2+...+h_{1,n-1}x_{n-1}+h_{1n}\} \times$$
$$\times (h_{21}h_{32}...h_{n,n-1})^{-1}. \quad (123)$$

The value so derived is perfectly satisfactory for computing a zero of $\det(\mathbf{H}-p\mathbf{I})$, and Muller's method or Laguerre's method (§ 11(iv) of Chapter 4) give good results for a well-conditioned problem. The *vector* obtained from (122), however, with $p = \bar{\lambda}$, the computed eigenvalue, may again suffer from considerable *induced instability*. We consider this, and some other induced instabilities, in the next few sections.

Induced instabilities

(i) *Transformation methods*

35. We have already mentioned the necessity for row interchanges in the transformation methods of §§ 28 and 29. The corresponding technique without these interchanges is liable to exhibit induced instability. It is, moreover, possible to transform the **H** of (105) to an unsymmetric triple-diagonal form, by operations embodied in the equation

$$
\overset{\mathbf{C}}{\begin{bmatrix} x & x & & \\ x & x & x & \\ & x & x & x \\ & & x & x \end{bmatrix}} = \begin{bmatrix} 1 & 0 & 0 & 0 \\ 0 & 1 & 0 & 0 \\ 0 & 0 & 1 & m_{34} \\ 0 & 0 & 0 & 1 \end{bmatrix} \begin{bmatrix} 1 & 0 & 0 & 0 \\ 0 & 1 & m_{23} & m_{24} \\ 0 & 0 & 1 & 0 \\ 0 & 0 & 0 & 1 \end{bmatrix} \times
$$

$$
\times \overset{\mathbf{H}}{\begin{bmatrix} h_{11} & h_{12} & h_{13} & h_{14} \\ h_{21} & h_{22} & h_{23} & h_{24} \\ & h_{32} & h_{33} & h_{34} \\ & & h_{43} & h_{44} \end{bmatrix}} \begin{bmatrix} 1 & 0 & 0 & 0 \\ 0 & 1 & -m_{23} & -m_{24} \\ 0 & 0 & 1 & 0 \\ 0 & 0 & 0 & 1 \end{bmatrix} \begin{bmatrix} 1 & 0 & 0 & 0 \\ 0 & 1 & 0 & 0 \\ 0 & 0 & 1 & -m_{34} \\ 0 & 0 & 0 & 1 \end{bmatrix},
$$

$$(124)$$

where, for example,

$$ m_{23} = h_{13}/h_{12}, \qquad m_{24} = h_{14}/h_{12}, \quad \text{etc.} \tag{125} $$

It is *not* now possible to incorporate interchanges, since this is incompatible with the triple-diagonal form, and this process can therefore also induce instability.

The use of orthogonal matrices does not cause any particular problems of stability, except that in the Householder method there is a division by a term $a \pm b$, with an ambiguity of sign. In the interests of stability we choose the sign so that $|a \pm b|$ is as large as possible. Corresponding to the remark of the previous paragraph, however, there is no method, in the unsymmetric problem, of reducing **H** to **C** by the similarity use of orthogonal matrices.

36. Some transformation methods proceed by the construction of a sequence of orthogonal vectors. For example, in the method of Lanczos for symmetric matrices, we construct the vectors from the relations

$$\left.\begin{array}{l} \mathbf{y}^{(r+1)} = \mathbf{A}\mathbf{y}^{(r)} - \alpha_r\mathbf{y}^{(r)} - \beta_r\mathbf{y}^{(r-1)}, r = 1, 2,..., n \\ \mathbf{y}^{(0)} = 0, \qquad \mathbf{y}^{(1)} \text{ arbitrary} \end{array}\right\}. \tag{126}$$

The choice of coefficients

$$\alpha_r = \mathbf{y}^{(r)\prime}\mathbf{A}\mathbf{y}^{(r)}/\mathbf{y}^{(r)\prime}\mathbf{y}^{(r)}, \qquad \beta_r = \mathbf{y}^{(r-1)\prime}\mathbf{A}\mathbf{y}^{(r)}/\mathbf{y}^{(r-1)\prime}\mathbf{y}^{(r-1)}, \tag{127}$$

ensures that $\mathbf{y}^{(r+1)}$ is effectively orthogonal not only to $\mathbf{y}^{(r)}$ and $\mathbf{y}^{(r-1)}$ but also to all previous vectors $\mathbf{y}^{(s)}$, $s < r$. The triple-diagonal form $\mathbf{C}$ then comes from the equation $\mathbf{A}\mathbf{Y} = \mathbf{Y}\mathbf{C}$, $\mathbf{Y} = (\mathbf{y}^{(1)}, \mathbf{y}^{(2)},..., \mathbf{y}^{(n)})$.

Now it is vital, in this process, that all the vectors $\mathbf{y}^{(r)}$ should be of reasonable size, say with largest coefficent unity, and that the vectors normalized in this way should be orthogonal to the working precision. It frequently happens that some vectors obtained by this process will become small, and when scaled to satisfy our normalization condition will not be orthogonal to all previous vectors. We must therefore perform a process of reorthogonalization with respect to all previous vectors, and without this, and the labour entailed, this method and other similar methods may have considerable induced instability. The corresponding technique for unsymmetric matrices has similar and even more pronounced disadvantages.

As an example of cancellation consider the first step of the Lanczos process, with four-figure floating-decimal arithmetic applied to the matrix

$$\mathbf{A} = \begin{bmatrix} 0 \cdot 5 & -0 \cdot 1 & -0 \cdot 2 \\ -0 \cdot 1 & 0 \cdot 3 & -0 \cdot 2 \\ -0 \cdot 2 & -0 \cdot 2 & 0 \cdot 5 \end{bmatrix}, \tag{128}$$

with starting vector

$$\mathbf{y}^{(1)\prime} = (1 \cdot 000, -0 \cdot 9801, 0 \cdot 4985). \tag{129}$$

With fl_2 arithmetic for the computation of the scalar products we find

$$\left.\begin{array}{l} (\mathbf{A}\mathbf{y}^{(1)})\prime = (0 \cdot 4983, -0 \cdot 4937, 0 \cdot 2453) \\ \mathbf{y}^{(1)\prime}\mathbf{A}\mathbf{y}^{(1)} = 1 \cdot 104, \qquad \mathbf{y}^{(1)\prime}\mathbf{y}^{(1)} = 2 \cdot 209 \end{array}\right\}, \tag{130}$$

which give $\alpha = (\mathbf{y}^{(1)\prime}\mathbf{A}\mathbf{y}^{(1)})/(\mathbf{y}^{(1)\prime}\mathbf{y}^{(1)}) = 0 \cdot 4998$ and, with fl_2 arithmetic again,

$$(\mathbf{A}\mathbf{y}^{(1)} - \alpha\mathbf{y}^{(1)})\prime = (-0 \cdot 001500, -0 \cdot 003846, -0 \cdot 003850). \tag{131}$$

This is certainly orthogonal to (129) in the sense that the scalar product $0 \cdot 00035...$ *is* small, but when we normalize (131) to the required size, giving the vector

$$\mathbf{y}^{(2)'} = (0 \cdot 3896,\ 0 \cdot 9990,\ 1 \cdot 000), \tag{132}$$

the scalar product now has the large value $-0 \cdot 09102$, and we do not have orthogonality to working precision. This must be achieved by reorthogonalization, taking

$$\mathbf{z}^{(2)} = \mathbf{y}^{(2)} - \gamma \mathbf{y}^{(1)}, \tag{133}$$

choosing

$$\gamma = \mathbf{y}^{(1)'} \mathbf{y}^{(2)} / \mathbf{y}^{(1)'} \mathbf{y}^{(1)} = -0 \cdot 04120, \tag{134}$$

and obtaining the normalized vector

$$\mathbf{z}^{(2)'} = (0 \cdot 4221,\ 0 \cdot 9393,\ 1 \cdot 000), \qquad \mathbf{y}^{(1)'} \mathbf{z}^{(2)} = -0 \cdot 000008. \tag{135}$$

(ii) *Vectors of transformed matrices*

37. We have already remarked that the computation of the eigenvalues of the transformed matrices, of triple-diagonal and Hessenberg forms, is a very stable process. Methods for the corresponding computation of eigenvectors, however, can have very considerable *induced* instability.

As an illustration we take an example from Wilkinson (1965). The triple-diagonal matrix

$$\mathbf{A} = \begin{bmatrix} 10 & 1 & & & & \\ 1 & 9 & 1 & & & \\ & 1 & 8 & 1 & & \\ & & & 1 & -9 & 1 \\ & & & & 1 & -10 \end{bmatrix}, \tag{136}$$

has its largest eigenvalue λ equal to $10 \cdot 7461941829...$, and this is obtained easily and accurately by the methods of § 33. Now suppose we accept a rounded value $\bar{\lambda}$ as being 'sufficiently' accurate, and proceed to compute the eigenvectors as the solution of the homogeneous linear equations

$$\left.\begin{aligned} (10 - \bar{\lambda})x_1 + x_2 &= 0 \\ x_1 + (9 - \bar{\lambda})x_2 + x_3 &= 0 \\ \text{------} \\ x_{19} + (-9 - \bar{\lambda})x_{20} + x_{21} &= 0 \\ x_{20} + (-10 - \bar{\lambda})x_{21} &= 0 \end{aligned}\right\}. \tag{137}$$

We can find only the ratios of the vector components, or equivalently we can fix any non-zero x_r to have the arbitrary value unity. If $\bar{\lambda}$ is in fact an exact eigenvalue, and no mistakes are made in the arithmetic, we can then omit any one equation in (137), solve the rest, and be sure that the omitted equation is satisfied exactly. In particular, if we take $x_1 = 1$ we can compute x_2 from the first equation, x_3 from the second, up to x_{21} from the penultimate twentieth equation, in a very simple way. The question is whether this method suffers from induced instability, springing from the small error in $\bar{\lambda}$ and the commission of other rounding errors.

The figures quoted by Wilkinson reveal catastrophic induced instability. With $\bar{\lambda} = 10.74619420$, with an error not exceeding two units in the tenth significant figure, and with no further mistakes in arithmetic, we find vector components of $\bar{\mathbf{x}}$, compared with the correct vector $\mathbf{x}$, of which a selection is given by

$$
\left.
\begin{array}{ccccccc}
r & 1 & 4 & 7 & 12 & 15 & 21 \\
\bar{x}_r & 1 & 0.0859026 & 0.00051681 & 0.3812... & 0.7686 \times 10^3 & 0.1920 \times 10^{11} \\
x_r & 1 & 0.0859025 & 0.00050815 & 0.00000001 & 0 & 0
\end{array}
\right\}. \quad (138)
$$

The vector, it should be said, is *not* particularly sensitive to small perturbations $\delta\mathbf{A}$, that is the problem is *not* ill-conditioned.

38. Wilkinson reveals the instability in the following (backward-type) analysis. When we have solved the first twenty equations, and substituted in the twenty-first, the result is not zero, since otherwise we have the correct vector. Suppose the result is k. Then we have actually solved exactly the full set of equations given by

$$(\mathbf{A} - \bar{\lambda}\mathbf{I})\bar{\mathbf{x}} = k\mathbf{e}^{(n)}, \quad (139)$$

where $\mathbf{e}^{(n)}$ is the last column of the unit matrix. The exact solution of (139) is in fact

$$\bar{\mathbf{x}} = \sum_{r=1}^{n} \frac{\alpha_r \mathbf{y}^{(r)}}{\lambda_r - \bar{\lambda}}, \quad (140)$$

where $k\mathbf{e}^{(n)}$ is expanded as a linear combination of normalized eigenvectors of $\mathbf{A}$, that is

$$
\left.
\begin{array}{ll}
k\mathbf{e}^{(n)} = \sum_{r=1}^{n} \alpha_r \mathbf{y}^{(r)}, & \mathbf{A}\mathbf{y}^{(r)} = \lambda_r \mathbf{y}^{(r)} \\
\mathbf{y}^{(r)'}\mathbf{y}^{(r)} = 1, & r = 1, 2, ..., n
\end{array}
\right\}. \quad (141)
$$

Moreover the coefficients in (140) are given by

$$\alpha_r = \mathbf{y}^{(r)'} k\mathbf{e}^{(n)}. \quad (142)$$

Now if $\bar{\lambda}$ is very close to λ_1, say, and no other λ_r is near to λ_1, then (140) is in general dominated by its first term, and we have effectively $\bar{x} = y^{(1)}$, the required eigenvector. But this assumes that α_1 is not small, of the order of $\lambda_1 - \bar{\lambda}$, and if it is so small our computed $\bar{x}$ may be a more or less unknown combination of all the eigenvectors. In our case this happens if $ke^{(n)}$ is nearly orthogonal to $y^{(1)}$, that is if the last component of $y^{(1)}$ is very small. Our true $y^{(1)}$ exhibits precisely this behaviour, and the method fails completely.

We note that in the general case the omission of any particular equation may fail for very similar reasons, and the possibility of induced instability means that a quite different method is advocated, the so-called inverse iteration which we describe briefly in § 41 below. We note also the great similarity between the present induced instability and the linear-equations inherent instability discussed in § 4.

39. It is also interesting to observe that we can explain this particular failure in terms of our ubiquitous recurrence relations. We are trying to solve the recurrence relation

$$x_{r-1} + (11 - r - \lambda)x_r + x_{r+1} = 0, \qquad r = 1, 2, ..., 21, \qquad (143)$$

with the boundary conditions

$$x_0 = 0, \qquad x_{22} = 0. \qquad (144)$$

Now in Chapter 3 we have observed that the general solution of (143), with a known λ and with specified x_0 and x_1, is given by

$$x_r = A_1 q_r^{(1)} + A_2 q_r^{(2)}, \qquad (145)$$

where $q_r^{(1)}$ and $q_r^{(2)}$ are the two independent solutions of the homogeneous system. We found that this initial-value problem is ill-conditioned if $q_r^{(1)}$ is increasing faster than $q_r^{(2)}$, and we 'require' the less dominant solution. Here, of course, the given combination of x_0 and x_1 is expected to 'suppress' $q_r^{(1)}$ by making A_1 zero, but this is difficult to attain without very accurate values of x_0 and x_1 and very accurate arithmetic in the step-by-step process. Similarly, the combination of step-by-step solutions for the boundary-value problem failed because of the effect on the arithmetic of the dominating $q_r^{(1)}$.

Now in the eigenvalue problem, represented by (143) and (144), the method of § 33 for finding an eigenvalue effectively starts with $x_0 = 0$, satisfying the first condition, and with $x_1 = 1$ which 'normalizes' the solution, and for a given $\lambda = p$ computes $x_2, x_3, ..., x_{21}$, and then finds $x_{22} = x_{22}(p)$, a function of p. We are trying to find a value of $p = \bar{\lambda}$ such that $x_{22}(\bar{\lambda}) = 0$. In the case in which $q_r^{(1)}$ in (145) is increasing we are effectively here *trying to find a* $\bar{\lambda}$ *such that the* dominating $A_1 q_r^{(1)}$ is suppressed.

This can be just as difficult as in the ordinary case in which we need x_0 and x_1 with great accuracy. In this particular example, indeed, x_{22} is very sensitive to small changes in $\bar{\lambda}$, and it is this fact which makes the largest eigenvalue very easy to obtain in our particular example. We here have something like $x_{22}(\lambda+\delta) \doteqdot +10^k$, $x_{22}(\lambda-\delta) \doteqdot -10^k$, where λ is the true eigenvalue, δ is very small, and k is a large integer. Since we want $x_{22} = 0$ the interval $(\lambda-\delta, \lambda+\delta)$, in which the true eigenvalue lies, is very small and we have an accurate $\bar{\lambda}$. Conversely, the eigenvector is very badly determined, and we have a paradoxical situation that the more accurately we can determine the eigenvalue the less accurately do we find the eigenvector *by this particular technique*.

For (143) the solution behaves locally like

$$q_1^{(r)} = p_1^r, \qquad q_2^{(r)} = p_2^r, \qquad p^2+(11-r-\bar{\lambda})p+1 = 0, \qquad (146)$$

and, with $\bar{\lambda} = 10\cdot7...$, p_1 exceeds unity in absolute value for all $r \geqslant 3$. The computed vector, as we would therefore expect, quickly reveals errors for values of r greater than 3.

We leave it as an exercise to show, by the analysis of § 38 and also by that of this section, that the omission of the first equation in (137), and the *backward* solution of the rest, gives a perfectly good vector. In practice, however, the vector will not generally have the monotonic behaviour exhibited in our example, and the analysis of § 38 is then more appropriate. The analysis of this section, however, throws further light on the motivation for the step-by-step variant of Dekker, mentioned by Wilkinson (1965) for this particular problem. Our analysis is also very relevant for the eigenvalue problem relevant to ordinary differential equations, in which the eigenfunction has smooth behaviour, and which we discuss further in Chapter 10.

(iii) *Matrix deflation*

40. In the last section the fact that the computed $\bar{\lambda}$ was not the exact eigenvalue could, as we saw, cause the computed vector to have very poor accuracy with a particular method of solution, though this could be avoided with the use of a stable method.

The fact that $\det(\mathbf{C}-\bar{\lambda}\mathbf{I})$ is not exactly zero, and could be large even when $|\lambda-\bar{\lambda}|$ is small, can have other adverse effects, notably in the process of 'matrix deflation'. In connection with the determination of the zeros of polynomials we have already observed, in Chapter 4, that polynomial deflation must be used with care, and there is a precisely similar situation in our present context.

Consider, for example, the Hessenberg form $\mathbf{H} = \mathbf{H}_4$ in (114), and suppose that we have computed, very accurately, one eigenvalue λ_1 and eigenvector. Without going into details, it can be shown that we can then transform $\mathbf{H}_4$ to the form

$$
\mathbf{B} = \begin{bmatrix} x & x & x & \square \\ x & x & x & 0 \\ 0 & x & x & 0 \\ x & x & x & \lambda_1 \end{bmatrix} = \left[\begin{array}{ccc|c} & & & \square \\ & \mathbf{H}_3 & & 0 \\ & & & 0 \\ \hline x & x & x & \lambda_1 \end{array} \right].
\tag{147}
$$

In the last column the two zeros really are zeros, but the $\square$ value is proportional to $\det(\mathbf{H}_4 - \bar{\lambda}\mathbf{I})$. If this is exactly zero the remaining eigenvalues are those of the reduced Hessenberg form $\mathbf{H}_3$, but as we have seen $\square$ can be large even if $\bar{\lambda}$ is very near to λ, and the resulting solutions can in consequence be quite meaningless. Not all processes of deflation, we should add, exhibit these phenomena, but they are dangerous and must be used with care and preferably only with rigorous guarantee of stability.

Iterative methods

41. As a final technique we should mention the use of iterative methods, which are valuable, as in the linear equation case, when the matrix has a rather special form (for example large and sparse), and when only a few eigensolutions are required.

If all the eigenvalues are real (as in the symmetric case) and distinct in value and in modulus, the 'direct' iteration

$$
\mathbf{x}^{(r+1)} = \mathbf{A}\mathbf{x}^{(r)}, \qquad \mathbf{x}^{(0)} \text{ arbitrary,}
\tag{148}
$$

gives vectors $\mathbf{x}^{(r)}$ which converge, as $r \to \infty$, to the eigenvector of $\mathbf{A}$ corresponding to the eigenvalue of largest modulus. The eigenvalue is ultimately the ratio of corresponding components of $\mathbf{x}^{(r+1)}$ and $\mathbf{x}^{(r)}$.

More usually we seek the smallest eigenvalue, and this is obtained from the 'inverse' iteration defined by

$$
\mathbf{x}^{(r+1)} = \mathbf{A}^{-1}\mathbf{x}^{(r)}, \qquad \mathbf{x}^{(0)} \text{ arbitrary.}
\tag{149}
$$

The vector $\mathbf{x}^{(r)}$ now converges to the eigenvector corresponding to the eigenvalue of smallest modulus, and the latter is the ultimate ratio of corresponding components of $\mathbf{x}^{(r)}$ and $\mathbf{x}^{(r+1)}$.

With inverse iteration we can find the eigenvalue closest to a given number p by replacing $\mathbf{A}^{-1}$ in (149) by $(\mathbf{A}-p\mathbf{I})^{-1}$. In all cases, of course, we do not invert the relevant matrix, but obtain its triangular decomposition, with interchanges to preserve stability, and the solution of successive sets of linear equations, with the same matrix on the left, is then an economic proposition.

42. Inverse iteration is a particularly valuable process for computing eigenvectors, and we can avoid the induced instability discussed in §§ 37 and 38. Having obtained p as a good approximation to λ, say by the Sturm sequence method, we use the iteration

$$(\mathbf{A}-p\mathbf{I})\mathbf{x}^{(r+1)} = \mathbf{x}^{(r)}, \tag{150}$$

and following the discussion of § 38 we see that the required safeguard for stability is that the first 'guess' $\mathbf{x}^{(0)}$ should contain a satisfactory component of the true eigenvector $\mathbf{y}$ corresponding to this particular eigenvalue. The analysis of § 38 shows that the method of that section is virtually a first step of inverse iteration, which fails because $\mathbf{x}^{(0)}$ is not sufficiently 'arbitrary'.

A satisfactory procedure, which in practice introduces the necessary arbitrary element, is to use (150) with a special first step. If $(\mathbf{A}-p\mathbf{I}) = \mathbf{LU}$ (with row permutations included where necessary), we effectively solve in succession the equations

$$\mathbf{Lz}^{(r+1)} = \mathbf{x}^{(r)}, \qquad \mathbf{Ux}^{(r+1)} = \mathbf{z}^{(r+1)}. \tag{151}$$

This is the general step, which is satisfactory if $\mathbf{x}^{(r)}$ has a suitable component of the required eigenvector. We achieve this in the first step by taking $\mathbf{z}^{(r+1)}$ to be the vector all of whose components are unity, which implies an 'arbitrary' $\mathbf{x}^{(r)}$ which we need not calculate. Though this process is not theoretically fool-proof, there is no recorded instance of its failure!

43. A final important iterative method, which we cannot discuss in detail, succeeds in reducing the matrix by similarity transformation to triangular form in an infinite sequence of operations, to be terminated when the elements that should be zero are sufficiently small. The eigenvalues are therefore the diagonal elements of the triangular form in the real case, or the zeros of (2×2) determinants in the complex case. There are two variations of this method. In the first, the $L–R$ method we compute successive $\mathbf{A}^{(s)}$ from the sequence

$$\left. \begin{aligned} \mathbf{A}^{(1)} &= \mathbf{L}^{(1)}\mathbf{U}^{(1)}, & \mathbf{A}^{(2)} &= \mathbf{U}^{(1)}\mathbf{L}^{(1)},\ldots \\ \mathbf{A}^{(s-1)} &= \mathbf{L}^{(s-1)}\mathbf{U}^{(s-1)}, & \mathbf{A}^{(s)} &= \mathbf{U}^{(s-1)}\mathbf{L}^{(s-1)},\ldots \end{aligned} \right\}, \tag{152}$$

where **L** and **U** are respectively lower and upper triangular matrices. Each step involves the matrix decomposition discussed in § 13, followed by a matrix multiplication in reverse order. The second, the Q–R method, uses orthogonal matrices, in the sequence

$$\mathbf{A}^{(s-1)} = \mathbf{Q}^{(s-1)}\mathbf{U}^{(s-1)}, \qquad \mathbf{A}^{(s)} = \mathbf{U}^{(s-1)}\mathbf{Q}^{(s-1)}, \tag{153}$$

where **U** is upper triangular and **Q** orthogonal.

Two points call for comment. First, as might be expected, (153) is stable without particular precaution, whereas row interchanges are essential in (152) to preserve stability in the matrix decomposition. Second, the method is best applied to matrices of special form, such as the triple-diagonal form, the Hessenberg form, or the band-type form representable by a matrix such as

$$\mathbf{B} = \begin{bmatrix} x & x & x & & & & \\ x & x & x & x & & & \\ x & x & x & x & x & & \\ & x & x & x & x & x & \\ & & x & x & x & x & x \\ & & & x & x & x & x \\ & & & & x & x & x \end{bmatrix}, \tag{154}$$

which might occur in the numerical solution of certain types of differential equations. The point is that in these cases the 'form' is preserved in successive $\mathbf{A}^{(s)}$, so that we can take full advantage of the zeros and economize on labour and machine time. A full account of the methods is given by Wilkinson (1965).

Accuracy and correction of solution

44. As in the linear-equation problem, so here we should ask for an estimate of the accuracy of our alleged solutions obtained by stable methods. Consider first the symmetric *mathematical* problem, and assume that we have an alleged eigenvalue $\bar{\lambda}_1$ and eigenvector $\mathbf{x}^{(1)}$. Estimates of accuracy *can* be obtained from the residual vector

$$\mathbf{r} = \mathbf{A}\mathbf{x}^{(1)} - \bar{\lambda}_1\mathbf{x}^{(1)}, \tag{155}$$

and we can show that if $\mathbf{x}^{(1)\prime}\mathbf{x}^{(1)} = 1, \mathbf{r}'\mathbf{r} = \varepsilon^2$, then

$$|\lambda_1 - \bar{\lambda}_1| \leqslant \varepsilon. \tag{156}$$

The value of ε will depend on the rounding errors in the computation and the mathematical error $\delta_M A$ in the given coefficients. Both can be taken into account in the determination of ε in (156).

For a physical problem, with uncertainties $\delta_P A$ in the coefficients, we can also reasonably estimate the number of meaningful figures in the solution by finding the largest possible value of the components of $\mathbf{r}$ in (155), and hence of ε in (156).

With regard to the eigenvector, we can also show that

$$(\mathbf{x} - \mathbf{x}^{(1)})'(\mathbf{x} - \mathbf{x}^{(1)}) \leqslant (\varepsilon/a)^2, \tag{157}$$

where a is the smallest value of $|\lambda_r - \lambda_1|$, $r \neq 1$, and the left-hand side of (157) is just the sum of the squares of the components of the eigenvector. Again both mathematical and physical problems are included in this analysis.

There is usually no point in 'improving the accuracy' of the results of the physical problem, since (156) and (157) give the number of meaningful figures in these results. For the mathematical problem, however, we can improve the eigenvalue by using the Rayleigh estimate

$$\lambda_R = \mathbf{x}^{(r)'} \mathbf{A} \mathbf{x}^{(r)}, \tag{158}$$

in which we use a more accurate matrix with some double-precision arithmetic. The eigenvector can then be improved by inverse iteration.

45. For the unsymmetric problem it is difficult to find the accuracy of one eigensolution in a physical problem, or to correct it in a mathematical problem, without a knowledge of the complete eigensystem. At present, for the physical problem, the number of meaningful figures in any solution is probably best estimated by repeating the computation with a matrix rounded to one fewer figure than the original, and comparing results.

We can estimate the accuracy of the solution of the mathematical problem, and correct it, by considering the residuals of all the alleged eigensolutions. The method is based on the fact that if $\mathbf{x}^{(r)}$ and λ_r are alleged solutions, and the residuals, defined by

$$\mathbf{r}^{(s)} = \mathbf{A} \mathbf{x}^{(s)} - \bar{\lambda}_s \mathbf{x}^{(s)}, \tag{159}$$

are columns of the matrix $\mathbf{R}$, then

$$\mathbf{AX} - \mathbf{XD} = \mathbf{R}, \tag{160}$$

where $\mathbf{D}$ is the diagonal matrix with elements $\bar{\lambda}_r$. It follows that

$$\mathbf{X}^{-1} \mathbf{AX} = \mathbf{D} + \mathbf{X}^{-1} \mathbf{R}, \tag{161}$$

so that the true eigenvalues of $\mathbf{A}$ are those of $\mathbf{D}+\mathbf{X}^{-1}\mathbf{R}$, a nearly diagonal matrix. Again we can use an accurate $\mathbf{A}$, with a little double-precision arithmetic to find $\mathbf{R}$, and we can find $\mathbf{X}^{-1}\mathbf{R}$ accurately by the methods of § 18. For the remaining details and analysis we must refer to the relevant parts of Wilkinson (1965).

III. The least-squares problem

46. As an example of the least-squares technique we consider the problem of curve fitting, the determination of the coefficients in the polynomial

$$y = \sum_{k=0}^{n} a_k x^k, \tag{162}$$

such that, for a set of observations (y_r, x_r), $r = 1, 2,..., N$, the quantity

$$S = \sum_{r=1}^{N} \{y_r - \sum_{k=0}^{n} a_k x_r^k\}^2 \text{ is a minimum.} \tag{163}$$

For the case $N = 6$, $n = 3$, for example, we seek to satisfy as well as possible, in the least-squares sense, the equations

$$\left.\begin{aligned}
a_0+a_1x_1+a_2x_1^2+a_3x_1^3 &= y_1 \\
a_0+a_1x_2+a_2x_2^2+a_3x_2^3 &= y_2 \\
\text{------------------------------} \\
a_0+a_1x_6+a_2x_6^2+a_3x_6^3 &= y_6
\end{aligned}\right\}. \tag{164}$$

Denoting this equation by $\mathbf{Aa} = \mathbf{y}$, in obvious notation, where $\mathbf{A}$ is a $(N \times n+1)$ matrix, the vector $\mathbf{a}$ which satisfies (163) is the solution of the *normal equations* given by

$$\mathbf{A'Aa} = \mathbf{A'y}, \tag{165}$$

the matrix $\mathbf{A'A}$ being square of order $n+1$.

Now for n of only moderate size it turns out that this method can *suffer from induced instability.* Suppose, for example, that the x_r^s, the coefficients of $\mathbf{A}$, are known and stored exactly in single-length registers. An element of $\mathbf{A'A}$ is then a double-length number, and the least significant half is very important. If we round the product to single-length, which is what fl or even fl_2 arithmetic would require, the solution of the rounded equations $\overline{\mathbf{A'Aa}} = \overline{\mathbf{A'y}}$ can be quite different from the correct solution of (165). The situation is quite analogous to that of the eigenvalue problem discussed in § 32.

47. As an illustration suppose that we take $x_r = 0.2(r-1)$ at equal intervals in the range $(0, 1)$, with $N = 6$, and let us seek the best cubic approximation with the arbitrary values

$$y_1 = 0 \cdot 7234, \quad y_2 = 0 \cdot 6427, \quad y_3 = 0 \cdot 4093$$
$$y_4 = 0 \cdot 2726, \quad y_5 = 0 \cdot 2007, \quad y_6 = 0 \cdot 1495 \qquad (166)$$

The exact normal equations have matrix and vector

$$
\begin{array}{cccc|c}
& \mathbf{A'A} & & & \mathbf{A'y} \\
6 & 3 & 2 \cdot 2 & 1 \cdot 8 & 2 \cdot 2982 \\
3 & 2 \cdot 2 & 1 \cdot 8 & 1 \cdot 5664 & 0 \cdot 76588 \\
2 \cdot 2 & 1 \cdot 8 & 1 \cdot 5664 & 1 \cdot 416 & 0 \cdot 46728 \\
1 \cdot 8 & 1 \cdot 5664 & 1 \cdot 416 & 1 \cdot 31296 & 0 \cdot 3424768
\end{array}
\qquad (167)
$$

The matrix is positive definite, so that we can perform the symmetric decomposition $\mathbf{A'A} = \mathbf{LL'}$ without worries about induced instability. The solutions, however, are very sensitive to small changes in the data or small induced errors in the arithmetic. The accurate solution of (167), to four figures, is

$$a_0 = 0 \cdot 7349, \quad a_1 = -0 \cdot 4839, \quad a_2 = -0 \cdot 9848, \quad a_3 = 0 \cdot 8927. \quad (168)$$

But the accurate solution of equations derived from (167) by rounding the coefficients to four significant figures, which is what the floating-point machine would do, is

$$a_0 = 0 \cdot 7274, \quad a_1 = -0 \cdot 3544, \quad a_2 = -1 \cdot 3084, \quad a_3 = 1 \cdot 0974, \quad (169)$$

and the solution of this problem using four-figure fl_2 arithmetic throughout is given by

$$a_0 = 0 \cdot 7303, \quad a_1 = -0 \cdot 3891, \quad a_2 = -1 \cdot 227, \quad a_3 = 1 \cdot 047. \quad (170)$$

These results show that the problem is ill-conditioned, and that we need to use extra precision, both in the storage and the arithmetic, to achieve satisfactory answers to the mathematical problem. For larger values of n the matrix $\mathbf{A'A}$ becomes increasingly nearly singular, and the computed results may bear no relation to the true answers.

48. The difficulty is overcome with the introduction of *orthogonal polynomials*. If we write (162) in the form

$$y = \sum_{k=0}^{n} c_k \phi_k(x), \qquad (171)$$

where $\phi_k(x)$ is a polynomial of degree k, then equation (165) becomes

$$\mathbf{C'Cc} = \mathbf{C'y}, \qquad (172)$$

where the general element of the matrix C is $\phi_k(x_r)$, $k = 0, 1, \ldots, n$, $r = 1, 2, \ldots, N$. The (i, j) element of the matrix $C'C$, and the ith element of the vector $C'y$, are then given by

$$(C'C)_{ij} = \sum_{r=1}^{N} \phi_i(x_r)\phi_j(x_r), \qquad (C'y)_i = \sum_{r=1}^{N} \phi_i(x_r)y_r. \qquad (173)$$

If now we choose the polynomials $\phi_k(x)$ to be orthogonal, meaning here that

$$\sum_{r=1}^{N} \phi_i(x_r)\phi_j(x_r) = 0, \qquad i \neq j, \qquad (174)$$

then the matrix $C'C$ is diagonal, and the solution of (172) is easily given by

$$c_i = \sum_{r=1}^{N} \phi_i(x_r)y_r / \sum_{r=1}^{N} \phi_i^2(x_r). \qquad (175)$$

We state without proof the fact that the orthogonal polynomials can be generated from the recurrence relation

$$\phi_{k+1}(x) = (2x+\beta_k)\phi_k(x)+\gamma_{k-1}\phi_{k-1}(x), \qquad \phi_0(x) = \tfrac{1}{2}, \ \phi_{-1}(x) = 0, \qquad (176)$$

where

$$\beta_k = \frac{-2\sum\limits_{r=1}^{N} x_r\phi_k^2(x_r)}{\sum\limits_{r=1}^{N} \phi_k^2(x_r)}, \qquad \gamma_{k-1} = \frac{-\sum\limits_{r=1}^{N} \phi_k^2(x_r)}{\sum\limits_{r=1}^{N} \phi_{k-1}^2(x_r)}. \qquad (177)$$

(See Forsythe (1957) for details of the proof of this result and the choice of the constants involved.)

49. For our particular example we easily find

$$\phi_0(x) = 0\cdot 5, \qquad \phi_1(x) = x-0\cdot 5, \qquad \phi_2(x) = \tfrac{1}{3}(6x^2-6x+0\cdot 8),$$

$$\phi_3(x) = \tfrac{1}{3}(12x^3-18x^2+6\cdot 576x-0\cdot 288), \quad (178)$$

and then, correct to four significant figures, we obtain

$$c_0 = 0\cdot 7994, \quad c_1 = -0\cdot 6189, \quad c_2 = 0\cdot 1771, \quad c_3 = 0\cdot 2232. \quad (179)$$

The result, in the polynomial form (162), is then

$$y = 0\cdot 7350-0\cdot 4838x-0\cdot 9850x^2+0\cdot 8928x^3, \qquad (180)$$

which is almost the exact solution (168). We have used virtually no double-precision arithmetic, though the use of fl_2 arithmetic has obvious advantages. It is also worth noting that in the general case the orthogonal polynomials depend only on the data points x_r, and can be obtained in advance, once and for all, with all necessary precision and without undue labour.

Conclusions

50. We hope that the material of this chapter has demonstrated, once again: (i) the care, experience, knowledge, and numerical sense that are needed with matrix computations; (ii) the existence of many methods in the matrix field, some of which are uniformly bad, some of which are very good, and some of which have their own advantages in particular contexts; (iii) a summary of the ways in which induced instability can ruin our methods; and (iv) a verification that the same types of induced instability arise in many different contexts.

In particular, we have tried to stress the important difference between inherent and induced instability. Failure to appreciate this has, to our knowledge, led to some very strange arguments in favour of doubtful computing methods!

Our description, we realize, is far from complete, and indeed we have not even ventured to describe the details of the transformation methods of Givens, Householder, Lanczos, etc., or of the various iterative methods for linear equations and the eigenvalue problem. All these are discussed in an elementary way by Fox (1964), and Wilkinson (1965) and Varga (1962) have more comprehensive treatment of the eigenvalue problem and the linear-equations iterative methods respectively. Wilkinson (1963) also gives more details, in a reasonably elementary way, of the error analysis for matrix problems.

Exercises 5

1. Compute four-figure approximations to the eigenvalues of the matrix of equation (1), showing that the *eigenvalue* problem for this matrix is well-conditioned with respect to small changes in its coefficients.

2. Show that the smallest eigenvalue and corresponding vector in Exercise 1 are

$$\lambda_1 = 0\cdot00002131, \quad \mathbf{x}^{(1)'} = (0\cdot0718, -0\cdot5151, 1, -0\cdot5711).$$

Note that the matrix is singular if an eigenvalue is zero, and that we are here close to this situation. Show that the vector $\mathbf{b}$ in (10) is nearly orthogonal to $\mathbf{x}^{(1)}$, which causes the severe ill-conditioning in the example of § 2.

Corresponding to the analysis of equations (17)–(19), the vector $\mathbf{c}'$ is (1, 1, 1, 1) in (13). Note that $\mathbf{c}$ is also nearly orthogonal to $\mathbf{x}^{(1)}$, so that (14) has some meaningful significant figures.

Find the vector $\mathbf{z} = \mathbf{c} - \alpha\mathbf{x}^{(1)}$ that is orthogonal to $\mathbf{x}^{(1)}$, and show that, with the problem of § 3, the value of $\mathbf{z}'\mathbf{y} = 2\cdot831$, with an absolute error not exceeding about $0\cdot009$, and hence a relative error of at most 1 part in 300.

3. Find the inverse of the matrix in equation (20), and rewrite §§ 2–4 with this matrix as example.

4. The *relative* errors in the results marked 7 and 8 in Table 5.1 are approximately

$$
\begin{aligned}
(7) &\quad 0{\cdot}14 \quad 0{\cdot}11 \quad 0{\cdot}093 \quad 0{\cdot}080 \quad 0{\cdot}070 \\
(8) &\quad 0{\cdot}012 \quad 0{\cdot}009 \quad 0{\cdot}008 \quad 0{\cdot}007 \quad 0{\cdot}006
\end{aligned} \Biggr\}.
$$

Why would we expect to gain roughly an extra figure in *relative* accuracy at each stage, at least for sufficiently large r in (22)? What can be said about the absolute error?

5. Repeat the computation of § 6 with the diagonal elements in (23) changed from $-1{\cdot}732$ to $-2{\cdot}001$. Verify that no interchanges are needed, and that the results are quite accurate.

6. From the array (24) write down the lower and upper triangular matrices that we allege to be the triangular decomposition of the matrix in (24). Hence record the exact perturbed equations (23) which, with exact arithmetic, would produce (24). Solve this perturbed set, verifying that the errors of the results (25) are mainly incurred in the production of (24) rather than in the back-substitution.

7. Find the perturbed equations of Exercise 6 by combining the individual perturbations according to the analysis of §§ 7 and 8 and the example of § 9.

8. Perform the arithmetic of § 6 with partial pivoting, show that the results are good, and that the perturbations in the equations from which the triangular set would be produced exactly are much smaller than those of Exercise 6.

9. Try to produce the method, mentioned at the end of § 13, for finding a matrix decomposition $\mathbf{A} = \mathbf{LU}$ in fl_2 arithmetic and with the equivalent of 'interchanges' and 'partial pivoting'.

10. We have solved the equations $\mathbf{Ax} = \mathbf{b}$, and now wish to add another row and column to the matrix and another element in the vector $\mathbf{b}$, and to solve this new set of equations. Discuss an economic method of performing the arithmetic.

11. Find the decomposition $\mathbf{A'A} = \mathbf{LL'}$ of the matrix in (167). Show that the corresponding decomposition of the matrix of § 6 will fail in real arithmetic. (The matrix in (23) is not positive definite, and some of the elements of the triangular matrix $\mathbf{L}$ are pure imaginary numbers.)

12. We wish to solve equations (70) in which to every element in $\mathbf{A}$ and $\mathbf{b}$ we add the number $0{\cdot}00005$. Obtain the solution to four figures, using the method of § 19 with the $\mathbf{L}$ matrix of (71) and the first approximation $\mathbf{x}^{(0)}$ of (73).

13. Invert the matrix $\mathbf{A}^{(1)}$ of (70), using the $\mathbf{L}$ of (71) and the fact that the rth column $\mathbf{x}^{(r)}$ of $\mathbf{A}^{-1}$ is the solution of $\mathbf{L'x}^{(r)} = \mathbf{L}^{-1}\mathbf{e}^{(r)}$, where $\mathbf{e}^{(r)}$ is the rth column of the unit matrix. Correct the computed inverse by applying the method of § 19.

14. Solve the equations $\mathbf{Ax} = \mathbf{b}$, where $\mathbf{A}$ is the matrix of (1) and $\mathbf{b}$ is the vector of (10), by iterating with the scheme $\mathbf{x}^{(r+1)} = (\mathbf{I} - \mathbf{A})\mathbf{x}^{(r)} + \mathbf{b}$. Knowing the eigenvalues of $\mathbf{A}$ (from Exercise 1), why are we sure that this process will converge? Use the convergence-accelerating device of § 25 when this becomes possible.

15. Find by the method of § 33 the smallest eigenvalue, to four significant figures, of the matrix in (1) with coefficients rounded to four significant figures. Assuming no error in the computation, what can we say about the corresponding eigenvalue of the original matrix in (1)?

16. Find the eigenvector corresponding to the eigenvalue computed in Exercise 15 by the process of inverse iteration given by (150), starting
   (i) with the vector $\mathbf{x}^{(0)'} = (1, 0{\cdot}7227, 0{\cdot}5697, 0{\cdot}4714)$,
   (ii) with the recommended method of § 42.
Why is the first method unsatisfactory?
   Use the results of § 44 to estimate the accuracy of the computed eigenvalue and eigenvector.

17. Complete the Lanczos process for the matrix of (128), using four-figure floating-decimal arithmetic without reorthogonalization. Show that the computed eigenvalues have large inaccuracies. Repeat the process with reorthogonalization, verifying the necessity thereof.

18. Perform the analysis mentioned in the last paragraph of § 39, and perform the arithmetic to verify the conclusion.

19. In the least squares process of § 46 show that the (i, j) element of the normal matrix is

$$(\mathbf{A}'\mathbf{A})_{ij} = \sum_{r=1}^{N} x_r^{i+j-2}.$$

If in § 47 we have observations of y at equal intervals in $(0, 1)$, giving N points, show that as $N \to \infty$ the normal matrix of order $n+1$ tends to the form

$$N \times \begin{bmatrix} 1 & \tfrac{1}{2} & \tfrac{1}{3} & \tfrac{1}{4} & \cdots \\ \tfrac{1}{2} & \tfrac{1}{3} & \tfrac{1}{4} & \tfrac{1}{5} & \cdots \\ \tfrac{1}{3} & \tfrac{1}{4} & \tfrac{1}{5} & \tfrac{1}{6} & \cdots \\ \tfrac{1}{4} & \tfrac{1}{5} & \tfrac{1}{6} & \tfrac{1}{7} & \cdots \\ \cdot & \cdot & \cdot & \cdot & \end{bmatrix}.$$

(This is the matrix of (1). It is called the Hilbert matrix, and the linear-equations problem with this matrix is notoriously ill-conditioned.)

20. The attempt to *produce* a positive definite matrix from a square matrix, to 'assist' in the solution of the linear equations $\mathbf{Ax} = \mathbf{b}$ by forming $\mathbf{A'Ax} = \mathbf{A'b}$, is a particularly retrograde step. Not only is this uneconomic in time (the formation of $\mathbf{A'A}$ has more work than the solution of $\mathbf{Ax} = \mathbf{b}$, but any illconditioning in the original problem is intensified in the transformed problem.
   Experiment with equations (70), forming $\mathbf{A'A}$ and $\mathbf{A'b}$ with fl_2 arithmetic, and (i) rounding to four figures, (ii) keeping all eight figures and working with eight figures in the solving process.
   (The situation is very analogous to that discussed in previous contexts, of the importance of *correlated* errors. Any roundings in the normal equations are not independent, and it is these 'hidden' figures that determine the accuracy of our results.)

6

Polynomial Approximation

Introduction

1. THIS chapter looks at some theoretical questions, but takes its place in a book concerned with practical methods because some knowledge of the fundamental theory of polynomial approximation is necessary for its application, and is not part of the equipment of most users of computers. The numerical methods discussed in the rest of this book are based on the approximation of functions by polynomials; for example, Simpson's rule for numerical integration produces the integral of a quadratic polynomial approximation to the integrand. We shall therefore begin by a brief study of the problem of obtaining such approximations.

Best approximation

2. In particular we should like to be able to construct polynomial approximations that are in some sense the best possible. We shall usually measure the accuracy of the approximation $p_n(x)$ to $f(x)$ in the interval $[a, b]$, where $p_n(x)$ is a polynomial of degree n, by the value of the quantity

$$E_n = \max |e_n(x)|, \qquad a \leqslant x \leqslant b, \tag{1}$$

where

$$e_n(x) = f(x) - p_n(x). \tag{2}$$

Notice that if the polynomial is written explicitly, in the form

$$p_n(x) = a_0 + a_1 x + a_2 x^2 + \ldots + a_n x^n, \tag{3}$$

then the 'error' E_n may be regarded as a function of the parameters $a_0, a_1, \ldots, a_n$. The problem of finding the best approximation then reduces to that of finding the set of parameters $a_0, a_1, \ldots, a_n$ which produces a minimum for the function $E_n(a_0, a_1, \ldots, a_n)$.

The important property of the best approximation $p_n(x)$, which always exists and is unique if $f(x)$ is a continuous function, is the *oscillation property*. This states that there is a set of at least $n+2$ points x_i such that

$$a \leqslant x_1 < x_2 < \ldots < x_{n+2} \leqslant b, \tag{4}$$

and $e_n(x)$ attains its extreme values $\pm E_n$ alternately at these points, so that

$$e_n(x_r) = f(x_r) - p_n(x_r) = (-1)^r E_n. \tag{5}$$

Table 6.1 illustrates this result by presenting the best cubic approximation to $\ln(1+x)$ over the interval $[0, 1]$. The maximum error is $0\cdot0004$,
and is attained alternately at five points. Notice that three of these
points are internal points of the interval $(0, 1)$, and the other two are
the end points of this interval. The three internal points are 'local
maxima', (or minima) in the usual sense, that is where the derivative
vanishes, but the end points constitute extreme values of $e_n(x)$ only
because x is prevented from going outside the interval; this behaviour
is typical, and the end points of the interval will usually, but not
invariably, constitute two of the set of $n+2$ points at which $e_n(x)$ has
alternate maximum and minimum values $\pm E_n$.

TABLE 6.1

$p_3(x) = 0\cdot0004 + 0\cdot9836x - 0\cdot4002x^2 + 0\cdot1097x^3$
$e_3(x) = 10^4\{\ln(1+x) - p_3(x)\}$

x	0	0·02	0·04	0·06	0·10	0·14	0·18	0·22	0·26	0·30	0·40	0·50
$e_3(x)$	-4	-2	$+1$	$+2$	$+4$	$+4$	$+4$	$+2$	$+1$	-1	-4	-4
x	0·60	0·70	0·74	0·78	0·82	0·86	0·90	0·94	0·96	0·98	1·0	
$e_3(x)$	-2	$+1$	$+3$	$+4$	$+4$	$+4$	$+3$	$+1$	0	-2	-4	

The exchange algorithm

3. The oscillation property is characteristic of the best approximation, and provides at once a possible means of constructing the required
$p_n(x)$. We may begin with some estimate of the likely positions of the
points $x_1,\ldots, x_{n+2}$, and consider the equations

$$e_n(x_r) = f(x_r) - (a_0 + a_1 x_r + \ldots + a_n x_r^n) = (-1)^r E_n, \tag{6}$$

for $r = 1, 2,\ldots, n+2$. Knowing the values of $f(x_r)$, equation (6) gives
a system of $n+2$ linear equations for the unknowns $a_0, a_1,\ldots, a_n$ and E_n.
The solution of these equations provides the coefficients of a polynomial approximation to $f(x)$. We may now tabulate the corresponding
error term $e_n(x)$ and find all its extreme values in $[0, 1]$. If the positions
of these extreme values coincide with the estimated x_r the required
best approximation has been found. Otherwise we may use these
points as a new set of estimates of the x_r and repeat the process to find
a new set of coefficients a_i and hence a new approximation. There is an
algorithm which determines uniquely the choice of the new x_r and which
guarantees convergence to the required solution. We do not pursue
this, (see, for example, Handscomb 1966) but note the obvious fact
that the amount of computation involved is enough to warrant the
consideration of alternative possibilities.

Good approximation

4. The second result we quote without proof from the fundamental theory of approximation is the theorem of De la Vallée Poussin. Suppose that $p_n(x)$ is the best approximation to $f(x)$ over the interval $[a, b]$, and that $q_n(x)$ is some other polynomial of the same degree, which has the property that there exists a sequence of $n+2$ alternate maxima and minima, as in the oscillation property, but not all of the same magnitude. Let m be the least and M the greatest of the magnitudes of these extrema. Then

$$m \leqslant E_n \leqslant M, \tag{7}$$

where E_n is the maximum error of $p_n(x)$.

Clearly M is the maximum error of the approximation $q_n(x)$, and the statement $E_n \leqslant M$ requires no proof, for it is simply the definition of $p_n(x)$ as the best approximation, which minimizes E_n. We also notice that the alternate maxima of $f(x)-q_n(x)$ cannot all have the same magnitude, since then $q_n(x)$ would have the oscillation property and would therefore be identical to $p_n(x)$. The important statement in this theorem is that $m \leqslant E_n$, the consequences being immediate.

Notice that in practice we seldom require the best approximation in the sense that the degree n is prescribed, but much more often require the approximation of smallest degree whose error is not greater than some prescribed 'tolerance' ε. Instead of wanting to minimize E_n for a fixed n, we therefore wish to minimize n for a given ε. But now of course n can take only integer values, so that the solution of this problem is far from being unique, and there will be an infinity of polynomials of the same degree, all having the required accuracy.

5. Consider again the problem of approximating to $f(x) = \ln(1+x)$ over the interval $[0, 1]$. Some approximations, found by a simple process discussed in §§ 16–18 of Chapter 7, are shown in Table 6.2.

TABLE 6.2

x	0·0	0·1	0·2	0·3	0·4	0·5	0·6	0·7	0·8	0·9	1·0
$e_3(x)$	-44	$+40$	$+29$	-10	-40	-44	-23	$+13$	$+41$	$+34$	-43
$E_3(x)$	-61	$+48$	$+48$	$+10$	-25	-38	-26	$+3$	$+30$	$+30$	-28
$E_4(x)$	-8	$+8$	$+1$	-5	-5	0	$+4$	$+5$	0	-4	$+4$

$e_3(x) = 10^5 \times$ error of best cubic approximation,
$E_3(x) = 10^5 \times$ error of $q_3(x)$,
$E_4(x) = 10^5 \times$ error of $q_4(x)$,
$q_3(x) = (3+4800x-1920x^2+512x^3)/4896$,
$q_4(x) = (1+11840x-5520x^2+2560x^3-640x^4)/11890$,
and these approximations are obtained in Exercise 13 of Chapter 7.

In each case we notice that there is a sequence of $n+2$ alternate maxima and minima, decreasing in magnitude from one end of the range to the other. Suppose that we require an approximation with a maximum error of 0·0001. We see that $q_4(x)$ satisfies this condition, and by the theorem of De la Vallée Poussin we know that $0·00028 <$ $E_3 < 0·00061$. Hence the approximation we have obtained of degree 3 is not of sufficient accuracy, and *neither is any other polynomial of this degree*. We may therefore accept $q_4(x)$ as an approximation satisfying the given conditions, knowing that no polynomial of lower degree will be acceptable. There is no need to attempt to improve the accuracy of $q_3(x)$, for example by the exchange algorithm, because we know that the final error would still be too large; and there is no need to improve the accuracy of $q_4(x)$, which already has the required 'tolerance'.

We are therefore led to the idea of a *good* approximation, which is one for which the error $f(x)-q_n(x)$ attains a sequence of $n+2$ alternate maxima and minima whose magnitude does not vary by a large factor. Having obtained a good approximation we know that the best approximation would not reduce the error considerably. The definition is clearly not very precise, for we have not defined exactly what is meant by a 'large factor'. In practice, however, this is a useful concept, for we shall find that methods for obtaining polynomial approximations fall into two classes, those that produce good approximations in this technical sense, and those that do not. Situations in which the distinction might be difficult to make do not often arise.

There will of course remain problems in which it is worth while to obtain the best possible approximation, in the sense of minimizing E_n, for example in constructing a set of library routines for a new computer. But for many practical problems in which such approximations are not often used a good approximation will often be adequate.

Power series

6. These ideas are illustrated by the two most obvious methods of obtaining polynomial approximations. First, suppose that $f(x)$ can be expressed as the convergent power series

$$f(x) = \sum_{r=0}^{\infty} a_r x^r. \tag{8}$$

Then if we terminate the series after the term in x^n we obtain a polynomial approximation of degree n. We consider again the expansion of

$\ln(1+x)$, given by

$$\ln(1+x) = x - \frac{x^2}{2} + \frac{x^3}{3} - \dots - \frac{(-x)^n}{n} + \dots . \tag{9}$$

If we terminate this expansion after the nth term, the error may be expressed in the form

$$e_n(x) = \int_0^x \frac{(-t)^n}{1+t} \, dt. \tag{10}$$

The integrand in this expression is everywhere one-signed, and the error $e_n(x)$ is therefore a monotonic function with just two extrema occurring at the ends of the interval, here at 0 and 1. This result is quite independent of the degree n, and we cannot therefore regard this truncated power series as a 'good' approximation in our technical sense.

It might be thought that this example depends on the known fact that the series for $\ln(1+x)$ converges rather slowly. The exponential series

$$e^x = 1 + \frac{x}{1!} + \frac{x^2}{2!} + \dots \tag{11}$$

converges comparatively rapidly, but it is clear that if we truncate it after the term in x^n the remainder is a sum of positive multiples of powers of x, and is again obviously monotonic in the interval $[0, 1]$. Again, therefore, the error $e_n(x)$ has only two extrema for all values of n, instead of the $n+2$ that are needed to produce a good approximation. In this example we have a better approximation in one sense, that the series (11) converges more rapidly than (9) and gives a smaller error if truncated after the same number of terms; but in our technical sense it is not a *good* approximation, and as we shall see in Chapter 7 it can easily be improved with little labour.

These examples are typical, and it is clear that if the power series is rapidly convergent, so that the remainder after n terms is dominated by the first neglected term, then this remainder will be monotonic and will have only the two extrema.

Interpolation

7. Another simple method of constructing an approximating polynomial $q_n(x)$ is to choose $n+1$ points x_i in the interval $[a, b]$, and to form the polynomial that takes the same values as $f(x)$ at each of these points. It is well known that these $n+1$ conditions, given by

$$a_0 + a_1 x_i + \dots + a_n x_i^n = f(x_i), \qquad i = 0, 1, \dots, n, \tag{12}$$

are sufficient to determine the $n+1$ coefficients a_r uniquely, giving the Lagrange interpolating polynomial. The error term $e_n(x)$ now vanishes at each of these $n+1$ points, and therefore has a maximum or minimum between each pair of adjacent zeros. If the end points a and b are not among the points x_i there will also be extrema at these points, giving the total number of $n+2$. We therefore have the correct number of extrema for a good approximation. Questions relating to the size of these extrema, and to the effect of different possible choices of the x_i, are considered briefly in the next chapter, but we note here the considerable improvement over the truncated power series of the previous section. Notice also that the simple choice of equally-spaced points x_i, chosen as usual to include the end points $x_0 = a$ and $x_n = b$, leads to only n extrema, and thus does not produce a good approximation in our technical sense.

Exercises 6

1. Show that the best 'constant' approximation to the continuous function $f(x)$ in $a \leqslant x \leqslant b$ is

$$c = \tfrac{1}{2}\left\{ \min_{a \leqslant x \leqslant b} f(x) + \max_{a \leqslant x \leqslant b} f(x) \right\},$$

and that the maximum error is

$$E_0 = \tfrac{1}{2}\left\{ \max_{a \leqslant x \leqslant b} f(x) - \min_{a \leqslant x \leqslant b} f(x) \right\}.$$

2. For a certain continuous function $f(x)$ it is known that for the best linear approximation $p_1(x) = ax+b$, in $-1 \leqslant x \leqslant 1$, the points of maximum error include the end points $x = 1$, $x = -1$. Show that

$$a = \tfrac{1}{2}\{f(1)-f(-1)\}, \qquad b = \tfrac{1}{4}\{f(1)+f(-1)+2f(x_c)-2ax_c\},$$

$$f'(x_c) = a,$$

and the maximum error is

$$M = |b+ax_c-f(x_c)|.$$

3. Show that the best linear approximation to $\sin 4\pi x + ax + b$, in $0 \leqslant x \leqslant 1$ is $p_1(x) = ax+b$, for any a and b. (Notice that the end points are *not* here points of maximum error.)

4. Find a continuous function for which a linear approximation, in $0 \leqslant x \leqslant 1$, has one end point as a point of maximum error.

5. Perform the exchange algorithm to compute the best linear approximation to e^x in $-1 \leqslant x \leqslant 1$. The procedure is as follows:
 (i) Guess three points x_1, x_2, and x_3, at which the error may have successive values $+M$, $-M$, $+M$.
 (ii) Solve the equations $e^{x_r} - (ax_r + b) = (-1)^r M$, $r = 1, 2, 3$.
 (iii) Find the maxima of $e^x - (ax + b)$.
 (iv) Replace one of the x_1, x_2, x_3 by a new point, obtained from (iii), so that the errors at x_1, x_2, and x_3 have successively opposite signs.
 (v) Repeat steps (i) to (iv) until the process converges.
This is not quite the exchange algorithm quoted by Handscomb (1966), which allows several of the x_r to be changed simultaneously. Repeat the computations by this method.

   Starting with $x_1 = -\frac{1}{2}$, $x_2 = 0$, $x_3 = \frac{1}{2}$, repeat the process but stop when the maximum error $\leqslant 0.3$.

6. The term $\frac{5}{6}x$ is reputed to be a good linear approximation to $\ln(1+x)$ in $0 \leqslant x \leqslant 1$. Show that the best linear approximation has a maximum error less than 0·140, but greater than 0·015, approximately.

7

Chebyshev Approximation

Introduction

1. In the previous chapter we introduced the idea of a 'good' polynomial approximation $p_n(x)$ to a continuous function $f(x)$ in a finite range $[a, b]$, observing that a characteristic of a good approximation is a type of oscillation property, effectively produced by the presence of $n+2$ alternating maxima and minima of the error $e_n(x) = f(x) - p_n(x)$.

We observed that a truncated power (Taylor's) series does not in general give a good approximation in this sense, and the purpose of this chapter is to show how good approximations can be produced in a variety of contexts. Basic to the discussion is the Chebyshev polynomial, and we begin by examining its important properties.

The Chebyshev polynomial

2. The function $\cos n\theta$ is a polynomial of degree n in $\cos \theta$. It has an oscillation property, that in $0 \leqslant \theta \leqslant \pi$ the function has alternate equal maximum and minimum values of ± 1 at the $n+1$ points

$$\theta_r = \frac{r\pi}{n}, \qquad r = 0, 1, ..., n. \tag{1}$$

Writing $x = \cos \theta$, we deduce that the Chebyshev polynomial

$$T_n(x) = \cos(n \cos^{-1}x), \qquad -1 \leqslant x \leqslant 1, \tag{2}$$

is a polynomial of degree n with alternate maxima and minima at the $n+1$ points

$$x_r = \cos \frac{r\pi}{n}, \qquad r = 0, 1, ..., n. \tag{3}$$

The immediate importance of this oscillation property is involved in the problem of approximating to the simple polynomial x^n by a polynomial of smaller degree. It is apparent that if k_n is the coefficient of x^n in $T_n(x)$, then the polynomial

$$p_{n-1}(x) = x^n - k_n^{-1}T_n(x) \tag{4}$$

is not only a good approximation but indeed the best polynomial approximation of degree $n-1$, because the error

$$x^n - p_{n-1}(x) = k_n^{-1}T_n(x) \tag{5}$$

has the required oscillation property, with $n+1$ alternate and equal maxima and minima required for a polynomial approximation of degree $n-1$.

3. It is convenient to list here some basic properties of the Chebyshev polynomial for the range $-1 \leqslant x \leqslant 1$. Successive polynomials satisfy the three-term recurrence relation

$$T_{n+1}(x) = 2xT_n(x) - T_{n-1}(x), \tag{6}$$

and with $T_0(x) = 1$, $T_1(x) = x$, we easily deduce the first few results

$$T_2(x) = 2x^2 - 1, \qquad T_3(x) = 4x^3 - 3x, \qquad T_4(x) = 8x^4 - 8x^2 + 1. \tag{7}$$

It is clear that the coefficient k_n of x^n in $T_n(x)$ is 2^{n-1}.

Other algebraic relations include the formulae for products, given by

$$\left.\begin{array}{l} x^r T_s(x) = 2^{-r} \sum\limits_{i=0}^{r} \binom{r}{i} T_{s-r+2i}(x) \\[2mm] T_r(x)T_s(x) = \tfrac{1}{2}\{T_{r+s}(x) + T_{|r-s|}(x)\} \end{array}\right\}. \tag{8}$$

We shall also need the indefinite integral relations

$$\int T_0(x)\,\mathrm{d}x = T_1(x), \qquad \int T_1(x)\,\mathrm{d}x = \tfrac{1}{4}T_2(x),$$

$$\int T_r(x)\,\mathrm{d}x = \frac{1}{2}\left\{\frac{T_{r+1}(x)}{r+1} - \frac{T_{r-1}(x)}{r-1}\right\}, \tag{9}$$

and the 'orthogonality' relations

$$\left.\begin{array}{ll} \int\limits_{-1}^{1}(1-x^2)^{-\frac{1}{2}}T_r(x)T_s(x)\,\mathrm{d}x = 0, & r \neq s \\[2mm] \qquad\qquad\qquad = \pi, & r = s = 0 \\[2mm] \qquad\qquad\qquad = \tfrac{1}{2}\pi, & r = s \neq 0 \end{array}\right\}. \tag{10}$$

The equations (6)–(10) are most easily verified by changing the variable from x to θ, where $x = \cos\theta$.

4. For the more general interval $[a, b]$ we merely make the linear transformation

$$u = (a+b-2x)/(a-b), \tag{11}$$

and the interval in the new variable u is just $[-1, 1]$. For the special interval $[0, 1]$ it is convenient to use a special notation. We write $u = 2x - 1$, and

$$T_n^*(x) = T_n(u) = T_n(2x-1). \tag{12}$$

Equations (6) and (7) then take the form

$$T_{n+1}^*(x) = 2(2x-1)T_n^*(x) - T_{n-1}^*(x), \tag{13}$$

$$\left.\begin{array}{l} T_0^*(x) = 1, \qquad T_1^*(x) = 2x-1, \qquad T_2^*(x) = 8x^2-8x+1 \\ T_3^*(x) = 32x^3-48x^2+18x-1,\dots \end{array}\right\}, \tag{14}$$

and the coefficient of x^n in $T_n^*(x)$ is 2^{2n-1}. We might also record the interesting result

$$T_n^*(x) = T_{2n}(x^{\frac{1}{2}}), \tag{15}$$

of which a particular case appears in equations (7) and (14).

The other algebraic relations become

$$\left.\begin{array}{l} x^r T_s'^*(x) = 2^{-2r} \sum\limits_{i=0}^{2r} \binom{2r}{i} T_{s-r+i}^*(x) \\ T_r^*(x)T_s^*(x) = \frac{1}{2}\{T_{r+s}^*(x) + T_{|r-s|}^*(x)\} \end{array}\right\}, \tag{16}$$

the integral relations are changed to

$$\left.\begin{array}{l} \displaystyle\int T_0^*(x)\,dx = \frac{1}{2}T_1^*(x), \qquad \int T_1^*(x)\,dx = \frac{1}{8}T_2^*(x) \\ \displaystyle\int T_r^*(x)\,dx = \frac{1}{4}\left\{\dfrac{T_{r+1}^*(x)}{r+1} - \dfrac{T_{r-1}^*(x)}{r-1}\right\} \end{array}\right\}, \tag{17}$$

and the orthogonality relation is now given by

$$\left.\begin{array}{ll} \displaystyle\int\limits_0^1 \{x(1-x)\}^{-\frac{1}{2}}T_r^*(x)T_s^*(x)\,dx = 0, & r \neq s \\ \hphantom{\displaystyle\int\limits_0^1 \{x(1-x)\}^{-\frac{1}{2}}T_r^*(x)T_s^*(x)\,dx} = \pi, & r = s = 0 \\ \hphantom{\displaystyle\int\limits_0^1 \{x(1-x)\}^{-\frac{1}{2}}T_r^*(x)T_s^*(x)\,dx} = \frac{1}{2}\pi, & r = s \neq 0 \end{array}\right\}. \tag{18}$$

Economization of power series

5. We have seen that the truncated power series for a continuous function $f(x)$ will not generally satisfy our criterion for a good approximation. The error, of course, may be small if we are prepared to include enough terms, but we can often reduce considerably the necessary number of terms, without increasing the error significantly, by the process called 'economization'. This method effectively produces a good approximation in our technical sense, and is based on the fundamental property of the Chebyshev polynomial.

Suppose that we have a convergent power series for $f(x)$, with a guarantee that the remainder, after truncation to a polynomial of degree n, does not exceed ε, that is

$$|f(x)-p_n(x)| = |f(x)-(a_0+a_1x+\ldots+a_nx^n)| < \varepsilon \quad \text{in} \quad [-1, 1]. \quad (19)$$

We seek a polynomial $p_{n-1}(x)$, of lower degree, so that

$$|f(x)-p_{n\,1}(x)| = |f(x)-(b_0+b_1x+\ldots+b_{n-1}x^{n-1})| < \varepsilon', \quad (20)$$

where ε' is not much bigger than ε.

The basic problem, of course, is the approximation of a_nx^n by a polynomial of degree $n-1$, and this problem we have already solved. It is then clear that our required approximation is given by

$$p_{n-1}(x) = \sum_{r=0}^{n-1} b_r x^r = p_n(x)-2^{1-n}a_nT_n(x), \quad (21)$$

and that

$$|f(x)-p_{n-1}(x)| = |f(x)-p_n(x)+2^{1-n}a_nT_n(x)| \\ \leqslant |f(x)-p_n(x)|+2^{1-n}|a_n|. \quad (22)$$

The polynomial $p_{n-1}(x)$ of degree $n-1$ therefore has a possible maximum error of at most $2^{1-n}|a_n|$ greater than that of $p_n(x)$, and of course our $p_{n-1}(x)$ is the best approximation to $p_n(x)$ in virtue of the oscillation property of $T_n(x)$.

6. We can obviously continue this process, replacing $p_{n-1}(x)$ by an approximation $p_{n-2}(x)$, etc., stopping when the maximum error is just within our requirement in any context. Successive polynomials, of course, are not *quite* the best approximations of lower degrees even to the polynomial $p_n(x)$, because the errors are combinations of Chebyshev polynomials.

Alternatively, we can cast our given $p_n(x)$ directly in the form

$$p_n(x) = \tfrac{1}{2}c_0T_0(x)+c_1T_1(x)+\ldots+c_nT_n(x), \quad (23)$$

(the conventional factor $\tfrac{1}{2}$ in the first coefficient having definite advantages in some contexts) and economize by ignoring successive terms $c_nT_n(x), c_{n-1}T_{n-1}(x),\ldots, c_rT_r(x)$, such that

$$|c_n| + |c_{n-1}| + \ldots + |c_r| + \varepsilon < \bar{\varepsilon}, \quad (24)$$

where $\bar{\varepsilon}$ is our tolerated error. We are quite safe, because certainly

$$\left|\sum_r^n c_iT_i(x)\right| < \sum_r^n |c_iT_i(x)| < \sum_r^n |c_i|. \quad (25)$$

7. Consider, as an example, the determination of a polynomial approximation to e^x in $[-1, 1]$, with an error not exceeding 0·005. We have

$$e^x = 1 + x + \tfrac{1}{2}x^2 + \tfrac{1}{6}x^3 + \tfrac{1}{24}x^4 + \tfrac{1}{120}x^5 + \dots \qquad (26)$$

If we truncate after the terms given explicitly the error is a maximum at $x = 1$, with value of about 0·0016. The neglect of the term in x^5 gives a maximum error of about 0·01, too large for our purpose. The question is whether it is possible to find a polynomial of degree less than 5 whose error does not exceed 0·005.

We have

$$T_5(x) = 16x^5 - 20x^3 + 5x, \qquad (27)$$

so that

$$\begin{aligned}
p_5(x) - (1 + x + \tfrac{1}{2}x^2 + \tfrac{1}{6}x^3 + \tfrac{1}{24}x^4) &= \tfrac{1}{120}x^5 \\
&= \tfrac{1}{120}\{\tfrac{1}{16}T_5(x) + \tfrac{5}{4}x^3 - \tfrac{5}{16}x\},
\end{aligned} \qquad (28)$$

and we deduce that

$$\left.\begin{aligned}
p_5(x) &= \tfrac{1}{1920}T_5(x) + p_4(x) \\
p_4(x) &= 1 + \tfrac{383}{384}x + \tfrac{1}{2}x^2 + \tfrac{17}{96}x^3 + \tfrac{1}{24}x^4
\end{aligned}\right\}. \qquad (29)$$

The error of $p_4(x)$ cannot then exceed $\tfrac{1}{1920}$ plus that of $p_5(x)$, certainly less than 0·0021, and our economization has succeeded. We have not just discarded the term in x^5 in (26), but 'allowed' for most of it by changing slightly some of the earlier coefficients.

We leave it as an exercise to show that the corresponding cubic polynomial, obtained by an obvious extension of our method, has an error which is slightly larger than our requirement.

Interpolation

8. As a second application of the Chebyshev theory we return to the problem of interpolation, which we discussed briefly in Chapter 6. We decided that the polynomial $p_n(x)$, which agrees with $f(x)$ at the $n+1$ points $x_0, x_1, \dots, x_n$, not including the terminal points of the range, qualifies as a good approximation in our sense. It is known that the error may be expressed in the form

$$f(x) - p_n(x) = \frac{1}{(n+1)!}(x - x_0)(x - x_1)\dots(x - x_n)f^{(n+1)}(\xi), \qquad (30)$$

where ξ is in the interval containing $x_0, x_1, \dots, x_n$ and x, which we here take as $[-1, 1]$.

We may ask for the choice of the x_r which minimizes the error in (30), and in the general case it is clear that we are restricted to minimizing the factor multiplying $f^{(n+1)}(\xi)$. This is a polynomial of degree $n+1$, and we now know that the best thing to do is to make this a multiple of $T_{n+1}(x)$, so that the matching points $x_0, x_1, ..., x_n$ should be taken at the zeros of the Chebyshev polynomial $T_{n+1}(x)$.

The 'Chebyshev matching' may give quite a significant improvement in accuracy over that obtained by matching at the natural set of $n+1$ equidistant points, including the end points, which as we have seen in Chapter 6 does not give the 'full' oscillation property. For example, with $n = 5$, the maximum value of the relevant factor, excluding the term $(n+1)!$, is $\frac{1}{32} = 0{\cdot}03125$ with the Chebyshev fit, while for the equal-interval fit, with $x_0 = -1$, $x_1 = -0{\cdot}6$, $x_2 = -0{\cdot}2$, $x_3 = 0{\cdot}2$, $x_4 = 0{\cdot}6$, $x_5 = 1$, the corresponding polynomial has successive extrema $-0{\cdot}07$, $0{\cdot}02$, $-0{\cdot}01$, $0{\cdot}02$, $-0{\cdot}07$, and hence more than twice the error, at most, of the Chebyshev fit. At some points, on the other hand, notably near the middle of the interval, the equal-interval fitting method gives a smaller error. We remark further, though without proof, that as we increase the number of matching points we do not by either method necessarily converge to the correct value at other points. Convergence will, however, be guaranteed for the Chebyshev-zeros method at least for all functions with continuous second derivatives, whereas with equal intervals the method will fail for a much larger class of functions, even, for example, for the apparently innocuous function $(1+x^2)^{-1}$.

The Chebyshev series

9. We observed, in §§ 5–7, that the economization of a power series was effected not just by neglecting some particular term but by changing appropriately the coefficients of earlier terms, and successive applications of this process involves considerable labour. On the other hand, by starting with a series of Chebyshev polynomials, as in (23), economization was effected just by removing successive high-order terms. Moreover, if a series like (23) converges rapidly at some stage, that is

$$|c_n| \ll |c_{n-1}| \ll |c_{n-2}| \ll ..., \tag{31}$$

then successive 'economized' polynomials are quite close to the best polynomials of successive degrees.

An equation like

$$f(x) = \tfrac{1}{2}c_0 T_0(x) + c_1 T_1(x) + ... + c_n T_n(x) + ... = \sum_{r=0}^{\infty}{}' c_r T_r(x), \tag{32}$$

of which (23) is the truncated equivalent, is an expansion in terms of the independent set of polynomials $T_r(x)$. These polynomials have the orthogonality property defined by (10), in $-1 < x < 1$, and this simplifies the computation of the coefficients c_r. Clearly

$$c_r = \int_{-1}^{1} (1-x^2)^{-\frac{1}{2}} T_r(x) f(x)\, dx \bigg/ \int_{-1}^{1} (1-x^2)^{-\frac{1}{2}} T_r^2(x)\, dx, \qquad (33)$$

and each coefficient is computed independently of the others. For $r = 0$ equation (33) gives the value of $\frac{1}{2}c_0$.

We call (32) an orthogonal expansion of $f(x)$ in terms of the Chebyshev polynomials, or just the 'Chebyshev series'. Other expansions are possible, but the Chebyshev case has two important properties. For most functions $f(x)$ that arise in practice, convergence is ultimately faster than that of any other orthogonal-polynomial expansion, so that truncation gives not only a polynomial near to the optimum for that degree, but we also have a very good estimate of the maximum error.

10. As an example consider the expansion of $(1+x)^{-1}$ in $0 < x < 1$. Here we must use the $T_r^*(x)$ polynomials, with orthogonality defined in (18):

$$(1+x)^{-1} = \frac{1}{2}c_0 T_0^*(x) + c_1 T_1^*(x) + \ldots + c_r T_r^*(x) + \ldots,$$

$$c_r = \frac{\displaystyle\int_0^1 \{x(1-x)\}^{-\frac{1}{2}}(1+x)^{-1} T_r^*(x)\, dx}{\displaystyle\int_0^1 \{x(1-x)\}^{-\frac{1}{2}}\{T_r^*(x)\}^2\, dx}. \qquad (34)$$

By changing the variable from x to θ, with $2x-1 = \cos\theta$, we can easily evaluate the integral, and find

$$\left.\begin{array}{l}(1+x)^{-1} = \sqrt{2}(\frac{1}{2}T_0^*(x) - \lambda T_1^*(x) + \lambda^2 T_2^*(x) - \ldots) \\[6pt] \lambda = 3 - 2\sqrt{2} \sim 0{\cdot}17 \end{array}\right\}, \qquad (35)$$

a series with very rapid convergence. Truncation to a cubic polynomial, for example, gives an error not exceeding about $0{\cdot}0015$ in $0 < x < 1$.

For this function, of course, the Taylor's series diverges at $x = 1$, and we have no possibility of performing the process of economization. This is an extreme case of a slowly convergent series, for example

$$(1+0{\cdot}9x)^{-1} = 1 - 0{\cdot}9x + (0{\cdot}9x)^2 - \ldots, \qquad (36)$$

in which more than 100 terms are needed to guarantee an error $<5\times10^{-6}$. Economization is now possible, but extremely laborious, and the corresponding Chebyshev series, computed as shown, achieves the same accuracy when truncated to only 8 terms.

Discrete ordinates

11. The computation of the coefficients of the Chebyshev series depends on our ability to evaluate certain definite integrals. This is rarely possible in closed form, and we may need to use formulae for numerical integration (see Chapter 9) or some other process of approximating to these integrals.

A rather simple method can be obtained from the 'summation orthogonality property' of Chebyshev polynomials. It is not difficult to show that if $x_k = \cos \dfrac{k\pi}{n}$, then

$$\sum_{k=0}^{n}{}'' T_r(x_k)T_s(x_k) = 0, \qquad \text{for} \quad r \neq s, \quad r \leqslant n, \quad s \leqslant n, \qquad (37)$$

where the notation is defined by

$$\sum_{k=0}^{n}{}'' a_k = \tfrac{1}{2}a_0 + a_1 + \ldots + a_{n-1} + \tfrac{1}{2}a_n. \qquad (38)$$

Consider now the computation of the coefficients in the Chebyshev series (32). If we multiply by $T_r(x)$, and sum over the x_k, $k = 0, 1, \ldots, n$, we do not isolate just the coefficient c_r, since in fact we have also

$$T_{2pn \pm r}(x_k) = \cos(2pn \pm r)\frac{k\pi}{n} = \cos\left(\frac{\pm rk\pi}{n}\right) = T_r(x_k). \qquad (39)$$

In virtue, however, of the relations

$$\left.\begin{aligned} \sum_{k=0}^{n}{}'' T_r(x_k)T_s(x_k) &= n \quad (r = s = 0 \quad \text{or} \quad r = s = n) \\ &= \tfrac{1}{2}n \quad (r = s \neq 0 \quad \text{or} \quad n) \end{aligned}\right\}, \qquad (40)$$

we easily find by this method the equation

$$\frac{2}{n} \sum_{k=0}^{n}{}'' f(x_k)T_r(x_k) = c_r + c_{2n-r} + c_{2n+r} + c_{4n-r} + c_{4n+r} + \ldots, \qquad (41)$$

and for sufficiently large n the left-hand side is a good approximation to c_r or to $2c_n$ (for $r = n$).

12. The choice of a satisfactory value of n is not obvious, and it is generally advisable to do two computations and to rely on consistency (which is here reasonably satisfactory). In particular if we double the first value of n, then nearly half the values of x_k are common to both computations, and the extra amount of arithmetic is not exhorbitant.

For the function $(1+x)^{-1}$ in $0 \leqslant x \leqslant 1$, for example, the choice of $n = 3$ gives, via the relevant change of variable, the five-figure approximation

$$(1+x)^{-1} \sim 0 \cdot 70714\,T_0^*(x) - 0 \cdot 24286\,T_1^*(x) + 0 \cdot 04286\,T_2^*(x) - $$
$$-0 \cdot 00714\,T_3^*(x), \quad (42)$$

and $n = 6$ gives

$$(1+x)^{-1} \sim 0 \cdot 70711\,T_0^*(x) - 0 \cdot 24264\,T_1^*(x) + 0 \cdot 04163\,T_2^*(x) - $$
$$-0 \cdot 00714\,T_3^*(x) + 0 \cdot 00123\,T_4^*(x) - 0 \cdot 00021\,T_5^*(x) + 0 \cdot 00004\,T_6^*(x). \quad (43)$$

Now equations (41), for $r = 0(1)3$ and with $n = 3$, give from (42) the equalities

$$\left.\begin{aligned}
\tfrac{1}{2}c_0 + c_6 + c_{12} + c_{18} + \ldots &= 0 \cdot 70714 \\
c_1 + c_5 + c_7 + c_{11} + \ldots &= -0 \cdot 24286 \\
c_2 + c_4 + c_8 + c_{10} + \ldots &= 0 \cdot 04286 \\
c_3 + c_9 + c_{15} + c_{21} + \ldots &= -0 \cdot 00714
\end{aligned}\right\} \quad (44)$$

and these are confirmed, within at most one unit in the fifth decimal, by the results of (43) with the assumption that $c_7 = c_8 = \ldots = 0$. The apparent rate of convergence in (43) reasonably confirms this assumption, and we decide that the (truncated) series (43) gives a maximum error of only a few units in the fifth decimal place.

It is interesting to notice, incidentally, that the approximate c_3 in (42) is very accurate indeed. This can be deduced from (41), represented by the last of (44), and these equations also show that the *penultimate* computed coefficient, c_2 for $n = 3$, is likely to have the largest error. This is also confirmed by the results (42) and (43).

Rational functions

13. Special methods are available for the polynomial approximation of rational functions, the ratios of two polynomials, in a finite range which we take to be $-1 \leqslant x \leqslant 1$. Again it is more convenient to consider the Chebyshev series

$$f(x) = \sum_{r=0}^{\infty}{}' a_r T_r(x), \quad (45)$$

where, as usual, the prime indicates that we take $\tfrac{1}{2}a_0 T_0(x)$ for the first term. Then, for a function

$$f(x) = \frac{q(x)}{s(x)} = \frac{\displaystyle\sum_{r=0}^{q}{}' b_r T_r(x)}{\displaystyle\sum_{r=0}^{s}{}' c_r T_r(x)}, \quad (46)$$

the coefficients in (45) are found by writing

$$\sum_{r=0}^{\infty}{}' a_r T_r(x) \sum_{r=0}^{s}{}' c_r T_r(x) = \sum_{r=0}^{q}{}' b_r T_r(x), \tag{47}$$

and equating corresponding coefficients of $T_r(x)$ for $r = 0, 1,\ldots$. This gives rise to an infinite set of linear algebraic equations for the computation of the a_r. By truncating this to a *finite* set we can find not only a polynomial approximation of given degree to $f(x)$, but also the error of this approximation.

A specific example best illustrates the process, and we might as well use our standard function $f(x) = (1+x)^{-1} = \{\tfrac{3}{2}T_0^*(x) + \tfrac{1}{2}T_1^*(x)\}^{-1}$, in the range $0 \leqslant x \leqslant 1$. By using equation (16) we easily deduce the infinite set of equations

$$\left.\begin{array}{l} \tfrac{3}{4}a_0 + \tfrac{1}{4}a_1 \qquad\qquad\qquad = 1 \\[4pt] \tfrac{1}{4}a_0 + \tfrac{3}{2}a_1 + \tfrac{1}{4}a_2 \qquad\qquad = 0 \\[4pt] \qquad \tfrac{1}{4}a_1 + \tfrac{3}{2}a_2 \;+\tfrac{1}{4}a_3 \qquad = 0 \\[4pt] \hline \qquad\qquad \tfrac{1}{4}a_2 \;+\tfrac{3}{2}a_3 + \tfrac{1}{4}a_4 = 0 \end{array}\right\}, \tag{48}$$

in which the meaning of the partitioning lines is clarified in § 14 below.

The general equation is the recurrence relation

$$\tfrac{1}{4}a_{r-1} + \tfrac{3}{2}a_r + \tfrac{1}{4}a_{r+1} = 0, \qquad r = 1, 2,\ldots, \tag{49}$$

and we have one 'initial condition', the first of (48). From our work in Chapter 3 we know that the solution of (49) is

$$a_r = A_1 p_1^r + A_2 p_2^r, \qquad p^2 + 6p + 1 = 0, \tag{50}$$

in which $|p_1| < 1$ and $|p_2| > 1$. We must clearly take $A_2 = 0$, since we know that the Chebyshev coefficients ultimately decrease, and the constant A_1 is determined from the initial condition. The solution (35) follows immediately.

14. In general the recurrence relation is not easily soluble in closed form, and we prefer to attack the linear equations of type (48) directly. These are always of the same form, a number of initial equations, depending on the degrees of $q(x)$ and $s(x)$ in (46), followed by an upper triangular set of equations. Now suppose we deliberately try to find a finite polynomial approximation of degree n, by solving the leading $(n+1, n+1)$ subset of equations in the infinite set of type (48). If $n = 2$, for example, we are assuming that $a_3 = a_4 = \ldots = 0$, and we observe that every equation in (48) is satisfied except the fourth.

In the spirit of backward error analysis we try to find what problem our solution actually and exactly satisfies. With no rounding errors in the computation, we find

$$a_0 = \tfrac{140}{99}, \qquad a_1 = -\tfrac{24}{99}, \qquad a_2 = \tfrac{4}{99}, \tag{51}$$

and can assert that the quadratic

$$p_2(x) = \tfrac{1}{99}\{70T_0^*(x) - 24T_1^*(x) + 4T_2^*(x)\} \tag{52}$$

is the exact solution of the equation

$$(1+x)p_2(x) = 1 + \tfrac{1}{4}a_2 T_3^*(x) = 1 + \tfrac{1}{99}T_3^*(x), \tag{53}$$

the coefficient of the last term in (53) being the number to be added on the right of the fourth equation in (48) to guarantee its satisfaction.

Error estimation is immediate. We have

$$p_2(x) = \frac{1}{1+x} + \frac{1}{99}\frac{T_3^*(x)}{1+x}, \tag{54}$$

so that the error nowhere exceeds $\tfrac{1}{99}$, its size at $x = 0$.

In general, of course, there may be more terms in the bottom left corner of the partitioning arrangement of an equation like (48), and these effectively determine the error of our polynomial approximation. We shall always be able to say, in relation to (46), that

$$p_n(x) \sum_{r=0}^{s}{}' c_r T_r(x) = \sum_{r=0}^{q}{}' b_r T_r(x) + \sum_{i_1}^{i_2} \tau_i T_i(x), \tag{55}$$

where i_1 and i_2 are known and the τ_i are known linear combinations of the coefficients of $p_n(x)$. The error is then

$$p_n(x) - f(x) = \frac{\sum \tau_i T_i(x)}{\sum' c_r T_r(x)} = \frac{\sum \tau_i T_i(x)}{s(x)}, \tag{56}$$

and its absolute value is certainly less than $\sum |\tau_i|/\min |s(x)|$.

15. We may note, in passing, that Chebyshev series or good polynomial approximations can often be obtained by the integration of similar known series. From (35), a series for $(1+x)^{-1}$ in $0 \leqslant x \leqslant 1$, integration using (17) gives

$$\ln(1+x) = \int_0^x (1+t)^{-1}\,dt = \ln\left(\frac{3+2\sqrt{2}}{4}\right)T_0^*(x) + 2(\lambda T_1^*(x) - \tfrac{1}{2}\lambda^2 T_2^*(x) + \ldots), \tag{57}$$

and we have the required Chebyshev series for $\ln(1+x)$.

Similarly, integration of the approximation (54) gives

$$
\begin{aligned}
\ln(1+x) &= \int_0^x p_2(t)\,\mathrm{d}t - \frac{1}{99}\int_0^x \frac{T_3^*(t)}{1+t}\,\mathrm{d}t \\
&= \frac{1}{297}\{112\,T_0^*(x) + 102\,T_1^*(x) - 9\,T_2^*(x) + T_3^*(x)\} - \frac{1}{99}\int_0^x \frac{T_3^*(t)}{1+t}\,\mathrm{d}t.
\end{aligned}
\tag{58}
$$

The corresponding approximation to $\ln(1+x)$, given by the first term on the right, has an error of absolute amount

$$
|e_n(x)| = \frac{1}{99}\left| \int_0^x \frac{T_3^*(t)}{1+t}\,\mathrm{d}t \right|.
\tag{59}
$$

Differential equations

16. Finally, many of the simpler functions of analysis satisfy simple ordinary differential equations, with polynomial coefficients, and an extension of the method of the last section gives a quick and easy way of obtaining good polynomial approximations. For example, the function $\ln(1+x)$ is the solution of the differential system (equation and associated condition) given by

$$
(1+x)y' = 1, \qquad y(0) = 0, \qquad 0 < x < 1.
\tag{60}
$$

Our recommended procedure, for a first-order differential equation of form

$$
q_1(x)y' + q_2(x)y = q_3(x),
\tag{61}
$$

is first to integrate once to produce the equation

$$
q_1(x)y + \int \{q_2(x) - q_1'(x)\}y\,\mathrm{d}x = \int q_3(x)\,\mathrm{d}x + A,
\tag{62}
$$

where A is an arbitrary constant. Consider now the computation of the Chebyshev series

$$
y = \sum_{r=0}^{\infty}{}' a_r T_r(x),
\tag{63}
$$

relevant to the range $-1 < x < 1$. Since the $q_r(x)$ in (62) are polynomials, we can apply (8) and (9) to express (62) in the form

$$
\sum_{r=0}^{\infty}{}' b_r T_r(x) = \sum_{r=0}^{q}{}' c_r T_r(x),
\tag{64}
$$

where q depends on the degree of $q_3(x)$ in (61), the coefficient c_0 includes the arbitrary constant A in (62), and b_r is a linear combination of a finite number of the required a_r. Equating b_r to c_r, for $r = 1, 2, \ldots$ ($r = 0$ being excluded because we are not interested in the arbitrary constant A) we obtain an infinite set of linear equations for the coefficients a_r. The associated condition, for example the second of (60), gives another (first) equation consisting of an infinite combination of the a_r. The solution of all these equations would give the Chebyshev series.

17. For (60), for example, the integrated form is

$$(1+x)y - \int y \, dx = x + A, \qquad (65)$$

and the equations for the Chebyshev coefficients (for the range $0 < x < 1$) are found to be

$$\left.\begin{aligned}
\tfrac{1}{2}a_0 - a_1 + a_2 \quad - a_3 + \ldots \quad &= 0 \\
0a_0 + \tfrac{3}{2}a_1 + \tfrac{1}{2}a_2 \quad &= \tfrac{1}{2} \\
\tfrac{1}{8}a_1 + \tfrac{3}{2}a_2 + \tfrac{3}{8}a_3 \quad &= 0 \\
\tfrac{1}{6}a_2 + \tfrac{3}{2}a_3 + \tfrac{1}{3}a_4 \quad &= 0 \\
\tfrac{3}{16}a_3 + \tfrac{3}{2}a_4 + \tfrac{5}{16}a_5 &= 0
\end{aligned}\right\}. \qquad (66)$$

The general equation is

$$\left(\frac{1}{4} - \frac{1}{4r}\right)a_{r-1} + \tfrac{3}{2}a_r + \left(\frac{1}{4} + \frac{1}{4r}\right)a_{r+1} = 0, \qquad (67)$$

a simple example of a recurrence relation with *non-constant* coefficients, which of course we can rarely solve in closed form.

Again, however, we can deliberately seek a polynomial approximation by solving a leading subset of equations (66). For example, an approximation of degree two assumes that $a_3 = a_4 = \ldots = 0$, and we easily find that

$$p_2(x) = \tfrac{1}{35}\{13T_0^*(x) + 12T_1^*(x) - T_2^*(x)\}. \qquad (68)$$

From our backward error analysis, moreover, we see from (66) that this is the exact solution of the equation, corresponding to (65), given by

$$(1+x)p_2(x) - \int p_2 \, dx = x + \alpha + \tfrac{1}{6}a_2 T_3^*(x), \qquad (69)$$

where α can be determined from the fact that we have taken $p_2(0) = 0$, that is our approximation satisfies exactly the given condition. The error $e_2(x) = p_2(x) - y$ then satisfies the equation

$$(1+x)e_2(x) - \int e_2(x) \, dx = \tfrac{1}{6}a_2 T_3^*(x) + \beta, \qquad (70)$$

where β is calculable.

18. We have therefore solved a slightly perturbed problem with the exact given condition. A useful refinement also 'perturbs' the given condition, in our example by *assuming* that $\int e_2(x)\,\mathrm{d}x = 0$, *making* $\beta = 0$, and hence choosing

$$(1+x)e_2(x) = \tfrac{1}{6}a_2 T_3^*(x) \quad \text{at} \quad x = 0. \tag{71}$$

This gives the perturbed initial condition

$$p_2(0) = -\tfrac{1}{6}a_2, \tag{72}$$

and the new equations, corresponding to the leading subset of (66), are given by

$$\left.\begin{aligned}
\tfrac{1}{2}a_0 - a_1 + a_2 &= -\tfrac{1}{6}a_2 \\
0a_0 + \tfrac{3}{2}a_1 + \tfrac{1}{2}a_2 &= \tfrac{1}{2} \\
\tfrac{1}{8}a_1 + \tfrac{3}{2}a_2 &= 0
\end{aligned}\right\}. \tag{73}$$

The solution is

$$p_2(x) = \tfrac{1}{210}\{79T_0^*(x) + 72T_1^*(x) - 6T_2^*(x)\}. \tag{74}$$

The main point about these operations is that, even for quite small values of n, the error is very close to a multiple of a Chebyshev polynomial which, as we have seen on numerous occasions, is a quality of some importance. In fact the errors in (68) and (74), compared with $\ln(1+x)$, are given by

x	0·0	0·1	0·2	0·3	0·4	0·5	0·6	0·7	0·8	0·9	1·0
$10^4 e_2(68)$	0	−62	−86	−87	−73	−55	−37	−26	−26	−41	−74
$10^4 e_2(74)$	+48	−14	−38	−39	−26	−7	+10	+21	+21	+6	−27

$$\tag{75}$$

We see not only that (74) has a smaller maximum error than (68), but also that it qualifies as a good approximation in our technical sense, having 4 alternate maxima and minima.

19. Similar methods can be used for second-order equations, and there is only one significant cautionary point. We have to be careful when the coefficient of the highest derivative vanishes somewhere in the range, as for example with Bessel's equation

$$xy'' + y' + xy = 0, \quad -1 \leqslant x \leqslant 1, \quad y(0) = 1, \quad y'(0) = 0. \tag{76}$$

It turns out that it is here convenient to find a polynomial approximation in the form $p_n(x) = \sum_{r=0}^{n} a_r x^{2r}$. We can still integrate twice, but we can cancel the offending term x after the first integration, finding, for example for $n = 4$, that we can satisfy the perturbed equation

$$p_4(x) + \int \frac{1}{x} \left(\int x p_4(x) \, dx \right) dx = \tau_6 T_6(x), \qquad e_4(0) = 1 - \tau_6. \qquad (77)$$

The resulting solution is virtually the best polynomial expression of this order.

Full details of these processes, together with other applications of Chebyshev polynomials and a list of earlier references, are given in Fox and Parker (1968). See also Clenshaw (1962).

Exercises 7

1. By using equation (10) of Chapter 6, show that the error of the cubic approximation $p_3(x) = x - \frac{1}{2}x^2 + \frac{1}{3}x^3$, to $\ln(1+x)$ in $0 < x < 1$, cannot exceed about $0 \cdot 140$. Find, by economization, a linear approximation whose maximum error cannot exceed about $0 \cdot 150$.

2. Prove the results of §§ 3 and 4.

3. Express the first four powers of x as (i) series $\sum_{r=0}^{n}{}' a_r T_r(x)$ in $-1 < x < 1$, and (ii) as series $\sum_{r=0}^{n}{}' a_r T_r^*(x)$ in $0 < x < 1$.

4. Show that $\sum_{r=0}^{n}{}' a_r T_r(x) = \frac{1}{2}\{b_0(x) - b_2(x)\}$, where the $b_r(x)$ are obtained from the (backward) recurrence system given by

$$b_r(x) = 2x b_{r+1}(x) - b_{r+2}(x) + a_r, \qquad b_{n+1}(x) = 0 = b_{n+2}(x).$$

(Hint: use the fact that $T_{r+1}(x) - 2x T_r(x) + T_{r-1}(x) = 0$, so that

$$\sum_{r=0}^{n} a_r T_r(x) = b_0(x) T_0(x) + b_1(x)\{T_1(x) - 2x T_0(x)\}.)$$

What is the corresponding result for $\sum_{r=0}^{n}{}' a_r T_r^*(x)$?

5. Discuss the error analysis to obtain the maximum error in the computation of $\sum_{r=0}^{n}{}' a_r T_r(x)$ by the method of Exercise 4, for any x in the relevant range.

6. If $f(x) = \sum_{r=0}^{\infty}{}' a_r T_r(x)$, show that

$$\int_{-1}^{1} f(x) \, dx = 2 \left(\frac{1}{2} a_0 - \frac{1}{1.3} a_2 - \frac{1}{3.5} a_4 - \cdots \right),$$

and find the similar result for the $T_r^*(x)$ expansion.

Given that

$$|x| = \frac{2}{\pi} + \frac{4}{\pi} \sum_{r=1}^{\infty} \frac{(-1)^{r+1}}{4r^2-1} T_{2r}(x), \qquad \text{in } -1 \leqslant x \leqslant 1,$$

show that

$$\frac{\pi}{4} = 1 - \frac{2}{1^2 \cdot 3^2} + \frac{2}{3^2 \cdot 5^2} - \frac{2}{5^2 \cdot 7^2} + \dots .$$

7. Perform the exercise of the last paragraph of § 7.

8. Given the result (35), show that, in $-1 \leqslant x \leqslant 1$,

$$\tan^{-1} x = 2\{\mu T_1(x) - \tfrac{1}{3}\mu^3 T_3(x) + \tfrac{1}{5}\mu^5 T_5(x) - \dots\}, \qquad \mu = \sqrt{2}-1.$$

(Notice that this is of the same nature as the Taylor's series

$$\tan^{-1} x = 2\{x - \tfrac{1}{3}x^3 + \tfrac{1}{5}x^5 - \dots\}.$$

The replacement of powers of x by Chebyshev polynomials gives a much faster rate of convergence.)

Show also that

$$\tan^{-1} x = x \sum_{r=0}^{\infty}{}' a_{2r} T_{2r}(x), \qquad a_{2r} = (-1)^r \sum_{s=r}^{\infty} \frac{4}{2s+1} \mu^{2s+1}, \qquad \mu = \sqrt{2}-1.$$

(Hint: find and use the relation $T_{2r+1} = 2x\{T_{2r} - T_{2r-2} + \dots + (-1)^r \tfrac{1}{2} T_0\}$.)

9. Repeat the computation of § 12 with $n = 2$ and $n = 4$, and estimate the accuracy of the approximation for $n = 4$.

10. Show that the Chebyshev series for $\ln (1+x)$ in $0 \leqslant x \leqslant 1$ converges faster at $x = 1$ than the Euler transformation of the Taylor's series (see Exercise 1 (iv) of Chapter 1).

11. Find, by the method of §§ 13 and 14, a quadratic approximation to $(1+x+x^2)^{-1}$ in $-1 \leqslant x \leqslant 1$, and determine its maximum error. Is this (i) a good approximation, (ii) the best approximation, in the sense of Chapter 6?

12. Find, by the methods of §§ 16 and 17, a cubic approximation to the solution $y = (1+x)e^{-x}$ of the differential system $(1+x)y' + xy = 0$, $y(0) = 1$.

Use the initial condition exactly, showing that the result is not a good approximation in the sense of Chapter 6, and then find a perturbation of the initial condition that does provide a good approximation. How near is the latter to the best cubic approximation?

13. Apply the method of § 18 to obtain approximations of degrees three and four to $\ln (1+x)$ in $0 \leqslant x \leqslant 1$. (See § 5 of Chapter 6.)

8

Interpolation and Differentiation. Finite Differences and Lagrangian Methods

Introduction

1. IN the previous chapter we discussed some methods for finding polynomial approximations, in a finite range of x, for functions $f(x)$ defined in various ways. Apart from one implicit definition, as the solution of a differential equation of a certain restricted class, our other definitions were explicit, and the main purpose of the polynomial approximation was to facilitate the computation of our function for any given argument in the basic finite range. Polynomials, of course, are quite easy to evaluate, particularly by the process of nested multiplication, and so is the finite Chebyshev series, for example by the use of recurrence relations given in Exercise 4 of Chapter 7.

This type of approximation is therefore particularly valuable for functions of frequent occurrence, such as the elementary functions that are computed from subroutines permanently stored in the computer and easily called into action in most automatic programming languages. But we may also have more complicated functions, for example Bessel functions, which appear frequently in certain problems and for which the storage of the coefficients of the polynomial or Chebyshev approximation again facilitates their computation with minimum effort and storage. In this respect our approximation is an economic replacement of the *mathematical table*, which in earlier times was the basic tool of computation.

2. In a mathematical table the function $f(x)$ is given numerically at a large number of arguments, usually at equal intervals in a given range. The uses of such a table include the ability to interpolate directly or inversely, that is to compute $f(x)$ at a non-tabular value of x, or to find the non-tabular x for which $f(x)$ has a prescribed value, to compute some derivative of $f(x)$ at any particular point, usually a tabular point, and to compute the definite integral of $f(x)$ between any two (usually tabular) points.

It is desirable here to discuss these methods, partly because the printed mathematical table is still needed in certain problems, but also because many of the requirements outlined, particularly inverse interpolation, differentiation and integration, are still best performed by the prior construction of such a table, at least in a restricted range of x. There are two main methods, the use of finite differences and the use of Lagrangian formulae, and these we proceed to discuss. Again we shall rarely try to derive the various expressions, but concentrate on their methods of use and the accuracy obtainable with them. In this chapter we consider interpolation and differentiation, leaving until Chapter 9 the problem of numerical integration.

Lagrangian methods

(i) *Interpolation*

3. It is convenient to start with Lagrangian methods, because we have already, in Chapter 6, mentioned the Lagrangian interpolation formula. The nth degree polynomial $p_n(x)$, given by

$$p_n(x) = l_0(x)f_0 + l_1(x)f_1 + \ldots + l_n(x)f_n, \tag{1}$$

where

$$f_i = f(x_i), \qquad l_i(x) = \prod_i(x) \Big/ \prod_i(x_i),$$

$$\prod_i(x) = (x - x_0)\ldots(x - x_{i-1})(x - x_{i+1})\ldots(x - x_n), \tag{2}$$

agrees with $f(x)$ at the $(n+1)$ points $x_0, x_1, \ldots, x_n$. Its error is given elsewhere by the formula

$$e_n(x) = f(x) - p_n(x) = \frac{\prod(x)}{(n+1)!}\, f^{(n+1)}(\xi), \qquad \prod(x) = (x - x_0)\ldots(x - x_n), \tag{3}$$

where ξ is in the interval containing $x_0, \ldots, x_n$, and x. The error is everywhere zero, of course, if $f(x)$ is a polynomial of degree n or less.

We have already remarked that a mathematical table will usually have a great number of entries, and when we use (1) for interpolation purposes the range x_0 to x_n will represent only a small part of the table.

We do not, in fact, use the same polynomial for the whole table, but preferably apply (1) for values of x as near as possible to the centre of the range x_0 to x_n, with different polynomials in other parts of the table. In particular the pivotal points will often be at equal intervals h, and it is then convenient to renumber the pivotal points and to write the interpolation formula in the form

$$p_n(x) = p_n(x_0+ph) = \sum_{r=-s}^{q} l_r(p)f(x_r), \qquad x_r = x_0+rh. \qquad (4)$$

Here $p_n(x)$ is our local polynomial approximation, with degree depending on q and s, and x_0 is a 'local' origin for the interpolation formula. We use (4) for interpolation near x_0, say between x_0 and x_1, in which case we prefer to have $q = s$ or $s+1$, and with $0 < p < 1$ we virtually have the same number of pivotal values on each side of our interpolation point.

4. Now we do not know, without further information about the function f, how many pivotal points are needed to ensure that the error (3) is negligible to our working precision. In the equal-interval case exemplified in (4), the error is

$$e_n(x) = \left\{ \frac{h^{q+s+1}p(p-1)...(p-q)(p+1)(p+2)...(p+s)}{(q+s+1)!} \right\} f^{(q+s+1)}(\xi), \qquad (5)$$

and two consequences follow. First, this form of interpolation is useless in a region in which $f(x)$ has some infinite derivative of small enough order. Second, the size of h is an important consideration. If h is too large, there is no virtue in increasing the values of q or s in (4), the qualitative point being that if the function behaves 'wildly' in the neighbourhood of x_0 then a knowledge of $f(x)$ at points remote from x_0 adds no particularly useful information. There *may* be a good polynomial approximation of small degree in the neighbourhood of x_0, but it must be based on more information *near* x_0, that is we need a smaller value of h.

If $f(x)$ is itself a polynomial of degree n, of course, then any value of h is satisfactory with any $n+1$ points x_r.

This information is usually provided with mathematical tables. Implicitly, the chosen interval is everywhere satisfactory, and explicitly we are told the values of q and s in (4) that will guarantee that the error (5) is less than a stated amount. Moreover the 'interpolation coefficients' $l_r(p)$ are available in tabular form, as polynomial functions of p, and our interpolation process is reasonably straightforward. One may note, however, that if we do not know in advance the required values of q and s, and start with small values equivalent to a polynomial approximation of low degree, then subsequent increase in q and s, equivalent to increasing the degree of the polynomial and taking more

11

pivotal points in (4), is not just equivalent to adding one or two more terms of a series. All earlier coefficients also change, and in fact the coefficients $l_r(p)$ in (4) depend also on q and s. This phenomenon is very similar to that of economizing a power series, and in due course we shall find methods more analagous to the economization of a series of Chebyshev polynomials.

5. We must also examine, of course, the question of rounding-error analysis (as distinct from the *truncation error* represented by (5)). Even if the computation of $f(x_r)$ is performed perfectly accurately the stored values will be rounded, with a possible error of half a unit, positive or negative in the last figure. If the error in $f(x_r)$ is ε_r, then from this source the accumulated error in the computed interpolant is

$$\varepsilon_p = \sum_{r=-s}^{q} l_r(p)\varepsilon_r, \tag{6}$$

with an upper bound

$$|\varepsilon_p| < \sum_{r=-s}^{q} |\varepsilon_r l_r(p)| < \eta \sum_{r=-s}^{q} |l_r(p)|, \tag{7}$$

where η is the maximum of the individual rounding errors $|\varepsilon_r|$.

It turns out that $\sum_{r=-s}^{q} |l_r(p)|$ is not very large (certainly less than 3) for $0 < p < 1$ and $q = s$ or $s+1$, for any 'reasonable' values of q, say not exceeding 5, so that the rounding error is reasonably small.

When s is very different from q, which is inevitable near the ends of a table, then this error can be very much larger. We saw in § 8 of Chapter 7, moreover, that the numerical factor in the truncation error (5) has its greatest values near the terminal points of a given range, and both these facts confirm our intuitive feeling, mentioned in § 3, that whenever possible we use effectively equal amounts of information on both sides of our interpolating point.

Neville's automatic interpolation

6. A process that is more convenient for the computing machine, which steadily and easily provides results of polynomial approximations of increasing degree, and therefore to some extent gives an automatic criterion for terminating the process, is the successive 'cross-mean' method of Neville. It is not restricted to the equal-interval case (neither, of course, is the previous method in theory), and it needs no computation of coefficients like $l_r(p)$ in (4).

The method produces a tableau of which a section is given by

$$
\left.
\begin{array}{llll}
x_{-2} & x-x_{-2} & f_{-2} & \\
& & & p_{-2,-1} \\
x_{-1} & x-x_{-1} & f_{-1} & & p_{-2,-1,0} \\
& & & p_{-1,0} & & p_{-2,-1,0,1} \\
x_{0} & x-x_{0} & f_{0} & & p_{-1,0,1} \\
& & & p_{0,1} & & p_{-1,0,1,2} \\
x_{1} & x-x_{1} & f_{1} & & p_{0,1,2} \\
& & & p_{1,2} \\
x_{2} & x-x_{2} & f_{2}
\end{array}
\right\}, \qquad (8)
$$

in which, for example,

$$
p_{0,1} = \frac{(x-x_0)f_1 - (x-x_1)f_0}{x_1 - x_0}, \qquad p_{-1,0,1} = \frac{(x-x_{-1})p_{0,1} - (x-x_1)p_{-1,0}}{x_1 - x_{-1}}.
$$

$$(9)$$

The quantity $p_{0,1}$ is the result of linear Lagrangian interpolation with the points x_0 and x_1, $p_{-1,0,1}$ is the quadratic polynomial through the points x_{-1}, x_0, and x_1, and so on. If successive columns converge to the same value we have some measure of accuracy and a criterion for stopping the process. The tableau is relevant to interpolation near x_0, and we are particularly interested in the behaviour of the elements in the lines between and including x_0 and x_1. In the formation of successive columns we will normally add extra pivotal points, as required, on each side of x_0. This, of course, is not essential to the practical realization of the process, and near the ends of a range we may be restricted, with less confidence about the result, to 'one-sided' interpolation.

The pivotal values need not be in any particular order, and in practice they are better arranged as shown in Table 8.1, which illustrates interpolation at $x = 1·23$ from a given table of e^x at interval 0·2. Here, of course, we are interested in the successive values along the leading diagonal, and we reasonably accept 3·4213 as an accurate value, subject to a small rounding error in the last figure. (The size of this rounding error is discussed in Exercises 1 and 2.)

7. Now apart from this small rounding error, we must consider whether this process will in fact give the correct result. We are basing

TABLE 8.1

x_j	$1.23-x_j$	f				
1·2	+0·03	3·3201				
			3·4304			
1·4	−0·17	4·0552		3·4219		
			3·4870		3·4212	
1·0	+0·23	2·7183		3·4123		3·4213
			3·5749		3·4204	
1·6	−0·37	4·9530		3·4408		
			3·6915			
0·8	+0·43	2·2255				

our conclusion on 'consistency', which in various places in this book we condemn as being unsatisfactory without independent rigorous justification. We are also assuming convergence, that is that some polynomial of sufficiently high degree, based on the given pivotal values, will give a satisfactory approximation.

In fact we can get 'temporary consistency', for example two of our successive values, and (rarely) even more, can be virtually the same with the correct result some distance away. The reasons for this will become apparent in § 17. We may never get convergence, for reasons mentioned in the first paragraph of § 4. Moreover we can get convergence to quite the wrong solution.

The first two of these remarks are illustrated in Table 8.2, in which we are trying to interpolate at $x = 0.5$ the value of $(1+x^2)^{-1}$, from pivotal values tabulated at integer arguments.

There is no sign of convergence, and the correct value is indeed smaller than each of the last three oscillating entries. We note, in addition,

TABLE 8.2

x_j	$0.5-x_j$	f					
0	0·5	1·000					
			0·750				
1	−0·5	0·500		0·875			
			0·500		0·800		
−1	1·5	0·500		0·575		0·856	
			0·350		0·575		0·814
2	−1·5	0·200		0·575		0·603	0·849
			0·200		0·462		0·603
−2	2·5	0·200		0·275		0·603	
			0·150		0·275		
3	−2·5	0·100		0·275			
			0·100				
−3	3·5	0·100					

the temporary consistencies of results in the second diagonal, which would relate to the attempt to perform this interpolation without knowledge of the pivotal value at $x = 0$.

Here, of course, the function varies very rapidly near the origin, and cannot be closely approximated by a polynomial of *any* degree computed from pivotal values *at this interval*. We should try a smaller interval, and this will ultimately be satisfactory.

Our last cautionary remark is more difficult to resolve mechanically. Suppose, for example, that we tabulate the function $\sin \pi x$ at the points $x = 0, 1, 2, \ldots$. Every value is zero, and so is the result of any interpolation. We have converged, but to the wrong result, and our polynomial is the exact representation of some other (simpler) function that has the same pivotal values at these points. In the last resort, therefore, the remainder term, a multiple of $f^{(n+1)}(\xi)$, is a very important quantity, and we neglect it at our peril!

(ii) *Inverse interpolation*

8. Inverse interpolation seeks the value of x for which $f(x)$ has a given value. If we interchange the roles of x and $f(x)$ we have a case of direct interpolation, and we can apparently use Neville's method just as in the direct problem. This, however, turns out to be of very doubtful value. The basis of direct interpolation is the ability to approximate to the tabulated function by a polynomial, and it by no means follows that if $f(x)$ is a polynomial in x then x can be represented adequately as a polynomial in $f(x)$.

Consider, for example, the table of values

x	-0.2	0.0	0.2	0.4	0.6	0.8	1.0	1.2
$f(x)$	-0.7328	-0.7071	-0.6528	-0.3981	0.5721	3.1165	8.4372	18.0797

$$(10)$$

and the attempt to find the value of x for which $f(x) = 0$. This is clearly in the range $0.4 < x < 0.6$, and our Neville (inverse) interpolation computation, analogous to that of Table 8.2, is shown in Table 8.3.

Clearly we can make no sensible estimate, and of course even the mechanical process would break down completely if any two elements in the column $0 - f(x)$ were the same, obviously a quite common event. We show in § 21 a perfectly satisfactory method of solving this problem.

TABLE 8.3

$f(x)$	$0-f(x)$	x				
-0.3981	0.3981	0.4				
			0.4821			
0.5721	-0.5721	0.6		0.5898		
			0.4132		0.5726	
-0.6528	0.6528	0.2		0.4378		-0.2572
			0.3039		1.2167	
3.1165	-3.1165	0.8		2.1793		
			0.1479		2.0364	
-0.7071	0.7071	0.0		0.1893		
			0.0773			
8.4372	-8.4372	1.0				
			-0.1041			
-0.7328	0.7328	-0.2				
			-0.1455			
18.0797	-18.0797	1.2				

(iii) *Numerical differentiation*

9. We have so far used the polynomial (1), explicitly or implicitly, for the process of interpolation for a function tabulated at 'pivotal points' x_r. The derivative of this polynomial will give some approximation to $f'(x)$, and this is likely to be a 'good' approximation in our technical sense. We have

$$f(x) = p_n(x) + e_n(x), \qquad f'(x) = p'_n(x) + e'_n(x). \tag{11}$$

Here, as we have seen, $e_n(x)$ is likely to have n internal local maxima and minima at each of which $e'_n(x)$ vanishes, so that, including the end points, $f'(x) - p'_n(x)$ has a sequence of $n+1$ alternate maximum and minimum values. Their amplitudes, of course, will rarely achieve our criterion for the best approximation.

Differentiation of (3) gives

$$f'(x) = p'_n(x) + \frac{1}{(n+1)!} \cdot \frac{d}{dx}\{\textstyle\prod(x) f^{n+1}(\xi)\}. \tag{12}$$

Since we rarely know ξ as a function of x it is difficult to estimate the right-hand side of (12) except at the pivotal values, where $\prod(x)$ vanishes, and we have, for example,

$$f'(x_r) = p'_n(x_r) + \frac{(x_r - x_0)\dots(x_r - x_{r-1})(x_r - x_{r+1})\dots(x_r - x_n)}{(n+1)!} f^{(n+1)}(\xi). \tag{13}$$

We therefore normally compute derivatives only at tabular points, and if they are wanted elsewhere we carry out from these a process of direct interpolation.

10. Again it is intuitively obvious that the drawing of an accurate tangent is more possible if we have a reasonable amount of information on both sides of the relevant point, and this is verified by some formulae for the important equal-interval case. We find, for example,

$$\left. \begin{aligned} f_0' &= \frac{1}{2h}(-f_{-1}+f_1) - \tfrac{1}{6}h^2 f'''(\xi) \\ f_0' &= \frac{1}{12h}(f_{-2}-8f_{-1}+8f_1-f_2) + \tfrac{1}{30}h^4 f^{\rm v}(\xi) \end{aligned} \right\}, \tag{14}$$

for the three- and five-point formulae respectively, the coefficient of f_0 being always zero and the other coefficients antisymmetric in this 'centred' case.

For the more 'one-sided' formulae we quote the results

$$\left. \begin{aligned} f_0' &= \frac{1}{2h}(-3f_0+4f_1-f_2) + \tfrac{1}{3}h^2 f'''(\xi) \\ f_0' &= \frac{1}{12h}(-25f_0+48f_1-36f_2+16f_3-3f_4) + \tfrac{1}{5}h^4 f^{\rm v}(\xi) \end{aligned} \right\}, \tag{15}$$

noting the larger factor in the 'remainder term'.

This phenomenon is the same as that in interpolation, and so is the greater effect of rounding errors in (15) compared with (14). If each f_r is tabulated with an error ε_r, of largest size η, we find that the rounding errors in (14) are respectively not greater than η/h and $\tfrac{3}{2}\eta/h$, whereas in the corresponding formulae (15) we have the very much larger respective maximum values of $4\eta/h$ and $10\tfrac{2}{3}\eta/h$.

11. We notice here, however, a phenomenon different from that of interpolation, in the presence of the factor h^{-1} in the rounding error. This increases as h decreases, whereas the truncation error or remainder term, the other component of the total error in the computed derivative, has the opposite behaviour. Whereas, therefore, in interpolation we prefer the smallest practicable interval, so that the truncation error is negligible, in differentiation there is a critical size for the interval, below which the rounding error becomes the dominant term. We shall not normally want to estimate this critical interval, but note the importance of using as large an interval as possible to minimize the rounding error, and a corresponding high-order formula (that is involving many pivotal points) to keep the truncation error small. The phrase 'as large an interval as possible' refers, as in a previous similar context, to our ability to approximate to $f(x)$, at this particular interval, by *some* polynomial based on the given values at the given pivotal points.

These phenomena, as one would expect, are more pronounced with derivatives of higher order. We have, for example,

$$
\left.\begin{aligned}
f_0'' &= \frac{1}{h^2}(f_{-1}-2f_0+f_1)+\tfrac{1}{12}h^2 f^{iv}(\xi) \\[2mm]
f_0'' &= \frac{1}{12h^2}(-f_{-2}+16f_{-1}-30f_0+16f_1-f_2)+\tfrac{1}{90}h^4 f^{vi}(\xi)
\end{aligned}\right\}, \quad (16)
$$

for the 'centred' formulae, and

$$
\left.\begin{aligned}
f_0'' &= \frac{1}{h^2}(2f_0-5f_1+4f_2-f_3)+\tfrac{11}{12}h^4 f^{iv}(\xi) \\[2mm]
f_0'' &= \frac{1}{12h^2}(45f_0-154f_1+214f_2-156f_3+61f_4-10f_5)+\tfrac{137}{180}h^4 f^{vi}(\xi)
\end{aligned}\right\}, (17)
$$

corresponding to (15). The only other comment we need make here is that the attempt to estimate any derivative in the neighbourhood of a singularity of the function will usually be even more catastrophic than the attempt to interpolate the function value in this region.

Finite-difference methods

(i) *Difference tables*

12. We turn now to a discussion of finite-difference methods for the equal-interval case which, we shall find, are less convenient for the computing machine than the corresponding Lagrangian methods, but remove at least some of the major uncertainties about the accuracy of the results. The two most important facts about a difference table are (i) that for a polynomial of degree n the differences of orders greater than n are all zero, and (ii) the differences of other smooth functions behave like rounded polynomials, or at least like a set of interlacing polynomials, possibly of gradually varying degrees, in which the tabular values have possible errors of half a unit in their last figures.

These remarks are illustrated in Tables 8.4 and 8.5. Table 8.4 shows the differences of x^4 at unit interval, and of $\tfrac{1}{10}x^4$ rounded to integer values. Table 8.5 gives the differences of a three-figure table of e^x. In all cases the bracketed figures are obtained by extending the table in the relevant direction. Near the origin in Table 8.4, of course, symmetry effectively provides this extension in an easy way. The

TABLE 8.4

x	x^4		δ^2		δ^4			$\tfrac{1}{10}x^4$ (rounded)		δ^2		δ^4		δ^6
0	0		2		24			0		0		+4		−8
		1		12		0			0		2		−4	
1	1		14		24			0		2		0		+10
		15		36		0			2		2		+6	
2	16		50		24			2		4		+6		−14
		65		60		0			6		8		−8	
3	81		110		24			8		12		−2		(+18)
		175		84					18		6		(+10)	
4	256		194					26		18		(+8)		(−22)
		369							36		(14)		(−12)	
5	625							62		(32)		(−4)		(+24)

TABLE 8.5

x	e^x (rounded)		δ^2		δ^4	
0·0	1·000		(40)		(+3)	
		221		(10)		(−4)
0·2	1·221		50		(−1)	
		271		9		(+7)
0·4	1·492		59		+6	
		330		15		−7
0·6	1·822		74		−1	
		404		14		+9
0·8	2·226		88		+8	
		492		22		−6
1·0	2·718		110		2	
		602		24		+1
1·2	3·320		134		3	
		736		27		+9
1·4	4·056		161		12	
		897		39		−9
1·6	4·953		200		3	
		1097		42		
1·8	6·050		242			
		1339				
2·0	7·389					

differences, incidentally, we shall commonly give in units of the last figure of the values of $f(x)$, without inserting the decimal point.

In the second part of Table 8.4 we see that the fourth differences are oscillating, but their average is certainly positive, whereas fifth and higher differences are oscillating about a zero average. Fifth and higher differences are here non-zero only through the presence of rounding errors in the pivotal values. A single error of one unit at any point gives rise to 'errors' in the differences as shown in the first part of Table 8.6, and the worst case, of successive errors of $+\tfrac{1}{2}$ and $-\tfrac{1}{2}$, is shown in the second part. The coefficients in the first case are those of the polynomial $(1-x)^n$, and in the second case they have the values $\pm 2^{n-1}$ in the nth difference.

TABLE 8.6

0				0	$+\frac{1}{2}$				
	0		0			-1			
0		0		$+1$	$-\frac{1}{2}$		$+2$		
	0		$+1$			$+1$		-4	
0		$+1$		-4	$+\frac{1}{2}$		-2		$+8$
	$+1$		-3			-1		$+4$	
1		-2		$+6$	$-\frac{1}{2}$		$+2$		-8
	-1		$+3$			$+1$		-4	
0		$+1$		-4	$+\frac{1}{2}$		-2		$+8$
	0		-1			-1		$+4$	
0		0		$+1$	$-\frac{1}{2}$		$+2$		
	0		0			$+1$			
0				0	$+\frac{1}{2}$				

13. We can therefore have nth differences, oscillating about zero with a maximum of 2^{n-1}, in a perfectly accurate but rounded polynomial, and we would expect to get reasonably accurate results from such a table if we use only those columns of differences previous to this oscillating column. For functions which are not polynomials we say that the differences are convergent when they oscillate within the limits of 2^{n-1} in the nth column of differences, and we are prepared to treat such functions as interlacing polynomials of degree $n-1$ in any particular region.

For example, in Table 8.5, the fourth differences near the origin are oscillating, but with a positive average. The fifth differences are oscillating about zero, and near the origin we can treat e^x, to three-decimal accuracy and at this interval, as a polynomial of degree 4. This is still the case for larger values of x shown in our table, though from the behaviour of the differences we should expect, and this is indeed the case, that for smaller values of x a polynomial approximation of degree three would suffice, and that for larger values the degree of the polynomial will have to increase.

We note, in passing, the value of a difference table in checking the accuracy of the pivotal entries. At some stage the small oscillation, of amplitude at most 2^{n-1}, may be disturbed by a larger oscillation represented by the first of Table 8.6 multiplied by the error, and we shall be able to deduce the location of the error and its approximate size. The first *even* oscillating difference is more valuable for this purpose than the first *odd* oscillating difference.

14. Now not all difference tables, even for 'well-behaved' functions, exhibit the desirable property of converging differences. As we have already remarked in connection with Lagrangian formulae, the interval may be too large, in some regions, to permit the use of a polynomial approximation based on the given pivotal values. This is illustrated in the first part of Table 8.7 with respect to the function $(1+x^2)^{-1}$, which we tried to treat in Table 8.2 by Lagrangian methods. The differences do not converge near the origin, though the table is perfectly satisfactory for values of x larger than about 6, where a fourth-degree polynomial will suffice for three-decimal accuracy.

TABLE 8.7

x	$(1+x^2)^{-1}$		δ^2		δ^4		δ^6
0	1·000		−1000		+2400		−7200
		−500		+1200		−3600	
1	0·500		+200		−1200		+4659
		−300		0		+1059	
2	0·200		+200		−141		−816
		−100		−141		│ 243	
3	0·100		+59		+102		−316
		−41		−39		−73	
4	0·059		+20		+29		+48
		−21		−10		−25	
5	0·038		+10		+4		+25
		−11		−6		0	
6	0·027		+4		+4		−2
		−7		−2		−2	
7	0·020		+2		+2		
		−5		0			
8	0·015		+2				
		−3					
9	0·012						

x	$(1+x^2)^{-1}$	δ^2	δ^4	δ^6
0·0	1·000	−76	+28	−14
0·2	0·962	−62	+21	−20
0·4	0·862	−27	−6	+17
0·6	0·735	+2	−16	+18
0·8	0·610	+15	−8	−7
1·0	0·500	+20	−7	+5

This difficulty is overcome by using a smaller interval in the offending region, as shown in the second part of Table 8.7, in which only even differences are tabulated.

15. So far, then, we have with the use of differences solved two of the difficulties of Lagrangian formulae. First, we can discover, through the convergence of differences, whether there is a satisfactory polynomial approximation defined by the data or, to put it in another useful way, *to how many figures* a polynomial representation is possible. In the first part of Table 8.7, for example, we should have to round to three fewer figures to get convergent differences; in the second part the differences just converge, but for the same function tabulated to four decimals at this interval the differences do not converge. The second resolved difficulty is the decision about what degree of polynomial approximation is necessary, and we have decided that this degree is that of the order of differences just prior to the column which oscillates about zero.

It is, of course, not very easy to find this information in the computer. Mechanical inspection, and resulting decisions, are relatively slower than the use of the human eye, and we know of no really satisfactory programme that does all we require. The storage of the differences, formerly a nuisance in small machines, is of course now much less of a handicap.

Two problems remain, in common with those for Lagrangian methods. First, we need more information about the function to make sure, for example, that it is not 'contaminated' by another function which vanishes at all the pivotal points, or, for that matter, by a systematic 'error', such as a contaminating polynomial of low degree whose presence is not revealed by the differences. Second, the use of differences is dangerous, and quite unreliable, in the vicinity of singularities. In particular, functions that do not exist on one side of a particular argument may have differences that *appear* to converge. It is important, however, that we should be able to calculate the bracketed quantities like δ^2, δ^4, etc. in Table 8.5 on lines opposite any given point, and this would be impossible in Table 8.5 if the function were not defined at negative values of x. In the notation of the next section, we must be able to compute the *central differences* at any given point if we are to use the table with confidence in the neighbourhood of this point.

16. The standard notations for differences are exemplified by Table 8.8. Numbers in the same places have the same values; for example

$$\Delta_{-2} = \nabla_{-1} = \delta_{-\frac{3}{2}}, \qquad \Delta_0^2 = \nabla_2^2 = \delta_1^2. \tag{18}$$

The Δ are called forward differences, the ∇ backward differences, and the δ central differences. With the latter we also find in the literature an averaging notation, typified by

$$\mu\delta_0 = \tfrac{1}{2}(\delta_{-\frac{1}{2}} + \delta_{\frac{1}{2}}), \qquad \mu\delta_{\frac{1}{2}}^2 = \tfrac{1}{2}(\delta_0^2 + \delta_1^2), \tag{19}$$

which effectively define the δ_n, $\delta_{n+\frac{1}{2}}^2$ differences not present in the difference table. The literature also uses a notation such as Δf_{-2} in place of our Δ_{-2}, and we shall use either form according to the context.

TABLE 8.8

f_{-3}			f_{-3}			f_{-3}		
	Δ_{-3}			∇_{-2}			$\delta_{-\frac{5}{2}}$	
f_{-2}		Δ^2_{-3}	f_{-2}		∇^2_{-1}	f_{-2}		δ^2_{-2}
	Δ_{-2}			∇_{-1}			$\delta_{-\frac{3}{2}}$	
f_{-1}		Δ^2_{-2}	f_{-1}		∇^2_0	f_{-1}		δ^2_{-1}
	Δ_{-1}			∇_0			$\delta_{-\frac{1}{2}}$	
f_0		$\Delta^2_{-1}\ldots$	f_0		$\nabla^2_1\ldots$	f_0		$\delta^2_0\ldots$
	Δ_0			∇_1			$\delta_{\frac{1}{2}}$	
f_1		Δ^2_0	f_1		∇^2_2	f_1		δ^2_1
	Δ_1			∇_2			$\delta_{\frac{3}{2}}$	
f_2		Δ^2_1	f_2		∇^2_3	f_2		δ^2_2
	Δ_2			∇_3			$\delta_{\frac{5}{2}}$	
f_3			f_3			f_3		

(ii) *Direct interpolation*

17. We can now illustrate the use of the difference table for interpolation at some point between x_0 and x_1, say. There are many formulae in the literature, but here we concentrate on the most useful and on those which have most connection with Lagrangian methods. First we mention the Gauss formula, given by

$$f(x_0+ph) = f_0+p\delta_{\frac{1}{2}}+\frac{p(p-1)}{2!}\delta^2_0+\frac{p(p^2-1^2)}{3!}\delta^3_{\frac{1}{2}}+\frac{p(p^2-1^2)(p-2)}{4!}\delta^4_0+\ldots.$$
(20)

It is connected with the Lagrange formula in the sense that truncation after the nth difference gives the value of the polynomial that passes through the $n+1$ points $f_0\ f_1,\ f_{-1},\ f_2,\ldots$, which alone determine this nth difference. In this respect successive truncations should give, apart from small rounding errors, precisely the same values as those along the main diagonal of the Neville interpolation table. For Table 8.1, for example, the differences would appear as

x	e^x		δ^2		δ^4		
0·8	2·2255		(894)		(33)		
		4928		(196)		(+14)	
1·0	2·7183		1090		(47)		
		6018		243		(+4)	
1·2	3·3201		1333		51		(21)
		7351		294		(+16)	
1·4	4·0552		1627		(67)		
		8978		(361)		(+13)	
1·6	4·9530		(1988)		(80)		

and we would preferably like a few more entries to give the differences shown in brackets. Clearly a fifth-degree polynomial is satisfactory, at this interval and to this precision, and for $x = 1 \cdot 23$ we have $p = 0 \cdot 15$ in (20) and the series

$$f(1 \cdot 23) = 3 \cdot 3201 + 0 \cdot 15(0 \cdot 7351) - 0 \cdot 0638(0 \cdot 1333) - 0 \cdot 0244(0 \cdot 0294) +$$

$$+ 0 \cdot 0113(0 \cdot 0051) + 0 \cdot 0049(0 \cdot 0016). \quad (22)$$

The addition of successive terms gives effectively the values on the main diagonal in Table 8.1, with rounding-error differences of at most one unit in the last figure. The final term in (22) makes no contribution to this precision, so that at this point a fourth-degree polynomial approximation is quite adequate.

The possibility of 'temporary consistency' in the Neville process is now quite apparent, resulting from some very small difference in an appropriate place. This, of course, is quite common even when several higher-order differences make a significant contribution.

18. Another useful formula is that of Bessel, given by

$$\left.\begin{array}{l} f(x_0 + ph) = f_0 + p\delta_{\frac{1}{2}} + 2B_2(p)\mu\delta_{\frac{1}{2}}^2 + B_3(p)\delta_{\frac{1}{2}}^3 + 2B_4(p)\mu\delta_{\frac{1}{2}}^4 + \ldots \\ B_2(p) = \tfrac{1}{4}p(p-1), \quad B_3(p) = \tfrac{1}{6}p(p-1)(p-\tfrac{1}{2}) \\ B_4(p) = \tfrac{1}{48}(p+1)p(p-1)(p-2), \ldots \end{array}\right\}. \quad (23)$$

The main importance of this formula is the existence not only of extensive tables of the coefficients but also of tables of the contributions from second and higher differences over quite wide ranges, that is the values of $2B_2(p)\mu\delta_{\frac{1}{2}}^2$, etc., for a range of both p and the magnitudes of the differences. All this information, and a wealth of other material about finite-difference tables and applications, is given in *Interpolation and Allied Tables* (1956).

Finally, we mention the Newton forward-difference formula (and there is an obvious backward-difference equivalent), given by

$$f(x_0 + ph) = f_0 + p\Delta_0 + \frac{p(p-1)\Delta_0^2}{2!} + \frac{p(p-1)(p-2)\Delta_0^3}{3!} + \ldots. \quad (24)$$

If this is applied to the example of § 17 we would take $x_0 = 0 \cdot 8$, $p = 2 \cdot 15$, and produce exactly the same result as before. Stopping at Δ_0^4, the result is exactly the value of the polynomial through the points $0 \cdot 8$, $1 \cdot 0$, $1 \cdot 2$, $1 \cdot 4$, and $1 \cdot 6$ in (21). We note, however, that successive truncation of (24) does not give the successive values of the Neville table, which could be obtained from (24) only with successively different values of x_0 and p. This formula has the disadvantage, therefore, that if for some reason we decided to include a higher-order difference we should have to recompute everything along a different sloping line, whereas with central differences we merely add one extra term.

The Newton formula might best be used near the ends of a range, whenever the central-differences are not available, but we repeat that the results of such a computation must be regarded with considerable reserve.

19. It remains to discuss the rounding and truncation error. The former is precisely that of the Lagrangian formula (4), discussed in § 5. It is important to observe that we cannot estimate a useful upper bound from the difference formula on the basis that each difference has a possible error of 2^{n-1} from maximum rounding errors in the function values. For the Gauss formula this would give, for the error in the interpolant,

$$|\varepsilon_p| \leq \eta\{1 + |p| + 2\,|\tfrac{1}{2}p(p-1)| + 4\,|\tfrac{1}{6}p(p^2-1^2)| + \ldots\}, \qquad (25)$$

where η has the definition of § 5. *This may be a considerable overestimate*, because the errors in the differences are not independent. Only those in the function values have this property, and we must therefore go back to § 5 for a valuable error estimate.

It is interesting to observe, in this respect, that even for quite large values of p in the Newton formula (24), say for $p \doteq 5$ which produces, approximately,

$$f(5) = f_0 + 5\Delta_0 + 10\Delta_0^2 + 10\Delta_0^3 + \ldots, \qquad (26)$$

the rounding error is still small (of the order of 1·5 units in the last figure) if we use fl_2 type arithmetic, avoiding frequent roundings. For then there is a significant cancellation in the errors of Δ_0, Δ_0^2,.... For p small on the other hand, the rounding error can be paradoxically large, since the coefficients of the Lagrange formula have larger values for this lop-sided formula.

20. Turning to the truncation error, we have effectively decided that this is negligible provided our difference table is convergent and that we use it properly. The reason for this is contained in the result

$$\Delta^n f_r = h^n f^{(n)}(\xi), \qquad (27)$$

where ξ is some point in the range which produces this nth difference.

Since our difference formulae are essentially different versions of the Lagrange formula the truncation error is the same, and for Gauss's formula we can write, for example,

$$f(x) - p_2(x) = \frac{p(p^2 - 1^2)}{3!} h^3 f'''(\xi), \qquad (28)$$

where $p_2(x)$ is the value of the sum of the first three terms on the right of (20). We observe that this result is contained in the Lagrangian error in equation (5).

Here ξ lies somewhere between the points $x_{-1} = x_0 - h$ and $x_1 = x_0 + h$, and if the central differences are available at all these points we have some estimates of $f'''(\xi)$. These are good estimates if the differences are converging, so that polynomial approximation is possible, and if the function does not vary significantly between the pivotal values, that is, is not 'contaminated' by functions like $\sin \pi x$ or $x(x - h)(x - 2h)\ldots$. (We cannot, unfortunately, escape from this dilemma.)

For well-behaved functions the point ξ is near the centre of the range. For example, in (21) we have, for the third difference opposite the point 1·3, the formula

$$0 \cdot 0294 = h^3 f'''(\xi) = 0 \cdot 008 f'''(\xi), \qquad (29)$$

where $1 \cdot 0 \leq \xi \leq 1 \cdot 6$. In fact with $f(x) = e^x$ we find $\xi \doteqdot 1 \cdot 3$, a point very close to the centre of this range. Moreover we have from the table a number of values of the third differences in this range and therefore estimates of the third derivative. Interpolation at $x = 1 \cdot 23$, neglecting third and higher differences, then gives from (28) the error

$$f(1 \cdot 23) - p_2(1 \cdot 23) = \frac{(0 \cdot 15)(0 \cdot 15^2 - 1)}{6} \delta^3 f \sim -0 \cdot 025 \delta^3 f. \qquad (30)$$

With the third differences given explicitly in (21) we have the limits 0·0196 and 0·0361 for $\delta^3 f$, and hence limits of about 0·0005 and 0·0009 for the error of this quadratic interpolation.

Near the ends of a range, of course, we cannot estimate the required derivative without a knowledge of the *central* differences. (See, for example, a relevant remark in § 6 of Chapter 9). With this knowledge, and using all the relevant differences, we virtually eliminate the truncation error completly, since $\Delta^n f_r$ in (27) is *effectively* constant, and higher differences are *effectively* zero.

(iii) *Inverse interpolation*

21. The difference table gives us a satisfactory method for solving the problem of inverse interpolation. Consider, for example, the problem of equation (10) and Table 8.3, for which we have the difference table

x	$f(x)$		δ^2		δ^4	
$-0\cdot2$	$-0\cdot7328$					
		257				
$0\cdot0$	$-0\cdot7071$		286			
		543		1718		
$0\cdot2$	$-0\cdot6528$		2004		3433	
		2547		5151		$+3$
$0\cdot4$	$-0\cdot3981$		7155		3436	
		9702		8587		-2 . (31)
$0\cdot6$	$0\cdot5721$		15742		3434	
		25444		12021		0
$0\cdot8$	$3\cdot1165$		27763		3434	
		53207		15455		
$1\cdot0$	$8\cdot4372$		43218			
		96425				
$1\cdot2$	$18\cdot0797$					

It is reasonably evident that our function can be closely approximated in the neighbourhood of the zero by a polynomial of degree four, and our process of inverse interpolation looks for the relevant zero of this polynomial. In Chapter 3 we observed great possibilities of ill-conditioning in this problem, but here we have a very special polynomial. Using Bessel's interpolation formula, for example, we have to solve the polynomial equation

$$0 = f_0 + p\delta_{\frac{1}{2}} + 2B_2(p)\mu\delta_{\frac{1}{2}}^2 + B_3(p)\delta_{\frac{1}{2}}^3 + 2B_4(p)\mu\delta_{\frac{1}{2}}^4, \qquad (32)$$

in which $x_0 = 0\cdot4$ in (31).

The important point is that the Bessel coefficients are small, and vary slowly with p, so that the iteration

$$-p_{n+1}\delta_{\frac{1}{2}} = f_0 + 2B_2(p_n)\mu\delta_{\frac{1}{2}}^2 + B_3(p_n)\delta_{\frac{1}{2}}^3 + 2B_4(p_n)\mu\delta_{\frac{1}{2}}^4 \qquad (33)$$

will usually converge rapidly, starting with $p_0 = -f_0/\delta_{\frac{1}{2}}$. Here we obtain the successive results

$$p = 0\cdot4103,\ 0\cdot5419,\ 0\cdot5501,\ 0\cdot5500, \qquad (34)$$

and we confidently take $x = 0\cdot5500$ as the required zero.

12

22. It is necessary to decide how many figures are meaningful in the computed p, in virtue of possible rounding errors in the function values. In the worst possible case, in which the errors in f are alternately $\pm\frac{1}{2}$, in units of the last figure, and if we make the incorrect but safe assumption that the corresponding effects on the differences are independent, then we have

$$\text{maximum error in } \{2B_2(p)\mu\delta_{\frac{1}{2}}^2 + B_3(p)\delta_{\frac{1}{2}}^3 + 2B_4(p)\mu\delta_{\frac{1}{2}}^4\}$$

$$= \max\{4\,|B_2(p)| + 4\,|B_3(p)| + 16\,|B_4(p)|\} < 0.5, \qquad (35)$$

in units of the last figure. With f_0 having a possible error of 0.5, and $\delta_{\frac{1}{2}}$ having a possible error of unity, we have the result

$$p = \frac{q \pm \varepsilon_1}{\delta_{\frac{1}{2}} \pm \varepsilon_2}, \qquad (36)$$

where q is the computed value of the right-hand side of (33), and ε_1 and ε_2 are at most one unit in the last figures of q and $\delta_{\frac{1}{2}}$. The relative error in p is then

$$\left|\frac{\delta p}{p}\right| \leqslant \left|\frac{\varepsilon_1}{q}\right| + \left|\frac{\varepsilon_2}{\delta_{\frac{1}{2}}}\right|, \qquad (37)$$

and in our case we have

$$\left|\frac{\delta p}{p}\right| \leqslant \left|\frac{1}{5336}\right| + \left|\frac{1}{9702}\right| \sim 0.0003, \qquad |\delta p| \sim 0.00016, \qquad (38)$$

an error of less than two units in the fourth decimal of p. In fact the function is here the rounded value of $\sqrt{(80)x^4 + 0.2x - 0.7071}$, and the accepted zero 0.5500 is correct in all its figures.

23. The important quantity is clearly $\delta_{\frac{1}{2}}$, and if this is small we may have an ill-conditioned problem. If h is also small, of course, we might be able to tolerate a relatively large error δp. This suggests an alternative to this method which is sometimes more convenient for machine computation. The alternative is the simple idea of approximating to p by iterated inverse linear interpolation. The first step is as before, with

$$p = -f_0/(f_1 - f_0). \qquad (39)$$

With this value of p we compute the corresponding value of the function, repeat the linear interpolation for the smaller interval in which the zero now lies, and so on. This is very similar to a type of 'bisection' process mentioned, for example, in Chapter 4. Whether it is a faster method depends on the ease with which we can compute values of $f(x)$ for given x. In some problems this can be very time-consuming, and our method of § 21 may be superior even if we have to perform the inverse interpolating process by desk-machine work.

(iv) *Differentiation*

24. Finally, the difference table permits evaluation of derivatives at pivotal points with an automatic decision on where to terminate the series of differences. For the first derivative, for example, we have

$$f_0' = \frac{1}{h}(\mu\delta_{\frac{1}{2}} - \tfrac{1}{6}\mu\delta_{\frac{1}{2}}^3 + \tfrac{1}{30}\mu\delta_{\frac{1}{2}}^5 - \ldots), \tag{40}$$

where the corresponding Lagrangian forms (14) are obtained by expressing the differences in terms of function values and truncating the series at successive points. The truncation error is obtained by replacing $h^{-1}\mu\delta_{\frac{1}{2}}^n$ by the corresponding term $h^{n-1}f^{(n)}(\xi)$, as in (14).

As usual we prefer the central-difference formulae, but we can record more 'one-sided' formulae in which the forward- or backward-difference notation is more useful. Corresponding to (15), for example, we have

$$f_0' = \frac{1}{h}(\Delta_0 - \tfrac{1}{2}\Delta_0^2 + \tfrac{1}{3}\Delta_0^3 - \ldots), \tag{41}$$

with the same remark about the truncation error, and 'less one-sided' formulae include the relation

$$f_0' = \frac{1}{h}(\Delta_{-1} + \tfrac{1}{2}\Delta_{-1}^2 - \tfrac{1}{6}\Delta_{-1}^3 + \tfrac{1}{12}\Delta_{-1}^4 - \ldots), \tag{42}$$

the coefficient of Δ_{-1}^r being $(-1)^r/r(r-1)$, for $r \geqslant 2$.

Another useful formula, for the derivative at a 'half-way' point, is given by

$$f_{\frac{1}{4}}' = \frac{1}{h}(\delta_{\frac{1}{2}} - \tfrac{1}{24}\delta_{\frac{1}{2}}^3 + \tfrac{3}{640}\delta_{\frac{1}{2}}^5 - \ldots), \tag{43}$$

in which the early coefficients are quite a bit smaller than those of (40).

For second derivatives we have the general central-difference formula

$$f_0'' = \frac{1}{h^2}(\delta_0^2 - \tfrac{1}{12}\delta_0^4 + \tfrac{1}{90}\delta_0^6 - \ldots), \tag{44}$$

which includes all the Lagrangian formulae of type (16), and the fully one-sided formula

$$f_0'' = \frac{1}{h^2}(\Delta^2 - \Delta^3 + \tfrac{11}{12}\Delta^4 - \tfrac{5}{6}\Delta^5 + \tfrac{137}{180}\Delta^6 - \ldots), \qquad (45)$$

which includes all the Lagrangian formulae of type (17). Corresponding to (42) we also have

$$f_0'' = \frac{1}{h^2}(\Delta_{-1}^2 - \tfrac{1}{12}\Delta_{-1}^4 + \tfrac{1}{12}\Delta_{-1}^5 - \tfrac{13}{180}\Delta_{-1}^6 - \ldots). \qquad (46)$$

25. The error analysis, both of truncation and rounding, is identical with that of the Lagrangian methods discussed in §§ 10 and 11. For the rounding error we repeat that the Lagrangian form alone will give the required information. For example, if we truncate (42) after the third difference the corresponding Lagrangian form is

$$f_0' = \frac{1}{h}\{(f_0 - f_{-1}) + \tfrac{1}{2}(f_1 - 2f_0 + f_{-1}) - \tfrac{1}{6}(f_2 - 3f_1 + 3f_0 - f_{-1})\}$$

$$= \frac{1}{h}\{-\tfrac{1}{3}f_{-1} - \tfrac{1}{2}f_0 + f_1 - \tfrac{1}{6}f_2\}. \qquad (47)$$

There is considerably cancellation in the first of (47), and the maximum rounding error is $2\eta/h$, where η is the maximum error in (f_r).

If we treat the differences as independent, however, with possible maximum error of $2^n\eta$ in the nth difference, we obtain from the first three terms of (42) the grossly overestimated error value of $16\eta/3h$.

Conclusion

26. The discerning reader will, we hope, notice the continuation of the trail, established in the algebraic part of this book, called 'ill-conditioning, induced instability, consistency without accuracy, and lack of mathematical knowledge'. We saw a faint trace of ill-conditioning in inverse interpolation, a strong scent of induced instability in Lagrangian inverse interpolation, significant instances of incorrect consistency in most Lagrangian applications, and the need for mathematical investigation on the dangers of contamination by a 'hidden function', one which vanishes at all pivotal points or which otherwise fails to reveal itself in the differences.

Exercises 8

1. In the results of Table 8.1 the values of f_r have possible errors of half a unit in the last figure. If all the subsequent arithmetic is performed exactly, show that the maximum error in the final entry in the table is about 0·6 of a unit in the last figure.

(Hint: express the final value as a linear combination of pivotal values.)

2. If in Exercise 1 the arithmetic is performed in the fl_2 mode, with final rounding of each entry in the table to five decimal figures, show that the maximum error in the final entry can be nearly three units of the last figure.

(Hint: the rounding errors in f_r 'propagate' to give the result of Exercise 1. To this must be added the propagated effects of rounding errors, random in sign but with a maximum value of half a unit in the last figure, in every subsequent column. The results of Exercises 1 and 2, of course, depend on the position of the point of interpolation.)

3. Repeat the computation of Table 8.2 at a satisfactory interval.

4. In the following table two digits in a particular number have been interchanged (a common copying error):

x	0·0	0·2	0·4	0·6	0·8	1·0	1·2	1·4	1·6	1·8	2·0
$f(x)$	1·000	1·221	1·492	1·822	2·262	2·718	3·320	4·056	4·953	6·050	7·389

Determine this number and its probable correct value.

5. Show that, for a truncated difference formula in which the coefficients alternate in sign, the estimate of the rounding error *can* be obtained accurately from individual treatment of the maximum error in each difference (§ 19).

6. Perform the arithmetic of the method of § 23 for the inverse interpolation of § 21, obtaining the required value of x to four decimal places. How many evaluations are needed of the function $f(x) = \sqrt{80x^4 + 0·2x - 0·7071}$?

7. For interpolation at a 'half-way' point in a table of values at equal intervals, show that

$$f_{\frac{1}{2}} = \tfrac{1}{2}(f_0 + f_1) - \tfrac{1}{16}(\delta^2 f_0 + \delta^2 f_1) + \tfrac{3}{256}(\delta^4 f_0 + \delta^4 f_1) - \cdots.$$

Express this in Lagrangian form corresponding to successive truncation of the series.

8. We try to find $y^{\frac{1}{3}}$, for $y = 20$, by inverse interpolation in the table $y = x^3$, at equal intervals $x = 0, 1, 2, 3, 4, 5$. Experiment with the Neville process, showing that the results are meaningless, and use the method of § 21 to obtain a good result.

9. In the method of § 23 for inverse interpolation we imply, following each linear inverse interpolation, that the function $f(x)$ is recomputed from its definition. If $f(x)$ is computed by direct interpolation, with Bessel's formula (23), show that the methods of §§ 21 and 23 are identical, apart from rounding errors. Verify this by producing the results of equation (34) by the suggested adaptation of § 23.

10. If the solution of $f(x) = 0$ is obtained by linear inverse interpolation using the pairs of values $\{x_1, f(x_1)\}$, $\{x_2, f(x_2)\}$, show that the error in the computed x is

$$\frac{-f(x_1)f(x_2)f''(\xi)}{2\{f'(\xi)\}^3},$$

where ξ is in the interval (x_1, x_2), and $f'(x)$ does not vanish in this interval. (Hint: Find x as a function of $f(x)$ by direct linear interpolation.)

9

Numerical Integration

Introduction

1. THERE are two main problems of integration. The first is the evaluation of a definite integral

$$I = \int_a^b f(x)\, \mathrm{d}x, \tag{1}$$

where a and b are constants and $f(x)$ is a known function. The second is the computation of an indefinite integral, which we might express as the solution of the differential equation

$$\frac{\mathrm{d}I}{\mathrm{d}x} = f(x), \qquad I(x_0) \quad \text{given.} \tag{2}$$

Then

$$I(x) = I(x_0) + \int_{x_0}^x f(x)\, \mathrm{d}x, \tag{3}$$

and we seek to tabulate the function $I(x)$ for a range of values of x.

Our first problem is perhaps the more important of the two, and there are various possibilities that inhibit any assertion about a single best method for numerical integration (quadrature). For example, both a and b may be finite, and the integrand $f(x)$ may be well-behaved to the extent of having finite values and derivatives of all orders in the complete range $a \leqslant x \leqslant b$. This is the easiest case. Otherwise either a or b may be infinite, or $f(x)$ or one of its derivatives may have an infinite value at some point in the range. This is a 'singular' case and merits special treatment. We assume, of course, that we know or can find out that the problem is meaningful, that is that I is finite, so that we are excluding cases such as $\int_0^1 x^{-\frac{3}{2}}\, \mathrm{d}x$.

Finally there are some special cases, usually when the integrand is a product of a particular function and a general function, such as

$$\int_0^1 \ln x\, f(x)\, \mathrm{d}x, \qquad \int_0^\infty \mathrm{e}^{-x^2} f(x)\, \mathrm{d}x, \quad \text{etc.} \tag{4}$$

2. Apart from the rare possibility of being able to perform the quadrature by expressing the indefinite integral in closed form, as for example in

$$\int_0^{\pi/2} \sin x \, dx = [-\cos x]_0^{\pi/2} = 1, \tag{5}$$

we have various general methods and some special methods. The general methods include the computation and subsequent integration of a Chebyshev series or finite Chebyshev approximation for the integrand in the given range, which we indicated briefly in exercise 6 of Chapter 7. We shall here be concerned mostly with finite-difference methods and Lagrangian methods, together with extrapolation processes for the latter which yield better results with a minimum of effort. Finally, we shall discuss in less detail some special methods for special cases such as (4).

Finite-difference methods

3. Following our discussion of difference tables in Chapter 8, we shall assume that $f(x)$ can be tabulated at equal intervals in the range $a < x < b$, and at an interval for which the differences are convergent. We assume, moreover, that enough external values can be computed so that we can record the relevant central differences near and at the terminal points a and b. These requirements can certainly be met if the function is perfectly well-behaved in $a < x < b$, and if the nearest singularities are sufficiently remote from a and b.

We can then use, for integration between the adjacent points x_0 and $x_1 = x_0 + h$, the central-difference formula

$$\int_{x_0}^{x_1} f(x) \, dx = h\{\tfrac{1}{2}(f_0 + f_1) + (-\tfrac{1}{12}\mu\delta_{\frac{1}{2}}^2 + \tfrac{11}{720}\mu\delta_{\frac{1}{2}}^4 - \tfrac{191}{60480}\mu\delta_{\frac{1}{2}}^6 + \ldots)\}, \tag{6}$$

in which we truncate the series just before the first 'oscillating' difference.

4. This formula immediately solves our problem of indefinite integration given by (3), since we can write this in the form

$$I(x_r) = I(x_0) + \int_{x_0}^{x_{r-1}} f(x) \, dx + \int_{x_{r-1}}^{x_r} f(x) \, dx = I(x_{r-1}) + \int_{x_{r-1}}^{x_r} f(x) \, dx, \tag{7}$$

compute the last term in (7) from the relevant formula (6), and add it to the previously computed $I(x_{r-1})$. Table 9.1 gives a few steps in the computation of $I(x)$ obtained from the formula

$$I(x) = \int_0^x \cos x \, dx, \tag{8}$$

with the correct values of sin x given for comparison.

Note that we avoid significant rounding errors by tabulating $2/h$ times the successive contributions, and by making the additions with fl_2 type arithmetic. Note also that we use rather a large interval, necessitating the computation of a significant number of external values in order to give the required central differences and the information that the sixth differences are oscillating. There is always this compromise with the use of central differences.

TABLE 9.1

x	$\cos x$	δ^2	δ^4		δ^6	$\dfrac{2}{h} \cdot \displaystyle\int_{x_{r-1}}^{x_r} \cos x \, dx$	$I(x)$	$\sin x$
0·0	1·000	-244	$+56$		$+2$		0·000	0·0000
		-122		$+28$	$+1$	1·918		
0·5	0·878	-216	57		-30		0·480	0·4794
		-338		85	-29	1·448		
1·0	0·540	-131	28		$+8$		0·842	0·8415
		-469		113	-21	0·624		
1·5	0·071	-18	7		(-12)		0·998	0·9975
		-487		120	(-33)			
2·0	$-0·416$	$+102$			$(+12)$			
		-385						
2·5	$-0·801$				$(+6)$			

The rounding errors, of course, accumulate as x increases, but there is no significant induced instability. As usual, this can be estimated only from the corresponding Lagrangian formula, and we shall refer to this later in a number of contexts.

5. For the definite integral, from x_0 to x_n, we effectively add the relevant contributions from (6), and obtain the definite-integral central-difference formula

$$I = \int_{x_0=a}^{x_n=b} f(x) \, dx = h(\tfrac{1}{2}f_0 + f_1 + \ldots + f_{n-1} + \tfrac{1}{2}f_n) +$$
$$+ h(-\tfrac{1}{12}\mu\delta + \tfrac{11}{720}\mu\delta^3 - \tfrac{191}{60480}\mu\delta^5 + \ldots)(f_n - f_0), \tag{9}$$

where the last term denotes the difference between the bracketed difference expression at the beginning and end of the range.

From Table 9.1, for example, we easily find

$$\int_0^{1\cdot5} \cos x \; \mathrm{d}x = 0\cdot5[\tfrac{1}{2}(1\cdot000)+0\cdot878+0\cdot540+\tfrac{1}{2}(0\cdot071)+$$
$$+\{-\tfrac{1}{24}(-0\cdot956)+\tfrac{11}{1440}(0\cdot233)-\tfrac{191}{120960}(-0\cdot056)\}], \quad (10)$$

the difference contributions at the origin being identically zero because $\cos x$ is an even function of x. We compute this with fl_2 arithmetic to produce the rounded value $0\cdot998$. In general, of course, we have a smaller rounding error than that obtained from the corresponding summation of the *rounded* partial contributions in the indefinite integration process, though the error in the latter can always be avoided by retaining an extra 'guarding' figure in the summation.

Equation (9) is not the only possible central-difference formula. In fact if we choose the interval h so that there are $2n+1$ pivotal points in the range, including the end points, we can use the formula

$$I = \int_{x_0=a}^{x_{2n}=b} f(x) \; \mathrm{d}x = \tfrac{1}{3}h(f_0+4f_1+2f_2+4f_3+\ldots+2f_{2n-2}+4f_{2n-1}+f_{2n})+$$
$$+h(-\tfrac{1}{180}\mu\delta^3+\tfrac{31}{15120}\mu\delta^5-\tfrac{557}{907200}\mu\delta^7+\ldots)(f_{2n}-f_0), \quad (11)$$

the notation indicating an even number of intervals in $a \leqslant x \leqslant b$. The 'correcting' terms, those involving differences explicitly, in this formula begin at a higher order of differences and with smaller coefficients than those of (9), and this is in fact a very powerful formula.

6. We can also express the correcting terms in (9) and (11) in terms of forward differences at the lower limit and backward differences at the upper limit, and we find

$$I = \int_{x_0=a}^{x_n=b} f(x) \; \mathrm{d}x = h(\tfrac{1}{2}f_0+f_1+\ldots+f_{n-1}+\tfrac{1}{2}f_n)+$$
$$+h\{-\tfrac{1}{12}(\nabla_n-\Delta_0)-\tfrac{1}{24}(\nabla_n^2+\Delta_0^2)-\tfrac{19}{720}(\nabla_n^3-\Delta_0^3)-$$
$$-\tfrac{3}{160}(\nabla_n^4+\Delta_0^4)-\tfrac{863}{60480}(\nabla_n^5-\Delta_0^5)-\ldots\}, \quad (12)$$

and

$$I = \int_{x_0=a}^{x_{2n}=b} f(x) \; \mathrm{d}x = \tfrac{1}{3}h(f_0+4f_1+2f_2+4f_3+\ldots+2f_{2n-2}+4f_{2n-1}+f_{2n})+$$
$$+h\{-\tfrac{1}{180}(\nabla_{2n}^3-\Delta_0^3)-\tfrac{1}{120}(\nabla_{2n}^4+\Delta_0^4)-\tfrac{137}{15120}(\nabla_{2n}^5-\Delta_0^5)-\ldots\}.$$
$$(13)$$

The disadvantage of these formulae, just as with other applications of 'sloping-difference' formulae, is that we have less certainty about the order of the first oscillating difference, or for that matter whether the differences will ever oscillate at this interval or with this integrand. In particular it may be difficult to detect even an infinite first derivative. For example, Table 9.2 shows the difference table for the function $x \ln x$, which has an infinite derivative at $x = 0$. But the forward differences become quite small, and the inexperienced might cheerfully use the truncated formula

$$hf_0' = \Delta_0 - \tfrac{1}{2}\Delta_0^2 + \tfrac{1}{3}\Delta_0^3 - \tfrac{1}{4}\Delta_0^4 + \tfrac{1}{5}\Delta_0^5, \tag{14}$$

(equation (41) of Chapter 8) to find a finite value for this derivative!

TABLE 9.2

x	$x \ln x$		δ^2		δ^4		δ^6
0·0	0·00						
		-23					
0·1	$-0·23$		$+14$				
		-9		-9			
0·2	$-0·32$		$+5$		$+7$		
		-4		-2		-5	
0·3	$-0·36$		$+3$		$+2$		$(+2)$
		-1		0		(-3)	
0·4	$-0·37$		$+3$		(-1)		$(+5)$
		$+2$		(-1)		$(+2)$	
0·5	$-0·35$		$(+2)$		$(+1)$		

The situation is not quite so serious for integration, and indeed the use say of (12), stopping at the fifth differences, gives quite a good value for $\int_0^{0·5} x \ln x \, dx$. We reiterate, however, that we are far less confident of results obtained from sloping-difference formulae compared with those obtained with central differences, and particularly doubtful when the central differences do not exist.

7. We can also write the correcting difference expressions in terms of derivatives, and though this is not generally useful for practical purposes it has some important consequences which we discuss in §§ 21–23. The interesting fact is that the expressions involve the derivatives only at the two ends of the range, and the unwary may think that the function can have any behaviour whatever in the interior. This is quite incorrect, and for the guaranteed success of these formulae, we repeat, the integrand must be well-behaved everywhere

and the interval must be sufficiently small to guarantee convergent differences. If there is any internal discontinuity, in function or derivative, say at a particular point x_c, we must write

$$I = \int_a^b f(x)\,dx = \int_a^{x_c} f_1(x)\,dx + \int_{x_c}^b f_2(x)\,dx, \tag{15}$$

and treat the two parts quite separately.

For the production of smooth central differences near the joining point we use $f(x) = f_1(x)$ at a few points beyond $x = x_c$ for the first integral and $f(x) = f_2(x)$ for a few points previous to $x = x_c$ in the second integral, assuming, of course, that both $f_1(x)$ and $f_2(x)$ are defined in these regions. Otherwise we must use methods appropriate to 'singularities', discussed in § 18 *et seq.* below.

Lagrangian formulae, equal intervals

8. From the formulae involving differences we can obtain corresponding Lagrangian formulae by expressing some of the differences in terms of function values. From the sloping-difference formula (12), for example, the choice $n = 1$ gives the formula

$$I = \int_{x_0=a}^{x_1=b} f(x)\,dx = \tfrac{1}{2}h(f_0+f_1)+E_1(h), \tag{16}$$

where $E_1(h)$ is a correcting term. Note that $\nabla_1 = \Delta_0$, so that the first correction contribution disappears, and we cannot estimate the remaining terms because we have no second and higher differences. With $n = 2$ we find

$$I = \int_{x_0=a}^{x_2=b} f(x)\,dx = h(\tfrac{1}{2}f_0+f_1+\tfrac{1}{2}f_2)+h[-\tfrac{1}{12}\{(f_2-f_1)-(f_1-f_0)\}-$$
$$-\tfrac{1}{12}(f_2-2f_1+f_0)]+E_2(h) = \tfrac{1}{3}h(f_0+4f_1+f_2)+E_2(h). \tag{17}$$

This is also obtained from (13) with $n = 1$, and in both cases we lack information about the error $E_2(h)$.

Proceeding in this way, which is equivalent to approximating over the whole range a to b by polynomials of degrees 1, 2, 3,..., we obtain the so-called Newton–Cotes formulae. These, of course, are also obtained by direct integration of the Lagrange interpolation formulae, and this process gives some estimate of the error in terms of a *derivative* of the integrand. We find, for example,

$$
\int_{x_0=a}^{x_1=b} f(x)\,\mathrm{d}x = \tfrac{1}{2}h(f_0+f_1)-\tfrac{1}{12}h^3 f''(\xi) \quad \text{(Trapezium rule)}
$$

$$
\int_{x_0-a}^{x_2=b} f(x)\,\mathrm{d}x = \tfrac{1}{3}h(f_0+4f_1+f_2)-\tfrac{1}{90}h^5 f^{\mathrm{iv}}(\xi) \quad \text{(Simpson's rule)}
$$

$$
\int_{x_0=a}^{x_3=b} f(x)\,\mathrm{d}x = \tfrac{3}{8}h(f_0+3f_1+3f_2+f_3)-\tfrac{3}{80}h^5 f^{\mathrm{iv}}(\xi) \quad \text{(Three-eighths rule)}
$$

$$(18)$$

where in each case $a < \xi < b$. We repeat that we cannot estimate the derivatives from the differences, and need for this purpose independent computation of the derivatives of the integrand. We may also note the rather surprising 'accuracy' of Simpson's rule, a phenomenon shared by all even-interval formulae.

9. Apart from the difficulty of error estimation, higher-order Newton–Cotes formulae have other undesirable properties. The first is that whereas the sum of the coefficients is always equal to nh (since otherwise the formulae would fail even for the simple case $f(x) = 1$), the higher-order formulae have both positive and negative signs. The maximum rounding error, proportional to the sum of the moduli of the coefficients, can then be uncomfortably large. An example of this is given by the nine-point formula

$$
\int_{x_0}^{x_8} f(x)\,\mathrm{d}x = \frac{4h}{14175}(989f_0+5888f_1-928f_2+10496f_3-4540f_4+
$$
$$
+10496f_5-928f_6+5888f_7+989f_8). \quad (19)
$$

The second is more subtle, and we merely quote the fact that, as the number of subdivisions increases, the Newton–Cotes formulae do not necessarily give convergent results. Hildebrand (1956), for example, states that for the integral

$$
\int_{-4}^{4}(1+x^2)^{-1}\,\mathrm{d}x = 2\tan^{-1}4 = 2\cdot6516, \quad (20)
$$

to four decimals, the Newton–Cotes formulae corresponding to $x_0 = -4$, $x_n = +4$, give for $n = 2, 4, 6, 8, 10$ the successive results

$$
5\cdot490,\ 2\cdot278,\ 3\cdot329,\ 1\cdot941,\ 3\cdot596, \quad (21)
$$

which are oscillating with increasing amplitude about the correct value.

It might be thought surprising that we recommend with much less reservation a formula of type (12), which as we have seen ultimately reduces to the Newton–Cotes formula. The point is that we use with this formula an interval for which the differences converge, and in order to guarantee this the order of oscillating differences must be quite a bit smaller than the number of pivotal points, in which case we do not have a Newton–Cotes formula. In fact we are effectively using Newton–Cotes formulae *of low order* over partial ranges, and interlacing smoothly the relevant polynomials over the whole range, giving a composite trapezium-rule or Simpson-rule formula of types (12) and (13) respectively. The treatment of the latter by Lagrangian methods, and without using the correcting terms explicitly, is discussed in the next section.

The deferred approach to the limit. Romberg integration

10. Perhaps the most common method of quadrature is to use the extended trapezium rule (12) or the extended Simpson's rule (13), written without correcting terms in the respective forms

$$\left. \begin{aligned} T(h) &= h(\tfrac{1}{2}f_0 + f_1 + \ldots + f_{n-1} + \tfrac{1}{2}f_n), \\ S(h) &= \tfrac{1}{3}h(f_0 + 4f_1 + 2f_2 + \ldots + 2f_{2n-2} + 4f_{2n-1} + f_{2n}) \end{aligned} \right\}. \tag{22}$$

The accuracy of the results is assessed in one of the following ways.

(i) The assertion that 'ten points (or some other number) is obviously good enough to give something near the correct value (say to 1 per cent or some other percentage)'.

(ii) The computation of $T(h)$ or $S(h)$ for successively smaller values of h, relying on ultimate consistency to give the result 'correct to the number of figures to which successive values agree'.

(iii) Computation for different values of h, together with linear combinations of successive estimates to improve the approximations obtained.

Method (i), of course, is the refuge of the ignorant and those devoid of self-respect and scientific honesty. Method (ii) is more commendable, but requires care to avoid 'consistent inaccuracies'. Method (iii) is good, though consistent inaccuracies *can* occur, as of course they can with all methods which do not make *explicit* attempts to assess the error.

11. Method (iii) has the following basis. For integrands with finite values and finite derivatives of all orders within the interval of integration it is true that, for some sufficiently small interval h, the trapezium-rule computation $T(h)$ is related to the true value I of the integral by the expression

$$I = T(h) + A_T h^2 + B_T h^4 + C_T h^6 + \ldots. \tag{23}$$

For the Simpson rule we have the similar formula

$$I = S(h) + B_S h^4 + C_S h^6 + \dots \tag{24}$$

Here the terms A_T, B_S, etc. are constants whose values, as is reasonably clear from (12) and (13), are functions of the derivatives of the integrand at the terminal points.

In the trapezium-rule calculation the error $I - T(h)$ is dominated by a multiple of h^2, but if we compute $T(h_1)$ and $T(h_2)$, write

$$\left. \begin{aligned} I &= T(h_1) + A_T h_1^2 + B_T h_1^4 + \dots \\ I &= T(h_2) + A_T h_2^2 + B_T h_2^4 + \dots \end{aligned} \right\} \tag{25}$$

and eliminate the constant A_T, we find

$$\left. \begin{aligned} I &= T(h_1, h_2) - B_T h_1^2 h_2^2 + \dots \\ T(h_1, h_2) &= \frac{h_1^2 T(h_2) - h_2^2 T(h_1)}{h_1^2 - h_2^2} = T(h_2) + \frac{h_2^2}{h_1^2 - h_2^2} \{T(h_2) - T(h_1)\} \end{aligned} \right\} \tag{26}$$

Both $T(h_1)$ and $T(h_2)$ have errors of order h^2, but by a small amount of extra work involved in the second of (26) we have produced the new estimate $T(h_1, h_2)$ with an error dominated by a multiple of h^4. The important thing to notice is that this has been obtained without computing more values of the integrand than those involved in $T(h_1)$ and $T(h_2)$. In particular, if $h_2 = \frac{1}{2}h_1$, all the computed integrands are needed for the production of $T(h_2)$.

12. This idea, which can obviously be extended, is called by L. F. Richardson the 'deferred approach to the limit', and the systematic tabulation of this process is called Romberg integration. In particular, if we systematically halve the interval, taking h, $\frac{1}{2}h$, $\frac{1}{4}h$, etc., we can construct the tableau of which a section appears as

$$\left. \begin{array}{llll} T(h) & & & \\ & T(1, \tfrac{1}{2}) & & \\ T(\tfrac{1}{2}h) & & T(1, \tfrac{1}{2}, \tfrac{1}{4}) & \\ & T(\tfrac{1}{2}, \tfrac{1}{4}) & & T(1, \tfrac{1}{2}, \tfrac{1}{4}, \tfrac{1}{8}) \\ T(\tfrac{1}{4}h) & & T(\tfrac{1}{2}, \tfrac{1}{4}, \tfrac{1}{8}) & \\ & T(\tfrac{1}{4}, \tfrac{1}{8}) & & \\ T(\tfrac{1}{8}h) & & & \end{array} \right\} \tag{27}$$

The first column gives the trapezium-rule estimates. The quantities like $T(1, \tfrac{1}{2})$, with obvious notation, are the $T(h_1, h_2)$ computed from (26) with $h_2 = \frac{1}{2}h_1$, and for each successive pair of the $T(h_r)$. For example,

$$T(1, \tfrac{1}{2}) = T(\tfrac{1}{2}) + \tfrac{1}{3}\{T(\tfrac{1}{2}) - T(1)\}. \tag{28}$$

It is easy to see that the errors in these quantities are given by

$$
\left.
\begin{aligned}
I - T(1, \tfrac{1}{2}) &= -\tfrac{1}{4} B_T h^4 + \dots \\
I - T(\tfrac{1}{2}, \tfrac{1}{4}) &= -\tfrac{1}{4} B_T (\tfrac{1}{2} h)^4 + \dots
\end{aligned}
\right\}, \tag{29}
$$

and we can eliminate B_T to find

$$
T(1, \tfrac{1}{2}, \tfrac{1}{4}) = T(\tfrac{1}{2}, \tfrac{1}{4}) + \tfrac{1}{15}\{T(\tfrac{1}{2}, \tfrac{1}{4}) - T(1, \tfrac{1}{2})\}, \quad \text{etc.} \tag{30}
$$

These elements in the third column now differ from I by terms dominated by a multiple of h^6, so that we can compute

$$
T(1, \tfrac{1}{2}, \tfrac{1}{4}, \tfrac{1}{8}) = T(\tfrac{1}{2}, \tfrac{1}{4}, \tfrac{1}{8}) + \tfrac{1}{63}\{T(\tfrac{1}{2}, \tfrac{1}{4}, \tfrac{1}{8}) - T(1, \tfrac{1}{2}, \tfrac{1}{4})\}, \tag{31}
$$

which has an error of order h^8, and so on. The factors in (28), (30) and (31) are $1/(2^{2n}-1)$, for $n = 1, 2, 3$.

13. We illustrate this process, and some of our earlier methods and comments, by considering the computation of the integral

$$
I = \int_0^1 (0 \cdot 92 \cosh x - \cos x)\, dx, \tag{32}
$$

whose correct value, easily obtainable by mathematical methods, is $0 \cdot 2397141\dots$. Table 9.3 gives the tabulated values of the integrand and its differences at interval $h = \tfrac{1}{8}$, and three extra values are implied for the computation of the required central differences near $x = 1$. Those at $x = 0$ are obtained by obvious symmetry considerations.

TABLE 9.3

$8x$	$f(x)$		δ^2		δ^4		δ^6
0	$-0 \cdot 080000$		$+29998$		-16		-4
		$+14999$		-8		-2	
1	$-0 \cdot 065001$		29990		-18		$+21$
		44989		-26		$+19$	
2	$-0 \cdot 020012$		29964		$+1$		-8
		74953		-25		$+11$	
3	$0 \cdot 054941$		29939		$+12$		$+14$
		104892		-13		$+25$	
4	$0 \cdot 159833$		29926		$+37$		$+19$
		134818		$+24$		$+44$	
5	$0 \cdot 294651$		29950		$+81$		-17
		164768		105		$+27$	
6	$0 \cdot 459419$		30055		$+108$		$(+23)$
		194823		213		$(+50)$	
7	$0 \cdot 654242$		30268		$(+158)$		$(+17)$
		225091		(371)		$(+67)$	
8	$0 \cdot 879333$		(30639)		$(+225)$		(-23)
		(255730)		(596)		$(+44)$	

The differences are converging, and we terminate any difference formulae after the fifth difference. Both central-difference and sloping-difference formulae can be used with confidence. Each of the formulae (9), (11), (12), and (13) produces the result 0·2397141, and we have given an extra figure to show what a 'smoothing' operation integration can be, obtaining here one more correct figure than the number of correct figures in the data. (This cannot always be expected!)

Consider now the computation with Simpson's rule without correcting term. In virtue of the symmetry of the integrand we can even compute the Simpson value at interval of unity (it is $\frac{1}{3}(f(1)+2f(0))$), and we find the six-figure results

$$S(1) = 0·239778, \qquad S(\tfrac{1}{2}) = 0·239778$$
$$S(\tfrac{1}{4}) = 0·239719, \qquad S(\tfrac{1}{8}) = 0·239714 \tag{33}$$

We note immediately the consistent inaccuracy of the first two values. Such a calamity is avoided with the use of the correcting terms involving differences, or less certainly with *repeated* consistency at smaller intervals.

The systematic Romberg process pictured in (27) gives rise to the array of Table 9.4.

TABLE 9.4

$T(2) = 0·879333$

   0·239777

$T(1) = 0·399666$ 0·239778

   0·239778   0·239714

$T(\tfrac{1}{2}) = 0·279750$ 0·239715

   0·239719   0·239714

$T(\tfrac{1}{4}) = 0·249727$ 0·239714

   0·239714

$T(\tfrac{1}{8}) = 0·242217$

Here, of course, repeated consistency along the forward diagonal, and particularly in the columns, gives rise to confidence in the results, though examples could be constructed of pathological repeated inaccurate consistency. Inspection of the 'backward' diagonal, of course, gives no significant information, since these values *must* get closer together, in virtue of the coefficients in the formulae (28), (30), (31),..., by which they are derived, *however inaccurate they may be*.

14. The value of $T(1, \tfrac{1}{2}, \tfrac{1}{4}, \tfrac{1}{8})$ in (27) and Table 9.4, of course, uses precisely the same values of the integrand as does $T(\tfrac{1}{8})$, but the coefficients of the linear combination are different and serve to reduce

13

the order of the error. We find, for example,

$$T(1, \tfrac{1}{2}, \tfrac{1}{4}, \tfrac{1}{8}) = \left(\frac{b-a}{8}\right)(\tfrac{1}{2835})(868f_0 + 4096f_1 + 1408f_2 + 4096f_3 +$$
$$+ 1744f_4 + 4096f_5 + 1408f_6 + 4096f_7 + 868f_8), \quad (34)$$

where the limits of integration are a and b, here 0 and 1.

We do not propose to use the method in this way, but (34) shows that the rounding error in $T(1, \tfrac{1}{2}, \tfrac{1}{4}, \tfrac{1}{8})$ need not exceed $(b-a)\eta$, where η is the maximum error in a pivotal value of f. To achieve this, of course, we may need to keep a 'guarding' figure, not in the computed values of f but in the elements of the array like (27) derived from them. Equation (34) is worth comparing with the corresponding Newton–Cotes formula (19) of the 'same order', which has both positive and negative signs in the linear combination and hence a probability of a larger rounding error.

One might consider other possibilities of minimizing the number of computed function values while still eliminating a reasonable number of terms in the error. For example, if we take the interval $\tfrac{1}{6}(b-a)$, computing the values $f_0, f_1, f_2, f_3, f_4, f_5$ and f_6, we can get a trapezium-rule estimate, from these values, also with intervals $\tfrac{1}{3}(b-a)$, $\tfrac{1}{2}(b-a)$, and $(b-a)$. We can then eliminate the first three coefficients A, B, and C in (23), obtaining a result with error $0(h^8)$. The final corresponding Lagrangian formula is

$$840I = 1296T(\tfrac{1}{6}) - 567T(\tfrac{1}{3}) + 112T(\tfrac{1}{2}) - T(1)$$
$$= (b-a)\{41f_0 + 216f_1 + 27f_2 + 272f_3 + 27f_4 + 216f_5 + 41f_6\}. \quad (35)$$

All the signs are positive, and the maximum rounding error (assuming negligible error in the intermediate calculations), is again only $(b-a)\eta$. The first of (35), of course, shows the need for guarding figures in the derived tableau of type (27).

Again, however, a more substantial word of warning is needed. Not all selections of intervals will give this satisfactory result. For example, with the successive intervals $[(b-a)/n]$, with $n = 1, 2, 3, 4$, we find

$$2520I = -7T(1) + 896T(\tfrac{1}{2}) - 6561T(\tfrac{1}{3}) + 8192T(\tfrac{1}{4}). \quad (36)$$

The pivotal values belonging to $T(\tfrac{1}{3})$ have little in common with those of $T(1)$, $T(\tfrac{1}{2})$, and $T(\tfrac{1}{4})$, so that the different signs of the coefficients of $T(\tfrac{1}{3})$ and $T(\tfrac{1}{4})$ are very significant, and the rounding error is correspondingly somewhat larger. In this respect this sequence of intervals, or any subsequence, becomes increasingly unsatisfactory as n increases.

Lagrangian formulae, unequal intervals

15. We have seen that the use of a single Newton–Cotes type formula, for integration over the complete range, assumes that the single Lagrangian polynomial that matches the function at the equidistant pivotal points is a good approximation to the integrand, and that its integration gives a good approximation to the required definite integral. The formula is then exact if the integrand is a polynomial of degree n or less, where $n+1$ is the number of pivotal points in the Newton–Cotes formula

$$I = \int_{x_0=a}^{x_n=b} f(x)\,\mathrm{d}x \doteq \sum_{r=0}^{n} L_r f(x_r), \qquad x_r = x_0+rh, \tag{37}$$

and the coefficients L_r depend on r and n. It is obvious that we could find the coefficients for a given value of n by assuming the formula (37), making it exact for $f(x)$ equal to the simple respective polynomials x^0, x^1, x^2,..., x^n, and solving the resulting algebraic equations

$$\int_a^b x^s\,\mathrm{d}x = \sum_{r=0}^{n} L_r x_r^s, \qquad s = 0, 1,..., n. \tag{38}$$

Substitution of the results in the corresponding expression for $s = n+1$ will reveal the general magnitude of the error, though if n is even the Newton–Cotes formulae have the property that they are exact also for polynomials of degree $n+1$, and the error appears first for $s = n+2$.

Now for the quadrature problem, particularly with automatic computers, there is no particular merit in using equal intervals, and if we write (37) in the form

$$\int_a^b f(x)\,\mathrm{d}x \doteq \sum_{r=0}^{n} L_r f(x_r), \tag{39}$$

where both the L_r and x_r are unknowns, we can hope to make the formula exact for polynomials $f(x)$ of degree not exceeding $2n+1$. The result is a Gauss-type quadrature formula, which with the remainder term is given by

$$\int_a^b f(x)\,\mathrm{d}x = \sum_{r=0}^{n} L_r f(x_r) + K_{2n+2} f^{(2n+2)}(\xi). \tag{40}$$

The abscissae x_r, the 'weights' L_r and the coefficients K_{2n+2} are tabulated in various texts (see, for example, Stroud and Secrest 1966).

16. The Gauss formula will usually give better results, for the same amount of work, than the corresponding equal-interval formulae.

It can be shown that all the coefficients are always positive, so that the rounding error accumulation is small. On the other hand they share, with the Newton–Cotes formulae, the disadvantages of having no easy means of estimating the error and therefore of relying on 'consistency' of Gauss formulae of different orders. Moreover, the formulae for different orders have few pivotal points in common, and we do not get the same advantages as in the corresponding use of the trapezium rule and Simpson's rule.

The danger of inaccurate consistency is always present. Indeed Clenshaw and Curtis (1960), in addition to the result of (33), noted the inaccurate consistency of the three- and four-point Gauss formulae for the integral

$$I = \int_{-1}^{1} \frac{1}{x^4 + x^2 + 0 \cdot 9} \, dx. \tag{41}$$

The results are 1·585026 and 1·585060 respectively, the true value being 1·582233. It is in this paper that Clenshaw and Curtis recommended the computation of a finite Chebyshev series for the integrand, followed by term-by-term integration, by one of the methods discussed in Chapter 7. The computation is hardly more extensive, and there are fewer possibilities of consistent inaccuracy.

Special cases

17. The basic idea of Gauss-type formulae can be applied to find Lagrangian formulae for special integrals, such as

$$\int_{0}^{\infty} e^{-x} g(x) \, dx, \qquad \int_{-\infty}^{\infty} e^{-x^2} g(x) \, dx, \qquad \int_{-1}^{1} (1 - x^2)^{-\frac{1}{2}} g(x) \, dx, \tag{42}$$

which are members of the general form

$$I = \int_{a}^{b} w(x) g(x) \, dx, \tag{43}$$

for particular a, b, and $w(x)$. Here we do not try to represent the complete integrand by a polynomial, but only the part $g(x)$, and we find formulae which are exact if $g(x)$ is a polynomial of certain maximum degree. The formulae are of the type

$$I = \int_{a}^{b} w(x) g(x) \, dx = \sum_{r=0}^{n} L_r g(x_r), \tag{44}$$

where the x_r may be fixed in advance corresponding to the Newton–Cotes case, or allowed to find their optimum positions as in the Gauss case. In both cases, of course, we need to be able to evaluate exactly the integrals $\int_a^b w(x)x^s \, dx$ for integer s.

The books on numerical analysis discuss these problems, giving weights and abscissae for the more common cases such as (42), and the only point we wish to stress here is that considerable care is needed to get *and guarantee* a satisfactory result. The methods can be rather disappointing. For the second of (42), for example, with $g(x) = (1+x^2)^{-1}$, the optimum formula with $n = 15$ still has an error exceeding 1 in 10^4 of the true value, the rate of convergence as n increases is very slow, and we have no easy means of estimating the error. This is perhaps not surprising, in view of the difficulty we have already noticed of representing $(1+x^2)^{-1}$ by a polynomial in the neighbourhood of the origin.

An alternative, which essentially guarantees good results whenever the integrand is perfectly well-behaved, is to use Simpson's rule, perhaps with Romberg-type correction, noting the possibility of using larger intervals in regions of large x when the integrand becomes very small. This remark also needs a word of warning. In equations (23) and (24), applied to the second of (42), the constants A, B,..., all vanish, and it would appear that the unrefined trapezium or Simpson rule would give the correct value for any interval. These formulae, however, themselves have *remainder* terms in addition to the *correcting* terms given explicitly in (23) and (24), and these are negligible, as we remarked in §11, only for sufficiently small h. The series are *asymptotic*, not convergent.

Singularities

18. Finite-difference methods, however, also need special care when the integrand does not have good behaviour. In the first of (4) and the last of (42), for example, the integrand may be infinite at one or both terminal points, and in other cases one or more derivatives may be infinite at an end point. If the integrand is infinite at an end point we cannot evaluate the trapezium or Simpson approximations. If a derivative is infinite at an end point, but the integrand is finite, we can find the trapezium or Simpson approximation, but for the correction the central differences are not available at the offending end point. The use of the sloping-difference correction as in equations (12) and (13) is a possibility, though there is no guarantee of its success.

The other important thing to note is that the corrections to the trapezium rule do not here have the simple forms of equations (23) and (24), and any attempt to use the Romberg table based on these forms is doomed to failure and inaccurate conclusions. Consider, for example, the computation of

$$I = -\int_0^1 x^{\frac{1}{2}} \ln x \, dx, \qquad (45)$$

whose value is $\frac{4}{9}$. At the intervals $h = 1, \frac{1}{2}, \frac{1}{4}, \frac{1}{8}, \frac{1}{16}$ the trapezium-rule four-figure estimates are respectively 0, 0·2451, 0·3581, 0·4081, and 0·4295. The 'bogus' Romberg table looks like

$$
\left.
\begin{array}{ccccc}
0 & & & & \\
 & 0\cdot3268 & & & \\
0\cdot2451 & & 0\cdot4004 & & \\
 & 0\cdot3958 & & 0\cdot4271 & \\
0\cdot3581 & & 0\cdot4267 & & 0\cdot4376 \\
 & 0\cdot4248 & & 0\cdot4376 & \\
0\cdot4081 & & 0\cdot4374 & & \\
 & 0\cdot4366 & & & \\
0\cdot4295 & & & &
\end{array}
\right\}, \qquad (46)
$$

and we are very far from the truth. We show how to use a properly adjusted Romberg table in §§ 21–23. We note, in passing, an illustration of a previous remark about inaccurate consistency along the 'backward' diagonal.

19. Of the useful methods for dealing with singularities we mention first the possibility of making a change of independent variable to remove the singularity. For example,

$$I = \int_0^1 x^{-\frac{1}{2}} f(x) \, dx, \qquad (47)$$

which is infinite at $x = 0$ if $f(x)$ is non-zero there, is transformed with the change of variable $y^2 = x$ to

$$I = \int_0^1 2f(y^2) \, dy, \qquad (48)$$

which is perfectly satisfactory if $f(x)$ has 'good behaviour'.

For the last of (42) the transformation $x = \sin\theta$ similarly produces the satisfactory form

$$I = \int_{-1}^{1} (1-x^2)^{-\frac{1}{2}} g(x) \; \mathrm{d}x = \int_{-\pi/2}^{\pi/2} g(\sin\theta) \; \mathrm{d}\theta. \qquad (49)$$

These methods, of course, require some preliminary mathematical analysis, which we have previously praised and recommended strongly. Not all cases, however, lead to a satisfactory conclusion, and one obvious unsatisfactory possibility is the replacement of a finite range by an infinite range, which is no particular improvement.

20. A second method is to 'subtract out' the singularity. For example, to compute

$$I(x) = \int_{0}^{1} \{x^{\frac{1}{2}} + f(x)\} \; \mathrm{d}x, \qquad (50)$$

we integrate the 'difficult' part analytically, obtaining

$$I(x) = \tfrac{2}{3} + \int_{0}^{1} f(x) \; \mathrm{d}x. \qquad (51)$$

The second term, assuming $f(x)$ to be well-behaved, can then be computed satisfactorily by one of our standard methods.

The order of the singularity can often be 'improved' by integration by parts. For example,

$$I = \int_{0}^{1} x^{-\frac{1}{2}} \cos x \; \mathrm{d}x = (2x^{\frac{1}{2}} \cos x)_{0}^{1} + 2 \int_{0}^{1} x^{\frac{1}{2}} \sin x \; \mathrm{d}x. \qquad (52)$$

The first integrand has an infinity at $x = 0$, while in the second the infinity is pushed into the second derivative. Again, all these devices depend on the particular functions involved and on our mathematical ability. They are used, as discussed in Chapter 1, in the *formulation* of the problem to which we finally apply our numerical methods.

Special Lagrangian formulae, either of Newton–Cotes or Gauss type, can also be valuable in the singular case, and in this respect the methods of § 17 have general application.

21. Finally, we mention an adaptation of the Romberg process, particularly for integrals over a finite range, which is quite successful for certain types of singularity. The basic idea is to find the correct forms of the error terms in equations like (23) and (24), and to eliminate them successively by combining appropriately successive estimates for different values of the interval.

Fox (1967) has given details of how to find the error terms when the integrand has an infinite derivative of some order at one terminal point, a sufficiently general case. He considers the integral

$$I = \int_{x_0}^{x_n} f(x)\, dx, \tag{53}$$

assumes that $f(x)$ has some infinite derivative at x_0, and shows that the terms in the error $I - T(h)$ of the trapezium-rule computation are from this source obtained from the expression

$$E_T(h) = (\tfrac{1}{12}h^2 D - \tfrac{1}{12}h^3 D^2 + \tfrac{29}{720}h^4 D^3 - \ldots)f(x_1),$$

$$x_1 = x_0 + h, \qquad D^r = \frac{d^r}{dx^r}. \tag{54}$$

To these must be added the usual h^2, h^4, h^6 contributions from the other end of the range, if $f(x)$ is there well-behaved.

For example, if $f(x) = x \ln x$, and $x_0 = 0$, the successive derivatives at $x = h$ are $\ln h + 1$, h^{-1}, $-h^{-2}, \ldots$, and (54) shows that the error is the sum of terms $h^2 \ln h$, h^2, $h^4, \ldots$, with constants which we need not determine. We can therefore write

$$I - T(h_r) = A h_r^2 \ln h_r + B h_r^2 + C h_r^4 + \ldots, \tag{55}$$

and proceed to eliminate successive terms by an adapted Romberg method.

For the integrand of (45) we find the error terms

$$h^{\frac{3}{2}} \ln h, \; h^{\frac{3}{2}}, \; h^2, \; h^4, \ldots, \tag{56}$$

and

$$I - T(h_r) = A h_r^{\frac{3}{2}} \ln h_r + B h_r^{\frac{3}{2}} + C h_r^2 + D h_r^4 + \ldots. \tag{57}$$

We can now see how to adapt correctly the 'bogus' Romberg table (46). If

$$h_1 = 1, \qquad h_2 = \tfrac{1}{2}, \ldots, h_r = 2^{-(r-1)}, \tag{58}$$

and we eliminate the constant A from (57) with h_r and h_{r+1}, we find

$$T(h_r, h_{r+1}) = \frac{(r-1)T(h_{r+1}) - \dfrac{r}{2\sqrt{2}}T(h_r)}{r - \dfrac{r}{2\sqrt{2}} - 1} = T(h_{r+1}) -$$

$$-\frac{\dfrac{r}{2\sqrt{2}}\{T(h_{r+1}) - T(h_r)\}}{r - \dfrac{r}{2\sqrt{2}} - 1}. \tag{59}$$

This is a rather unsatisfactory formula, since it depends not just on the ratio of successive intervals but also on the actual size of the interval. Moreover, the remaining error is $B'_{(r)}h_r^{\frac{3}{2}}+C'_{(r)}h_r^2+...$, the 'constants' depending on r. We can recover the situation, and by-pass the first derived column of the Romberg table, by eliminating A and B simultaneously from (57), obtaining the formula

$$T(h_r, h_{r+1}, h_{r+2}) = \frac{T(h_{r+2})-2^{-\frac{1}{2}}T(h_{r+1})+\frac{1}{8}T(h_r)}{1-2^{-\frac{1}{2}}+\frac{1}{8}}, \tag{60}$$

which is independent of r. The error in this quantity is the combination $C'h^2+D'h^4$, where C' and D' are constants independent of h, and we can now complete the Romberg table in the usual way.

The correct table replacing (46) will then look like

$$\left.\begin{array}{llll} 0 & & & \\ & & & \\ 0{\cdot}2451 & 0{\cdot}4422 & & \\ & & 0{\cdot}4445 & \\ 0{\cdot}3581 & 0{\cdot}4439 & & 0{\cdot}4446 \\ & & 0{\cdot}4446 & \\ 0{\cdot}4081 & 0{\cdot}4444 & & \\ & & & \\ 0{\cdot}4295 & & & \end{array}\right\}, \tag{61}$$

and we have a good result. The error, one and a half units in the last figure, is due solely to rounding, and can be reduced by keeping a guarding figure in the Romberg-produced quantities.

22. Fox (1967) gives the results of Table 9.5 for the types of error terms for various integrals and for both the trapezium and Simpson's rule. For the latter, the expression corresponding to (54) is given by

$$E_S(h) = (\tfrac{1}{180}h^4D^3 - \tfrac{1}{180}h^5D^4 + \tfrac{2}{945}h^6D^5 - ...)f_1, \tag{62}$$

for the error terms at the offending terminal point. In Table 9.5 the integrals are defined by

$$I_1 = \int_0^1 x^{\frac{1}{2}}g(x)\,\mathrm{d}x, \quad I_2 = \int_0^1 x\ln x\,g(x)\,\mathrm{d}x, \quad I_3 = \int_0^1 x^{\frac{1}{2}}\ln x\,g(x)\,\mathrm{d}x, \tag{63}$$

where $g(x)$ is everywhere well-behaved.

We note that for integrals of this kind the unrefined Simpson rule may not be particularly superior to the trapezium rule. In fact for

TABLE 9.5

$I_1 - T(h)$	$h^{\frac{3}{2}}$	h^2	$h^{\frac{5}{2}}$	$h^{\frac{7}{2}}$	h^4...		
$I_1 - S(h)$	$h^{\frac{3}{2}}$	$h^{\frac{5}{2}}$	$h^{\frac{7}{2}}$	h^4	$h^{\frac{9}{2}}$...		
$I_2 - T(h)$	$h^2 \ln h$	h^2	h^3	$h^4 \ln h$	h^4	$h^5 \ln h$	h^5...
$I_2 - S(h)$	h^2	h^3	$h^4 \ln h$	h^4	$h^5 \ln h$	h^5...	
$I_3 - T(h)$	$h^{\frac{3}{2}} \ln h$	$h^{\frac{3}{2}}$	h^2	$h^{\frac{5}{2}} \ln h$	$h^{\frac{5}{2}}$	$h^{\frac{7}{2}} \ln h$	$h^{\frac{7}{2}}$ h^4...
$I_3 - S(h)$	$h^{\frac{3}{2}} \ln h$	$h^{\frac{3}{2}}$	$h^{\frac{5}{2}} \ln h$	$h^{\frac{5}{2}}$	$h^{\frac{7}{2}} \ln h$	$h^{\frac{7}{2}}$	h^4...

the integral

$$I = \int_0^1 x^{\frac{1}{2}}(1-x)^{\frac{1}{2}} \, dx, \tag{64}$$

which has an infinite derivative at both ends of the range, both rules have error terms $h^{\frac{3}{2}}$, $h^{\frac{5}{2}}$, $h^{\frac{7}{2}}$,..., with no integer powers at all.

23. Finally, Fox showed the possibility of using a Romberg table when the integrand itself has an integrable infinity. For this purpose he avoids a formula which uses the terminal point, and such a formula, involving $2n$ intervals like Simpson's rule, is given by

$$U(h) = 2h(f_1 + f_3 + \dots + f_{2n-1}) \tag{65}$$

(Hamming and Pinkham 1966). Corresponding to (54) and (62) we have the error expression

$$E_U(h) = (-\tfrac{1}{6}h^2 D + \tfrac{1}{6}h^3 D^2 - \tfrac{23}{360}h^4 D^3 + \dots)f_1. \tag{66}$$

For the integral

$$I = \int_0^1 x^{-\frac{1}{2}} \, dx = 2, \tag{67}$$

for example, equation (66), together with the contributions from the upper limit, shows that we can write

$$I - U(h) = Ah^{\frac{1}{2}} + Bh^2 + Ch^4 + \dots. \tag{68}$$

The correct Romberg table is easy to construct. We have, for the first derived column,

$$U(h, \tfrac{1}{2}h) = U(\tfrac{1}{2}h) + \frac{1}{2^{\frac{1}{2}} - 1}\{U(\tfrac{1}{2}h) - Uh)\}, \tag{69}$$

and these results have errors $B'h^2 + C'h^4 + \dots$. The remaining columns are then derived in the usual manner. Some results are shown in Table 9.6.

TABLE 9.6

$U(\tfrac{1}{2}) = 1{\cdot}4142$

$\qquad\qquad\qquad 1{\cdot}9714$

$U(\tfrac{1}{4}) = 1{\cdot}5774 \qquad\qquad 1{\cdot}9987$

$\qquad\qquad\qquad 1{\cdot}9919 \qquad\qquad\qquad 2{\cdot}0004$

$U(\tfrac{1}{8}) = 1{\cdot}6988 \qquad\qquad 2{\cdot}0003$

$\qquad\qquad\qquad 1{\cdot}9982$

$U(\tfrac{1}{16}) = 1{\cdot}7865$

We observe the remarkable improvement of the Romberg process, compared with the rather poor $U(\tfrac{1}{16})$, obtained with an insignificant amount of extra work.

Conclusion

24. We have tried to show the differences between good and bad methods for numerical integration and, without covering all possibilities, to indicate some of the main methods at present in existence. The discerning computor will, we hope, learn to select a good method, good that is for his particular problem, and to develop some numerical sense in its use. Quadrature is a large subject, and the last word has yet to be spoken. In 1967, for example, Davis and Rabinowitz produced a new book on quadrature, containing both advanced mathematical treatment and computational details. It says virtually nothing about finite-difference methods, and little about our modified Romberg method. Amid a wealth of valuable material, however, we select the following two quotations:

(i) 'No mathematical method should ever be ruled out of consideration from computing practice. Changing machine characteristics and more versatile programming languages have restored to good practice numerous mathematical devices previously considered too cumbersome or uneconomical. Thus, whereas current programming tends to avoid the difference calculus approach to numerical analysis, and this is reflected in the selection of the material in this book, we may yet see the difference calculus restored.'

(ii) 'We should realize that, in principle, an automatic integrator does nothing that might not reasonably be done by a programmer forced to work in the absence of any theoretical analysis of his integral. A series of printouts, monitored either by eye or by the machine, leads him squarely and surely to the same dilemma: What faith can he put in the alleged value? There is no answer other than to build up experience and set modest goals.'

Exercises 9

1. Compute

$$\int_0^1 (1+x^2)^{-1}\, dx$$

from the formulae (9), (11), (12), and (13), using an interval $h = 2^{-n}$ with an estimated value of n needed to guarantee three-figure accuracy.

2. We have (Table 9.1) a table of $\cos x$, and we wish to construct a table of $\sin x$ from one of the pieces of information (i) $\sin x = -d(\cos x)/dx$, (ii) $\sin x = \int \cos x\, dx$. With numerical methods, which of (i) or (ii) would give the better result? Verify your answer with the use of Table 9.1.

3. Compute the four-figure value of

$$\int_0^1 f(x)\, dx,$$

where

$$f(x) = \sin x, \qquad 0 \leqslant x \leqslant \tfrac{1}{2},$$

$$f(x) = e^{x-\frac{1}{2}} + \sin x - 1, \qquad \tfrac{1}{2} \leqslant x \leqslant 1.$$

4. Use the Romberg process to compute

$$\int_{-4}^4 (1+x^2)^{-1}\, dx = 2 \cdot 6516.$$

(Successive trapezium-rule values, with $h = 4, 2, 1, \tfrac{1}{2}, \ldots$ are

$$4 \cdot 2353, \quad 2 \cdot 9176, \quad 2 \cdot 6588, \quad 2 \cdot 6505, \quad 2 \cdot 6513, \ldots.$$

Note the change from decreasing behaviour after the interval $h = 0 \cdot 5$, and the danger of assuming wrongly, from a knowledge of the first four values, that $I < 2 \cdot 6505$. Moreover there is clearly some interval $h > \tfrac{1}{2}$, whose trapezium-value is nearer to I than that of $h = \tfrac{1}{4}$. Here the Romberg table is virtually useless, since in the neighbourhood of $x = 0$ the interval $h = 0 \cdot 5$ is still too large for the validity of the assumption (23).)

5. In view of the failure of the method of Exercise 4, try the 'range-splitting'

$$I = 2 \int_0^{x_c} (1+x^2)^{-1}\, dx + 2 \int_{x_c}^4 (1+x^2)^{-1}\, dx,$$

using Romberg integration in both ranges. (It is here clearly uneconomic to reduce the interval successively, and by the same amounts, in all ranges of x.)

6. Compute the integral (32) by expressing the integrand as a Chebyshev series (valid in $-1 \leqslant x \leqslant 1$, since the integrand is an even function), and integrating the result.

7. Repeat Exercise 6 for the computation of the integral (41).

8. Find the values of L_r and x_r in equation (44), for $n = 1$, 2, and 3, for each of the integrals in (42), and also for $\int_0^1 g(x)\,dx$.

(For the first of (42) we have to solve, for $n = 2$, say, the equations

$$\int_0^\infty e^{-x}x^s\,dx = L_0 x_0^s + L_1 x_1^s + L_2 x_2^s, \qquad s = 0, 1, 2, 3, 4, 5.$$

This gives the equations (via a recurrence relation (!)) for $I_s = \int_0^\infty x^s e^{-x}\,dx$,

$$L_0 + L_1 + L_2 = 1, \tag{1}$$
$$L_0 x_0 + L_1 x_1 + L_2 x_2 = 1, \tag{2}$$
$$L_0 x_0^2 + L_1 x_1^2 + L_2 x_2^2 = 2, \tag{3}$$
$$L_0 x_0^3 + L_1 x_1^3 + L_2 x_2^3 = 6, \tag{4}$$
$$L_0 x_0^4 + L_1 x_1^4 + L_2 x_2^4 = 24, \tag{5}$$
$$L_0 x_0^5 + L_1 x_1^5 + L_2 x_2^5 = 120. \tag{6}$$

If we multiply equations (1)–(4) by 1, α, β, γ, respectively and add, we find that x_0, x_1, x_2 are roots of the cubic equation

$$1 + \alpha x + \beta x^2 + \gamma x^3 = 0,$$

if

$$1 + \alpha + 2\beta + 6\gamma = 0.$$

Similar treatment of equations (2)–(5) and (3)–(6) gives the equations

$$1 + 2\alpha + 6\beta + 24\gamma = 0,$$
$$2 + 6\alpha + 24\beta + 120\gamma = 0.$$

We find the cubic $1 - 3x + \frac{3}{2}x^2 - \frac{1}{6}x^3$, whose zeros we can find by the methods of Chapter 4. Then substitution in the first three equations, say, will give L_0, L_1, and L_2.)

9. Compute to four decimals the value of

$$\int_{-\infty}^\infty e^{-x^2}\,dx = \pi^{\frac{1}{2}} = 1 \cdot 77245\ldots,$$

using the trapezium rule at intervals 4, 2, 1, $\frac{1}{2}$,..., and replacing ∞ by a suitable finite number. (How do we determine this?) (Note the remarkable accuracy even for $h = 1$. The integrand does *not* have convergent differences at this interval. See Goodwin (1949) for an explanation of this phenomenon.)

10. Show that, for the integral

$$\int_0^1 x \ln x\,dx,$$

the elimination of the terms A and B in (55) is effected with the formula

$$T(1, \tfrac{1}{2}, \tfrac{1}{4}) = \tfrac{1}{9}\{16T(\tfrac{1}{4}) - 8T(\tfrac{1}{2}) + T(1)\},$$

and that this quantity has an error of order h^4.

11. Compute the integral (64) by Romberg integration, first with the trapezium rule and then with the Simpson rule. Observe that the latter does not here give faster convergence than the former.

12. Show that, when the integrand has no singularity, the Romberg column derived from the trapezium-rule values gives the corresponding Simpson-rule values.

13. For the computation of

$$\int_0^1 \ln x \, dx,$$

show that the error terms for the U formula of § 23 are multiples of h, h^2, h^3,.... Compute the U estimate for $h = \tfrac{1}{2}, \tfrac{1}{4}, \tfrac{1}{8}$, (to three decimal places) and fill in the Romberg table.

14. For the computation of

$$\int_0^1 \ln x \, g(x) \, dx,$$

by the U formula, derive the correcting terms similar to those of Table 9.5. (To find Table 9.5 we have to consider the contributions to the error from the U estimate of

$$\int_0^1 x^r \ln x \, dx, \qquad \text{for } r = 0, 1, 2, ...)$$

15. In the formula

$$I = \int_0^{2h} x^{\frac{1}{2}} f(x) \, dx = Af_0 + Bf_1 + Cf_2 + E, \qquad f_r = f(rh),$$

show that A, B, and C can be chosen to make the result exact if $f(x)$ is a polynomial of degree 2.

(We find, with error term, $I = (\sqrt{2}/105)h^{\frac{3}{2}}(8f_0 + 96f_1 + 36f_2) - (16\sqrt{2}/945)h^{\frac{7}{2}}f'''(\xi)$.)

16. Use the result of Exercise 15 to compute

$$\int_0^1 x^{\frac{1}{2}} \cos x \, dx,$$

which is 0·5312 to four figures.

17. The interval $h = \tfrac{1}{2}$ is too large, in Exercise 16, for the formula of Exercise 15 to produce the correct result to four figures. The 'trouble' lies in the early part of the range, and a reasonable compromise is to split the range at $x = \tfrac{1}{2}$, using $h = \tfrac{1}{4}$ with the given formula in the first part, and Simpson's rule in the second part where $h = \tfrac{1}{8}$ will suffice. Show that the resulting error cannot exceed 0·0003. (Hint: we need upper bounds for the third derivative of $\cos x$ in $0 \leqslant x \leqslant \tfrac{1}{2}$, and of the fourth derivative of $x^{\frac{1}{2}} \cos x$ in $\tfrac{1}{2} \leqslant x \leqslant 1$, the error of Simpson's rule being the multiple $\tfrac{1}{90}h^5$ of this quantity. The bound is conservative, and by this method we produce the correct result to four figures. This method, of course, is less attractive when simple analytic upper bounds are not available for the derivatives in the error terms.)

18. Evaluate the integral in Exercise 16 by the adapted Romberg process, using the relevant part of Table 9.5. Show that 'Romberg-trapezium' requires at least $T(\tfrac{1}{8})$ to guarantee four-figure accuracy.

10

Ordinary Differential Equations

Introduction

1. WE TURN finally to the numerical solution of ordinary differential equations, concentrating largely on equations of first and second order. The general first-order equation has the form

$$y' = f(x, y), \tag{1}$$

and needs one extra condition, for example y given at some value of x, to generate a unique solution. The general second-order equation is given by

$$y'' = f(x, y, y'), \tag{2}$$

and here we need two associated conditions to produce a unique solution.

The situation, of course, is very similar to that for recurrence relations discussed in Chapter 3. First, we shall denote by the phrase 'differential system' the combination of differential equation(s) and associated condition(s). Second, the first-order system is usually of initial-value type, whereas the second-order system has two possibilities. If we have two conditions specified at x_0, for example given values of $y(x_0)$ and $y'(x_0)$, then the system is of initial-value type. Boundary conditions, for example the specification of $y(x_0)$ and $y(x_n)$, give a system of boundary-value type. Third, the general solution of a *linear* differential equation of order n is given by

$$y(x) = \sum_{r=1}^{n} A_r y_r(x) + y_0(x), \tag{3}$$

where $y_0(x)$ is a particular integral and the $y_r(x)$ are independent (complementary) solutions of the homogeneous system. The arbitrary constants are determined from the associated conditions.

2. Many of our numerical methods, moreover, start by replacing the differential system by an approximating algebraic system. This is usually a recurrence system of initial-value or boundary-value type, though the system is linear or nonlinear according to the corresponding nature of the differential system. Apart from solving the algebraic system, we have here the extra problem of deciding how nearly this solution (the algebraic solution) agrees with the solution of the given differential system (the differential solution). All the major numerical methods exhibit this problem. (We are, of course, excluding the rare case in which we can solve the differential system directly by mathematical methods   This should always be considered, as we emphasized in Chapter 1). The methods include

(i) the determination of an approximating simpler function, such as a polynomial, over the whole range of interest;

(ii) the construction of a table of values $y(x_r)$, with arguments x_r separated by a generally constant interval h, the x_r covering the range of interest.

Method (i) we have discussed in Chapter 7 in relation to the computation of a truncated Chebyshev series for a particular class of differential systems, namely linear equations with polynomial coefficients and linear associated conditions. This is the only class for which this particular version of method (i) has significant advantages, and we shall not discuss it further here.

3. We shall concentrate on various types of method (ii), in which the algebraic system always comprises a set of algebraic equations, each of which is an approximation to the differential equation at a particular argument x_r. For example, the differential equations (1) or (2) may be replaced *locally* by an algebraic equation of type

$$L(Y_r)+g_r = E_r. \tag{4}$$

Here $L(Y_r)$ is some combination, possibly non-linear, of two or more pivotal values Y_r, g_r is a known quantity, and E_r is the *local truncation error*. The quantities Y_r, evaluated at interval h, are approximations to the true solution $y(x_r)$. The main differences between the methods are in the formation of the algebraic problem and the treatment of the local truncation error. We shall find that some methods give rise to induced instability, and these, of course, we must reject. First, however, we consider the problem of inherent instability.

Inherent instability

4. The possibilities of inherent instability, at least for linear systems, are effectively the same as those for recurrence systems discussed in Chapter 3, so that our treatment here can be brief. Corresponding to §§ 3–11 of Chapter 3 we have the following situation. For the first-order system

$$y' = ay, \qquad y(0) \quad \text{given}, \qquad a = \text{constant}, \tag{5}$$

the solution is $y = e^{ax}y(0)$. If $a > 0$ small changes in $y(0)$ give large *absolute* changes in $y(x)$ for large x, and the problem is absolutely ill-conditioned though relatively well-conditioned. If $a < 0$ the problem is both absolutely and relatively well-conditioned. With the equation (5) and condition specifying the value of $y(x_n)$, for which we seek the solution in $0 \leqslant x \leqslant x_n$, the situation is completely reversed.

For the system

$$y' = ay + 1 - ax, \qquad y(0) \quad \text{given}, \qquad a = \text{constant}, \tag{6}$$

the solution is $y = Ae^{ax}y(0) + x$. If a is positive the solution is dominated by the complementary solution, which increases faster than the particular integral. For most values of $y(0)$ the problem is relatively well-conditioned, but as $y(0) \to 0$, giving $A = 0$ and the particular integral $y = x$, the *physical* problem, represented by small uncertainties in $y(0)$, becomes increasingly ill-conditioned in both absolute and relative senses. The corresponding mathematical problem, for $y(0) = 0$, is difficult to solve accurately by numerical methods, and for this purpose we would prefer a reformulation of the problem so that $y(x_n)$ is specified for some large x_n. For $a < 0$ the situation is again completely reversed.

5. For the second-order problem, of initial-value type, the discussion is analogous to that of §§ 12–17 of Chapter 3. The equation

$$y'' - k^2 y = 0 \tag{7}$$

has the general solution
$$y = A_1 e^{kx} + A_2 e^{-kx}. \tag{8}$$

The constants may be determined from the initial conditions specifying $y(0)$ and $y'(0)$. If A_1 has a reasonable size the problem is relatively well-conditioned. As $A_1 \to 0$, so that we 'want' the decreasing solution, the physical problem is ill-conditioned and the corresponding mathematical problem is difficult to solve accurately. Specification of $y(x_n)$ and $y'(x_n)$ completely reverses this situation.

For the equation
$$y'' + k^2 y = 0, \tag{9}$$

with complementary solutions $\sin kx$ and $\cos kx$, neither of these is dominant, and initial conditions, either at x_0 or at x_n, both give well-conditioned problems. The different nature of 'oscillatory' and 'exponential' solutions is quite analogous to that of the recurrence problem, and indeed the approximation

$$h^2 y_r'' = \delta^2 y_r = y_{r+1} - 2y_r + y_{r-1} \tag{10}$$

gives rise, corresponding to equations (7) and (9), to the recurrence relation

$$y_{r+1} - (2 \pm h^2 k^2) y_r + y_{r-1} = 0, \tag{11}$$

which we discussed from this point of view in several places in Chapter 3.

For the non-homogeneous system

$$y'' - k^2 y = -k^2 x, \tag{12}$$

with general solution

$$y = A_1 e^{kx} + A_2 e^{-kx} + x, \tag{13}$$

initial conditions specifying y and y' either at x_0 or x_n will fail to produce an accurate solution for the particular integral $y = x$, and for this purpose we prefer a boundary-value formulation, with y specified both at x_0 and x_n. This, again, is quite analogous to the discussion of § 17 in Chapter 3.

6. The possible inherent instability of the second-order boundary-value problem, finally, is also similar in form to that of the corresponding recurrence problem discussed in § 26 of Chapter 3. The system

$$y'' + k^2 y = 1, \qquad y(0) = 0, \qquad y(x_n) = 1, \tag{14}$$

has the general solution

$$y = A_1 \sin kx + A_2 \cos kx + k^{-2}, \tag{15}$$

and the particular solution generated by the boundary conditions has for the arbitrary constants the values

$$A_2 = -k^{-2}, \qquad A_1 = \frac{1 - k^{-2}(1 - \cos kx_n)}{\sin kx_n}. \tag{16}$$

Ill-conditioning here corresponds to the possibility that A_1 or A_2 can be very large, and this can clearly happen for some k and some x_n. The important quantity is kx_n, and if this is a multiple of π then A_1 is infinite. If kx_n has slight variations near a multiple of π, then A_1 can be large and in any case is badly determined.

This, again, is directly comparable with the corresponding recurrence situation. The inability to determine an arbitrary constant means that the *homogeneous* problem, here defined by

$$y'' + k^2 y = 0, \qquad y(0) = 0, \qquad y(x_n) = 0, \tag{17}$$

has a non-trivial solution, here $y = A_1 \sin kx$, when kx_n is a multiple of π. It also corresponds directly with the singularity of the matrix of recurrence relations mentioned in § 26 of Chapter 3, that is with the fact that the homogeneous problem has a non-trivial 'eigensolution'.

In this respect the oscillatory case is more dangerous than the exponential case. Moreover, though we have not yet mentioned the possibility of induced instability, the discussion of problem formulation in the general case, in which the solution may have different forms in different regions, also corresponds directly with the discussion of § 27 of Chapter 3.

7. We did not discuss the non-linear case in Chapter 3, but this is rather important with respect to differential equations. The effect on the solution of small variations in a particular parameter can conveniently be studied by forming a linear equation by differentiation. As a simple example, suppose that we seek the effect of small changes in p in the given system

$$y'' + f(x, y, y', p) = 0, \qquad y(0) = p, \qquad y'(0) = q, \qquad (18)$$

when we have an approximate solution for a particular value of p. What we look for is the function $\partial y(x)/\partial p = z(x)$, and by differentiating (18) we obtain for this the linear system

$$z'' + \frac{\partial f}{\partial y'} z' + \frac{\partial f}{\partial y} z + \frac{\partial f}{\partial p} = 0, \qquad z(0) = 1, \qquad z'(0) = 0, \qquad (19)$$

where y and y' are obtained from the computed approximate solution. If z turns out to be large then the original system is correspondingly ill-conditioned.

I. Initial-value problems

8. We now consider various methods for solving initial-value systems of first and second orders. It is convenient to divide the methods into

    (i) those which use derivatives;
    (ii) those which use finite differences;
    (iii) those of Lagrangian type.

Methods of types (i) and (ii) effectively have no truncation error. Methods of type (iii) are essentially variations of truncated versions of (i) and (ii), and therefore either

    (a) use a sufficiently small interval so that the local truncation error, and hence its accumulated effect, are negligible to some required precision,

(b) correct a first approximation by subsequent treatment of the truncation error, or

(c) use a sequence of decreasing intervals, relying on consistency and/or performing a type of 'deferred approach to the limit' to improve the rate of convergence of the sequence of results.

We first describe the methods in general terms, and then discuss their efficiencies, dangers such as the possibilities of induced instability, and so on.

Methods that use derivatives

9. The 'derivative methods' essentially compute the Taylor's series. This is obtained first at x_0, the initial point, and is used to calculate the solution and its relevant derivatives at the next pivotal point $x_1 = x_0 + h$. This point is then taken as new origin, and the process repeated until the complete range is covered.

For the first-order equation (1), with a specified value of $y(x_0)$, the equation itself gives $y'(x_0)$, the second derivative is obtained by differentiating (1) in the form

$$y_0'' = \frac{\partial f_0}{\partial x} + y_0' \frac{\partial f_0}{\partial y}, \qquad y_r = y(x_r), \qquad f_r = f(x_r, y_r), \qquad (20)$$

and so on. We then compute

$$y_1 = y(x_0 + h) = y_0 + hy_0' + \frac{h^2}{2!}y_0'' + \cdots, \qquad (21)$$

and this is all that is required for the continuation of the process from the new origin $x_1 = x_0 + h$.

For the second-order equation (2), with specified y_0 and y_0', the second derivative is obtained directly from (2), higher derivatives by differentiation, and we compute both the function from (21) and the derivative from

$$y_1' = y_0' + hy_0'' + \frac{h^2}{2!}y_0''' + \cdots, \qquad (22)$$

which are the quantities needed for the continuation of the process from the point x_1.

10. These methods have certain obvious advantages. First, if we are prepared to compute enough derivatives we can avoid any truncation error. Second, we are not restricted to equal intervals, and we can change the interval easily and at will. There are disadvantages. For example, the computation of higher derivatives is not particularly easy in general. Sometimes we can find a recurrence relation (by methods similar to those of Exercise 1(vii) in Chapter 1), and at some future time we may be able to get the machine to perform automatic differentiation, at which stage a remark at the end of Chapter 9 is very relevant. Another drawback is that the Taylor's series may converge only slowly (as we remarked in Chapter 7 in connection with the computation of the Chebyshev series) and many terms might be needed in the series for the function and its derivative. In other words the method is less satisfactory whenever the function is not well-represented by a few terms of the Taylor's series, and this is specially inconvenient for 'simple' functions like e^{-kx}, for moderate-sized positive k, whose Taylor's series is alternating in sign, converging slowly, and suffering from cancellation of positive and negative terms.

Methods that use finite differences

11. Finite-difference methods also attempt to avoid truncation error, and their basis is similar to that of processes for numerical integration discussed in Chapter 9. In the latter problem, of course, the table of pivotal values can be recorded immediately, whereas in our present problem we are building up the table as part of the computation. When we have reached the point x_r we have only backward differences of y_r, and the central differences become available only at some later stage. At the beginning of the computation we have no differences at all, so that we must start by calculating several early values by the Taylor's-series methods of §§ 9 and 10.

Suppose that this has been done, and that we have enough entries to indicate that the differences are convergent and that we can ignore differences beyond a certain order. For the first-order case (1) we can then proceed from x_r to x_{r+1} by using the integration formula

$$y_{r+1} = y_r + (1 + \tfrac{1}{2}\nabla + \tfrac{5}{12}\nabla^2 + \tfrac{3}{8}\nabla^3 + \ldots)hy_r', \qquad (23)$$

which involves only quantities which we have already computed. We have observed in Chapters 8 and 9, however, that 'sloping-difference' formulae can give rise to a rather large rounding error. In (23), for example, if the computed hy_r' have possible rounding errors of half a unit, the quantity given explicitly in brackets can have an error of as much as $3\tfrac{1}{2}$ units, and the combined propagated effect of these errors could be quite large.

A somewhat better formula than (23), with a smaller rounding error, is

$$y_{r+1} = y_r + (1 - \tfrac{1}{2}\nabla - \tfrac{1}{12}\nabla^2 - \tfrac{1}{24}\nabla^3 - \ldots)hy'_{r+1}, \qquad (24)$$

though for its use we need a knowledge of y'_{r+1}. This is effectively obtained by an iterative process for the solution of the generally non-linear equation

$$y_{r+1} = y_r + (1 - \tfrac{1}{2}\nabla - \tfrac{1}{12}\nabla^2 - \tfrac{1}{24}\nabla^3 - \ldots)hf_{r+1}, \qquad (25)$$

and the first step of the iteration uses the approximation obtained from (23) and the corresponding value of $y'_{r+1} = f_{r+1}$ obtained from the differential equation. The rounding error from the terms given explicitly in the less 'lopsided' formula (25) is less than one unit of hy'_r. Equation (23), the *predictor*, and (24), the *corrector*, are the basic equations of the Adams–Bashforth method.

For the second-order system (2) we record both hy'_r and $h^2y''_r$ and their differences. At the stage in which we have computed y_r, hy'_r, and $h^2y''_r$, we use first the formula

$$hy'_{r+1} = hy'_r + (1 + \tfrac{1}{2}\nabla + \tfrac{5}{12}\nabla^2 + \tfrac{3}{8}\nabla^3 + \ldots)h^2y''_r, \qquad (26)$$

which is the predictor for hy'_{r+1}. We can now use the 'corrector' (24) to obtain y_{r+1}, and we can then compute $h^2y''_{r+1}$ from the differential equation. At this stage we can iterate with the correctors, first for hy'_{r+1}, and then for y_{r+1}.

12. These processes have all the advantages of finite-difference methods. We can check that a satisfactory interval is being used, so that the functions behave locally like polynomials; we know how many differences must be used in the finite-difference expressions; we are avoiding truncation error; and we are keeping reasonably small the rounding errors involved. We would, of course, prefer to use throughout central-difference integration formulae, since these give less rounding error and more certainty about the polynomial-type behaviour in the neighbourhood of the current argument x_r at which we are applying the formulae. Such methods do exist and have been used extensively (see, for example, *Modern computing methods*, 1961, and *Interpolation and allied tables*, 1956), and may well be resurrected when the necessary advances have been made in the machine hardware and software. At present the extra necessity for extrapolation and subsequent correction, over and above the need for automatic differencing and examination of the differences, makes their automatic use rather prohibitive.

Lagrangian methods

(i) *Truncated Taylor's series.   Runge–Kutta methods*

13. Various types of Lagrangian methods are obtained effectively by truncating the formulae corresponding to the 'exact' methods of §§ 9–12. First we consider two forms of the truncated Taylor's-series method, observing that for practical purposes we prefer *not* to have to differentiate the differential equation in order to compute the required derivatives.

For the first-order system direct truncation of the Taylor's-series method, with the object of avoiding differentiation, can lead only to the so-called Euler method, with general formula

$$y_{r+1} = y_r + hy'_r, \tag{27}$$

for proceeding from x_r to x_{r+1}. For the second-order case we could use

$$y_{r+1} = y_r + hy'_r + \frac{h^2}{2!}y''_r \tag{28}$$

for the function, and

$$y'_{r+1} = y'_r + hy''_r \tag{29}$$

for the derivative, without having to perform any formal differentiation.

14. The truncation errors in (27)–(29) can be large except for prohibitively small intervals, and we would prefer some formulae which, while avoiding differentiations, have smaller truncation errors. Such formulae are provided by the various Runge–Kutta methods, which for the first-order system (1) effectively approximate to the derivatives of y_r by evaluating certain combinations of values of $y' = f(x, y)$ at certain points in the range x_r to x_{r+1}. There are formulae of orders one (the Euler case) and higher, each of which effectively gives local results equivalent to those obtained by truncating the Taylor's series after the terms in h, h^2, h^3, and h^4 (though the truncation error is not just that of the Taylor's series).

The most convenient Runge–Kutta method is a fourth-order method, which for the first-order equation (1) proceeds from x_r to x_{r+1} via the computation

$$\left.\begin{aligned}
k_1 &= hf(x_r, y_r) \\
k_2 &= hf(x_r + \tfrac{1}{2}h,\ y_r + \tfrac{1}{2}k_1) \\
k_3 &= hf(x_r + \tfrac{1}{2}h,\ y_r + \tfrac{1}{2}k_2) \\
k_4 &= hf(x_r + h,\ y_r + k_3) \\
y_{r+1} &= y_r + \tfrac{1}{6}(k_1 + 2k_2 + 2k_3 + k_4)
\end{aligned}\right\} \tag{30}$$

For the second-order equation (2), with specified y, y' at x_0, we conveniently treat the problem as two simultaneous first-order systems, given by

$$\left.\begin{aligned} y' &= z \\ z' &= f(x, y, z) \end{aligned}\right\}, \tag{31}$$

with specified values of y_0 and z_0. These are special forms of the more general set of two simultaneous first-order equations

$$\left.\begin{aligned} y' &= f_1(x, y, z) \\ z' &= f_2(x, y, z) \end{aligned}\right\}, \tag{32}$$

for which the equations corresponding to (30) are given by

$$\left.\begin{aligned} k_1 &= hf_1(x_r, y_r, z_r) \\ m_1 &= hf_2(x_r, y_r, z_r) \\ k_2 &= hf_1(x_r+\tfrac{1}{2}h, \, y_r+\tfrac{1}{2}k_1, \, z_r+\tfrac{1}{2}m_1) \\ m_2 &= hf_2(x_r+\tfrac{1}{2}h, \, y_r+\tfrac{1}{2}k_1, \, z_r+\tfrac{1}{2}m_1) \\ k_3 &= hf_1(x_r+\tfrac{1}{2}h, \, y_r+\tfrac{1}{2}k_2, \, z_r+\tfrac{1}{2}m_2) \\ m_3 &= hf_2(x_r+\tfrac{1}{2}h, \, y_r+\tfrac{1}{2}k_2, \, z_r+\tfrac{1}{2}m_2) \\ k_4 &= hf_1(x_r+h, \, y_r+k_3, \, z_r+m_3) \\ m_4 &= hf_2(x_r+h, \, y_r+k_3, \, z_r+m_3) \\ y_{r+1} &= y_r+\tfrac{1}{6}(k_1+2k_2+2k_3+k_4) \\ z_{r+1} &= z_r+\tfrac{1}{6}(m_1+2m_2+2m_3+m_4) \end{aligned}\right\}. \tag{33}$$

The Runge–Kutta methods therefore achieve some of our aims without losing the advantages of easy starting and easy adjustment of interval of the original Taylor's-series method. Their disadvantages we discuss in §§ 19 and 31 below.

(ii) *Truncated finite-difference methods. Special and general predictor-corrector methods*

15. In a somewhat similar but more obvious way we can obtain, from the finite-difference processes of § 11, Lagrangian methods of different orders by deliberately truncating the series of differences in (23) and (24) and expressing the results in Lagrangian form. For example, we can find from (23) the various 'predictor formulae'

$$\left.\begin{aligned} y_{r+1}-y_r &= hy_r' \\ y_{r+1}-y_r &= \tfrac{1}{2}h(3y_r'-y_{r-1}') \\ y_{r+1}-y_r &= \tfrac{1}{12}h(23y_r'-16y_{r-1}'+5y_{r-2}') \end{aligned}\right\}, \tag{34}$$

and from (24) the corresponding corrector formulae

$$\left.\begin{aligned} y_{r+1}-y_r &= \tfrac{1}{2}h(y'_{r+1}+y'_r) \\ y_{r+1}-y_r &= \tfrac{1}{12}h(5y'_{r+1}+8y'_r-y'_{r-1}) \\ y_{r+1}-y_r &= \tfrac{1}{24}h(9y'_{r+1}+19y'_r-5y'_{r-1}+y'_{r-2}) \end{aligned}\right\}, \quad (35)$$

where everywhere y' is related to y through the differential equation.

These formulae have the usual advantages that no difference tables are formed, and the usual Lagrangian disadvantages that we have no immediate knowledge about what intervals to use and what order of formulae are appropriate.

16. We might call these the 'special' predictor-corrector methods. The 'corrector' of course, is the more important formula, being the one wo actually satisfy, and the correctors (35) are just various formulae for integrating between adjacent pivotal points. The first of (35), for example, is evidently the trapezium rule without correction.

Another special 'corrector' is the unrefined Simpson rule, which gives

$$y_{r+1}-y_{r-1} = \tfrac{1}{3}h(y'_{r+1}+4y'_r+y'_{r-1}), \quad (36)$$

and with this we might use the predictor

$$y_{r+1}-y_{r-3} = \tfrac{4}{3}h(2y'_r-y'_{r-1}+2y'_{r-2}), \quad (37)$$

to produce the predictor-corrector method of Milne. The apparent advantage of (36), compared with the first of (35), as the equation we actually solve in proceeding from x_r to x_{r+1}, is that the local truncation error is smaller. Its truncation error, in fact, is of the same order as that of the last of (35), whereas it involves less arithmetic and has a smaller rounding error (noting that (36) covers *two* steps).

17. Now if we stop (24) after the term in $\nabla^{n-1}y'_{r+1}$ the local truncation error is a multiple of $h^{n+1}y^{(n+1)}(\xi)$, and the formula looks like

$$y_{r+1}-y_r = h(\beta_0 y'_{r+1}+\beta_1 y'_r+\dots+\beta_{n-1}y'_{r-n+2}), \quad (38)$$

where the n constants β_s have known values. Alternatively, in some analogy with the production of Newton–Cotes quadrature formulae, we might ask for what maximum degree of polynomial $y(x) = p_q(x)$ we can satisfy (38) exactly. Since there are n constants to find the maximum degree is clearly $q = n$. In some analogy with the production of Gauss-type quadrature formulae we might take instead of (38) the more general form

$$y_{r+1}+\alpha_1 y_r+\alpha_2 y_{r-1}+\ldots+\alpha_{n-1} y_{r-n+2} = h(\beta_0 y'_{r+1}+\ldots+$$
$$+\beta_{n-1} y'_{r-n+2}), \quad (39)$$

which has $2n-1$ constants but involves no more pivotal points. By suitable choices of the constants we could obviously obtain a much smaller truncation error of order h^{2n-1}, making (39) exact for a polynomial of degree $q = 2n-2$. For example, we could find

$$11y_{r+1}+27y_r-27y_{r-1}-11y_{r-2} = 3h(y'_{r+1}+9y'_r+9y'_{r-1}+y'_{r-2}), \quad (40)$$

which has seven independent constants and is exact if $y(x)$ is a polynomial of degree six or less.

One could use (40) as the general formula for proceeding from x_r to x_{r+1}, solving it by iteration with or without the assistance of a special predictor. We shall show later, however, that *such methods must be used with extreme care. They can suffer from catastrophic induced instability*, and there is always a conflict between the achievement of stable methods and the desire for small local truncation errors.

Treatment of the truncation error

18. We have remarked that only the Lagrangian methods have local truncation error, and of course the accumulation and propagation of the local errors may give a significant difference, after some steps, between the computed solution and the true solution of the differential system. There are various ways of dealing with this situation, many of them analogous to the corresponding problem for numerical quadrature. Standard methods include:

(i) guessing an interval, using simple formulae, and hoping that 'everything will be alright';

(ii) adjusting the interval, systematically and mechanically, so that the local truncation error is negligible;

(iii) taking subsequent account of the errors by a process of 'deferred correction', using the same intervals as those of the first approximation;

(iv) obtaining complete solutions at different intervals, examining for consistency, and perhaps improving convergence by a 'deferred approach to the limit' idea.

We reject method (i), and examine briefly the nature, advantages and disadvantages of the other three methods.

(i) *Local treatment*

19. In method (ii) of § 18 we effectively estimate the local truncation error. For the fourth-order Runge–Kutta method the truncation error is the factor h^5 multiplying a rather complicated expression involving derivatives of $f(x, y)$. Formulae have been produced, however, which with a little extra computation give an approximation to the required estimate if the functions involved are sufficiently smooth. Merson (1957) computes the quantities

$$\left.\begin{aligned}
k_1 &= hf(x_r, y_r)\\
k_2 &= hf(x_r + \tfrac{1}{3}h, y_r + \tfrac{1}{3}k_1)\\
k_3 &= hf(x_r + \tfrac{1}{3}h, y_r + \tfrac{1}{6}k_1 + \tfrac{1}{6}k_2)\\
k_4 &= hf(x_r + \tfrac{1}{2}h, y_r + \tfrac{1}{8}k_1 + \tfrac{3}{8}k_3)\\
k_5 &= hf(x_r + h, y_r + \tfrac{1}{2}k_1 - \tfrac{3}{2}k_3 + 2k_4)
\end{aligned}\right\}, \tag{41}$$

involving one more 'substitution' in the differential equation, and shows that the error in the accepted value,

$$y_{r+1} = y_r + \tfrac{1}{6}k_1 + \tfrac{2}{3}k_4 + \tfrac{1}{6}k_5, \tag{42}$$

is not very different from

$$e_{r+1} = \tfrac{1}{15}k_1 - \tfrac{3}{10}k_3 + \tfrac{4}{15}k_4 - \tfrac{1}{30}k_5. \tag{43}$$

This quantity clearly depends on h, and the interval is made sufficiently small so that the local error is negligible. Though the method performs satisfactorily in many cases its assumptions can neither be checked nor guaranteed to hold in general, and the reader is advised to watch the literature for more and better developments of this kind.

20. In a rather similar way the difference between the predicted and corrected values, in the methods of § 15 et seq., will give an indication of the local error in these processes whenever the truncation errors in both formulae have the same order, with different constants. For example, in Milne's method of equations (36) and (37) we can write

$$\left.\begin{aligned}
y_{r+1}^{(p)} &= y_{r-3} + \tfrac{4}{3}h(2y_r' - y_{r-1}' + 2y_{r-2}') + \tfrac{14}{45}h^5 y^{(v)}(\xi_1)\\
y_{r+1}^{(c)} &= y_{r-1} + \tfrac{1}{3}h(y_{r+1}' + 4y_r' + y_{r-1}') - \tfrac{1}{90}h^5 y^{(v)}(\xi_2)
\end{aligned}\right\}, \tag{44}$$

where ξ_1 and ξ_2 are unknown points in the relevant ranges, and the superscripts p and c denote predictor and corrector. The difference between the *computed* values is about $\tfrac{29}{90}h^5 y^{(v)}(\xi)$, provided that the fifth derivative is sensibly constant in the relevant range, so that the error in the corrected value is about $\frac{1}{29}$ of this difference. Again we can select the interval so that this is negligible, though frequent interval changes are rather uneconomic in methods based on equal intervals. One might even 'correct' the corrector, rather similarly to the 'deferred approach to the limit' process. More details of such methods are given in Fox (1962) and the works quoted in the bibliography of that book. Here we are more interested in general principles and we suppress the details.

(ii) *Global treatment. Deferred correction and other Lagrangian methods*

21. Though the local treatment of §§ 19–20 usually gives respectable results, and is certainly superior to the 'guessing' methods, we are on firmer ground with the methods of 'deferred correction', which seek to improve an approximate solution, obtained by some Lagrangian method at a particular interval h, by performing the solution of a slightly perturbed problem at the same interval. This is precisely in the spirit of 'backward error' analysis, except that we compute the perturbations accurately insteady of assessing their upper bounds.

Suppose, for example, that we have obtained an approximate solution to the differential equation $y' = f(x, y)$, with $y(x_0)$ given, and that this solution is represented by a table of values $Y(x_r)$ at arguments $x_r = x_0 + rh$. The Lagrangian method we have used, moreover, we assume to be good enough to produce a smooth table, in the sense that the differences of Y_r converge at this interval h, and that the solution is not 'contaminated' by functions like $\sin(r\pi/h)$.

We can then compute $f(x_r, Y_r)$ at each pivotal point, and carry out an *accurate* process of numerical integration to find $\int_{x_0}^{x_r} f(x, Y)\, \mathrm{d}x$. If this is equal to $Y_r - y_0$ we have the correct solution of the differential system. Otherwise we can see that our computed Y is the exact solution of the system

$$Y_r = y(x_0) + \int_{x_0}^{x_r} f(x, Y) + C(x_r), \tag{45}$$

where $C(x_r)$ has been computed. The error $e_r = Y_r - y_r$ then satisfies the system

$$e_r = \int_{x_0}^{x_r} \{f(x, Y) - f(x, y)\}\, \mathrm{d}x + C(x_r). \tag{46}$$

If $f(x, y)$ is linear in y, say of the form $g(x)+yk(x)$, then (46) becomes

$$e_r = \int_{x_0}^{x_r} k(x)e(x) \, \mathrm{d}x + C(x_r), \tag{47}$$

and we can solve this by precisely the same method as we used to obtain Y_r, thereby producing a better solution $y_r = Y_r - e_r$. The iteration can be repeated as often as necessary.

For a non-linear function $f(x, y)$, we must 'linearize' the correcting equation, assuming that e_r^2 is negligible, and find

$$e_r = \int_{x_0}^{x_r} e \frac{\partial f}{\partial y}(x, Y) \, \mathrm{d}x + C(x_r), \tag{48}$$

which again we can solve by our standard method.

The advantages of this global process are that the truncation corrections $C(x_r)$ can be computed with the use of central differences, which now exist except possibly near the ends of the range, and that we can use a large interval with confidence, subject only to the convergence of the differences.

22. Now the Lagrangian methods so far discussed, which are based on finite differences, have all involved formulae for numerical integration. Our correcting process then requires the differences of Y'_r for the first-order problem, and of both Y'_r and Y''_r for the second-order problem. This difficulty can be avoided if we use finite-difference expressions for derivatives rather than for integrals, so that we express the local truncation error in terms of differences of the solution rather than of its derivatives.

This gives rise to a set of Lagrangian methods which are valuable in their own right, even if we do not propose to make a global correction. For the second-order problem (2), for example, we have the 'correct' difference formula

$$h^{-2}(\delta^2 - \tfrac{1}{12}\delta^4 + \tfrac{1}{90}\delta^6 - \ldots)y_r = f\{x, y_r, h^{-1}(\mu\delta - \tfrac{1}{6}\mu\delta^3 + \ldots)y_r\}. \tag{49}$$

If we suppress all but the first term of the difference expressions we can then write

$$Y_{r+1} - 2Y_r + Y_{r-1} = h^2 f\left\{x, Y_r, \frac{1}{2h}(Y_{r+1} - Y_{r-1})\right\}, \tag{50}$$

as the required simple Lagrangian formula for proceeding from point x_r to point x_{r+1}. It is, of course, a non-linear equation for Y_{r+1}, but is not particularly different in this respect from the 'corrector' formula of previous methods. It can be solved by iteration, and a knowledge of the differences of Y_r, at previous points, will serve to 'predict' a good starting value.

If the first derivative is not present in the equation, a fairly common case, the equation corresponding to (50) does not contain Y_{r+1} on the right, and we have an explicit formula for the evaluation of Y_{r+1}. But in this case we can record a more powerful implicit formula than (49), given by

$$h^{-2}(\delta^2 + \tfrac{1}{240}\delta^6 + \ldots)y_r = \tfrac{1}{12}(f_{r-1} + 10f_r + f_{r+1}), \tag{51}$$

so that, instead of (50), we have the Lagrangian formula

$$Y_{r+1} - 2Y_r + Y_{r-1} = \tfrac{1}{12}h^2\{f(x_{r-1}, Y_{r-1}) + 10f(x_r, Y_r) +$$
$$+ f(x_{r+1}, Y_{r+1})\}, \tag{52}$$

involving no more points than (50) but with a much smaller truncation error. This, incidentally, is undoubtedly the best method of solving the particular equation

$$y'' = f(x, y), \tag{53}$$

with any kinds of associated conditions.

23. Corresponding to (49) and (50) the deferred correction process effectively has the following basis. We are trying to solve

$$y_{r+1} - 2y_r + y_{r-1} + C_1(y_r) = h^2 f\left\{x_r, y_r, \frac{1}{2h}(y_{r+1} - y_{r-1}) + C_2(y_r)\right\},$$
$$C_1 = -\tfrac{1}{12}\delta^4 + \tfrac{1}{90}\delta^6 \ldots, \ C_2 = h^{-1}\{-\tfrac{1}{6}\mu\delta^3 + \tfrac{1}{30}\mu\delta^5 - \ldots\} \tag{54}$$

and for this purpose we are using the iterative scheme

$$y_{r+1}^{(n+1)} - 2y_r^{(n+1)} + y_{r-1}^{(n+1)} + C_1(y_r^{(n)})$$
$$= h^2 f\left\{x_r, y_r^{(n+1)}, \frac{1}{2h}(y_{r+1}^{(n+1)} - y_{r-1}^{(n+1)}) + C_2(y_r^{(n)})\right\}, \tag{55}$$

where $y_r^{(0)} = Y_r$ in (50), and $C_1 y_r^{(-1)} = C_2 y_r^{(-1)} \equiv 0$.

Alternatively, we can substitute our first approximation $Y_r(x)$ into the differential equation, compute its derivatives accurately by finite differences, and show that $Y_r(x)$ satisfies exactly the equation

$$Y'' = f(x, Y, Y') + C(x), \tag{56}$$

everything being evaluated at pivotal points x_r. Then at these points the function $e(x) = Y(x) - y(x)$ satisfies approximately the linearized equation

$$e'' = e\frac{\partial f}{\partial Y} + e'\frac{\partial f}{\partial Y'} + C(x), \tag{57}$$

which we can solve by our simple Lagrangian method to obtain a better approximation to $y(x)$ at the pivotal points.

24. With this type of method, we repeat, we can use a relatively large interval, take full subsequent account of the truncation errors, and *know* that we have achieved this. Compared with most of our previous methods we do not need any significant special starting procedure, except that in the second-order case we need y_1 as well as y_0. The initial conditions normally specify y_0 and y_0' (which of course is just right for the Runge–Kutta method). For various reasons (see § 27) it is here desirable *not* to use the Taylor's series to obtain y_1, but to use a finite-difference approximation such as

$$y_0' = \frac{1}{h}(\mu\delta y_0 - \tfrac{1}{6}\mu\delta^3 y_0 + \dots) = \frac{1}{2h}(y_1 - y_{-1}) + C_3(y_0),\qquad(58)$$

in its simple Lagrangian form

$$Y_0' = \frac{1}{2h}(Y_1 - Y_{-1}).\qquad(59)$$

With the use of the differential equation at the point x_0 and with $C_3(Y_0)$ ignored in the first solution, this will enable us to start, and $C_3(Y_0)$ is later incorporated as an additional term in the first step of the correcting process. We notice, as a computational point, that we can extend the solution Y backwards from x_0, and forwards beyond x_n, in order to compute the central differences involved in the correcting terms C_1, C_2, and C_3 even near the ends of the range.

25. For the first-order case the central-difference formula for the first derivative would give the approximate Lagrangian equation

$$Y_{r+1} - Y_{r-1} = 2hf(x_r, Y_r),\qquad(60)$$

and for reasons which we shall mention later (see § 38) this is not a particularly attractive formula. We can, and should, use the trapezium-rule 'corrector' written in the form

$$\left.\begin{aligned}y_{r+1} - y_r &= \tfrac{1}{2}h(f_{r+1} + f_r) + C(y_r)\\ C &= -\tfrac{1}{12}\delta^3_{r+\frac{1}{2}} + \tfrac{1}{120}\delta^5_{r+\frac{1}{2}} - \dots\end{aligned}\right\},\qquad(61)$$

in which the truncation correction is again expressed in terms of differences of the function. The method, and its deferred correction, needs no further description.

(iii) *Different intervals and the deferred approach to the limit*

26. Finally, we have the possibility, as in the corresponding problem of numerical quadrature, of solving the problem with the same method but with successively smaller intervals, and observing the convergence of the computed values at the common pivotal points of the successive solutions. Since here we have a *vector* of numbers to inspect, the possibility of consistent inaccuracy is less likely than in the quadrature formula.

We may also accelerate the convergence by a Romberg-type process, though this has to be used with considerable care. The general idea is that if $Y(x, h)$ is the computed solution at interval h at a particular point x, then

$$y(x) - Y(x, h) = g(h), \tag{62}$$

where $g(h)$ is a function of h. If we can find its form, for example in a series like

$$g(h) = Ah^2 + Bh^4 + ..., \tag{63}$$

then an obvious Romberg-type method can be used to accelerate the convergence of our interval-reduced sequence of results, at least for the common pivotal points.

The general 'rule of thumb' is as follows. If the Lagrangian formula we actually solve has a *local* truncation error of order h^p, then for a first-order equation the dominant term in (62) is Ah^{p-1}, and for a second-order equation it is Ah^{p-2}. If p is large, for example $p = 5$ in the fourth-order Runge–Kutta method for a first-order equation, then the dominant term in the error, here Ah^4, is so small that we hardly need consider higher-order terms. Computation with intervals h, $\frac{1}{2}h$, and $\frac{1}{4}h$, with extrapolation from the first and second pairs, will usually give correct information at least about the number of figures worth quoting in the results. If the dominant term in $g(h)$ in (62) is of order h^q, we refer to this process as 'h^q-extrapolation.'

Rules of thumb, of course, are notoriously unreliable, and these statements have been proved, and can therefore be guaranteed, only for cases in which everything is very 'smooth'. This remark excludes any singularity either in the differential equation or in the solution of the problem.

27. For the Lagrangian methods of §§ 22–25, in which we use central-difference formulae for derivatives or integrals and retain only the dominant terms in the Lagrangian expressions, the error is somewhat larger, and we would like extra information about the nature of $g(h)$ in (62). It can be shown that if we use central-difference expressions for any derivative which appears, both in the differential equation *and the associated conditions* (see the remark preceding equation (58)), then $g(h)$ in (63) contains only even powers of h. For the method represented by equation (50), for example, we have

$$y_r - Y_r = Ah^2 + Bh^4 + Ch^6 + ..., \qquad (64)$$

and for (52), the recommended method for the second-order equation lacking its first derivative, we have

$$y_r - Y_r = Bh^4 + Ch^6 + ... \qquad (65)$$

For the method stemming from (61), the trapezium-rule method for a first-order equation, the error is also of the form (64).

We stress that these statements effectively require the use of central differences throughout. For example they are not true, for the second-order case with specified y_0 and y_0', if we compute y_1 accurately from the Taylor's series (explaining a remark in § 24 just previous to equation (58)), and they are not true if we replace (59), for the derivative condition, by something like

$$Y_0' = \frac{1}{2h}(-3Y_0 + 4Y_1 - Y_2). \qquad (66)$$

Lack of singularity both in differential equation and in the solution specified by the associated conditions is also necessary, and in this respect Mayers (1964) gives the following interesting results.

28. The function $y = \frac{1}{4}x^2 \ln x$ satisfies the boundary-value system

$$xy'' - y' - x = 0, \qquad y(0) = y(1) = 0, \qquad (67)$$

and Mayers showed that the dominant terms in the error of a Lagrangian method using equations corresponding to (50) are proportional to h^2 and $h^2 \ln h$. The same function also satisfies the equation

$$x^2 y'' - 2y - \frac{3}{2}x^2 = 0, \qquad y(0) = 0, \qquad y(1) = 0, \qquad (68)$$

and with the same method the dominant errors are multiples of h^2 and h^4.

In these cases both the equation and the solution have 'singularities'. A perhaps more interesting result of Mayers relates to the system

$$xy'' + y' = x^2, \qquad y(0) = 0, \qquad y(1) = \frac{1}{9}, \qquad (69)$$

whose solution is $y = \frac{1}{9}x^3$. Here the equation is singular, with a complementary solution $A \ln x$. The particular solution is perfectly well-behaved, and yet the dominant error terms are multiples of h^2 and $h^2/\ln h$.

15

More research is needed on the deferred approach to the limit, but these results show that its use is dangerous (giving rise to inaccurate consistency in all probability) without proper mathematical investigation. Though the situation is somewhat similar to that of the corresponding quadrature analysis of Chapter 9, it is in fact much more complicated. We hardly need add that none of our numerical methods have any hope of giving accurate results in the neighbourhood of a significant singularity of the *solution* of the differential system.

Induced instabilities

29. We come now to a more important question, of evaluating our methods with respect to possible *induced instabilities*. As we remarked in § 2 most of our methods, particularly the Lagrangian methods, reduce the differential system to an approximating algebraic system, giving rise to two types of possible induced instability. The first is in the solution of the algebraic system, which we have discussed in Chapters 3 and 5. The second is the extent to which the accurate algebraic solution differs from the differential solution. This is not just a question of the size of the local truncation error, since we shall show that induced instabilities can occur even when the local truncation error is effectively negligible.

Our algebraic system usually appears in the form of recurrence relations, whose properties we discussed in the linear case in Chapter 3. It is practicable and convenient to treat the induced instability problem also for *linear* differential systems, and we are therefore interested in differential equations like

$$y' = ay + b, \qquad y'' + ay' + by = c. \tag{70}$$

Their exact solutions, combinations of particular integrals and complementary functions, are given by

$$y = y_0(x) + A_1 y_1(x), \qquad y = y_0(x) + A_1 y_1(x) + A_2 y_2(x). \tag{71}$$

The exact solution of the corresponding algebraic problem is also composed of a particular solution and combinations of complementary solutions, the number of which depend on the order of the recurrence relation. In general we shall have a solution looking like

$$y_r = y_r^{(0)} + A_1 y_r^{(1)} + A_2 y_r^{(2)} + \ldots + A_s y_r^{(s)}, \tag{72}$$

and in the particular case in which the recurrence relation has constant coefficients we know that $y_r^{(s)} = p_s^r$, where p_s is a zero of a certain polynomial.

30. Some consequences are intuitively evident. First, for a differential system of first order we would in a sense be content with a recurrence system of first order, since then both differential and algebraic problems have just one complementary solution. Second, we should expect, if our method is good, that these two complementary solutions would be very similar, and at the very least have the same sort of general behaviour. Third, if our algebraic system has more than one complementary solution we must be concerned about the behaviour of these 'bogus' parasitic solutions. For the second-order system we have the obvious analogous problems.

There are then two possibilities of induced instability. First, even when the algebraic system has the same number of complementary solutions as the differential system, their behaviour may be different. Second, if the algebraic system has parasitic solutions their behaviour may 'swamp' the required solution. We proceed to discuss our methods from these two points of view.

(i) *Induced partial instability*

31. First we examine those methods which produce no parasitic solutions. The first of these is the truncated Taylor's series, and if we apply this to the first-order equation

$$y' = ay + b \tag{73}$$

it is easy to see that the algebraic problem has the single complementary solution given by

$$y_r = Ap^r, \qquad p = \left(1 + ah + \frac{a^2h^2}{2!} + \ldots + \frac{a^nh^n}{n!}\right), \tag{74}$$

in which we have truncated the Taylor's series after the nth derivative.

Now if a is positive (and of course we are taking h to be positive), then $p > 1$ for any h, and the behaviour of the algebraic solution is exponentially increasing, like that of the differential equation. In this respect the method is stable. If a is negative, on the other hand, the true complementary solution is exponentially decreasing, and hence for the algebraic problem we need $|p| < 1$. Evidently $p \sim e^{ah} < 1$ for sufficiently small h, while $|p| \to \infty$ as $h \to \infty$. Hence there is a critical value of $|ah|$ above which $|p| > 1$. For Euler's method of § 13, for example, we have $n = 1$, and $|ah| < 2$ for $|p| < 1$. For the Runge–Kutta fourth-order method, with $n = 4$, we find $|ah| < 2 \cdot 7$ approximately.

For solutions of decreasing exponential type, therefore, the truncated Taylor's series methods, including the Runge–Kutta variety, exhibit what we call *partial* induced instability, being stable only for a restricted size of interval h. The critical size is rather large, and it might be thought that we could never want to use such an interval. But there is a significant class of problems, with so-called 'stiff' equations, with solutions typified by

$$y = \mathrm{e}^{-x} + A\mathrm{e}^{-50x}. \tag{75}$$

For any A the second term ceases to contribute for reasonably-sized x, and at this stage we would expect to be able to use a larger interval, one for which e^{-x} alone can be approximated locally by a polynomial. The fact that e^{-50x} is a complementary solution, however, means that we have to use the restricted interval $h < 2 \cdot 7/50$ with the Runge–Kutta method throughout the whole computation. Even if A is forced to be zero by the initial condition this restricted interval is needed for stability, a rather prohibitive condition.

32. The second-order equation with constant coefficients, treated as two first-order equations, is a member of the class of problems defined by

$$\mathbf{y}' = \mathbf{A}\mathbf{y}, \qquad \mathbf{y}(0) \quad \text{given}, \tag{76}$$

where $\mathbf{y}$ is a vector and $\mathbf{A}$ a matrix. If $\mathbf{A}$ has any real negative eigen-values $-\lambda_r$, then the partial instability requirement requires that

$$h < 2 \cdot 7/\max |\lambda_r|, \tag{77}$$

which again can be prohibitively small in a region in which these rapidly-decreasing complementary solutions have ceased to contribute to the working precision. The difficulty is not restricted to real roots. If $\mathbf{A}$ has an eigen value $-\lambda_r + i\mu_r$, where λ_r is large and positive, the complementary differential solution oscillates with rapidly-decreasing amplitude, whereas the corresponding algebraic solution will oscillate with increasing amplitude for intervals greater than some critical size. These results indicate the necessity for mathematical and computational care, recommended for this type of problem in § 4 of our first chapter.

33. It is important to note that the Runge–Kutta and allied processes are *explicit*, in that the value of y_{r+1}, in both the linear and non-linear cases, is computed directly from information derived only from the point x_r. Implicit methods, we find, suffer less from partial instability. In particular the trapezium-rule method defined in the first of (35) is in general implicit, though for our equation (73) we can compute y_{r+1}

directly and find that the complementary solution has the form

$$y_r = Ap^r, \qquad p = (1+\tfrac{1}{2}ah)/(1-\tfrac{1}{2}ah). \qquad (78)$$

For $a > 0$ this is an exponentially-increasing function, and for $a < 0$ it is exponentially decreasing for any value of h. Although p may not be a good approximation to $e^{-|ah|}$ for large $|ah|$, it is at least <1 in absolute value, and for the problems of the last section the trapezium-rule method, with no induced instability, can be used with confidence at any interval at which the true solution is well-represented by a polynomial.

34. Turning to the second-order case solved by our special Lagrangian methods of § 22, consider the equation

$$y'' + k^2 y = g(x), \qquad (79)$$

with complementary solutions $\sin kx$ and $\cos kx$. The method of equation (50) gives rise to the recurrence relation

$$Y_{r+1} - (2 - h^2 k^2) Y_r + Y_{r-1} = h^2 g_r, \qquad (80)$$

whose complementary solutions are

$$Y_r^{(1)}, \; Y_r^{(2)} = p_1^r, \, p_2^r; \qquad p^2 - (2 - h^2 k^2)p + 1 = 0. \qquad (81)$$

It is not difficult to see that p_2 is negative, with $|p_2| > 1$, if $|hk| > 2$, so that again we have here an induced partial instability.

We leave it as an exercise to show that, for the more accurate method of equation (52), which also has no parasitic solutions, the corresponding critical interval is $|hk| = \sqrt{6}$.

35. We turn now to an analysis of the methods (the so-called multi-step methods) which introduce parasitic solutions. The general recurrence relation for a first-order system is of the form of equation (39), the general 'corrector'. The predictor, of course, plays no part if we iterate in the corrector until we have solved it accurately. We find two main cases. In the first, the parasitic solutions enter because more β-coefficients other than β_0 and β_1 are non-zero, whereas $\alpha_2, \alpha_3, \ldots$ are zero in (39). In the second, more of the α-coefficients are non-zero.

The first case is exemplified by the Adams–Bashforth corrector (24) expressed in Lagrangian form (35). The first of (35), which is just the trapezium-rule method discussed in § 33, has no induced instability for any h, and the others exhibit only partial instability, with certain critical values of h. It has in fact been proved that this is true of all methods for first-order equations, that nothing worse than partial induced instability is associated with any method whose parasitic solutions are introduced only on the right of an equation like (39), the point being effectively that this parasitic introduction disappears as $h \to 0$.

(ii) *Induced strong and weak instabilities*

36. The second case, of parasitic solutions introduced via the left-hand side of (39), not associated with the factor h, is far more serious, and can give more catastrophic forms of induced instability. Consider for example the formula (40), which has a very small local truncation error, and its application to equation (73). The complementary solutions of the recurrence relation depend on the roots of the cubic equation

$$(11-3ha)p^3+(27-27ha)p^2-(27+27ha)p-(11+3ha) = 0. \quad (82)$$

For $h = 0$ the zeros are 1, $-3 \cdot 1...$, $-0 \cdot 32...$, and for small ha Newton's process gives the results

$$1+ha, \quad -3 \cdot 1+0 \cdot 7ha, \quad -0 \cdot 32+0 \cdot 1ha, \quad (83)$$

for the zeros of (82) to the first order in h. For all ha there is one root of modulus greater than $1 \cdot 5$.

The first of (83) corresponds to the single true complementary solution of the differential equation, and the others are parasitic solutions. We see that at least one parasitic solution will make its presence felt for all values of ha, that the situation gets worse as $h \to 0$, and that the induced instability is manifest for any type of solution. This is called *strong induced instability*, and of course methods exhibiting this property should certainly not be used.

37. There is a general theory (Dahlquist 1956, 1959) whose main points are as follows.

(i) In an equation like (82), for stability all the roots p for $h = 0$ must satisfy $|p| \leqslant 1$. (There is, of course, always one root $p = 1$.)

(ii) This is impossible if, in the notation of § 17, $q > n+1$ for odd n, and $q > n$ for even n, where h^{q+1} is the order of the local truncation error of (39).

(iii) If $q = n+1$ for odd n, then there is a form of induced instability, *weak* instability, which will occur *for any h* and which is dangerous for *some* problems.

An example of (iii) is the use of the corrector in the Milne method, given by equation (36). Here $n = 3$ and $q = 4$. If we apply (36) to our standard equation (73) we find that the complementary solutions depend on the roots of the quadratic equation

$$(1 - \tfrac{1}{3}ah)p^2 - \tfrac{4}{3}ahp - (1 + \tfrac{1}{3}ah) = 0. \tag{84}$$

The zeros are approximately

$$p_1 \sim e^{ah}, \qquad p_2 \sim -e^{-\tfrac{1}{3}ah}, \tag{85}$$

the first of which corresponds to the differential solution and the second of which is parasitic. If $a > 0$, so that the true solution is exponentially increasing, we are not worried by the parasitic solution, but if $a < 0$ the parasite is dominant and we have instability for any value of h, however small. Milne's method is therefore satisfactory, or at least needs no special care and attention, only when the solution is exponentially increasing.

38. The strong and weak induced instabilities are also manifest in the special Lagrangian methods of the type of §§ 22–26. Consider, for example, the use of an equation like (49) in which we incorporate one more than the dominant term in the difference expressions, with a view to improving the order of the local truncation error. Applied to equation (79) this would give, for the complementary functions, the solutions of

$$(\delta^2 y_r - \tfrac{1}{12}\delta^4 y_r) + h^2 k^2 y_r = 0 = -\tfrac{1}{12}y_{r+2} + \tfrac{4}{3}y_{r+1} - (\tfrac{5}{2} - h^2 k^2)y_r +$$
$$+ \tfrac{4}{3}y_{r-1} - \tfrac{1}{12}y_{r-2}. \tag{86}$$

To the first order in $h^2 k^2$ the four zeros of the relevant quartic equation are the zero of the quadratics

$$p^2 - (2 - h^2 k^2)p + 1 = 0, \qquad p^2 - (14 + h^2 k^2)p + 1 = 0. \tag{87}$$

The first effectively contains the true solutions, and the second is parasitic. One root of the second of (87) is clearly considerably greater than unity for any $h^2 k^2$, and we have a case of strong induced instability. In this respect it is interesting to note that the special method given by equation (52), which succeeds in reducing the truncation error, has managed to do this without introducing parasitic solutions.

Finally, and to explain the remark following equation (60), we see that the use of the *mean* first-difference for the first-order equation, giving rise to equation (60) and to the recurrence

$$y_{r+1} - 2ahy_r - y_{r-1} = 0, \tag{88}$$

for the complementary solution of our standard first-order equation (73), has introduced a parasitic solution. The situation is clearly similar to that of Milne's method, and the roots of the relevant quadratic are

$$p_1 = e^{\theta}, \qquad p_2 = e^{-\theta}, \qquad ah = \sinh \theta. \tag{89}$$

The first of these corresponds to the true solution, and the second is parasitic. The parasite is no worry if θ and therefore ah are positive, but otherwise the parasite dominates at any interval and we again have *weak* induced instability.

(iii) *The non-linear case*

39. Our discussion of instability has concentrated on the case of linear differential systems with constant coefficients. In the linear case with variable coefficients, and in the non-linear case, we must be content with examination of the local behaviour. For the linear first-order equation

$$y' = f(x)y + g(x), \tag{90}$$

for example, our discussion is essentially unchanged if we replace the constant a in (73) by the 'local constant' $f(x_r)$. Methods with strong instability will maintain that unfortunate quality, but partial and weak instability may be present in some regions of the argument x and not in others.

In the non-linear case we can do little better than assume local linear behaviour. For example, the general equation (1) can be approximated locally by

$$y' = f(x_r, y_r) + (x - x_r)\frac{\partial f_r}{\partial x} + (y - y_r)\frac{\partial f_r}{\partial y}, \tag{91}$$

and it follows that the important quantity governing stability is the local value of $\partial f/\partial y$.

40. The evaluation and use of the local quantities governing partial instability in particular does, of course, involve considerable labour, especially for a system of non-linear simultaneous first-order equations corresponding to the linear case of § 32. Here the elements of the relevant matrix **A** are certain partial derivatives, and the eigenvalues of A are different at different arguments x_r. We therefore call attention to the problem without suggesting its treatment, and we have to admit that there is considerable scope for research in the production of satisfactory computer programmes.

One interesting fact, however, is that the quantities governing partial instability also affect the convergence of the iterative treatment of the corrector formulae. For the second Adams-Bashforth corrector in (35), for example, we will normally solve for y_{r+1} by the iterative process

$$y_{r+1}^{(n+1)} - y_r = \tfrac{1}{12}h(5f_{r+1}^{(n)} + 8f_r - f_{r-1}), \tag{92}$$

in which the required y_{r+1} appears generally non-linearly in f_{r+1}. It is not difficult to show that convergence will occur if and only if $h\left|\dfrac{\partial f}{\partial y}\right| < 2\cdot 4$, at $y = y_{r+1}$. Partial instability may occur (depending of course on the nature of the true solution) if

$$h\left|\frac{\partial f}{\partial y}\right| > 6, \tag{93}$$

so that we have to reduce the interval, to secure the convergence of the corrector solved in this manner, *before* the onset of induced partial instability.

41. Factors such as this are taken into account in one of the most recent methods, that of Nordsieck (1962). This is a predictor-corrector method based on the Adams–Bashforth formulae, and has some safeguards against both truncation and induced-instability errors. For example, it examines the differences $\nabla^s y_r'$ to estimate the local truncation error, judges the possibility of partial instability by examining the convergence of the corrector, and adjusts the interval accordingly.

The method of (92), of course, may fail even when there is no induced instability, for example with the trapezium-rule process defined in the first of (35). Convergence occurs here only if

$$h\left|\frac{\partial f}{\partial y}\right| < 2 \quad \text{at} \quad y = y_{r+1}, \tag{94}$$

and this may be a serious restriction on the efficiency of the trapezium-rule method. We can avoid this trouble by solving the corrector formula by a method of effective guaranteed convergence, such as the Newton process described in Chapter 4. This, of course, certainly requires the computation of $\partial f/\partial y$.

II. Boundary-value and eigenvalue problems

Linear problems

42. Discussion of the boundary-value problem can be relatively brief, since the important points are effectively covered in the material of Chapters 3 and 5 and of the earlier part of this chapter. (See also Fox 1957.) We concentrate on the second-order problem, given by

$$y'' = f(x, y, y'), \qquad y_0' = g_0(x_0, y_0), \qquad y_n' = g_n(x_n, y_n), \qquad (95)$$

where f, g_0, and g_n are given functions.

The linear problem,

$$y'' + ay' + by = c, \qquad y_0' + \alpha_0 y_0 = \beta_0, \qquad y_n' + \alpha_n y_n = \beta_n, \qquad (96)$$

is of course particularly simple, and there are two main methods. In the first, we compute a linear combination of two initial-value solutions so that one of the boundary conditions in (96) is satisfied, and adjust an arbitrary constant so that the second condition is satisfied.

Suppose, for example, that we recur from the origin x_0. Then, among other possibilities, we can take the initial-value solutions $y^{(1)}$ and $y^{(2)}$ defined by

$$\left. \begin{aligned} y^{(1)''} + ay^{(1)'} + by^{(1)} = c, \qquad y_0^{(1)'} + \alpha_0 y_0^{(1)} = \beta_0, \qquad y_0^{(1)} = 0 \\ y^{(2)''} + ay^{(2)'} + by^{(2)} = 0, \qquad y_0^{(2)'} + \alpha_0 y_0^{(2)} = 0, \qquad y_0^{(2)} = 1 \end{aligned} \right\}, \qquad (97)$$

for which the combination $y^{(1)} + Ay^{(2)}$ certainly satisfies the differential equation and the boundary condition at x_0. The constant A is then determined from the satisfaction of the second boundary condition, and we have

$$y_n^{(1)'} + \alpha_n y_n^{(1)} + A(y_n^{(2)'} + \alpha_n y_n^{(2)}) = \beta_n. \qquad (98)$$

The solutions $y^{(1)}$ and $y^{(2)}$ can be computed by any of the respectable methods so far discussed, though the initial conditions in (97) are 'tailored' to the Runge–Kutta method since we can easily derive both y_0 and y_0' from (97). The Lagrangian predictor-corrector type methods, which need several starting values $y_0, y_1, y_2, \ldots$, for both $y^{(1)}$ and $y^{(2)}$, are clearly considerably less attractive since they require the use of the Taylor's series evaluated at several points.

The special Lagrangian methods of § 22 are quite attractive. Equations of type (49) produce for the first of (97) the approximate recurrence relations

$$\left. \begin{aligned} (1 + \tfrac{1}{2}ha_r)y_{r+1}^{(1)} - (2 - h^2 b_r)y_r^{(1)} + (1 - \tfrac{1}{2}ha_r)y_{r-1}^{(1)} = h^2 c_r \\ y_1^{(1)} + 2h\alpha_0 y_0^{(1)} - y_{-1}^{(1)} = 2h\beta_0, \qquad y_0^{(1)} = 0 \end{aligned} \right\}, \qquad (99)$$

and we can clearly make a start by eliminating $y_{-1}^{(1)}$ from the second of (99) and the first of (99) for $r = 0$.

In the common case of specified boundary values, $y_0 = \beta_0$, $y_n = \beta_n$, we can replace the conditions in (97) by the simple forms

$$y_0^{(1)} = \beta_0, \quad y_0^{(1)\prime} = 0; \quad y_0^{(2)} = 0, \quad y_0^{(2)\prime} = 1. \tag{100}$$

Corresponding to (99) we can take

$$y_0^{(1)} = \beta_0, \quad y_1^{(1)} = 0; \quad y_0^{(2)} = 0, \quad y_1^{(2)} = 1, \tag{101}$$

and compared with the second of (99) we have no truncation error at the point x_0. These easier conditions, we note, do *not* make the predictor-corrector methods more attractive.

43. A second possibility, of course, is to use a boundary-value type method analogous to that for boundary-value recurrence systems. This is hardly appropriate for Runge–Kutta or predictor-corrector-type methods of any class, but is clearly quite appropriate for the special Lagrangian methods of § 22. In fact equations of type (99), applied at all pivotal points x_0 to x_n, with the terminal points excluded in the special case of fixed boundary values, clearly give rise to a set of linear algebraic equations with matrix of triple diagonal form. This we know how to solve, we can do it accurately by the appropriate methods of Chapter 5, and we therefore obtain the complete solution of the algebraic system (which of course has a truncation error) in one fell swoop. The case of absent first derivative gives rise, with the more accurate formulae of type (52), to a problem of precisely the same form.

We discuss in §§ 45 and 46 below the relative advantages of these various methods, including their stability properties and treatment, where relevant, of the truncation errors.

Non-linear problems

44. If the problem is non-linear we cannot take two initial-value solutions and combine them linearly to satisfy another condition. Effectively we have a problem of inverse interpolation. Suppose, to avoid inessential complications, that we have the simple boundary-value system

$$y'' = f(x, y, y'), \quad y_0 = \beta_0, \quad y_n = \beta_n. \tag{102}$$

Then the unknown parameter is y_0' (suitable for the Runge–Kutta-type method), or y_1 (suitable for the methods of § 22). Suppose we call this parameter p, and consider the corresponding initial-value problem.

The computed value of y_n is clearly a function of p, and we are trying to solve the non-linear equation

$$y_n = y_n(p) = \beta_n. \tag{103}$$

Many of the methods discussed in Chapter 8 are suitable for this purpose. In particular, Newton's method, giving quadratic convergence, is quite possible if we are prepared to compute $q_n = (\mathrm{d}/\mathrm{d}p)y_n(p)$. This is the final value of $q_r(x)$, where $q_r(x)$ satisfies the differential system

$$q'' = q\frac{\partial f}{\partial y} + q'\frac{\partial f}{\partial y'} \qquad q_0 = 0, \qquad q_0' = 1 \quad \text{or} \quad q_1 = 1. \tag{104}$$

The matrix-type method is also possible, though our system of algebraic equations is now non-linear, and we must use a Newton-type process for solving them.

Truncation error. Instabilities. Computational comments

45. Apart from the partial, strong and weak instabilities already mentioned for initial-value problems, the use of initial-value techniques, particularly for the linear boundary-value problem, can have precisely the same form of induced instability as the corresponding methods discussed in Chapter 3 for the boundary-value recurrence system. This will happen when one of the complementary solutions of the differential equation is increasing rapidly, whereas the actual contribution from this source is finally suppressed by the boundary conditions.

In this event, moreover, the Runge–Kutta and predictor-corrector methods have extra disadvantages, in that they will try to get the initial-value solutions quite accurately and therefore need quite a small interval for the accurate representation of this rapidly-increasing complementary solution. We then do more work than is necessary because the final solution may be well represented at a much larger interval, a situation not only possible but quite common in boundary-value problems.

The initial-value processes based on equations of type (99) avoid this last difficulty to some extent, but they do not avoid the induced instability. The matrix method indicated in § 43 has the best of all worlds. In its first approximation it obtains a good representation of the true solution, and there are obvious ways of correcting it, that is for coping with the truncation error.

46. First, if we use central differences throughout, even for a derivative boundary condition as in (99), and if the equation and the solution contain no singularities, then the method of the deferred approach to the limit discussed in § 27 is still applicable.

Second, we can carry out a deferred correction more or less as in § 23. Central differences for the truncation error are available at internal points of the range, and near the ends we obtain them by extending the solution at external points by step-by-step methods, having all the necessary information for this purpose.

Third, the 'pivotal' method of solving the linear algebraic equations will even give us some idea about the inherent instability of the problem.

Finally, the matrix method, with equations obtained from truncated finite-difference formulae for derivatives, is completely free from partial, weak, or even strong instabilities. We have already mentioned the advantage of implicit methods and the matrix method is the ultimate implicit method! Provided the true differential solution satisfies reasonably well the algebraic equations we use, then if the problem is inherently well-conditioned the simultaneous solution of these algebraic equations will give a perfectly good result.

This last remark is very important, and we have made similar comments in other contexts. We cannot, we repeat, consign to oblivion a particular *equation*, but only a particular *method* of using that equation in a particular context. Whereas, for example, the use of (86) in a step-by-step process is fatal, its use in a boundary-value matrix process is perfectly all right. The solution of (86) even in a step-by-step method, moreover, is perfectly satisfactory if performed in the iterative sequence

$$\delta^2 y_r^{(n+1)} + h^2 k^2 y_r^{(n+1)} = \tfrac{1}{12}\delta^4 y_r^{(n)}, \tag{105}$$

which is the basis of the deferred-correction method for initial-value problems. The point here is that no parasitic *complementary* solutions are produced in the application of (105).

For non-linear boundary-value problems, of course, the matrix method still has many of the advantages outlined, though it is computationally more difficult, involving the solution of non-linear algebraic equations. But this is in fact often quite practicable, and the deferred correction method can be applied, in a form analogous to the corresponding treatment of initial-value problems in § 24, by solving *linear* simultaneous equations.

Eigenvalue problems

47. Finally, we mention briefly the eigenvalue problem, defined for example by the system

$$y'' + ay' + (b + \lambda)y = 0, \qquad y_0 = y_n = 0. \tag{106}$$

There are other forms, but the problem is basically linear and of boundary-value type, with a homogeneous equation and homogeneous boundary conditions. A trivial solution is $y(x) \equiv 0$, and we seek one or more non-trivial solutions $y^{(r)}(x)$ and the eigenvalues λ_r for which these exist.

The matrix method produces immediately an approximating algebraic eigenvalue problem, which we can solve by one of the methods of Chapter 5. Normally we require a few (perhaps just one) of the smallest eigenvalues and corresponding eigenfunctions, so that the process of inverse iteration is very appropriate. We can incorporate the local truncation error either by a process of deferred correction or by a deferred approach to the limit technique. If in (106) we use the simplest central-difference formulae, and neither the equation nor the solution has any singularity, then the computed $\lambda(h)$ satisfies the error equation

$$\lambda - \lambda(h) = Ah^2 + Bh^4 + \dots. \tag{107}$$

If the first derivative is lacking in (106), and we apply the relevant equation corresponding to (52), then A is zero in (107).

If the equation has a singularity, even if the solution is well-behaved, then (107) may not apply, and its unguarded use can lead to inaccurate consistency. For example, in an eigenvalue problem involving a partial differential equation, with a singularity at the boundary, we produced the successive results

$$\left. \begin{array}{cccc} h & \tfrac{1}{4} & \tfrac{1}{6} & \tfrac{1}{8} \\ \lambda(h) & 15{\cdot}22122 & 15{\cdot}19661 & 15{\cdot}19535 \end{array} \right\}. \tag{108}$$

Elimination of A in (107) gives the pair of values 15·1999 and 15·1996, and further elimination of B produces the result 15·1995. (See Fox 1962, p. 310 for these results and their context.) Most computors would claim high accuracy for the value 15·1995, and yet the correct value (not known to us in 1961!) is in fact 15·1973.

48. The initial-value method is here quite attractive, particularly when the range x_0 to x_n is large or even infinite. Corresponding to the discussion of § 44 we can proceed as follows. With an arbitrary value of λ, and with $y_0 = 0$, y_0' or $y_1 = 1$ (which is not an 'unknown', the choice of unity fixing or normalizing the size of the solution), we can perform an initial-value process and find $y(x_n)$. This is in fact a function of λ, and we seek one of its zeros. This can be performed by inverse interpolation, or by Newton's process which here gives

$$\lambda_{r+1} = \lambda_r - \frac{y(x_n)}{\dfrac{\partial}{\partial \lambda_r} y(x_n)}. \tag{109}$$

The quantity $(\partial/\partial \lambda_r)y(x_n)$ is the value of

$$z(x_n) = \frac{\partial}{\partial \lambda_r} y(x_n), \tag{110}$$

which can be obtained from the initial value problem

$$z'' + az' + (b + \lambda_r)z + y = 0, \qquad z_0 = 0, \qquad z'_0 \ \text{or} \ z_1 = 0. \tag{111}$$

49. Unfortunately this method, in certain contexts, can suffer from the type of induced instability completely analogous to that associated with an algebraic eigenvalue problem, discussed in § 39 of Chapter 5. The general solution of (106) is

$$y(x) = A_1 y_1(x) + A_2 y_2(x), \tag{112}$$

and both the complementary functions and the arbitrary constants (or at least their ratio) depend on λ. Now it may well happen that one of these functions, say $y_2(x)$, increases very rapidly, and in order that the boundary condition $y(x_n) = 0$ should be satisfied we must have $A_2 = 0$. It is the correct λ which causes A_2 to be suppressed. Now if we start with a small perturbation, $\lambda_1 = \lambda + \delta\lambda$, A_2 is not quite suppressed, and the step-by-step solution gets very large and say positive for large x. On the other hand the choice $\lambda_2 = \lambda - \delta\lambda$ will cause a corresponding large but negative value at large x. The correct λ is somewhere in the interval $\lambda - \delta\lambda$, $\lambda + \delta\lambda$, and will be quite accurately determined. The eigenfunction, however, is not determined accurately for large values of x, and paradoxically is most poorly determinable for the case of very well-determinable λ, as in the algebraic problem.

50. The remedy for this difficulty depends somewhat on the nature of the problem. Quite commonly, however, we have the system

$$y'' + \{f(x) - \lambda\}y = 0, \qquad y_0 = 0, \qquad y_n = 0, \qquad n \to \infty. \tag{113}$$

For the required λ the quantity $f(x) - \lambda$ will be positive in a region x_0 to x_c, for some x_c, and for $x > x_c$ this quantity is everywhere negative.

Just as in the recurrence case, discussed in § 27 of Chapter 3, we re-formulate this problem. Clearly the increasing solution starts at x_c, so that we are perfectly safe in solving by initial-value techniques from x_0 to x_c. After that the instability sets in. On the other hand we can solve by initial-value methods by working backwards from x_n (in the infinite case for very large n) and matching the solutions at x_c.

We now effectively have two parameters, the unknown λ and the unknown derivative at x_n (since we cannot fix *both* y_0' and y_n'). A possible procedure is as follows. We solve by 'forward' integration, from x_0 to x_c, the system

$$y_f'' + \{f(x) - \lambda\}y_f = 0, \qquad y_f(0) = 0, \qquad y_f'(0) = 1 \quad \text{or} \quad y_f(x_0 + h) = 1.$$
$$\text{(114)}$$

We solve by 'backward' integration, from x_n to x_c, the system

$$y_b'' + \{f(x) - \lambda\}y_b = 0, \qquad y_b(x_n) = 0,$$
$$y_b'(x_n) = p \quad \text{or} \quad y_b(x_n - h) = p, \quad \text{(115)}$$

and we have to determine the parameters λ and p. The determination comes from the matching of the function and its derivative at x_c, that is we seek to solve the equations

$$y_f(x_c) - y_b(x_c) = 0, \qquad y_f'(x_c) - y_b'(x_c) = 0. \qquad \text{(116)}$$

Now y_f and y_f' are functions of λ, y_b and y_b' of λ and p. The Newton process makes corrections to first estimates from the solution of the linear equations

$$\left.\begin{aligned} \delta\lambda\left(\frac{\partial y_f}{\partial \lambda} - \frac{\partial y_b}{\partial \lambda}\right) - \delta p\frac{\partial y_b}{\partial p} + y_f - y_b = 0 \\[2mm] \delta\lambda\left(\frac{\partial y_f'}{\partial \lambda} - \frac{\partial y_b'}{\partial \lambda}\right) - \delta p\frac{\partial y_b'}{\partial p} + y_f' - y_b' = 0 \end{aligned}\right\}, \qquad \text{(117)}$$

all quantities being evaluated at $x = x_c$. The unknown coefficients of these linear equations can be obtained, with the notation

$$\frac{\partial y}{\partial \lambda} = s, \qquad \frac{\partial y}{\partial p} = q, \qquad \text{(118)}$$

from the systems

$$\left.\begin{aligned} s_f'' + \{f(x) - \lambda\}s_f - y_f = 0, &\quad s_f(0) = 0, &\quad s_f'(0) = 0 \text{ or } s_f(x_0 + h) = 0 \\ s_b'' + \{f(x) - \lambda\}s_b - y_b = 0, &\quad s_b(x_n) = 0, &\quad s_b'(x_n) = 0 \text{ or } s_b(x_n - h) = 0 \\ q_b'' + \{f(x) - \lambda\}q_b = 0, &\quad q_b(x_n) = 0, &\quad q_b'(x_n) = 1 \text{ or } q_b(x_n - h) = 1 \end{aligned}\right\}.$$
$$\text{(119)}$$

Clearly $q_b = p^{-1}y_b$, and therefore need not be computed, and equations (117) reduce to

$$\left.\begin{aligned} \delta\lambda(s_f - s_b) - \delta p p^{-1} y_b + y_f - y_b = 0 \\ \delta\lambda(s_f' - s_b') - \delta p p^{-1} y_b' + y_f' - y_b' = 0 \end{aligned}\right\}, \qquad (120)$$

everything being evaluated at $x = x_c$. Moreover we can, in the finite-difference method, avoid the computation of the derivatives at x_c by matching at two adjacent pivotal points, such as x_c and $x_c \pm h$.

This idea of differentiating the differential equation and associated conditions, which we mentioned in § 7 in connexion with the determination of inherent instability, incidentally has many other similar applications.

51. A second possibility for avoiding the induced instability problem has again been suggested in the analogous problem of Chapter 3. We can proceed as follows.

(i) Solve by forward integration the system (114), obtaining in particular a value $y_f(x_c)$, and choosing x_c *near* the point at which $f(x) = \lambda$, but so that $y_f(x_c) \neq 0$.

(ii) Solve by matrix methods the system

$$y_m'' + \{f(x) - \lambda\}y_m = 0, \qquad y_m(x_c) = y_f(x_c), \qquad y_m(x_n) = 0. \quad (121)$$

A solution exists, since the *algebraic* equations are not homogeneous with $y_m(x_c) \neq 0$, and the matrix is not singular because λ is not an eigenvalue of this particular matrix.

(iii) The derivative agreement $y_f'(x_c) = y_m'(x_c)$ is true only for the correct λ, and we believe that we can now safely leave to the reader details of various methods for adjusting λ so that this condition is satisfied.

III. Summary and examples

52. We have discussed various methods, and their advantages and disadvantages, for a variety of first- and second-order systems. We hope that the remarks of Chapter 1 have been demonstrated, that there is no single best method and that the computor should have at his command a knowledge of at least several methods from which he can choose the most appropriate in any particular context.

We attempt a tentative summary of appropriate methods.

(i) For linear equations whose coefficients are polynomials, and with any form of associated conditions, the construction of a Chebyshev series is usually the best method. This is also true for the eigenvalue problem of this class, provided that the range x_0 to x_n is not too large.

(ii) For problems of second order, in which the equation lacks the first derivative, the method suggested by equation (52), in both initial-value and boundary-value cases, is highly recommended.

(iii) For general linear systems, and for some non-linear systems in which the derived forms of the differential system are easy to obtain, the methods of §§ 22–25, with deferred correction, are also very applicable in both initial-value and boundary-value problems.

(iv) For complicated non-linear initial-value problems, Nordsieck's method is probably superior to the current class of Runge–Kutta methods.

(v) For complicated non-linear boundary-value problems, the choice of combination of initial-value techniques, compared with the matrix method, will depend on any known information about the nature of the solution.

(vi) For eigenvalue problems the matrix method is valuable in general, and the methods of §§ 50 and 51 depend on *a priori* knowledge of the behaviour of the solution.

(vii) The method of the deferred approach to the limit should be used only when we can guarantee a knowledge of the nature of the correcting terms.

(viii) In all cases we aim to publish results only to the number of figures which we can be certain are correct.

53. Finally, we consider a few numerical examples to illustrate some of the methods and commentaries thereon of this chapter. Linear illustrations are included in the exercises, so that it is here convenient to examine some harder and mainly non-linear problems. Most of the arithmetic has been performed on a desk machine, with no attempt to simulate true floating-point arithmetic.

Example 1. *Partial instability, finite-difference method*

54. We have discussed the phenomenon of partial instability in linear problems, and further examples are included in the exercises at the end of this chapter. The first example of this section is related to the non-linear extension of the first results of § 34. There we observed that the use of the approximation

$$h^2 y_r'' = y_{r+1} - 2y_r + y_{r-1} \qquad (122)$$

gives partial instability for the step-by-step solution of $y'' + k^2 y = g(x)$, if $|hk| > 2$.

For the non-linear equation $y'' = f(x, y)$ the phenomenon of induced instability is related to the 'variational equation'

$$\eta'' - \eta \frac{\partial f}{\partial y} = 0, \tag{123}$$

and we therefore expect partial instability in a range in which $h \, |\partial f/\partial y|^{\frac{1}{2}} \geq 2$.

The function $y = x/(1+x)$ satisfies the differential equation

$$y'' = \frac{1}{y^3} - \left\{ \frac{(1+x)^6 + 2x^3}{x^4(1+x)^2} \right\} y. \tag{124}$$

For large x the value of $\partial f/\partial y$ tends to a constant. We have

$$\frac{\partial f}{\partial y} = \frac{-3}{y^4} - \frac{(1+x)^6 + 2x^3}{x^4(1+x)^2} \to -4 \quad \text{as} \quad x \to \infty. \tag{125}$$

Partial instability is then expected at some stage if $|h| > 1$.

Table 10.1 gives the results of computations, with intervals $h = 10/n$, $n = 40, 20, 12,$ and 8, in which we start with the correct values of y at $x = 50$ and $x = 50 + h$. Comparison with the exact solution verifies our expectations. The local truncation error of the exact solution is negligible in all cases.

TABLE 10.1

x	Exact solution	$h = \frac{1}{4}$	$h = \frac{1}{2}$	$h = \frac{5}{6}$	$h = \frac{5}{4}$
50	0·98039	0·98039	0·98039	0·98039	0·98039
55	0·98214	0·98215	0·98215	0·98214	0·98293
60	0·98361	0·98361	0·98362	0·98361	1·34073
65	0·98485	0·98485	0·98485	0·98485	−250·5173

Example 2. Partial instability, Runge–Kutta method

55. The system

$$y' = -40 \cdot 2y + 19 \cdot 6z + \frac{\cos x}{1+x} - \frac{\sin x}{(1+x)^2} + \frac{40 \cdot 2 \sin x}{1+x}$$

$$z' = 19 \cdot 6y - 10 \cdot 8z - \frac{19 \cdot 6 \sin x}{1+x} \Biggr\} , \tag{126}$$

$$y(0) = 3, \quad z(0) = 1$$

has the solution

$$y = e^{-x} + 2e^{-50x} + \frac{\sin x}{1+x}, \quad z = 2e^{-x} - e^{-50x}. \tag{127}$$

If we wish to solve by step-by-step methods to the point at which the oscillating term is the dominant part of the solution, we expect to need a small interval in the neighbourhood of the origin and that larger intervals will be satisfactory for larger values of x. For example, working to three decimals with the fourth-order Runge–Kutta method, changing the interval at various stages and checking that this is satisfactory, we find the results of Table 10.2.

TABLE 10.2

x	0·0	0·005	0·010	0·015	0·020	0·025	0·030	0·035	0·040	0·045	0·050
y	3·000	2·558	2·213	1·945	1·736	1·573	1·446	1·347	1·270	1·210	1·163
z	1·000	1·211	1·374	1·498	1·593	1·664	1·718	1·757	1·786	1·807	1·820

x	0·05	0·06	0·07	0·08	0·09	0·10
y	1·163	1·098	1·058	1·034	1·019	1·009
z	1·820	1·834	1·835	1·828	1·817	1·803

x	0·10	0·12	0·14	0·16	0·18	0·20
y	1·009	0·999	0·994	0·990	0·987	0·984
z	1·803	1·771	1·738	1·704	1·670	1·637

x	0·20	0·24	0·28	0·32	0·36	0·40	0·44	0·48	0·52	0·56	0·60
y	0·984	0·978	0·972	0·964	0·957	0·948	0·940	0·930	0·921	0·912	0·902
z	1·637	1·573	1·512	1·452	1·395	1·341	1·288	1·238	1·189	1·142	1·098

56. At the end of Table 10.2 both y and z are virtually correct to three decimals, and the local truncation error is very small. In fact even at interval 0·1 the third differences of the correct values of y and z are virtually negligible beyond $x = 0·6$. If we now increase the interval to $h = 0·1$, however, the results rapidly suffer from catastrophic error. We find the values

$$\begin{matrix} x & 0·6 & 0·7 & 0·8 & 0·9 & 1·0 \\ y & 0·902 & 0·755 & -0·809 & -21·9 & -310·7 \\ z & 1·098 & 1·083 & 1·727 & 12·18 & 156·5 \end{matrix} \right\}, \qquad (128)$$

which clearly have no relation to the truth.

The point is that in this system the partial instability depends on the eigenvalues of the matrix

$$\mathbf{A} = \begin{bmatrix} -40·2 & 19·6 \\ 19·6 & -10·8 \end{bmatrix}. \qquad (129)$$

The eigenvalues are -1 and -50, and for stability we therefore have the approximate critical interval size

$$50h < 2·7, \qquad h < 0·054. \qquad (130)$$

With the interval $h = 0·1$ the instability is quickly manifest even though the offending e^{-50x} is by this time making no contribution to the solution.

Example 3. Strong instability

57. Consider the application of the 'corrector' (equation (40)) given by

$$11y_{r+1}+27y_r-27y_{r-1}-11y_{r-2} = 3h(y'_{r+1}+9y'_r+9y'_{r-1}+y'_{r-2}),\quad (131)$$

for the solution of the system

$$y' = -y^2/(1+x),\qquad y(0) = 1,\qquad (132)$$

whose exact solution is $y = \{\ln(1+x)+1\}^{-1}$.

This corrector is the most accurate possible of this order, that is it has the smallest local truncation error of all formulae which involve four consecutive points. It would be possible to find a predictor with an accuracy of the same order, but this is hardly required if 'iteration in the corrector' converges rapidly, and one could use simple extrapolation embodied in the formulae

$$\left.\begin{array}{l} y_3 = 3y_2-3y_1+y_0 \\[4pt] y_{r+1} = 4y_r-6y_{r-1}+4y_{r-2}-y_{r-3}, \quad r \geqslant 3 \end{array}\right\}. \qquad (133)$$

For our non-linear equation we have

$$\frac{\partial f}{\partial y} = \frac{-2y}{1+x}, \qquad (134)$$

so that, in accord with the discussion of § 40, the rate of convergence of the corrector, depending on the quantity $|(3h/11)(\partial f/\partial y)|$, is clearly very satisfactory. For example, with $h = 0\cdot1$ and with the correct $y(0) = 1$, $y(0\cdot1) = 0\cdot9130$ and $y(0\cdot2) = 0\cdot8458$, we predict

$$y_p(0\cdot3) = 0\cdot7984,\quad \text{giving}\quad y'_p(0\cdot3) = -0\cdot4903, \qquad (135)$$

and the corrected values are

$$\left.\begin{array}{ll} y_c^{(1)}(0\cdot3) = 0\cdot7920, & y_c^{(2)}(0\cdot3) = 0\cdot7922 \\[4pt] y_c'^{(1)}(0\cdot3) = -0\cdot4825, & y_c'^{(2)}(0\cdot3) = -0\cdot4828 \end{array}\right\}, \qquad (136)$$

with no further change to this precision.

Calculation with $h = 0\cdot1$ and $h = 0\cdot05$ gives the results of Table 10.3, obtained with four-decimal *fl* arithmetic. We observe the rapid increase in error, and the characteristic feature of strongly unstable methods that the error *increases* as the interval *decreases*.

TABLE 10.3

x	0·3	0·4	0·5	0·6	0·7	0·8
y (exact)	0·7922	0·7482	0·7115	0·6803	0·6533	0·6298
interval 0·1	0·7922	0·7482	0·7117	0·6797	0·6552	0·6239
error $\times 10^4$	0	0	−2	+6	−19	+59
interval 0·05	0·7921	0·7475	0·7039	0·6038		
error $\times 10^4$	1	+7	+76	+765		

Example 4. Weak instability

58. We now illustrate Milne's method, at least with respect to its corrector

$$y_{r+1} = y_{r-1} + \tfrac{1}{3}h(y'_{r+1} + 4y'_r + y'_{r-1}), \qquad (137)$$

on the problem of the previous example. We start with the correct values at $x = 0$ and $x = h$, and for convenience use the correct result as predicted value at each subsequent stage.

In the analysis of § 37 the weak instability is associated with a negative value of a in the linear equation $y' = ay$, and for the non-linear case $y' = f(x, y)$ we are therefore interested in the sign of $\partial f/\partial y$. In our example $\partial f/\partial y$ is negative, and in the range $x = 0$ to 2 its value varies from about $-2\cdot 0$ to $-0\cdot 31$. The resulting parasitic solution appears as a multiple of $(-1)^r e^{-\frac{1}{3}rah} \sim (-1)^r e^{-\frac{1}{3}ax_r}$, which for a lying between -2 and $-0\cdot 31$ has no very large growth. Milne's method is therefore acceptable over this range.

The results, however, exhibit another undesirable feature of Milne's method. In this example the local truncation error is greatest in the first step (we have taken the interval $h = 0\cdot 2$), and this produces an error of $0\cdot 0004$ in $y(2h) = y(0\cdot 4)$. In subsequent steps the local truncation errors are negligible. The results, given in Table 10.4, show clearly how this error in $y(0\cdot 4)$ is propagated through the 'even' values y_{2r}, but hardly affects the 'odd' values y_{2r+1}. This is due to the fact that y_{r+1} is more sensitive than y_r to a small change in y_{r-1}, but it makes it difficult to assess the resulting error. In particular the differences of the computed solution, shown in the second part of Table 10.4, reveal all the effects of accidental 'blunders'!

Example 5. Non-linear boundary-value problem, boundary-value method

59. We consider the system

$$y'' = y^2 - 1, \qquad y(0) = 0, \qquad y(1) = 1, \qquad (138)$$

and illustrate two boundary-value methods for its solution. In the first we use the finite-difference equation

$$h^2 y''_r = \delta^2 y_r + C(y_r), \qquad C(y_r) = -\tfrac{1}{12}\delta^4 y_r + \tfrac{1}{90}\delta^6 y_r - \dots, \qquad (139)$$

TABLE 10.4

x	0·0	0·2	0·4	0·6	0·8	1·0	1·2	1·4	1·6	1·8	2·0	2·2	2·4
y (exact)	1·0000	0·8458	0·7482	0·6802	0·6298	0·5906	0·5591	0·5332	0·5114	0·4927	0·4765	0·4623	0·4497
y ($h = 0·2$)	1·0000	0·8458	0·7478	0·6803	0·6293	0·5906	0·5586	0·5333	0·5108	0·4928	0·4760	0·4624	0·4492
error $\times 10^4$	0	0	+4	−1	+5	0	+5	−1	+6	−1	+5	−1	+5

x	y		δ^2		δ^4
0·0	1·0000				
		−1542			
0·2	0·8458		+562		
		−980		−257	
0·4	0·7478		305		+117
		−675		−140	
0·6	0·6803		165		+98
		−510		−42	
0·8	0·6293		123		−14
		−387		−56	
1·0	0·5906		67		+56
		−320		0	
1·2	0·5586		67		−39
		−253		−39	
1·4	0·5333		28		+56
		−225		+17	
1·6	0·5108		45		−50
		−180		−33	
1·8	0·4928		12		+53
		−168		+20	
2·0	0·4760		32		−48
		−136		−28	
2·2	0·4624		+4		
		−132			
2·4	0·4492				

and propose to solve the algebraic equations typified by

$$y_{r+1} - 2y_r + y_{r-1} + C(y_r) = h^2 y_r^2 - h^2. \qquad (140)$$

For this we apply the iterative scheme

$$y_{r+1}^{(s+1)} - 2y_r^{(s+1)} + y_{r-1}^{(s+1)} + C(y_r^{(s)}) = h^2(y_r^{(s+1)})^2 - h^2, \qquad C(y_r^{(0)}) = 0, \quad (141)$$

at each stage of which we satisfy the given boundary conditions. This proposal accords with the suggestions of § 23.

At each stage, however, we have to solve a set of non-linear algebraic equations, and this is performed by another iterative process (the so-called 'inner iteration' in computer terminology, compared with the 'outer iteration' of (141)). For simplicity we write (141) in the form

$$y_{r+1} - 2y_r + y_{r-1} - h^2 y_r^2 = -h^2 - C(y) = f_r, \qquad (142)$$

the right-hand side being known. If z_r is an approximate solution of (142), then an improved solution is $z_r + w_r$, where the w_r satisfy the linear algebraic equations

$$w_{r+1} - 2(1 + h^2 z_r)w_r + w_{r-1} + (z_{r+1} - 2z_r + z_{r-1} - h^2 z_r^2 - f_r) = 0, \quad (143)$$

with $w_r = 0$ at the two boundary points. This is an obvious use of the Newton iterative method applied to *simultaneous* non-linear equations.

With the interval $h = 0 \cdot 2$, and with a first approximation

$$\left. \begin{array}{ccccccc} x_r & 0 & 0 \cdot 2 & 0 \cdot 4 & 0 \cdot 6 & 0 \cdot 8 & 1 \cdot 0 \\ z_r & 0 & 0 & 0 & 0 & 0 & 1 \end{array} \right\}, \qquad (144)$$

we have for the correction w_r the linear equations

$$\left. \begin{array}{rl} -2w_1 + w_2 & = -0 \cdot 04 \\ w_1 - 2w_2 + w_3 & = -0 \cdot 04 \\ w_2 - 2w_3 + w_4 & = -0 \cdot 04 \\ w_3 - 2w_4 & = -1 \cdot 04 \end{array} \right\}, \qquad (145)$$

where $w_r = w(rh)$. The solution, and the second approximation z_r, are given (exactly) by

$$\left. \begin{array}{ccccccc} x_r & 0 & 0 \cdot 2 & 0 \cdot 4 & 0 \cdot 6 & 0 \cdot 8 & 1 \cdot 0 \\ w_r & 0 & 0 \cdot 28 & 0 \cdot 52 & 0 \cdot 72 & 0 \cdot 88 & 0 \cdot 0 \\ z_r & 0 & 0 \cdot 28 & 0 \cdot 52 & 0 \cdot 72 & 0 \cdot 88 & 1 \cdot 0 \end{array} \right\}. \qquad (146)$$

At the next step of the inner iteration the linear equations are

$$\left.\begin{array}{r}-2{\cdot}0224w_1+w_2 \qquad\qquad\qquad = 0{\cdot}003136\\ w_1-2{\cdot}0416w_2+w_3 \qquad\qquad = 0{\cdot}010816\\ w_2-2{\cdot}0576w_3+w_4 \qquad = 0{\cdot}020736\\ w_3-2{\cdot}0704w_4 = 0{\cdot}030976\end{array}\right\}. \qquad (147)$$

We solve them by the elimination method of Chapter 5, noting the diagonally-dominant nature of the matrix so that we can safely take pivots down the diagonal. We find the new solution

$$\left.\begin{array}{llllllll}x_r & 0 & 0{\cdot}2 & 0{\cdot}4 & 0{\cdot}6 & 0{\cdot}8 & 1{\cdot}0\\ z_r & 0 & 0{\cdot}25945 & 0{\cdot}48158 & 0{\cdot}67293 & 0{\cdot}84230 & 1{\cdot}0\end{array}\right\}. \qquad (148)$$

There is very little extra change. The new diagonal elements of the equations for the new w_r change slightly to the respective values $-2{\cdot}02076$, $-2{\cdot}03853$, $-2{\cdot}05383$, $-2{\cdot}06738$, and the new values of w_r affect only the last two figures of z_r. To five decimals this result,

$$\left.\begin{array}{llllllll}x_r & 0 & 0{\cdot}2 & 0{\cdot}4 & 0{\cdot}6 & 0{\cdot}8 & 1{\cdot}0\\ y_r^{(1)} & 0 & 0{\cdot}25937 & 0{\cdot}48143 & 0{\cdot}67276 & 0{\cdot}84219 & 1{\cdot}0\end{array}\right\}, \qquad (149)$$

satisfies equations (141) with $s = 0$, $C(y_r^{(0)}) = 0$.

60. The next step is the computation of $C(y_r^{(1)})$ from the second of (139). For the central differences near the terminal points we need values of $y_r^{(1)}$ outside the range 0 to 1, and these we find by using (141) in a step-by-step process, still with $C(y_r^{(0)}) = 0$, so that the error in the external values is of precisely the same nature as those of the internal values. (If y' appears non-linearly in the differential equation, note that we have non-linear algebraic equations at this stage also.) These results, and the computed values of $C(y_r^{(1)})$, are shown in Table 10.5.

We now proceed to the next inner iteration, with a view to solving (141) with $s = 1$. We clearly use $y_r^{(1)}$ as the first approximation to $y_r^{(2)}$, and at this stage it is not necessary to alter the coefficients of the linear equations for the new w_r. The results of the first iteration give

$$\left.\begin{array}{llllllll}x_r & 0{\cdot}0 & 0{\cdot}2 & 0{\cdot}4 & 0{\cdot}6 & 0{\cdot}8 & 1{\cdot}0\\ w_r & 0 & -0{\cdot}00039 & -0{\cdot}00048 & -0{\cdot}00041 & -0{\cdot}00025 & 0\end{array}\right\}, \qquad (150)$$

TABLE 10.5

x_r	$y_r^{(1)}$		δ^2		δ^4		δ^6	$C(y_r^{(1)})$
−0·6	−0·99480							
		+35965						
−0·4	−0·63515		−2387					
		33578		−1254				
−0·2	−0·29937		−3641		+895			
		29937		−359		−267		
0·0	0·00000		−4000		+628		+28	(−0·00052)
		25937		+269		−239		
0·2	+0·25937		−3731		+389		+75	−0·00032
		22206		+658		−164		
0·4	0·48143		−3073		+225		+84	−0·00018
		19133		+883		−80		
0·6	0·67276		−2190		+145		+69	−0·00011
		16943		+1028		−11		
0·8	0·84219		−1162		+134		+76	−0·00010
		15781		+1162		+65		
1·0	1·00000		0		+199		+82	(−0·00016)
		15781		+1361		+147		
1·2	1·15781		+1361		+346			
		17142		+1707				
1·4	1·32923		+3068					
		20210						
1·6	1·53133							

and there is no further change, the addition of w_r to $y_r^{(1)}$ producing the results

$$x_r \quad\quad 0·0 \quad\quad 0·2 \quad\quad 0·4 \quad\quad 0·6 \quad\quad 0·8 \quad\quad 1·0$$
$$y_r^{(2)} \quad 0·00000 \quad 0·25898 \quad 0·48095 \quad 0·67235 \quad 0·84194 \quad 1·00000 \tag{151}$$

which satisfy (141), with $s = 1$, to five decimals.

61. At the next stage, of producing the new central differences of $y_r^{(2)}$, the extrapolation to points outside the range must use the $C(y_r^{(1)})$ correcting terms at the terminal points and some other points outside the range. Using the bracketed terms in Table 10.5, for example, we can find $y_r^{(2)}$ at the nearest external points $x = -0·2$ and $x = 1·2$, the respective values being $-0·29846$ and $1·15822$. To find more points we would need $C(y_r^{(1)})$ at more external points, and hence $y_r^{(1)}$ at still more external points. Too many 'outer iterations' therefore become prohibitive, though in most problems the number of internal points would be much larger and the extra 'external' work would be a smaller percentage of the total labour.

The differences of $y_r^{(2)} - y_r^{(1)}$, which serve to form the required additions to the $C(y_r^{(1)})$ of Table 10.5, are shown in Table 10.6.

It is reasonably clear that sixth and higher differences make no contribution at the internal points, and the change from $C(y_r^{(1)})$ to $C(y_r^{(2)})$ is little more than minus half a unit at each internal point. This causes

TABLE 10.6

x_r	$y_r^{(2)} - y_r^{(1)}$		δ^2		δ^4	$C(y_r^{(2)} - y_r^{(1)})$
$-0\cdot2$	$+0\cdot00091$					
		-91				
$0\cdot0$	$0\cdot00000$		$+52$			
		-39		-22		
$0\cdot2$	$-0\cdot00039$		$+30$		$+8$	$-0\cdot000007$
		-9		-14		
$0\cdot4$	$-0\cdot00048$		$+16$		$+7$	$-0\cdot000006$
		$+7$		-7		
$0\cdot6$	$-0\cdot00041$		$+9$		$+7$	$-0\cdot000006$
		$+16$		0		
$0\cdot8$	$-0\cdot00025$		$+9$		$+7$	$-0\cdot000006$
		$+25$		$+7$		
$1\cdot0$	$0\cdot00000$		$+16$			
		$+41$				
$1\cdot2$	$+0\cdot00041$					

changes in $y_r^{(2)}$, in the next outer iteration, of -1, -2, -2, -1 in the fifth decimal, and we conclude that the correct result, with little more than a rounding error in the last figure, is

$$\left.\begin{array}{ccccccc} x_r & 0\cdot0 & 0\cdot2 & 0\cdot4 & 0\cdot6 & 0\cdot8 & 1\cdot0 \\ y_r & 0\cdot00000 & 0\cdot25897 & 0\cdot48093 & 0\cdot67233 & 0\cdot84193 & 1\cdot00000 \end{array}\right\}. \quad (152)$$

To guarantee the last figure we should need to keep an extra figure in $C(y_r^{(1)})$ in Table 10.5, which would affect slightly the difference correction in Table 10.6. The effect on the answers of small errors in $C(y_r)$ depends, of course, on the degree of inherent instability in the problem, measured here by the size of the elements of the inverse of the matrix corresponding to the final coefficients in (147).

62. Another boundary-value method for this problem, involving less arithmetic, uses the powerful formula (52), whose local truncation error, approximately $\frac{1}{240}\delta^6 y_r$, is almost negligible in this problem. We have to solve the non-linear equations

$$y_{r+1} - 2y_r + y_{r-1} + \tfrac{1}{240}\delta^6 y_r - \ldots = \tfrac{1}{12}h^2(y_{r+1}^2 + 10y_r^2 + y_{r-1}^2) - h^2, \quad (153)$$

and the Newton iteration corresponding to (143) is here given by

$$(1 - \tfrac{1}{6}h^2 z_{r+1})w_{r+1} - 2(1 + \tfrac{5}{6}h^2 z_r)w_r + (1 - \tfrac{1}{6}h^2 z_{r-1})w_{r-1} + $$
$$+ \{z_{r+1} - 2z_r + z_{r-1} - \tfrac{1}{12}h^2(z_{r+1}^2 + 10z_r^2 + z_{r-1}^2) + h^2\} = 0. \quad (154)$$

Starting with the same approximation as in the previous method, we find the successive results

$$
\begin{array}{lllllll}
x_r & 0\cdot0 & 0\cdot2 & 0\cdot4 & 0\cdot6 & 0\cdot8 & 1\cdot0 \\
z_r^{(0)} & 0\cdot0 & 0\cdot0 & 0\cdot0 & 0\cdot0 & 0\cdot0 & 1\cdot0 \\
z_r^{(1)} & 0\cdot0 & 0\cdot27933 & 0\cdot51867 & 0\cdot71800 & 0\cdot87733 & 1\cdot0 \\
z_r^{(2)} & 0\cdot0 & 0\cdot25903 & 0\cdot48106 & 0\cdot67247 & 0\cdot84202 & 1\cdot0 \\
z_r^{(3)} & 0\cdot0 & 0\cdot25895 & 0\cdot48091 & 0\cdot67232 & 0\cdot84193 & 1\cdot0
\end{array}
\qquad (155)
$$

The last of these is very similar to the final result of the previous method, and it is not difficult to see, since the sixth differences are all positive, that the neglected $\frac{1}{240}\delta^6 y_r$ in (153) would cause a small increase in the values of z_r, in accord with the final previous result (152).

Example 6. Non-linear boundary-value problem, initial-value method
63. It is also of interest to consider the solution of Example 5 by a combination of initial-value techniques. The general idea is to estimate a value of $y'(0)$ or $y(h) = y_1$, so that we can use a step-by-step method and achieve the correct value $y(1) = 1$. Since the problem is non-linear we cannot 'superpose' two solutions, and iteration is necessary.

There are two main possibilities. First, we can compute $y(1)$ for values of the estimated $y(h)$, (with a finite-difference method) and perform a process of inverse interpolation to compute the correct $y(h)$. The other values of $y(rh)$ can then be obtained by direct interpolation, or by a final step-by-step process with the correct $y(h)$. The inverse interpolation can be performed either by successive linear processes or by the method of § 21 of Chapter 8.

For Example 5 the step-by-step process corresponding to (140), with $C(y_r)$ neglected, computes successive values directly from the recurrence

$$
y_{r+1} = 2y_r - y_{r-1} + h^2 y_r^2 - h^2. \qquad (156)
$$

We take $y_0 = 0$, $y_1 = p$, and choose successive values of p so that the computed $y(1)$ straddle the correct value $y(1) = 1$, and this choice can clearly be made in the process of the computation. Some results are shown in Table 10.7.

TABLE 10.7

x	y	y	y	y	y	y
0·0	0·00000	0·00000	0·00000	0·00000	0·00000	0·00000
0·2	0·00000	0·10000	0·20000	0·30000	0·40000	0·50000
0·4	−0·04000	0·16040	0·36160	0·56360	0·76640	0·97000
0·6	−0·11994	0·18183	0·48843	0·79991	1·11629	1·43764
0·8	−0·23930	0·16458	0·58480	1·02181	1·47603	1·94795
1·0	−0·39637	0·10841	0·65485	1·24547	1·88292	2·57004

TABLE 10.8

$y(0\cdot2)$	$y(1)$		δ^2		δ^4
0·0	−0·39637				
		50478			
0·1	+0·10841		4166		
		54644		252	
0·2	0·65485		4418		13
		59062		265	
0·3	1·24547		4683		19
		63745		284	
0·4	1·88292		4967		
		68712			
0·5	2·57004				

We now seek the value of $y(0\cdot2)$ which gives $y(1) = 1$, and for the purpose of inverse interpolation we form the differences shown in Table 10.8.

By the method of § 21 of Chapter 8 we know that the required $y(0\cdot2)$ has the value $0\cdot2+0\cdot1k$, and we find k in three successive iterations, with values $0\cdot58439$, $0\cdot59375$, and $0\cdot59369$. The required $y(0\cdot2)$ is then $0\cdot25937$, agreeing, as it should, with the corresponding value in Table 10.5.

If we now use this in a final step-by-step calculation, we produce the results

$$\left.\begin{array}{ccccccc} x & 0\cdot0 & 0\cdot2 & 0\cdot4 & 0\cdot6 & 0\cdot8 & 1\cdot0 \\ y & 0\cdot0 & 0\cdot25937 & 0\cdot48143 & 0\cdot67276 & 0\cdot84219 & 0\cdot99999 \end{array}\right\}. \quad (157)$$

This is reasonably satisfactory, but it is quite clear from equations like (147) that as an initial-value problem our example is ill-conditioned, and if we had to cover a significantly longer range we should have to obtain $y(0\cdot2)$ far more accurately, to more significant figures, in order to obtain the required accuracy in the neighbourhood of the second terminal point. This difficulty does not appear in the boundary-value method.

We leave as an exercise the correction of the result (157) with the incorporation of the difference correction.

64. In a second method we observe that if $y_1 = p$ then $y(1)$ is a function of p, and we seek that value of p for which $y(1) = 1$. This we can find with Newton iteration defined by

$$p_{r+1} = p_r - \frac{y(1)-1}{(\partial/\partial p_r)y(1)}. \quad (158)$$

The value of the denominator in (158) comes by differentiating the given system, in the form

$$q'' = 2yq, \qquad q(0) = 0, \qquad q(h) = 1, \qquad q = \partial y/\partial p, \qquad (159)$$

and performing the corresponding step-by-step process from the recurrence

$$q_{r+1}-2(1+h^2y_r)q_r+q_{r-1} = 0, \qquad q_0 = 0, \qquad q_1 = 1, \qquad (160)$$

to find $q(1) = (\partial/\partial p_r)y(1)$.

Starting, for example, with $p = 0\cdot1$, giving the second column of Table 10.7, we find that the corresponding values of q are given by

$$
\left.
\begin{array}{ccccccc}
x & 0\cdot0 & 0\cdot2 & 0\cdot4 & 0\cdot6 & 0\cdot8 & 1\cdot0 \\
q & 0 & 1 & 2\cdot00800 & 3\cdot04176 & 4\cdot11978 & 5\cdot25206
\end{array}
\right\}, \qquad (161)
$$

and (158) gives a new $p = 0\cdot26976$. Successive results are shown in Table 10.9.

TABLE 10.9

x	0·0	0·2	0·4	0·6	0·8	1·0
y	0·0	0·26976	0·50243	0·70610	0·88971	1·06498
q	0·0	1·0	2·02158	3·12441	4·40370	5·99645
y	0·0	0·25892	0·48052	0·67136	0·84023	0·99734
y	0·0	0·25936	0·48141	0·67270	0·84209	0·99985

We note the rapid (quadratic) convergence, and the fact that after some stage the *previous* value of $q(1)$ can be used for the production of a new p with only minor effects on the convergence. The fact that the corresponding initial-value problem is quite ill-conditioned is revealed in the difference between $y(1\cdot0)$ in the last row of Table 10.9 and the $y(1\cdot0)$ of equation (157), the only starting difference being $0\cdot00001$ in $y(0\cdot2)$. Finally, we note that the relative merits of our two initial-value methods may depend, among other things, on the complexity of the derived equation of type (159). This differentiation is avoided with the method of § 63, but the latter, on the other hand, needs perhaps more judgement and is less automatic.

Example 7. Eigenvalue problem, infinite range

65. For our last example we consider the computation of an eigensolution of the system

$$y''+(\lambda-4x^2-x^4)y = 0, \qquad y(0) = 0, \qquad y \to 0 \quad \text{as} \quad x \to \infty. \qquad (162)$$

With problems of this kind (the 'self-adjoint' systems) it is known that there is an infinity of positive eigenvalues, and the rth eigenvalue, in increasing order, has an eigenfunction with exactly $r-1$ zeros. This fact immediately helps us to locate the approximate position of any particular eigenvalue. Suppose, for example, that we seek the third eigensolution. Then with the approximation represented by

$$y_{r+1}-a_r y_r+y_{r-1} = 0, \qquad a_r = 2-h^2\lambda+h^2(4x_r^2+x_r^4), \qquad (163)$$

we can start with $y_0 = 0$, $y_1 = 1$ (which 'normalizes' the solution), and with various values of λ we proceed in a step-by-step manner to produce evidence for the location of the required value. With $h = 0.1$ we find results of which a sample is shown in Table 10.10.

TABLE 10.10

x	0·0	0·2	0·4	0·6	0·8	1·0	1·2	1·4	1·6	1·8
$y(\lambda = 20)$	0·00	1·80	2·25	1·04	−0·90	−2·29	−2·37	−1·32	0·18	1·72
$y(\lambda = 60)$	0·00	1·40	−0·05	−1·40	0·05	1·42	0·10	−1·23		
$y(\lambda = 30)$	0·00	1·70	1·54	−0·29	−1·83	−1·54	0·20	1·81	2·18	1·43

The solution for $\lambda = 60$ has three zeros, one too many for our requirement. The solution for $\lambda = 20$ has the required number of zeros, but the solution is clearly exponentially increasing beyond $x = 2.0$ (where the coefficient a_r in (163) exceeds 2·0). For $\lambda = 30$ we have the required two zeros, and in the 'exponential' region for $x > 2$ we have at this stage a decreasing solution, with some hope that the increasing complementary solution is reasonably-well suppressed. We therefore take $\lambda = 30$ as our first approximation.

With this value the solution has a point of inflexion at about $x = 2$. In $0 \leqslant x \leqslant 2$ the a_r in (163) is everywhere less than 2, so that the solutions are of non-increasing oscillatory form for which step-by-step methods are quite satisfactory. For $x > 2$ we have a combination of increasing and decreasing exponential-type solutions, and of course the forward step-by-step method in this region is unstable. We could recur backwards from 'infinity', and match the forward solution at $x = 2$, as discussed in § 50, but here we vary this procedure by solving by boundary-value methods in the region $x > 2$. The advantage of this process is that we do not need to specify in advance a satisfactory 'value' of infinity.

66. Suppose, then, that we integrate outwards, using (163) with a guessed value of λ, stopping at $x = 2$, near enough to the point of inflection. With this value of $y(2)$, and with $y(\infty) = 0$, we treat the equations (163) as a set of simultaneous equations, solving them by a method, described in § 67 below, which estimates the '∞ point' in the process. The only equation left unsatisfied is at $x = 2$, where we can compute

$$y_{k+1} - a_k y_k + y_{k-1} = R_k, \qquad x_k = 2. \tag{164}$$

The residual R_k is a function of λ, and we seek that λ for which $R_k(\lambda) = 0$. Newton's process gives, for a first correction to our guessed λ, the amount

$$\delta\lambda = -\frac{R_k(\lambda)}{(\partial/\partial\lambda)R_k(\lambda)}. \tag{165}$$

Now if $\partial y/\partial\lambda = z$, we have from (163) the variational equation

$$z_{r+1} - a_r z_r + z_{r-1} + h^2 y_r = 0, \qquad z_0 = 0, \qquad z_1 = 0. \tag{166}$$

If we solve this equation by the same methods as before, in the respective ranges, it is unsatisfied only at the point $x_k = 2$, where obviously

$$z_{k+1} - a_k z_k + z_{k-1} + h^2 y_k = \frac{\partial R_k}{\partial\lambda}, \tag{167}$$

the remaining quantity needed in (165).

67. There remains only the discussion of the linear-equation solving process in the range $x \geqslant x_k$. For simplicity we consider the equations for y_r, and write them in matrix form $\mathbf{Ay} = \mathbf{b}$, where the vector $\mathbf{y}$ has components $y_{k+1}, y_{k+2},...$, the vector $\mathbf{b}$ has components $b_{k+1}, b_{k+2},...$, in which in fact $b_{k+1} = -y_k$ and the other components are zero in the y equations. We write

$$\mathbf{A} = \begin{bmatrix} -a_{k+1} & 1 & & \\ 1 & -a_{k+2} & 1 & \\ & 1 & -a_{k+3} & 1 \\ \hdashline & & & \end{bmatrix} = \overset{\mathbf{L}}{\begin{bmatrix} 1 & & \\ l_{k+2} & 1 & \\ & l_{k+3} & 1 \\ \hdashline & & \end{bmatrix}} \times$$

$$\times \overset{\mathbf{U}}{\begin{bmatrix} u_{k+1} & v_{k+1} & \\ & u_{k+2} & v_{k+2} \\ & & u_{k+3} & v_{k+3} \\ \hdashline & & \end{bmatrix}}. \tag{168}$$

The elements of $\mathbf{L}$ and $\mathbf{U}$ are obtained from the equations

$$\left.\begin{aligned} u_{k+1} &= -a_{k+1}, \\ l_r u_{r-1} &= 1, \qquad l_r v_{r-1} + u_r = -a_r, \qquad r \geqslant k+2 \\ v_r &= 1, \qquad r = k+1, k+2,... \end{aligned}\right\} \tag{169}$$

The triangular decomposition without interchanges is perfectly stable, as we observed in Chapter 5, because $|a_r| > 2$ leading to $|l_r| < 1$ and $|u_r| > 1$. The solution of the linear equations is effected in two stages. First, we solve $\mathbf{Lq} = \mathbf{b}$ from the forward recurrence system

$$\left.\begin{array}{c} q_{k+1} = b_{k+1} \\ l_{k+2}q_{k+1} + q_{k+2} = b_{k+2} = 0 \\ \text{-----------------------------} \end{array}\right\}, \qquad (170)$$

the general equation having the form

$$q_{r+1} = -l_{r+1}q_r. \qquad (171)$$

We proceed with this recurrence until q_n is negligible, and at this stage we have correspondingly decided at which point to terminate the triangular decomposition.

The required solution then comes from the equations $\mathbf{Uy} = \mathbf{q}$, by backward recurrence from the system

$$\left.\begin{array}{c} u_n y_n = q_n \\ u_{n-1}y_{n-1} + y_n = q_{n-1} \\ \text{-----------------------------} \end{array}\right\}. \qquad (172)$$

Since $|u_n| > 1$, clearly y_n is negligible, which is what we want, when q_n is negligible, and there are no difficulties, of stability or otherwise, in the whole of this computation. The analysis for the equations for z_r brings in no extra points of difficulty.

68. Table 10.11 gives the results of the iterative process we have described, and at the end of the second step we have a good answer to the solution of the algebraic problem represented by equations (163) with $h = 0\cdot1$. We leave as an exercise the correction of this result to allow for the truncation error ignored in (163).

The convergence is rapid, and indeed we expect this iteration to have the quadratic quality of Newton's process. We must remember, however, the discussion in Chapter 4 on the effect on the convergence of errors in the computation of the function whose zero we seek to obtain. Although there is no significant accumulation of error in the step-by-step process there is bound to be a small accumulation of error, since although the complementary functions are not increasing they are correspondingly not decreasing. The computation for $\lambda = 28\cdot64$ was performed on a desk machine, with the coefficients a_r and the values of y_r rounded at each stage to four decimal places. If we use a more accurate $\delta\lambda = 0\cdot2154$ obtained at the previous stage, take the new $\lambda = 28\cdot6354$,

17

TABLE 10.11

	$\lambda = 30$		$\lambda = 28\cdot42$		$\lambda = 28\cdot64$	$\lambda = 28\cdot6354$
x	y	z	y	z	y	y
0·0	0·0	0·0	0·0	0·0	0·0	0·0
0·1	1·0000	0·0	1·0000	0·0	1·0000	1·0000
0·2	1·7004	−0·0100	1·7162	−0·0100	1·7140	1·7140
0·3	1·8934	−0·0340	1·9474	−0·0343	1·9399	1·9400
0·4	1·5254	−0·0669	1·6324	−0·0685	1·6174	1·6176
0·5	0·7100	−0·0954	0·8644	−0·1000	0·8425	0·8428
0·6	−0·3109	−0·1034	−0·1401	−0·1128	−0·1648	−0·1644
0·7	−1·2434	−0·0789	−1·1070	−0·0939	−1·1275	−1·1272
0·8	−1·8302	−0·0200	−1·7836	−0·0393	−1·7921	−1·7919
0·9	−1·9223	0·0626	−2·0063	0·0431	−1·9967	−1·9968
1·0	−1·5127	0·1481	−1·7371	0·1350	−1·7073	−1·7076
1·1	−0·7249	0·2117	−1·0611	0·2127	−1·0143	−1·0149
1·2	0·2347	0·2324	−0·1504	0·2540	−0·0947	−0·0955
1·3	1·1423	0·1992	0·7913	0·2445	0·8446	0·8437
1·4	1·8171	0·1140	1·5842	0·1811	1·6233	1·6225
1·5	2·1590	−0·0103	2·1119	0·0715	2·1267	2·1262
1·6	2·1568	−0·1545	2·3363	−0·0695	2·3200	2·3200
1·7	1·8697	−0·2999	2·2890	−0·2258	2·2384	2·2391
1·8	1·3939	−0·4337	2·0469	−0·3858	1·9614	1·9629
1·9	0·8269	−0·5531	1·7033	−0·5471	1·5828	1·5851
2·0	0·2390	−0·6668	1·3435	−0·7202	1·1857	1·1888
2·0	0·2390	−0·6668	1·3435	−0·7202	1·1857	1·1888
2·1	0·1698	−0·4720	0·9373	−0·4916	0·8293	0·8314
2·2	0·1128	−0·3122	0·6123	−0·3150	0·5430	0·5444
2·3	0·0701	−0·1935	0·3753	−0·1897	0·3335	0·3343
2·4	0·0409	−0·1123	0·2161	−0·1075	0·1924	0·1928
2·5	0·0224	−0·0614	0·1170	−0·0573	0·1043	0·1045
2·6	0·0115	−0·0315	0·0595	−0·0288	0·0532	0·0533
2·7	0·0056	−0·0152	0·0285	−0·0136	0·0255	0·0256
2·8	0·0025	−0·0069	0·0128	−0·0061	0·0115	0·0115
2·9	0·0011	−0·0030	0·0054	−0·0025	0·0049	0·0049
3·0	0·0004	−0·0012	0·0022	−0·0010	0·0019	0·0019
3·1	0·0002	−0·0004	0·0008	−0·0004	0·0007	0·0007
3·2	0·0001	−0·0001	0·0002	−0·0001	0·0002	0·0002

$$R_k = 0\cdot5139 \qquad\qquad R_k = -0\cdot0945 \qquad R_k = 0\cdot0009 \quad R_k = -0\cdot0011$$

$$\frac{\partial R_k}{\partial \lambda} = 0\cdot3242 \qquad\qquad \frac{\partial R_k}{\partial \lambda} = 0\cdot4409$$

$$\delta\lambda = -1\cdot58 \qquad\qquad \delta\lambda = +0\cdot22$$

compute the a_r and y_r to five decimals, and make a final rounding to four decimal places, we obtain the slightly different results of the last column of Table 10.11.

69. Finally, it is interesting to consider a method that avoids the solution of the variational equation for **z**. If we multiply (163) by z_r, (166) by y_r, subtract, and add the resulting equations for $r = 1, 2, \ldots$, the left-hand side is reduced to zero, and we obtain

$$z_k R_k - y_k \frac{\partial R_k}{\partial \lambda} + h^2 \sum_{r=1}^{\infty} y_r^2 = 0. \tag{173}$$

We can now achieve our objective by applying the Newton process not to R_k but to (R_k/y_k). Then

$$\delta\lambda = \frac{-(R_k/y_k)}{\dfrac{\partial}{\partial \lambda}(R_k/y_k)} = \frac{-y_k R_k}{y_k \dfrac{\partial R_k}{\partial \lambda} - z_k R_k} = \frac{-y_k R_k}{h^2 \displaystyle\sum_{r=1}^{\infty} y_r^2}, \tag{174}$$

a result which does not contain z explicitly.

Unfortunately the early rate of convergence of this method might be rather slow. For at an early stage y_k might be small, (R_k/y_k) large, and we have the situation partially discussed in relation to Fig. 4.1. In that diagram, if the tangent at P_1 is nearly vertical, then early corrections $\delta\lambda$ might be smaller than later corrections. This happens in our present example. By this process we converge to $\lambda = 28 \cdot 64$ in four steps (rather than two with the method of Table 10.11), and the second correction is considerably larger than the first, which takes us only from $\lambda = 30$ to $\lambda = 29 \cdot 71$.

Exercises 10

1. Consider the differential equation $y'' - 10\pi y = -10x$, with initial conditions $y(0) = 0$, $y'(0) = 1/\pi$. Perform enough step-by-step computations, by any method, including the fourth-order Runge–Kutta process applied to a pair of first-order equations, to demonstrate that the problem has a large degree of inherent instability.

2. Use the differential equation in Exercise 1, with boundary conditions $y(0) = 0$, $y(2) = 2/\pi$, and demonstrate that this boundary-value problem is very well-conditioned. (Use the approximation (10) for the second derivative and solve the resulting algebraic equations, with successive intervals $h = \frac{1}{2}, \frac{1}{4}, \frac{1}{8} \ldots$.)

3. Use a combination of step-by-step methods in Exercise 2, with interval $h = \frac{1}{8}$, to show that this method has significant induced instability.

4. Demonstrate the possibility of ill-conditioning in a boundary-value problem by attempting the method of Exercise 2 for the system $y'' + \pi^2 y = \pi^2 x$, $y(0) = 0$, $y(1) = 1$, with intervals $h = \frac{1}{2}, \frac{1}{4}, \frac{1}{8}$.

5. For the solution of the linear first-order equation $y' = P_1(x)y + Q_1(x)$, by the 'Taylor's-series method', show that

$$y(x+h) = \left(1 + hP_1 + \frac{h^2}{2!}P_2 + \ldots\right)y(x) + \left(hQ_1 + \frac{h^2}{2!}Q_2 + \ldots\right) = Py(x) + Q,$$

where $P_{r+1} = P'_r + P_1 P_r$, $Q_{r+1} = Q'_r + Q_1 P_r$. (Note that P and Q, for fixed h, depend only on x and can be tabulated before the integration begins. See Wilson (1949)).

6. The solution of the differential system

$$\begin{aligned} y' &= -10y + 6z, & y(0) &= \tfrac{4}{3}e \\ z' &= 13 \cdot 5y - 10z, & z(0) &= 0 \end{aligned}\Biggr\},$$

is $y = \tfrac{2}{3}e(e^{-x} + e^{-19x})$, $z = e(e^{-x} - e^{-19x})$.

For $x \geqslant 1$ the term e^{-19x} is negligible. Starting with $y(1) = \frac{2}{3}$, $z(1) = 1$, integrate forward by (i) the fourth-order Runge–Kutta method (equations (33)), (ii) Milne's method (equations (36) and (37)), (iii) the Adams–Bashforth method (equations (23) and (24)), (iv) the method of equations (40), and (v) the trapezium-rule method (equation (61) without a correction) at successive intervals $\frac{1}{2}, \frac{1}{4}, \frac{1}{8}, \ldots$, sufficiently far to demonstrate the partial instability phenomenon of methods (i) and (iii), the weak instability of method (ii), the strong instability of method (iv), and the complete stability of method (v). Improve the results of method (v) by applying the 'difference correction' in equation (61). (See Fox and Goodwin 1949).

7. Show that the fourth-order Runge–Kutta method, applied to $y' = f(x)$, is equivalent to Simpson's rule for numerical integration.

8. Show, by computation, that the unrefined application of method (v) in exercise 6 can be corrected by 'h^2-extrapolation'.

9. Show, by computation, that h^2-extrapolation is valid in the numerical solution of $y'' + y = 0$, $y(0) = 0$, $y'(0) = 1$, if we use the approximations

$$h^2 y''_0 = y_1 - 2y_0 + y_{-1}, \qquad 2hy'_0 = y_1 - y_{-1},$$

but that this will fail if we start with the correct value of y_1 obtained say by the use of Taylor's series, or with the approximation (66) for the first derivative. What order of extrapolation would we expect with the latter method?

10. Show by computation that in the solution of Exercise 9 with the method of equation (52) we can use 'h^4-extrapolation', provided that we make suitable provision for the derivative condition at $x = 0$. What is this 'suitable' provision? (See Fox (Ed.) 1962 for a discussion of the relevant general theory).

11. Verify, by computation, the induced instability of the method of equation (80) applied to (79), with $k = \pi$, $g(x) = x$, $y(0) = 0$, $y(h) = h\pi^{-2}$, $h = 0 \cdot 8$ say. Prove the final remark in § 34.

12. Demonstrate the strong instability of the step-by-step method of solving $y'' + y = 0$, $y(0) = 0$, $y'(0) = 1$, which uses

$$h^2 y_r'' = -\tfrac{1}{12} y_{r+2} + \tfrac{4}{3} y_{r+1} - \tfrac{5}{2} y_r + \tfrac{4}{3} y_{r-1} - \tfrac{1}{12} y_{r-2}$$

(as in § 38). Start with $h = 0 \cdot 1$ and $y_r = \sin x_r$ for $r = 0, 1, 2$, and 3.

13. Demonstrate that the use of the formula of exercise (12) is perfectly stable with the boundary conditions $y(0) = 0$, $y(h) = \sin h$, $y(2) = \sin 2$, $y(2-h) = \sin (2-h)$, and the solution of the relevant algebraic equations. (Take $h = \tfrac{1}{4}$, say.)

14. Demonstrate the weak instability of the method of equation (88) for the solution of Exercise 6, starting with correct values at $x = 1$ and $1+h$. (Take $h = 0 \cdot 2$, say.)

15. Compute the smallest eigenvalue and corresponding eigenvector of the system
$$y'' + \lambda y = 0, \qquad y(0) = 0, \qquad y(1) = 0,$$
by
(i) performing a step-by-step process for $y'' + \lambda_0 y = 0$ with $y(0) = 0$, $y'(0) = 1$ (or $y(h) = 1$) and a guessed λ_0;
(ii) solving by the same step-by-step process the equation $z'' + \lambda_0 z + y = 0$, with $z(0) = 0$, $z'(0) = 0$ (or $z(h) = 0$);
(iii) repeating with $\lambda_1 = \lambda_0 - y(1)/z(1)$.

16. Perform the computation suggested at the end of § 63.

17. Perform the computation suggested at the beginning of § 68.

Bibliography

BAKER, C. T. H., FOX, L., MAYERS, D. F., and WRIGHT, K. 1964. Numerical solution of Fredholm integral equations of first kind. *Comput. J.* **7**, 141–8.

CLENSHAW, C. W. 1962. Chebyshev series for mathematical functions. *Mathl. Tabl. natn. phys. Lab.* **5**. H.M.S.O., London.

—— and CURTIS, A. R. 1960. A method for numerical integration on an automatic computer. *Num. Math.* **2**, 197–205.

DAHLQUIST, G. 1956. Convergence and stability in the numerical integration of ordinary differential equations. *Mathematica scand.* **4**, 33–53.

—— 1959. Stability and error bounds in the numerical integration of ordinary differential equations. *K. tek. Högsk. Handl.* **130**.

DAVIS, P. J. and RABINOWITZ, P. 1967. *Numerical integration.* Blaisdell Publishing Co., New York.

DWYER, P. S. 1951. *Linear computations.* Wiley, New York and London.

FORSYTHE, G. E. 1957. Generation and use of orthogonal polynomials for data-fitting with a digital computer. *J. Soc. ind. appl. Math.* **5**, 74–88.

FOX, L. 1957. *The numerical solution of two-point boundary problems in ordinary differential equations.* Clarendon Press, Oxford.

—— 1964. *An introduction to numerical linear algebra.* Clarendon Press, Oxford.

—— 1967. Romberg integration for a class of singular integrands. *Comput. J.* **10**, 87–93.

—— 1962 (Ed.) *Numerical solution of ordinary and partial differential equations.* Pergamon Press, Oxford.

—— and GOODWIN, E. T. 1949. Some new methods for the numerical integration of ordinary differential equations. *Proc. Camb. phil. Soc. math. phys. Sci.* **45**, 373–388.

—— and GOODWIN, E. T. 1953. The numerical solution of non-singular linear integral equations. *Phil. Trans. R. Soc.* **A245**, 501–34.

—— and PARKER, I. B. 1968. *Chebyshev polynomials in numerical analysis.* Oxford University Press, London.

GOODWIN, E. T. 1949. The evaluation of integrals of the form

$$\int_{-\infty}^{\infty} f(x) e^{-x^2} \, dx.$$

Proc. Camb. phil. Soc. math. phys. Sci. **45**, 241–5.

—— and STATON, J. 1948. Table of

$$\int_{0}^{\infty} \frac{e^{-u^2}}{u+x} \, du.$$

Q. Jl Mech. appl. Math. **1**, 319–26.

HAMMING, R. W. and PINKHAM, R. S. 1966. A class of integration formulas. *J. Ass. comput. Mach.* **13**, 430–8.

HANDSCOMB, D. C. 1966 (Ed.) *Methods of numerical approximation.* Pergamon Press, Oxford.

HILDEBRAND, F. B. 1956. *Introduction to numerical analysis.* McGraw-Hill, New York and London.

Interpolation and allied tables. 1956. H.M.S.O., London.

MAYERS, D. F. 1964. The deferred approach to the limit in ordinary differential equations. *Comp. J.* **7**, 54–7.

MERSON, R. H. 1957. An operational method for the study of integration processes. *Proceedings of a Conference on Data Processing and Automatic Computing Machines,* Weapons Research Establishment, Salisbury, South Australia.

Modern computing methods. 1961. H.M.S.O., London.

MOLER, C. B. 1967. Iterative refinement in floating point. *J. Ass. comput. Mach.* **14**, 316–21.

MOORE, R. E. 1966. *Interval analysis.* Prentice-Hall, New Jersey.

MULLER, D. E. 1956. A method for solving algebraic equations using an automatic computer. *Mathl Tabl. natn. Res. Coun., Wash.* **10**, 208–15.

NORDSIECK, A. 1962. On numerical integration of ordinary differential equations. *Maths Comput.* **16**, 22–49.

STROUD, A. H. and SECREST, D. 1966. *Gaussian quadrature formulas.* Prentice-Hall, New Jersey.

VARGA, R. S. 1962. *Matrix iterative analysis.* Prentice-Hall, New Jersey.

WILKINSON, J. H. 1963. *Rounding errors in algebraic processes.* H.M.S.O., London.

—— 1965. *The algebraic eigenvalue problem.* Clarendon Press, Oxford.

WILSON, E. M. 1949. A note on the numerical integration of differential equations. *Q. Jl Mech. appl. Math.* **2**, 208–11.

Index